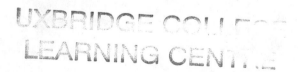

PROJECT PLANNING AND ANALYSIS FOR DEVELOPMENT

DAVID POTTS

LYNNE
RIENNER
PUBLISHERS

BOULDER
LONDON

Published in the United States of America in 2002 by
Lynne Rienner Publishers, Inc.
1800 30th Street, Boulder, Colorado 80301
www.rienner.com

and in the United Kingdom by
Lynne Rienner Publishers, Inc.
3 Henrietta Street, Covent Garden, London WC2E 8LU

Library of Congress Cataloging-in-Publication Data
Potts, David, 1953–
    Project planning and analysis for development / David Potts.
        p.   cm.
    Includes bibliographical references and index.
    ISBN 1-55587-649-8 (alk. paper)—ISBN 1-55587-656-0 (pbk.   :   alk. paper)
    1. Economic development projects—Developing countries—Planning.   2. Project
management.   I. Title.
    HC59.7 .P63   2002
    338.9'0068'4—dc21

                                                                    2002020151

British Cataloguing in Publication Data
A Cataloguing in Publication record for this book
is available from the British Library.

Printed and bound in the United States of America

The paper used in this publication meets the requirements
of the American National Standard for Permanence of
Paper for Printed Library Materials Z39.48-1984.

5   4   3   2   1

Contents

Tables and Figures

Tables

Figures

Acknowledgments

This book has been a long time in gestation, and numerous people have helped in its formation. Apart from the continued encouragement provided by my family, my greatest debt is to the many students who have experienced my teaching. What they have understood, what they have not understood, and the questions they have asked have caused me to revise my material many times.

I also owe a debt to many of my colleagues and former colleagues who have encouraged me to write this book and have discussed many of the issues with me. Particular thanks are due to John Weiss, who provided very perceptive comments on an earlier draft, and to Behrooz Morvaridi and P. B. Anard, who gave valuable comments on Chapters 14 and 17 respectively. The comments of a reviewer are also acknowledged.

Finally I would like to acknowledge the contribution of my former colleagues in the Ministry of Agriculture in Tanzania in the 1980s, where I first had the opportunity to put some of my ideas into practice. We may not have solved all the problems, but we had a good team and we asked a lot of questions!

Needless to say, none of the above people bears any responsibility for shortcomings and mistakes.

—*David Potts*

I

Introduction

The purpose of this book is to provide a guide to the approaches and techniques involved in the planning and analysis of development projects for those likely either to use them or to assess the work of others who have used them. The book is oriented to the context of developing countries, but much of what is written on techniques is also relevant to transitional and developed economies. The book concentrates on practical issues that arise in project analysis and is intended to be accessible to readers who may not be specialist economists.

The book is derived from teaching material developed over the past twenty years at the Bradford Centre for International Development (BCID, formerly the Development and Project Planning Centre, or DPPC) of the University of Bradford. The material has been used in various forms on the BCID's master's program, the Postgraduate Certificate in Project Planning, Appraisal, and Financing, and on a series of training courses conducted for the Public Investment Programme Units in Lithuania and Latvia.

Project Planning and Analysis in a Changing World

Project Planning and Analysis for Development has been written at a time when the project approach to development has been increasingly questioned, particularly by aid agencies. Questions have been raised about the policy context in which projects are implemented, the potential fungibility of funds allocated to projects, and the need to perceive projects in the context of sector-wide programs in which both policies and recurrent resources are also defined. Others have questioned the complexity of some of the techniques of cost-benefit analysis and the extent to which they can be used for the types of social and infrastructure investments that now dominate public investment. If aid funds are increasingly channeled into programs rather than projects, what role is there for project analysis?

There is no doubt that the importance of projects was overemphasized

I

during the heyday of project appraisal in the 1970s. Projects have always existed in a context, and the context will affect success in implementation. Nevertheless a very large part of the improvement in the welfare of human beings comes from investment in change, and a substantial part of the available resources is invested in projects. It is therefore important to be able to make an informed judgement on the magnitude of the likely benefits in comparison to the costs involved. Project analysis is concerned with investigating this question. Some responses to the questions raised about the relevance of project analysis are outlined below.

Part of project analysis is concerned with assessing the policy environment. This is particularly important at the project identification stage. Some of the policy-related issues involved in screening project proposals are outlined in Chapter 2. Policy is important, but without appropriate investment, the best policies in the world will not deliver sustained economic development.

Fungibility is an issue for aid donors who may be concerned that the funds made available for a particular project could allow other funds to be released for less worthy uses. This provides a convenient excuse for aid donors to stop doing detailed analysis of projects, but it does not take away the need for the recipient country to try to ensure that scarce investment resources are put to the best possible use. If aid donors have retreated from project analysis, then they have simply transferred the task to the recipient governments. The task has not gone away just because donors are doing less of it. Indeed it could be argued that the donor emphasis on program funding actually makes the need to boost the capacity for project analysis in the recipient countries more pressing. To the extent that the planning and appraisal of projects are increasingly undertaken within developing and transitional countries, it is to be hoped that "ownership" of projects by those countries will be enhanced, thus increasing the likelihood of success. This book is written in the hope that it will make some contribution to the process by improving the knowledge and skills of those assessing projects in developing and transitional economies.

Of course projects are often part of wider sector programs. Chapter 1 attempts to set projects in this wider context and suggests some of the activities that might be required to define projects within a program. Project analysis is about assessment of alternatives, and in principle there is no reason why the techniques and approaches used in project analysis cannot be used to appraise alternative versions of sector programs. What is more likely, however, is that alternative versions of sector programs will contain different combinations of projects and therefore that comparison of these projects will define the most appropriate program given the resources available. In some sectors investment resources may not be the critical factor and so some of the criteria for cost-benefit analysis may not be particularly relevant. However, project analysis is about far more than the mathematics of investment criteria.

Complexity is certainly an issue. The complexity of the analysis must bear some relation to the size and complexity of the project. In this book a variety of approaches to project analysis are discussed, some of which may only be relevant for medium- to large-scale projects. It is also possible to use particular approaches to differing levels of complexity. The book describes the approaches available and their strengths and weaknesses but does not prescribe what should be done in every circumstance. Ultimately the chosen approach depends on the judgment of the analyst and the organization he/she reports to. Relatively simple informal approaches may be appropriate for assessing small inexpensive projects with relatively small-scale impact. More rigorous analysis is required when either the resource costs of the project or the expected impact is more substantial.

Arguments related to the changing content of public investment can be answered in two ways. First of all, there are a number of well-defined approaches to both cost-benefit analysis and cost-effectiveness analysis in the sectors that continue to be funded publicly. These are described to some extent in Chapter 4 but more extensively in Chapter 9. The introduction of noneconomic criteria into project assessment is discussed in Chapter 14. A second response is to point out that cost-benefit analysis is not only about public-sector projects, and that many public-sector projects are intended to enable private-sector development.

Although the book is primarily about financial and economic analysis, it draws from other disciplines where these are seen to be important for the main themes. This is the case particularly in the discussion of project identification and design where issues of social acceptability and participation can be of fundamental importance. The underlying philosophy is that *all* disciplines can make a contribution to the planning and analysis of projects and that attempts to assert the supremacy of any particular discipline are fundamentally misconceived. Project planning and analysis are essentially about teamwork, and it is important that the members of any project planning team communicate with each other so that all relevant information is used effectively. The reality is often different.

A large part of the book is about economic cost-benefit analysis. My preferred approach is first to identify income changes and then to examine other welfare changes where they can be measured. The details of this approach are defined in the first part of Chapter 13 and may be compared to the existing mainstream procedures outlined in Chapter 11. Most Anglophone texts on cost-benefit analysis are rooted in a neoclassical interpretation of welfare economics in which differences between market prices and their economic value are sometimes described as distortions. Although the difference in terms of end result is unlikely to be significant, I have deliberately avoided using the term *market distortion* and have preferred to describe differences between price and economic value in terms of the opportunity cost of resources. This is partly because I believe that all attempts to define economic value contain logical flaws and can only describe a limited view of reality. This should not prevent us from trying to identify and quantify economic effects, but we should be careful about the validity of value judgments made on wider issues such as "getting the prices right." While I think it is quite possible to get the prices manifestly wrong, I am not convinced that there is such a thing as a "right" price.

The emphasis placed on identifying income changes also relates to the idea that a project is not a monolithic entity. All projects have different stakeholders who may be affected in widely different ways. We may wish to add up the effects on different groups to draw an overall conclusion, but if we ignore the differential impact of projects on incomes, we will fail to understand the motivations of the affected groups and will therefore fail to understand the social dynamics of the project.

An example of a hypothetical textile project is used throughout the quantitative parts of the book. The example is intended to illustrate techniques and issues, and certain features are simplified to reduce it to a manageable size. It should not therefore be considered a template for the analysis of textile projects. The association with textiles is for illustration only.

In an era when the role of the state is increasingly restricted to the provision of social infrastructure, it may seem odd to use a productive sector project as an example. There are a number of justifications for this choice. First and most important, the example is used to illustrate as complete a range of project analysis techniques as possible. The full range of financial statements cannot be obtained from a project without commercial objectives, although some financial statements (in particular the cash flow) may be relevant to any kind of project, whether commercial or not. The project example is also used to illustrate the analysis of linkages to small producers, a common requirement for any "enabling" project such as those providing extension services or rural infrastructure. The choice of an agroindustrial project allows this illustration to be made. It also allows the distinction to be made between inducing additional production and transferring production from one use to another, and it provides an illustration of how to trace the income effects of price changes.

The full range of quantitative techniques could have been illustrated by using different examples from different sectors. In certain specific aspects of project analysis, this approach has been used. However, the emphasis in this book is on the integration of different techniques in a consistent manner such that the relationship between financial analysis and economic analysis is clear and can be related to the income and welfare effects on different stakeholders.

A second justification for the example used is that cost-benefit analysis is not just a tool for public-sector projects. Financial analysis is relevant for all projects, whether public or private. Economic analysis can also be relevant to private-sector projects. Development banks often fund private-sector projects and should be convinced that such projects provide benefits to the national economy as a whole. Issues of planning permission also arise, particularly where projects have some environmental impact. Private investors should also be aware if their projects depend for their profitability on a government taxation policy that could change. All investors should be aware of the interests of affected stakeholders because these will determine the extent to which the intended investment will gain wider acceptance.

Two areas explored in this book tend to be neglected in many other texts. Throughout the book there is an emphasis on tracing income and welfare effects so that the distributional impact of projects can be assessed. This is important if projects are to be used to tackle the problem of poverty that affects all countries. The cost-benefit analysis literature of the 1970s and 1980s tended to concentrate on weighting systems, on which common agreement could not be found, rather than on the identification of the income effects themselves.

The literature of project analysis has also tended to pay little attention to the effects of inflation and changes in exchange rates despite the overwhelming evidence that failure to take these factors into account is a major cause of project failure.

Inevitably such a book cannot cover every issue. The most important omission in this book is that of project management and implementation. In planning projects it is essential to consider issues such as the scheduling of activities and planning for project management. The literature on these subjects tends to be separate from that on project appraisal, and for this reason I have not attempted to cover project management issues.

There is also some variation in the depth of coverage of topics in this book. In particular the coverage of the social analysis of projects is very introductory. The justification for its inclusion is that it is an area where some common understanding is required if different social science disciplines are to engage in constructive dialogue.

Outline of the Book

The book can be divided conceptually into four unequal parts. The first part concerns the identification and formulation of projects, the estimation of project costs and benefits, and basic principles of project appraisal. The second part is concerned with the financial analysis of projects. The third and largest part is concerned with the economic and social assessment of projects. The final part considers the implications of changes in assumptions and changes in prices.

Chapter 2 describes the context within which projects are developed. Some basic definitions are provided, and various models of the project sequence are discussed in the context of wider planning systems.

Chapter 3 is concerned with project identification and formulation. The various sources of project ideas are considered along with approaches to screening these ideas. Different approaches and techniques that can be used in project design and formulation are discussed, including stakeholder analysis, objective oriented project planning, and the logical framework. An appendix provides an illustration of the use of some of these approaches.

Chapter 4 sets out the basic principles of project analysis including the definitions of *with* and *without* the project and the main categories of project costs and benefits. The various measures of project worth are discussed as well as cost-effectiveness analysis. The implications for project appraisal of ideas about *blueprint* and *process* projects are also discussed.

Chapter 5 covers the financial analysis of commercial projects. The main financial statements are described, and the issues of liquidity and profitability are discussed. Chapter 5 also contains brief discussions of financial ratios and the pricing of public utilities.

Chapter 6 discusses some of the issues surrounding the analysis of incentives and response for small producers. The special features of small producers are considered, and approaches to dealing with factors such as reconciliation of conflicting labor demands and maximization of returns to scarce resources are examined. Aggregation of the effects of an *enabling* project on large numbers of small producers is also discussed.

Chapter 7 provides an overview of economic analysis and its rationale and looks at the definition and treatment of transfer payments.

Chapter 8 is concerned with linkages, externalities, and the environment. It includes a discussion of the treatment of linkage effects and the analysis of projects wherein a number of different agents are involved. The linkage between processing facilities and raw material suppliers is examined. The discussion of externalities includes a review of environmental impact assessment and the measurement and valuation of environmental effects.

Chapter 9 investigates the particular issues surrounding the assessment of the benefits of social and infrastructure projects. Where it is possible to value the benefits of such projects, an outline is given of the approaches available and the context in which they might be used. Where valuation is difficult, an indication of the possible approaches to benefit assessment is provided.

Chapter 10 looks at the concept of opportunity cost as the basis for the estimation of shadow prices and then proceeds to consider how the financial value of different categories of cost and benefit can be disaggregated into primary factors. Disaggregation of financial values into primary factors provides the basis for all shadow price estimates, irrespective of the unit of account or numeraire adopted. The information defined by the procedures outlined in Chapter 10 is therefore required, whatever shadow pricing system is adopted.

Chapter 11 discusses shadow prices and shadow pricing systems. The chapter starts off with an explanation of the concept of *numeraire* and proceeds to discuss estimation of the economic values for foreign exchange and different categories of labor and how these relate to the shadow pricing systems put forward by various authors. Different shadow pricing procedures are sometimes perceived to be intrinsically different, partly because different authors might recommend the use of different assumptions. From a procedural point of view, it can be demonstrated that, with equivalent assumptions, all procedures give equivalent results. Chapter 11 reviews existing mainstream procedures in turn. First of all, the use of a domestic price numeraire with composite conversion factors is illustrated. The world price numeraire system put forward by Little and Mirrlees is then shown as an alternative adaptation. Finally the UNIDO *Guidelines* approach is shown as an alternative procedure in which an overall breakdown into primary factors precedes the application of conversion factors. My own preference is for a modified version of the UNIDO approach. An explanation of this modified approach is given in Chapter 13, where distribution questions are addressed.

An appendix to Chapter 11 outlines how the technique of semi-input-output analysis can be used to make national shadow price estimates and provides a simplified example of a semi-input-output table.

Chapter 12 investigates the different approaches to determining the discount rate and the related issue of the economic valuation of investment resources. Time preference– and opportunity cost–based approaches are considered, and the economic valuation of investment resources is derived from the difference between the two.

Chapter 13 starts with a discussion of the estimation of the distribution of costs and benefits and describes the *modified UNIDO approach* to economic analysis, which can be used to define distribution effects. The possible use of such an approach in determining the contribution of projects to poverty reduction is then considered. The distribution weighting approaches of earlier cost-benefit analysis texts are also discussed.

In an appendix to Chapter 13, the potential use of the *effects method* is discussed. This approach was developed in France and forms the basis for economic analysis in the current *EU Manual*. Some of the problems in using the effects method are considered along with the changes required for full consistency of this approach with shadow pricing methods.

Chapter 14 considers the limitations of economic analysis. What can economic analysis tell us, and what issues does it exclude? Some of the issues involved in social impact assessment are discussed along with the technique of multicriteria analysis.

Chapter 15 looks at the techniques of sensitivity and risk analysis. How certain are we that our best estimates are correct? What are the implications of changes in assumptions? What is the probability that the project will succeed in meeting its objectives?

Chapter 16 looks at the implications of changing prices and exchange rates for the financial analysis of projects. How can we take account of changes in relative prices? What is the impact of expected inflation on the financial sustainability of the project? How do exchange rate changes affect payments for foreign loans? This is a difficult subject because of the complexities of inflation accounting, but it should not be ignored. A major cause of project failure is lack of money.

Chapter 17 concludes the book with a review of the main issues covered and some comments on the economic value system underlying cost-benefit analysis and the use of economic analysis. This leads on to the question as to whether project planning and analysis matters. Not surprisingly, given the title of the book, I argue that it does.

PART 1

Project Identification and Design

2

Projects and the Planning Process

Projects and Development

This book is concerned with project analysis for development. Implied in this title are views of what development is, what a project is, and what belongs in project analysis. All of these concepts are open to a wide range of interpretations. Therefore I will start with some definitions.

Development

In its broadest definition *development* can be regarded as the process of improving human welfare. A narrow economic definition of development would focus on gross domestic product (GDP). The United Nations Development Programme (UNDP) Human Development Index (HDI) also includes life expectancy and adult literacy as proxies for health and educational status.[1] It has been suggested that issues of income distribution among persons, regions, and gender categories should also be considered as well as the issues of environmental and institutional sustainability.[2]

Development therefore implies the improvement over time and on a sustainable basis of the level and distribution of income and the physical and human resource base. Whether these issues can be captured effectively in a single measure is open to debate; however, they do indicate some of the concerns that need to be addressed in the analysis of projects if the contribution of these projects to development is to be assessed.

Projects

Although the word *project* has a multitude of different interpretations, this book concerns development projects, which may be expected to have the following features:

- A project involves the investment of scarce resources for future benefit.
- A project can be planned, financed, and implemented as a unit.
- A project has a defined set of objectives and a specific start and end.
- A project has geographical or organizational boundaries.

Unfortunately investment resources are often spent on activities that do not satisfy the above criteria. The success or failure of such ill-defined "projects" can be extremely difficult to judge. They are often difficult to manage, and they can lead to a continuous drain on resources because no one knows when the activity being financed stops being a project.

Project Analysis

Project analysis is carried out for a purpose and from a point of view. The major purposes of project analysis are to determine from the viewpoints of the agents involved the answers to two questions: Will the project work as proposed? Is the project worthwhile? Obviously much of the first question covers technical issues that are outside the scope of this book; however, there is little purpose in answering the second question unless the first has been resolved satisfactorily. The focus of this book on techniques for project analysis should not obscure the fact that a sound technical analysis of projects is necessary for successful implementation. Some of the methods that can help the nonspecialist to examine the logic and assumptions of projects and to focus on the important issues in project design will be examined in Chapter 3.

Models of the Project Sequence

Although development projects vary considerably, most projects go through a similar sequence of activities. The differences lie primarily in the procedures and degree of detail of the various stages and the number and role of the different agents involved. The first and most well-known model of this sequence was called the *project cycle* (Baum 1970). The original version of the cycle had four components:

- The initial *identification* of the project (conceptualization of project ideas)
- *Preparation* of the project (also known as project formulation and design)
- Project *appraisal* and selection
- Project *implementation*

A subsequent version (Baum 1978) included a fifth component of *evaluation* of the project to close the cycle (see Figure 2.1). The idea was that evaluation of the project after completion would lead to the generation of ideas for new projects.

Six different aspects of the appraisal stage were defined: technical, financial, commercial, economic and social, managerial, and organizational. Later versions of the project cycle have added social, institutional, and environmental appraisal to the list.

According to the project cycle model, *project appraisal* is followed by negotiations and loan agreement leading on to project implementation. *Project analysis* primarily relates to the earlier stages of project identification, preparation, and appraisal although the tools of project appraisal can also be used in project evaluation.

The advantage of the Baum model is its simplicity, but Baum's description has been criticized on a number of grounds, including:

- It is too simplistic (although simplicity could also be seen as an advantage).
- It is related too specifically to procedures for World Bank projects.
- It does not allow for feedback (loops in the system) or rejection (closure or escape out of the system).

Figure 2.1   The Project Cycle

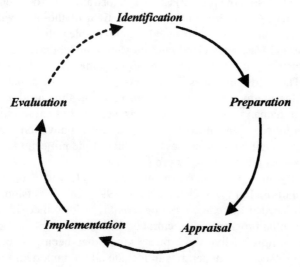

Source: Baum 1978.

Various other models have been developed by subsequent authors to account for observed shortcomings and different emphases.

Rondinelli (1977) provided an expanded version of the Baum cycle with more stages. The most important new features were the separation of appraisal from negotiation and approval, the introduction of project monitoring and control, and the inclusion of project completion and termination followed by transition to normal administration. This model pointed specifically to the need to plan for the termination of a project as well as its beginning.

The Development Project Management Center (DPMC) cycle (Development Project Management Center 1979) emphasized three phases (preauthorization planning, postauthorization planning, and output production and distribution). The phases were separated by distinct milestones that were described as *conception, authorization,* and *end of investment.* The helpfulness of these distinctions lies in the likelihood that the three phases will be conducted and managed by different people and that the three milestones indicate the need for some kind of decision. The distinction between phases and milestones differentiates between activities and events in a similar way to the network analysis technique that is sometimes used in project implementation planning.[3]

Goodman and Love (1979) developed a model called the *integrated project planning and management cycle.* The model had four distinct phases and showed feedback, flows of information and authority, and policy connections. The introduction of feedback was an important contribution because it introduced the idea that the process of project planning could go backward (to redesign the project) as well as forward. The focus on the policy environment was also significant in the light of the observation that project failure could often be attributed to unfavorable policies.

Behrens and Hawranek (1991) put forward a model that relates specifically to industrial projects but also focuses on some issues of more general relevance. The model indicates the various different studies that might be required in the preinvestment phase. It also indicates the need to consider investment in human resources (training) as well as physical resources. The need to plan for replacement expenditure and future innovation is also indicated, and, depending on the success or failure of the project, there may be a need for project rehabilitation or project expansion.

A slightly amended version of the Baum cycle was adopted by the Commission of the European Communities (1993). In this version, identification was preceded by *indicative programming,* with project ideas drawn up into a potential program on a sectoral or thematic basis.

A very comprehensive three-phase model has been put forward by MacArthur (1994). This model tries to include all the important features of previous models and to allow for the possibility that a project can be terminated at any stage. It also tries to show where the ideas for projects might come from.

Picciotto and Weaving (1994) have proposed a "New Project Cycle for the World Bank." Their model emphasizes the issues of participation and risk and the need for greater flexibility centered on the needs of the borrower and the beneficiaries (the "stakeholders") rather than those of the aid agency. It is related to the movement toward a more adaptive process approach to projects rather than the traditional blueprint approach. In their model, Picciotto and Weaving replace identification with *listening*. Listening is followed by *piloting, demonstrating,* and *mainstreaming*.

The various models of the project sequence tend to reflect the perspective and experience of the authors and organizations that produced them and the type of project they had in mind. The basic project cycle model has been adapted in different ways depending on the particular issues that were felt to be important by the authors. Their prime value is to highlight those issues and to provide a conceptualization of the process through which a project might pass.

The *Project Spiral* (see Figure 2.2) provides a framework with circles of decreasing size that meet at a single point designated as *Project Design*. The idea is that the process of project development is essentially convergent, ultimately leading either to implementation of some version of the project or to abandonment. However, at any stage of the process, it should be possible to redesign or abandon the project so that the process of convergence does not always have to work in one direction. The emphasis is on flexibility in project design so that the project can be adapted to the circumstances within which it exists. The emphasis on flexibility is consistent with current trends toward process projects.

The outer circle is the environment within which the project is identified. The project environment generates project ideas through a variety of processes including various planning processes as well as political pressure and the perception of opportunities and needs that may arise from "listening."[4] The factors determining the project environment also determine the policy environment within which the project will operate. Once the project idea is generated, it is conceptualized, prepared as a project proposal, and tested for feasibility. If it appears to be feasible, it may then proceed to the appraisal stage where the question of the desirability of the project is considered. If it is found to be desirable from all points of view, it may be implemented, but it will be monitored periodically and may also be subject to evaluation. At each of these stages the project design may be altered and subjected to some form of reappraisal. This process may lead to the identification of a new project, but it does not necessarily have to.

At all stages an awareness of the project environment is important because changes in the project environment may have implications for

Figure 2.2   The Project Spiral

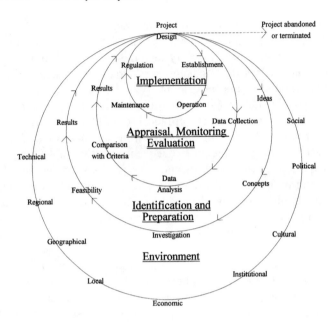

Source: Adapted from Baird and Potts 1978.

design. Such changes can be either positive or negative, but those involved in the processes of planning and implementation should be aware of the implications and able to take the necessary action.

Figure 2.2 focuses on the context within which projects operate, but it does not specify the planning processes that may be undertaken. Figure 2.3 shows a flow diagram of a project planning system including the different stages of planning that might be undertaken and the feedback to earlier stages.

Two features of Figure 2.3 are particularly important. First, there is an emphasis on *alternatives*. At early stages of the project planning process it is important to give consideration to all possible alternative means of achieving the given objectives. The second feature is the distinction between *feasibility* and *desirability*. Projects are feasible if they can work, but they are not necessarily desirable. Projects can also appear to be desirable but in practice may not be feasible. A good project should be both feasible and desirable from the points of view of all those who are affected significantly. Figure 2.3 also indicates that not all project ideas will eventually lead to projects. At each stage of the process it is likely that some project proposals will either be dropped or referred back for amendment.

Figure 2.3   A Model of a Project Planning System

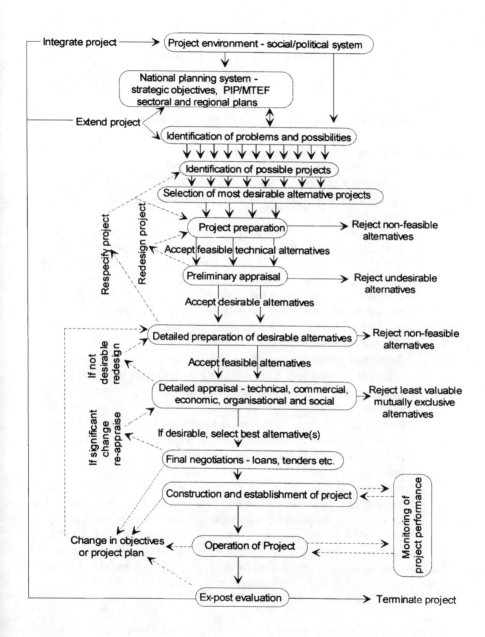

Source: Adapted from Baird and Potts 1978.

Projects and the Planning Process

Not all projects are derived from a formal planning process but many are. Where projects are derived from the planning process they are usually derived from medium-term plans. The nature and scope of medium-term planning have changed considerably in the past decade, and most countries have moved away from the fixed-period, five-year plan covering all economic activities and toward three-year rolling plans concentrating on public expenditure.

Dallago and Kovacs (1990) defined four types of planning:

- *Direct planning,* involving administrative allocation of resources, was practiced in the Soviet Union and other Council for Mutual Economic Assistance (CMEA, or COMECON) countries but is now used in very few countries. The role of project analysis in such systems is limited.
- *Indirect planning,* where the government controls certain parameters (some prices, interest rates, taxes, exchange rates, and allocation of public resources) and uses these parameters to influence the decisions of enterprises in the desired direction. Many of the CMEA countries were moving in this direction in the 1980s, and this approach was also adopted in a number of developing countries. The introduction of economic reforms has reduced considerably the range of prices that most governments try to control.
- *Regulative planning* is used not only to allocate state resources and to coordinate public-sector activities but also to influence the activity of the private sector through incentives and regulations to cooperate in plan implementation. This type of planning is used in many developing countries and also, to some extent, in some developed market economies, particularly in the areas of environmental control and the regulation of natural monopolies.
- *Indicative planning* involves forecasting the development of the economy and indicating expected government and state sector expenditure. This process provides information and creates an environment that influences the decisions of the private sector, although there may be no attempt to govern those decisions directly. Indicative planning is the main form of planning in developed capitalist economies. It attempts to tackle directly the problem of imperfect information that contributes to the failure of markets to give an optimal outcome.

The three last-mentioned approaches imply greater decentralization of decisionmaking over investment decisions and therefore a significant role for project analysis. Most countries use both public investment programs (PIPs) and some regulative and incentive measures to steer investment in the desired direction. More recently many countries have attempted to integrate the planning of public expenditure on investment and recurrent activities through a medium-term expenditure framework (MTEF).

Projects are normally included in the public investment planning process whenever they make a claim on the government budget. This is most obviously the case where part or all of a public-sector project is funded from government revenue. It may also be the case where either public- or private-sector projects make use of government loan guarantees. In most countries the government budget is severely constrained and so the direct and indirect budgetary or fiscal impact of a project is a significant factor.

The public investment program is usually drawn up on the basis of proposals from various public-sector organizations. These are usually put together on a sectoral basis to form a sectoral plan or program in which sectoral priorities are defined.

Projects that do not make a claim on budgetary resources may not be included in the public investment planning process, but they are quite likely to be subject to regulatory planning controls if they have significant environmental impact or involve monopoly pricing.

In larger countries small- and medium-scale projects may enter the planning process through regional and subregional plans and programs. This applies particularly to projects located in rural areas and involving nongovernmental organizations (NGOs).

Where projects are proposed by large organizations they may form part of a corporate plan. Where such organizations are multinational these plans may extend across national boundaries.

Figure 2.4 shows the connections between the various levels of planning and how they relate to project planning.

Sectoral Planning and Project Priorities

For planning purposes economies are usually divided into sectors. In practice the division into sectors usually corresponds with the administrative division into sectoral ministries. Such a division has the advantage that it corresponds with an administrative framework, but it has the disadvantage of lack of continuity when administrative divisions change. Often large sectors are broken down further into subsectors so that investment programs can be drawn up to cover closely related activities. The argument for undertaking sectoral planning rests on the assumption that the whole is likely to be greater than the sum of the parts when the pattern and sequence of investments are a coordinated rather than a random process.

Figure 2.4   Types and Levels of Planning

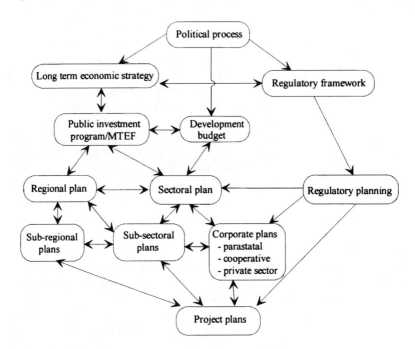

Sectoral planning provides the link between planning at the macro level and project planning. Its nature varies considerably from sector to sector, but there are some common features that are important for project identification. The major activities involved in drawing up a sectoral plan are likely to be:

The Sectoral Review

This is the first stage in formulating a plan and defines the environment within which any project must operate. The sectoral review might consist of:

- A description of activities and trends
- An assessment of existing resources such as land, human resources, fixed capital, financial capital, and foreign exchange
- An analysis of the constraints facing the sector, including those relating to policy, natural resources, human resources, capital investment, recurrent resources, and markets
- An assessment of potential opportunities

Definition of a Sector Strategy

Once the current situation is known, it is necessary to formulate a strategy for the future. This is likely to involve:

- Establishment of sector goals. Depending on the sector these could include maximizing the value of commercial production, provision of a specified good or service for the minimum cost or to the highest possible standard, improving the distribution of the benefits of development, or improving national security.
- Defining the means to achieve the sector goals. These might include policy measures, capital expenditure, and/or recurrent expenditure.
- Determining the feasibility of achieving the stated goals from the political, technical, organizational, and resource viewpoints.
- Making a preliminary assessment of the likely financial and/or economic costs and benefits of the measures proposed.
- Determining priorities against some agreed criteria. This is likely to lead to the identification of a number of priority projects.

The process is likely to be iterative. In the sectoral planning process, the criteria used for determining project priorities may involve relatively crude estimates and qualitative judgements. As projects are defined more clearly the perception of their priority may change. Nevertheless a sectoral plan at least will give a systematic justification for entering into the process of project identification and formulation.

Although the sectoral planning process is coordinated by the government, it should provide an opportunity for consultation with civil society both in providing information for the review and in helping to define sector goals and the means to achieve them. There is increasing recognition of the importance of such consultation implicit in the pressure for developing countries to adopt poverty reduction strategy papers (PRSPs), although the extent to which such consultation has any genuine influence on outcomes is open to question.

Further Reading

The various models of the project sequence can be found in the sources indicated. Some of the lessons of World Bank experience are set out in Baum and Tolbert (1985). A useful description of the concept of the project environment can be found in Cusworth and Franks (1993).

The classic texts on development planning in a mixed economy are Lewis (1966) and Tinbergen (1967). Caiden and Wildavsky (1974) provide an early description of the tension between planning and budgeting and the problems involved in reconciling capital and recurrent expenditure requirements. These issues are still relevant and underlie the movement toward the MTEF approach. The shift toward three-year rolling public investment programs is described by Allan and Hinchliffe (1992) based on experience in Papua New Guinea.

Much of the more recent literature tends to be based on individual country experience. More general statements of the current state of thinking in international agencies can be found by visiting their websites. A lot of valuable material can be found on the World Bank site (www.worldbank. org). A useful overview is given in the *Public Expenditure Management Handbook* (World Bank 1998).

Notes

1. The Human Development Index was introduced in the 1990 *Human Development Report* (UNDP 1990). Subsequent modified indices have been produced including distributional issues.

2. A useful survey of the issues is given in Colman and Nixson (1994: chap. 1).

3. An overview of these techniques is given in Cusworth and Franks (1993: chap. 6).

4. The concept of *project environment* is discussed in more depth in Cusworth and Franks (1993: chap. 2).

3

Project Identification and Formulation

Projects are identified in a variety of different ways partly depending on their ownership, the sector they come from, and the expected source of funding. Public-sector projects are usually derived from the planning process or from political imperatives whereas private-sector projects usually stem from the identification of an opportunity for profit.

Project identification requires that there is a demand (or more generally a need) for the outputs and the availability of resources to produce them. It is also necessary to define a technical solution as to how to translate the available resources into the required output. Definition of a technical solution generally implies identification of one or more problems that are preventing demands or needs from being satisfied. It is important that the technical solution address the problem.

Identification on the basis of demand is market based and is derived from studying demand or needs. A distinction is usually made between demand, which presupposes both ability and willingness to pay, and need, which does not. Adequate demand is required for all projects producing a commercial output.

The two major aspects of demand that need to be investigated are those of quantity and price. Quantity is more likely to be important for outputs that are expected to be sold primarily on the domestic market, while the question of price is more likely to be important for output intended for export or for import substitution.

Estimates of prices for traded goods can be adapted in many cases from existing international commodity price statistics. Both the Food and Agriculture Organization (FAO) of the United Nations and the United Nations Conference on Trade and Development (UNCTAD) publish regular bulletins on the prices of internationally traded commodities, and the World Bank produces projections of commodity prices.[1] Such data have to be adapted for local circumstances relating to factors such as quality and transport costs. Difficulties arise for nonhomogeneous products and those for which the market is small. Such cases may require preparation of a separate market study before proceeding further with project identification.

Estimation of the quantity of demand is particularly important for the infrastructure sectors where producers are often monopolies and where prices may be controlled or where some services, such as roads, may be free. For these sectors demand may be estimated from time series data where these are available or from cross-sectional data where comparison is made with other areas or even other countries facing similar situations. Attempts may be made to include various factors such as income or population growth in building models to predict demand.[2]

Project identification on the basis of needs is most likely to be important for social sector projects such as those in the health and education sectors, but it may also extend to infrastructure projects, such as rural water supply, which provide a service perceived as a basic need. An important issue is clarity in the definition of *need*. Without such clarity, it will be difficult to establish whether a project proposal actually addresses the need. For example, the definition of need as the provision of water to a certain number of people is not sufficiently specific. It is necessary to know how much water each household requires, what quality is required, what the water will be used for, and what level of service is likely to be acceptable to the intended users.

In the case of need-based projects the involvement of key stakeholders in defining the nature of the need can be critical. Incorrect perceptions of needs by people with inadequate knowledge of the project area can have serious implications for the sustainability and acceptance of a project. This chapter explores some of the approaches that can be used to ensure that the interests of key stakeholders are given due consideration.

Resource-based identification starts from a resource assessment and determines what the resource might be used for. Whereas demand or *need-based project identification* is usually a response to a problem that prevents demands or needs from being met, resource-based identification is concerned with finding opportunities for using whatever resources may be available. Surveys of land-use capabilities provide one source of resource-based identification. Other examples are studies of potential uses for waste materials or by-products and assessment of labor skills.

Project identification can result both from systematic and from unsystematic sources. Systematic project identification is normally derived from some form of planning process. Where available, sectoral plans should provide both an assessment of demands and needs and an assessment of available resources. A similar process may take place at a regional level, particularly in relation to resource and need assessment. Projects may also be identified through corporate planning by large enterprises in both the public and private sectors.

Other systematic sources of project identification are the processes of sector review and evaluation of completed projects undertaken by various funding agencies. Unfortunately the timing of these activities does not always correspond with the timing of the planning cycle in the recipient countries, and problems can arise both in the coordination of sources of ideas and in the definition of different versions of the same idea.

A distinction is often made between *top-down* and *bottom-up* approaches to planning. Top-down planning has the potential benefit of being systematic and comprehensive, but it carries the risk of lack of commitment from the people affected. In many countries greater effort is now being made to include people affected by projects in the identification process, either through the project planning process itself or through decentralized consultation procedures. Bottom-up planning through community participation and decentralized planning is more likely to lead to commitment by the affected population but may slow down the decisionmaking process. Extreme versions of either approach tend to lead to problems of inflexibility in the one case and indecision in the other.

Unsystematic project identification can arise either from political expediency or from opportunism. Projects identified in this way are sometimes criticized by planners because they can be disruptive and may not have been appraised properly. However, such projects are not always bad. If projects have political support there may be a political commitment to make things work, and the idea may reflect a serious local need. A lot of successful private-sector projects are simply the result of a bright idea. However well ordered and systematic the planning process is, there will always be projects that "short-circuit" the system. What is important is that there should be some means to distinguish the good ones from the bad ones to ensure that, as far as possible, only the good projects go ahead.

Project Profiles and Project Screening

There are usually far more project ideas than there are successful projects. It would be foolish to embark on a major project study without a good prospect that the project might eventually succeed. Before embarking on detailed studies it is important to:

- Specify the objectives in terms of the expected output of the project, preferably in terms of something that can be measured.
- Identify the main constraints currently preventing the achievement of the objectives specified.
- Identify alternative means of achieving the project objectives (or of overcoming constraints).

- Identify the resources required and the people affected or whose cooperation is required.

The next step is likely to be the preparation of a simple project report, which might be described as a project profile or as an identification report. Generally a project identification report is more substantial than a project profile and it usually relates to bigger projects, although it may serve more or less the same purpose. Project profiles are used both as a summary of proposed projects that might appear in a sectoral program and as an initial test of the potential value and priority of the project idea.

Preparation of a project profile should allow the project to be subjected to a process of screening against some form of criteria to decide whether it would be worthwhile to go any further into detailed project preparation. At this stage the criteria are likely to be partial and impressionistic. They might include some or all of the following factors:

- potential financial profitability
- potential for earning or saving foreign exchange
- impact on employment or incomes of target groups (e.g., those identified as poor)
- contribution to development of skills
- environmental impact
- social acceptability
- sustainability of project activities
- effect on other economic activities

Those proposals that seemed to have the greatest potential could then be developed further while those that seemed unlikely to be successful would be abandoned at an early stage without excessive expenditure of resources. Still others might be returned for rethinking if the project concept did not appear to have a clear rationale.

The further development of project ideas is sometimes called *project formulation*. In formulating project proposals it is important always to bear in mind the objectives of the project, including definition of the target beneficiaries, the constraints preventing achievement of the objectives, and the means by which the constraints can be overcome. There are some specific techniques that can help us to do this.

Stakeholder Analysis

An important activity in the design of a project is to identify the people, groups, or institutions likely to be affected. These are the project's stakeholders. Stakeholder analysis is particularly important for projects where some degree of participation is expected from beneficiaries in the design and/or the operation of the project. It is used to gain a better understanding of the interests and needs of the various groups affected as well as to assess their capability to enhance or to threaten project implementation.

In undertaking stakeholder analysis it is common to differentiate between primary and secondary stakeholders. Primary stakeholders are those affected by the project either in a positive or a negative way. Secondary stakeholders are those engaged in an intermediary role in the delivery of project benefits. Stakeholders can also be categorized according to function (contributor, implementer, or beneficiary). The Overseas Development Administration (ODA) (1995) uses the concept of *key stakeholders* to refer to those who can influence a project significantly or who are important for the objectives of the project to be met. The term *external stakeholder* is also used to refer to groups who are not directly involved either as beneficiaries or as implementers but who may have an interest in the outcome of the project.

Stakeholder analysis often involves the use of tables to summarize the position of different stakeholder groups in relation to the project. The first step is to identify potential stakeholders. This can be done using a *stakeholder table* (see Figure 3.1). This table lists the various stakeholders by category and indicates their interests where these are relevant to the project. These interests could include the expectations of stakeholders, the resources they are willing to commit, and any conflicts of interest. The potential impact on the project of those interests is given using positive, negative, and uncertain indicators (+, −, ?) and relative priority is indicated according to the nature of the project objectives. The indicator of relative priority is normally given on a scale of 1 (high priority) to 5 (low priority) and usually relates to the definition of primary, secondary, and external stakeholders.

The next step is to assess the power and influence of stakeholders. For formal institutions power and influence can be derived from legal status, leadership authority, control of resources, possession of knowledge, and strength of position in negotiation. For informal groups socioeconomic status, levels of organization and consensus, control of critical resources, informal influence, and levels of dependence are relevant. Power and influence can also be set out in a tabular format and related to importance (see Figure 3.2).

If a participatory approach to project design is intended, a logical place to start is an assessment of the degree of participation expected of each group at each stage of the project life. For this a *participation matrix* can be used (see Figure 3.3). The participation matrix gives an indication of the roles of different stakeholders in the development of the project. At each

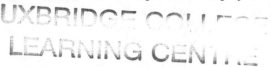

Figure 3.1   Stakeholder Table

Stakeholders	Interests	Potential Project Impact	Relative Priorities of Interest
Primary ·········· ·········· ··········			
Secondary ·········· ·········· ··········			
External ·········· ·········· ··········			

Source: ODA 1995b.

Figure 3.2   Classification of Stakeholders by Relative Importance and Influence on Project Objectives

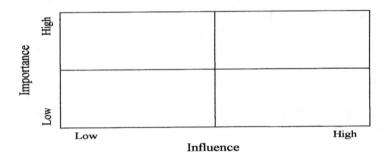

Source: ODA 1995b.

stage of the project it is possible for stakeholders to be informed (provided with information) to be consulted for information or opinions, to participate actively, to be delegated a subsidiary role, or to be controlled (not involved in planning but involved in implementation). The appropriate role for each stakeholder group will vary according to the stage reached by the project and according to the nature of the project.

Once the stakeholders in a project have been defined it is necessary to develop the project idea into a coherent proposal. There are two related approaches that can be used to help define the project. These are *objective oriented project planning* (OOPP) and the *logical framework*. It should be noted that the process is an iterative one. As the project is defined more closely the roles of different stakeholders become clearer. Stakeholder analysis is therefore a continuous process throughout the development of a project.

Figure 3.3   Participation Matrix

	Inform	Consult	Partnership	Delegate	Control
Identification					
Planning					
Implementation					
Monitoring and Evaluation					

Source: ODA 1995: 99.

Objective Oriented Project Planning

OOPP is an approach originally devised by the German aid agency Deutsche Gesellschaft für Technische Zusammenarbeit (GTZ) to generate project ideas in a systematic way and then to develop them.[3] It is a problem-centered method that is best suited to projects involving a number of different agents. The method is intended to improve communication and cooperation among agents involved in the development of the project. Ideally OOPP involves the participation of all significant interest groups and target groups in the process of developing a clear understanding of the current situation and its problems. It is from this common understanding that a solution is defined. The approach starts with analysis of four important aspects of the potential project:

Participation Analysis

In the first stage all persons, groups, and actors likely to be involved in the project are identified and characterized as actors; beneficiaries; or those affected, including both supporters and potential opponents. The characteristics, motivation, and potential of each category are described along with the possible implications for planning the proposed project. One important result of this process is the early identification of potential conflicts of interest. It should also be possible to identify the strengths and weaknesses of the groups and institutions likely to be involved in implementation. This will help to ensure that projects are undertaken by appropriate institutions and that issues of institutional capacity are addressed.

Problem Analysis

Here the idea is to identify the core problem to be tackled and then to establish the chain of causes and effects. The first step is to reach a common agreement on the nature of the core problem, which is expressed as a negative condition that will have to be resolved. Considerable importance is attached to establishing this consensus among those participating in the analysis. Once agreement is reached an attempt is made to build a problem tree in which multilevel cause-effect relationships are traced (Figure 3.4). In this process the problems of each interest group are listed, and the causal relationships among them are then defined. By tracing these relationships it should be possible to determine how particular measures might contribute to overcoming the problems identified.

Objectives Analysis

Once the core problem has been identified and causes and effects have been determined it is possible to define objectives by restating the problems (negative conditions) as positive conditions to be achieved. In the process the cause-effect relationships become means-ends relationships, and the hierarchy of problems in the problem tree becomes a hierarchy of objectives that define the future desired and achievable situation to be reached

Figure 3.4   A Problem Tree

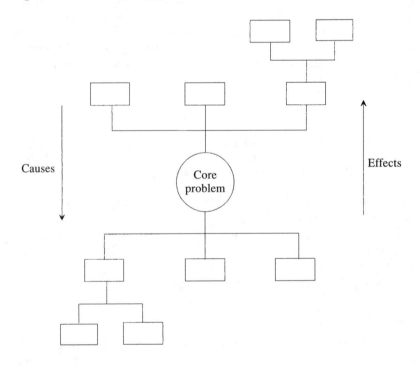

when the problems have been solved. When the objectives have been defined in this way it is necessary to re-examine the means-ends relationships to ensure that the means are actually sufficient to achieve the ends.

Alternatives Analysis

An important aspect of the identification and formulation stage in project analysis is to consider all the alternative ways of achieving a given set of objectives. In the context of OOPP this means that the project team must

- Identify those objectives that are not desirable or achievable
- Identify various means-ends ladders as possible strategies for achieving those objectives that are desirable and achievable
- Assess which of the alternative strategies provides the optimal strategy using agreed criteria

Various criteria could be used depending on the level of detail to which the alternative strategies have been prepared. The criteria outlined earlier in this chapter might be used, as might a more general indication of the priority of different courses of action within the sector program and the appropriateness of the strategy in relation to local conditions. A very important practical criterion is whether each of the strategies proposed is realistic and likely to be workable. The importance of considering each possible alternative at an early stage of the project planning process cannot be overemphasized.

Throughout the world there are thousands of projects where means have been confused with ends. The desire to counter this tendency contributed to the development of the *logical framework approach* to project design. This approach was developed independently of OOPP but was adopted by the proponents of OOPP as the next stage in the process.[4] An illustration of the application of both OOPP and the logical framework approach using GTZ terminology is provided in Appendix 3.1.

The Logical Framework

The logical framework approach was originally devised for the U.S. Agency for International Development (USAID), but subsequently it has been adopted in a modified format by a number of different agencies including GTZ, the UK Overseas Development Administration (ODA), the Canadian International Development Agency (CIDA), and the Norwegian Agency for Development Co-operation (NORAD). It is used in the design, preparation, monitoring, and evaluation of projects.

The logical framework format is a four-by-four matrix in which the logic of the project design is set out in the form of a vertical hierarchy of rows (Figure 3.5):

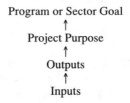

The logical framework also has columns showing indicators of achievement, means of verifying the achievements, and important assumptions for the success of the project. It provides a summary of what the project is and how it is supposed to work. The format discussed below indicates the original terminology and gives some of the alternative descriptions used by different agencies in brackets (ODA and GTZ respectively).

Figure 3.5   The Logical Framework Matrix

Project Design Summary Logical Framework

Project Title: _____

Narrative Summary	Ojectively Verifiable Indicators	Means of Verification	Important Assumptions
Program or sector goal: the broader objective to which this project contributes:	Measure of goal achievement:		Assmptions for achieving goal targets:
Project purpose:	Conditions that will indicate purpose has been achieved— end of project:		Assumptions for achieving outputs:
Outputs:	Magnitude of outputs:		Assumptions for achieving outputs:
Inputs:	Implementation target (type and quality):		Assumptions for providing inputs:

Narrative Summary
(Project Structure or Summary of Objectives and Activities)

The left-hand column summarizes the logic of the project. The highest level of objective is the program or sector goal (wider objective or overall goal). There is general agreement that there should not be too many sector goals, and some agencies (CIDA and GTZ) insist that there should be only one.

The second level of objective in the narrative summary is the project purpose (immediate objective). This is the result expected from the project, which will contribute to achievement of the goal. It could also be described as project impact. As with the sector goal there should not be too many project purposes, otherwise the purpose becomes confused. Again CIDA and GTZ suggest that there should be only one.

The third level of the narrative summary shows the project outputs (results/outputs). These are the specific results expected from project inputs, which in turn help the achievement of the purpose. This description often causes some confusion because, for the logical framework, the outputs of the project are the physical structures and institutions established by the project, not the production that results from setting up these structures. Thus the output of an irrigation project might be a completed irrigation system and an institution to manage the system, while the additional crops produced as a result of establishing the project would be described as the project purpose.

The lowest level of the narrative summary shows the project inputs (activities). These are the resources used by the project to produce the project output. Both GTZ and NORAD use the term *activities* to avoid repetition in the verifiable indicators column and to avoid excessively long lists. In the NORAD version the inputs are the goods and services required to undertake the activities, and these are entered in the indicators column.

Objectively Verifiable Indicators
(Indicators of Achievement and Value)

The second column of the logical framework shows the objectively verifiable indicators of achievement for each level. An indicator is a means of measurement, which allows judgements to be made about a situation. Indicators provide the criteria for assessing the progress of the project in terms of its stated objectives. Indicators have to be specified in such a way that their achievement is verifiable when project implementation is being monitored. Normally this means that they should be quantifiable.

Means of Verification (How Indicators Can Be Quantified or Assessed or Means/Sources of Verification)

The third column is concerned with sources of information. For each indicator a source should be specified. This column provides those monitoring or evaluating the project with advance knowledge of how the success of the project is to be verified and therefore helps in the design of information systems for project implementation.

Important Assumptions (Assumptions, Risks, and Conditions)

The vertical logic outlined in a logical framework contains a series of assumptions about the environment external to the project. The fourth column outlines for each level those assumptions that would affect the progress of the project but over which the project has no control. The importance of this column is that it requires the designer of the project to consider whether the assumptions being made are realistic, and it also indicates to the project manager some of the most important external factors to monitor during implementation. Definition of the extent to which factors are within the control of project management is not always obvious, and there are many factors that might be within the influence of project management but not necessarily within control. A safe working rule might be to include all those assumptions that are important, including those that can be influenced but not controlled.

There is some variation in the way in which proponents of the logical framework technique recommend that the assumptions be related to the different levels. In the original version of the logical framework the assumptions were set out in such a way that the realization of the assumption related to the achievement of the same level of the narrative summary. This meant that the lowest level of assumption related to the inception of the project without which the inputs could not be obtained. In this approach, which is the one followed in the manuals prepared for the UK ODA, the following connections could be made:

$$\text{assumptions (1) + decisions} \rightarrow \text{project inception (inputs) (1)}$$
$$\text{inputs (1) + assumptions (2)} \rightarrow \text{output (2)}$$
$$\text{output (2) + assumptions (3)} \rightarrow \text{purpose (3)}$$
$$\text{purpose (3) + assumption (4)} \rightarrow \text{goal (4)}$$

More recently other users have proposed that the assumption should relate to the next higher level of objective so that achievement of the lower-level objective plus the lower-level assumption leads to achievement of the higher-level objective. Thus,

$$\text{inputs (1) + assumptions (1)} \rightarrow \text{output (2)}$$
$$\text{output (2) + assumptions (2)} \rightarrow \text{purpose (3)}$$
$$\text{purpose (3) + assumption (3)} \rightarrow \text{goal (4)}$$

The top (fourth) level of assumption then would remain blank unless an overall long-run goal above the program or sector goal is defined. This approach has been put forward by GTZ and is also used in the manual prepared for the European Commission as well as in a computer software package developed specifically to facilitate the design of projects using a variant of OOPP and the logical framework approach.[5] The case study in Appendix 3.1 uses GTZ terminology but with the original ordering of assumptions.

Limitations and Problems in the Use of the Logical Framework

The logical framework is a useful tool but, like any tool, it has its limitations. Intelligent use of the logical framework should ensure that the design of the project is logical, but it does not ensure that the project is optimal. To some extent the issue of choosing an optimal strategy may have been dealt with if the OOPP process has preceded the use of the framework. Nevertheless the kind of qualitative assessment made at an early stage of project design does not guarantee that the best alternative has been chosen. This would suggest that, where genuine alternatives exist, analysis of alternatives should be taken beyond the stage of drawing up a logical framework.

The logical framework also gives no guidance on issues that it is not asked to address. It is therefore likely to be neutral in relation to important issues such as income distribution, employment, participation, and the environment unless these issues are addressed specifically in the objectives of the project. Again, these issues may have been considered through some form of stakeholder analysis or the OOPP process; however, without further analysis the scale of the implications may not be very clear.

The great value of the logical framework format is its ability to provide a clear summary of the basic features of a project proposal in a four-by-four matrix. This is also a limitation because there is a limit to the amount of information that realistically can be included in such a matrix. The framework is only a summary. It does not contain all the answers.

Although the agencies that have used the logical framework approach have generally found it useful, there have also been some problems. Its use in practice has been reviewed both by USAID and ODA.[6] Among the problems noted were:

- A tendency for users to engage in mechanical box filling rather than thinking.
- A failure to allow targets to be adapted to changing circumstances.
- Unnecessary rigidity caused by projects designed to "fit the framework."
- Overemphasis or misuse of quantitative targets.
- Difficulties in distinguishing between outputs and purposes. This

problem also extended to problems with projects where the hierarchy of objectives did not fit neatly into the four-level structure.
- Difficulties in specifying the means of verification for the achievement of sector goals.

Tools such as the OOPP approach and the logical framework can sometimes be misused through dogmatic interpretation. An important rule in
using such tools is that "the tail should not wag the dog." If some aspect of
a project is logically consistent but really does not seem to fit the tool, it is
the tool that should be adapted, not the project. As long as this flexibility is
retained these tools can be of great value in thinking through the design of
a project.

Building Flexibility:
Blueprint Projects and Process Projects

One of the important problems recognized in introducing the logical framework was the possible introduction of excessive rigidity in the planning and
implementation process. Once a plan is established there is a tendency to
regard targets as fixed regardless of whether changing circumstances continue to justify those targets. Unless a process of periodic review of project
objectives is established there is no reason for those implementing the project to learn from the mistakes being made.

Traditional *blueprint* projects involve drawing up a plan and implementing it. This type of approach is most appropriate for engineering projects that involve a very specific set of tasks that are unlikely to change with
circumstances. Such projects can be contrasted with projects that are
intended to change people's behavior, where the project outcome is based
on a set of hypotheses about how people will react to project activities. The
margin of error in people-based projects is likely to be much greater than
for engineering projects, as is the scope for changes in project design.
Projects of this kind are most common in the social sectors and in the agricultural and small-scale industrial sectors when the aim is to influence large
numbers of small producers. Where these conditions exist, an adaptive or
process approach to project design may be more appropriate. This is the
kind of approach that Picciotto and Weaving (1994) were attempting to put
forward with their New Project Cycle for the World Bank, partly in the
realization that blueprint approaches were not appropriate for certain kinds
of projects.

The essential feature of process projects is that the project design is
regarded as indicative rather than fixed. Because of this the project design
must include provision for periodic review to allow for learning from expe-

rience. Since such projects are supposed to be centered around people it is also necessary to include procedures for listening to the experiences of the people potentially affected by the project. A process project might then be expected to go through a succession of stages, each one being the subject of review to determine the precise nature of the next stage. These stages have been described as those of experimentation, piloting, demonstration, and replication or production (Rondinelli 1983).

In reality the dichotomy between blueprint and process projects is often not so clear-cut. Most reasonably large projects are planned in phases, and the content of one phase is likely to depend on the results of the previous stage even if the overall project is fairly tightly defined. Even loosely defined process projects will have an overall objective toward which the project is supposed to aim.

One issue that the debate over blueprint and process projects has brought into focus is the question of time. Inappropriate use of inflexible approaches to project design can lead to unrealistic projections of the amount of time required to implement a project. The result may be that considerable resources are expended with little result. The process approach would tend to have a longer time horizon with relatively little expenditure taking place until a pilot project had indicated that the project idea would be likely to succeed. Such approaches have implications for project funding because they suggest the need for a conditional commitment to funding a project over a much longer time period than has traditionally been the case.

A second issue that arises when considering process projects is that of participation. To what extent and at what stages should local participants be involved in the design, appraisal, and implementation of the project? How are decisions made about which participants and local institutions are going to be involved? How will the dialogue between the various actors take place and how will those involved ensure that a constructive outcome is obtained? There are no easy answers to these questions but they do point to the need for a clear understanding of the social and political context within which a project is proposed. Stakeholder analysis can help in obtaining such an understanding.

A third issue is the relationship between project components that are "blueprint" by their nature (e.g., engineering components) and those that are not. Where one depends on the other, the issue of timing becomes critical. This may have implications for the assumptions specified in any project framework and the periodic review of the timing of the implementation of project components.

Some might argue that the greater uncertainty involved in process projects would undermine the use of standard project appraisal methods. This does not have to be the case. There are ways of dealing with uncertainty however great it is. It is still important to be able to decide whether the expected future benefits have any chance of justifying the expenditure on the project however large the margin of error in the estimates.

Further Reading

Literature on project identification is fairly sparse. Some ideas can be gleaned from Behrens and Hawranek (1991), Benjamin (1981), and Mathur (1985). By contrast there is a large and growing literature on stakeholder analysis and the logical framework. This can be traced back to the work of Delp et al. (1977) and the USAID. MacArthur (1993) provides a useful review of available material on the logical framework. The connection between objective oriented project planning and the logical framework is covered in various GTZ publications as well as NORAD (1996) and Commission of the European Communities (1993). Stakeholder analysis techniques are covered in Overseas Development Administration (1995) and Howlett and Nagu (1997).

Appendix 3.1:
The Smallholder Tea Project—
An Illustration of the Application of
OOPP and the Logical Framework

Purpose of the Example

The example discussed below is intended to illustrate some of the issues that arise in trying to use OOPP and the logical framework. It is not intended to be a faultless display of the methods, and it deliberately raises some problems. Some rules were broken where it appeared convenient to do so, and some might argue that the project itself is misconceived. The emphasis is on using the techniques as frameworks for thinking in a structured way rather than as a set of strict rules.

The Project

The project illustrated is based on a real project proposal. The proposal arose because smallholder farmers in a certain area were frustrated at being unable to sell all the green leaf they could produce to the nearby private-sector factory to be processed into made tea. This frustration became more serious when the producer prices set by the government for green leaf rose to levels that encouraged farmers to revive their production. The farmers wanted the government-owned tea company to build a new factory so that they could sell green leaf from their existing area and plant new areas.

The private-sector factory was unable to purchase the farmers' green leaf because a combination of poor world tea prices, unfavorable exchange rate policy, and inadequate foreign exchange allocations had left the factory in such poor condition that it had difficulty processing the green leaf from its own estates. Added to this were problems in transporting the green leaf due to poor feeder roads and inadequate vehicle capacity. Although a change in exchange rate policy and liberalization of foreign exchange allocation had led the private-sector company to consider rehabilitation of the factory, its primary intention was to process green leaf from its own estates, not those of small farmers in the surrounding area. Smallholder green leaf was believed to be too expensive because of high producer prices and high transport costs and too risky to justify a major investment. As a result of this situation some antagonism had built up between the farmers and the private-sector factory.

The government, as represented by the nationalized tea company and the ministry of agriculture extension service, was keen for a smallholder tea processing project to go ahead, partly for political reasons and partly because of the importance of tea as a major source of foreign exchange. The problem can be investigated in an OOPP framework.

Participation Analysis

The main actors were the nationalized tea company and the ministry of agriculture. They were both keen for a project to go ahead in order to resolve the farmers' complaints and generate extra foreign exchange earnings. The ministry was unsure about the appropriate level of government involvement in the project because of budget constraints and would have welcomed some form of joint venture with private-sector participation. The nationalized tea company wanted to take full responsibility but recognized that funding might be a problem. Although the company had a reasonably good reputation, some doubts were expressed about its capacity to manage the implementation of a major new project.

The main beneficiaries would be the farmers. They wanted to see a new factory designed specifically to serve their needs. They were antagonistic to proposals involving the existing factory because they felt that it had not looked after their interests in the past.

The existing factory would be affected by a new factory. It had some reasons to oppose a new project because it would increase competition for the labor currently working on the estates and would also compete for smallholder green leaf. Yet competition for smallholder leaf was not a very important issue for the existing factory because smallholder green leaf did not give much profit given the existing relatively high producer prices and the low-quality tea being produced by aging machinery. Estate workers would benefit from a new factory because competition from smallholders for their labor at peak periods would improve their bargaining position and increase their income earning opportunities. Local people would also benefit if feeder roads were improved.

Problem Analysis

A problem tree is shown in Figure 3.6. There is some question as to what the core problem should be. At the general level it could be defined as "reduced tea production," but this could relate to any area and any type of tea production. The particular problem being addressed in this project related to smallholder farmers in a specific area. The core problem was therefore defined as "farmers unable to sell all the green leaf they wish to produce." This problem was primarily a result of inadequate factory capacity and inadequate facilities for green leaf transport. These problems were caused in turn by a combination of past government policies and a hostile external economic environment. It might also be possible to define the core problem as "reduced farmer incomes." This would open up the possibility of proposing a project that did not involve tea at all. The process of defining problems could be thought of as an iterative process with alternative views of the core problem being dealt with in the alternatives analysis.

Figure 3.6 illustrates a number of problems in drawing a problem tree. First of all there is a problem of cause and effect interacting with each other. Low world tea prices combined with an unfavorable exchange rate policy resulted in the existing factory getting low prices for its made tea. This contributed to low profitability, which resulted in the failure to maintain and replace aging factory equipment. Deteriorating equipment contributed to poor-quality tea, which in turn contributed to low tea prices. There was therefore a downward spiral of cause and effect, which is not very easily expressed in one-way relationships.

Figure 3.6 also shows a problem that does not relate directly to the core problem since it is an anticipated problem. If a new factory were to be established, farmers would want a supply of tea plants so that they could expand their areas. This is not a problem without the new factory because there would be no point in planting new areas if the output could not be sold. However, if a new factory were to be built, there would be no existing nurseries to provide farmers with tea plants to allow them to expand their area. Inadequate nursery capacity is therefore entered as a potential future problem. A similar anticipated problem would be inadequate fuelwood for processing if green leaf production were to expand. This has also been included as a potential future problem in Figure 3.6. One of the features of

Figure 3.6   Problem Tree for the Smallholder Tea Project

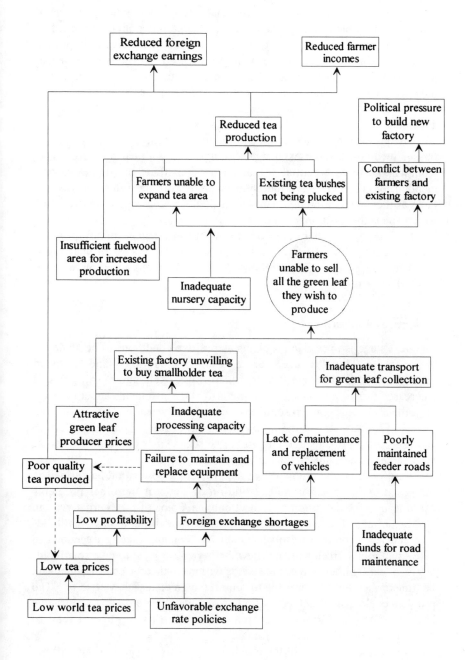

a problem tree is that it cannot encompass the time dimension. For that several problem trees would be required.

The issue of time specificity also relates to the two policy issues indicated in the problem tree. Unfavorable exchange rate policies were a feature of past rather than present conditions, but they were clearly important in contributing to the situation being addressed. Attractive green leaf prices were a reflection of the change in exchange rate policy. Of course they are only a problem from the point of view of the factory that has to buy the green leaf. From the point of view of the farmers they are an advantage.

The problem tree ends in three problems at the highest level relating to farmer incomes, foreign exchange earnings, and political pressures. This would imply three potential overall goals, something that is not recommended by GTZ. We have the choice of breaking the rules and leaving them as they are, combining them into a single composite goal, or deciding which one is the most important.

Difficulties like these are bound to occur in drawing up any problem tree. We could either let these difficulties cause the process of analysis to grind to a halt or we could recognize the issues and carry on with an "imperfect" model.

Objectives Analysis

The next stage is to restate problems as positive conditions to be achieved in the future. Thus "reduced foreign exchange earnings" and "reduced farmer incomes" become "increased foreign exchange earnings" and "increased farmer incomes." We might also make statements about removal of political pressures and resolution of conflict between the farmers and the factory. These aspects of the problem tree have been abandoned in further analysis on the grounds that they might be regarded as constraints on solutions rather than as objectives in themselves.

Further down the problem tree the project purpose could be defined as increased tea production, and resolution of some of the other problems could lead to the definition of project outputs. Some of the alternatives can also be defined. The problem "existing factory unwilling to buy smallholder green leaf" could be resolved either by "existing factory expanded to take smallholder green leaf" or "new factory constructed to take smallholder green leaf." Either of these measures will mean that the core problem can be transformed to "farmers able to sell all the green leaf they wish to." The problem could also be solved by finding an alternative crop that would give better returns to farmers than tea. However, this might not lead to "increased foreign exchange earnings."

Restatement of some of the problems as positive conditions also allows the identification of important assumptions. Transformation of "unfavorable exchange rate policies" to "favorable exchange rate policies" is an important assumption, but it lies outside the control of the project.

Alternatives Analysis

There are various possible ways of dealing with the core problem. The first is to propose construction of a new factory. Construction could be undertaken either by the nationalized tea company or by a private-sector investor or through a joint venture. Given the problems of public-sector financing of productive-sector projects in the 1990s, it would appear that the latter two approaches would have had the greatest chance of success. Since the project involved agricultural extension and rural feeder roads it might be that a private-sector investor would be reluctant to undertake all of the necessary investment. The history of past policy problems might also make private investors unwilling to invest without some form of participation or guarantee from the government. A joint venture might therefore be the preferred option. Some form of involvement of the farmers or of farmers' organizations in part ownership of the factory might also be desirable to increase farmer commitment as stakeholders in the success of the factory.

The factory could also be planned with different views of both the ultimate size of the factory and the time scale over which this size could be reached. In view of the uncertainty about farmers' plans to plant new areas, it would be sensible to plan in phases with a relatively small scale initially but with the possibility of further expansion. This would make the project in some respects a process project.

Another alternative would be to persuade the existing private-sector factory to include smallholders in their expansion plans. This might be the most economically satisfactory way of solving the problem, but neither the private-sector factory nor the farmers appeared to be very keen on the idea. In an area where there is only one tea factory, that factory is a monopoly buyer of green leaf, and this position may have contributed to the level of mutual distrust.

A third alternative would be to convince farmers to forget tea and grow something else. Since there wasn't an obvious alternative cash crop this alternative was not given further consideration.

The fourth alternative would be to do nothing at all and let the situation sort itself out. This alternative was politically problematic.

As a result of examining the alternatives, it was proposed to investigate the feasibility of building a new factory in phases with the ownership to be determined once the viability of the project had been established.

Project Planning Matrix (Logical Framework)

Figure 3.7 shows the project planning matrix for the project. The highest-level problems have become the overall goal, but in this case two goals

Figure 3.7 Project Planning Matrix (Logical Framework) for the Smallholder Tea Project

Summary of Objectives/Activities	Objectively Verifiable Indicators	Means of Verification	Important Assumptions
Overall goal:			
Increase foreign exchange earnings	Value of foreign exchange earned from additional tea	Tea market reports	World tea prices are within assumed range
Increase farmer incomes	Value of farmer earnings from sale of green leaf	Factory records	Favorable exchange rate policy
			Green leaf prices remain profitable to farmers
Project purpose:			
Increase production of made tea from smallholder green leaf	Quantity of made tea produced from smallholder green leaf	Factory records	Assumed ratio of green leaf to made tea is achieved
	Quantity of smallholder green leaf sold	Factory records	Assumed green leaf yields are achieved
			Weather conditions favorable
Improve quality of tea production	Prices achieved on export market	Tea market reports	New factory improves tea quality
Results/outputs:			
a) New tea factory	a) New factory installed and working	a) Project manager's reports	a) Equipment delivered is satisfactory
b) Improved green leaf transport system	b) Green leaf transported to the factory	b) Transport manager's reports	b) Improved roads are maintained
c) Distribution of tea plants to smallholders	c) Number of tea plants distributed	c) Village tea officers' reports	c) Smallholder farmers want to improve existing areas
			Smallholder farmers want to expand tea area
d) Establishment of fuelwood plantation	d) Area of fuelwood established	d) Plantation manager's reports	d) Suitable area exists for planting fuelwood
Activities:			
a) Construction of factory buildings	a) Building materials delivered	a) Engineer's reports	Foreign exchange available
b) Installation of factory machinery	b) Factory machinery delivered	b) Engineer's reports	Funds disbursed to schedule
c) Upgrading feeder roads	c) Road repairs contracted	c) Engineer's reports	Required labor skills available
d) Purchase of vehicles	d) Vehicles purchased	d) Transport officer's reports	
e) Provision of extension advice	e) Extension officers employed	e) Personnel officer's reports	
f) Establishment of nurseries	f) Nursery materials delivered	f) Plantation manager's reports	
g) Planting fuelwood trees	g) Planting materials delivered	g) Plantation manager's reports	

have been given. This is contrary to GTZ practice but can be justified on the grounds that the project has two aspects that are equally important. From the economic point of view the major purpose of the project is to earn foreign exchange from exporting tea. This could be achieved by any sort of tea project. This project also has a distributional aspect. It is intended to solve a problem of reduced farmer incomes. This will only be solved by a project that is oriented to the needs of the smallholder growers.

A similar issue arises at the level of project purpose. Low earnings are caused both by low production and by poor quality. The project therefore has two purposes. It is intended to improve the quantity and the quality of made tea. Of course this could be made into a single purpose by adding the word *and*, but this does not contribute anything to the analysis.

Some difficulties arise in distinguishing between outputs and activities. A distinction has been made between the green leaf transport system as an output and the purchase of vehicles as an activity. There are a number of intermediate steps between "distribution of tea plants to smallholders" and "increase production of made tea from smallholder green leaf." These include the planting of new areas by smallholders and the rehabilitation of existing areas. Neither of these steps is directly within the control of the project so they have to be entered as important assumptions about smallholder behavior.

The objectively verifiable indicators in Figure 3.7 have been indicated in general terms. For practical purposes it would be necessary to define these in terms of thousands of dollars or tons of tea; otherwise there would be no targets against which to measure achievement.

The means of verification also define some of the records that will have to be kept by the project and can help in determining the allocation of responsibilities and the design of the project management structure. Simply asking who is going to collect a certain piece of information helps to determine staff requirements.

The important assumptions indicate just how many factors can have a significant effect on the success of the project and what behavioral assumptions are being made. Some assumptions are not included because the logical framework does not examine alternatives. The assumption that some agreement cannot be reached between the smallholders and the existing factory is not included, but if it turned out to be false, it could undermine the whole case for the project.

There are some grey areas in defining the assumptions if a strict definition of what lies within the control of the project is adhered to. The assumptions related to the processing efficiency of the equipment and the quality of tea produced by that equipment are within the control of project management to a significant extent, but they also depend on the quality of the equipment delivered to the project, which might be regarded as outside the control of the management. If the contract for supplying the equipment included some performance guarantees, these issues might then be regarded as within management control. They could then be removed from the important assumptions.

The process of thinking about the assumptions can itself be used as a means of identifying areas where specific actions could reduce uncertainty, thereby improving the project design. The process of drawing up a logical framework can therefore be regarded as interactive with project design. The logical framework is unlikely to remain unchanged for the duration of the project preparation process.

Notes

1. Like all projections, the World Bank projections are subject to a considerable margin of error, and they have the disadvantage that they are used by a lot of people in a lot of countries. Projections of price improvements therefore tend to be self-adjusting because they encourage new producers to enter the market. Nevertheless it is unlikely that the individual project analyst will be able to come up with any better estimates.

2. Demand forecasting techniques are many and varied, and approaches are sometimes sector specific. As such they are beyond the scope of this book.

3. The original version of the technique is known by the German acronym ZOPP. Variants of the approach have been used by other agencies, including NORAD.

4. In the OOPP approach the logical framework is known as the project planning matrix.

5. The software package is called TeamUP. The package includes both the objective oriented project planning approach and the logical framework.

6. A useful summary of the various reviews is given in MacArthur (1993).

4

Basic Principles
of Project Analysis

Basic Concepts

In Chapter 2 a number of aspects of project appraisal were mentioned. These included analysis from the technical, financial, commercial, economic and social, managerial, and organizational standpoints. Environmental analysis could also be added to this list. A distinction was made between those aspects of appraisal that involve the question of project feasibility and those that relate to the question of project desirability.

Analysis of feasibility is about what will work. There are no generally applicable techniques for many of the technical aspects of feasibility, only the application of whatever approaches are relevant to the type of project concerned. Nevertheless there are some general questions that will need to be answered. A checklist of some of these questions is given in Figure 4.1.

Questions of desirability apply particularly to the financial and economic appraisal of projects where attempts are made to compare costs and benefits to decide whether the project is worthwhile. The desirability of a project can be interpreted from the point of view of the investor (financial analysis) or from a wider national perspective (economic analysis). In principle, economic analysis can be adapted to include environmental and social questions where such costs and benefits can be identified and measured. Figure 4.1 includes some of the desirability criteria that will be discussed later in this and other chapters.

There is a general set of techniques that can be used to assess the desirability of a project involving the comparison of costs and benefits to determine whether benefits exceed costs. This set of techniques is known as cost-benefit analysis (CBA). CBA was originally developed for public-sector projects in the United States but is now used widely for public- and private-sector projects throughout the world.

Sometimes, when benefits are not easy to measure or when a compari-

47

Figure 4.1   A Matrix of Criteria for Project Appraisal

Project Aspect	Feasibility	Desirability
Technical	Technical design criteria are satisfied Technical capacity of management and workforce adequate Output targets can be met	Local resources/skills used where appropriate Sustainable technology used Technical efficiency maximized
Financial	Cash balance is always positive (required finance is available and all financial commitments can be met) All parties have adequate financial incentives	Financial profitability measures satisfactory to all parties IRR to equity exceeds real interest rate Uncertainty and risk associated with project is minimized
Economic		EIRR exceeds target rate Domestic resource cost of foreign exchange lower than shadow exchange rate Cost-effective methods used for noncommerical projects Risk that project failure will damage economy is minimized
Social	Project acceptable in relations to existing laws and social norms	Target groups involved in project design and operation Distribution of costs and benefits of project contributes to government objectives
Institutional	Implementing agencies have authority and motivation to perform roles assumed	Preferred forms of organization are used Implementing agency operations are sustainable
Environmental	All negative effects are below legal/customary limits	All negative effects are minimized All positive effects are maximized
Political	Project is consistent with government policies and plans	Project has active political support

Source: Adapted from a similar matrix devised by J. D. MacArthur.

son is being made of two alternative ways of achieving the same objective, a variant of CBA techniques known as cost-effectiveness analysis (CEA) is used. CEA is used most commonly in social- and infrastructure-sector projects and for projects where there are choices of location or technology.

CBA and CEA both make use of a common unit of measure, usually (but not always) a unit of the currency of the country in which the analysis is being undertaken. Criteria for assessing the desirability of projects are then developed based on these units. CBA and CEA make use of both economic principles and accounting principles. This mixture of disciplines can lead to inconsistencies in the treatment of particular items. In this chapter I will try to establish some basic ground rules that are as consistent as possible with both disciplines.

Sometimes assessment of a project involves the comparison of CBA or CEA criteria, which are measured in money terms, with other criteria that cannot be measured in money terms. When such situations arise it may be possible to make use of multicriteria analysis (MCA).

CBA and CEA assume that the resources used in projects are scarce and therefore that they should be used in the most efficient way possible. If resources were not scarce, the issue of efficiency in their use would not be sufficiently important to justify the time spent on the analysis. Since time is also a resource, the degree of detail to which such analysis is taken will depend in part on the potential size of the costs and benefits of the project under consideration.

"With" and "Without" the Project

A fundamental principle of project analysis is that the value of a project is determined by making a comparison of the assumed situation *with* the project and the assumed situation *without* the project. The value of the project is measured by taking the difference between the two. The situation without the project is not necessarily the same as the situation before the project. The assumption, which is common in practice, that without the project is the same as before the project is justified only when the situation without the project is expected to be one of no change.

The without project situation is sometimes described as a *counterfactual hypothesis*. What would happen if we did not implement the project? In economic terms what we lose by implementing the project can be described as the project's *opportunity cost*. The opportunity cost principle provides the basis for most aspects of the economic analysis of projects.

Estimation of the without project situation is one of the most difficult aspects of project analysis and also one of the most neglected. Unfortunately there is very little guidance on what to assume since this will vary so greatly from one project to another. Nevertheless some basic principles should be observed. The without project assumption is sometimes important in financial analysis, but it is always important in economic analysis. To consider different aspects of the without project assumption it is helpful to divide projects into four types:

- "Green field" projects are completely new activities operating where the activity did not exist before.
- Expansion projects are those projects that are designed to lead to the expansion of an existing activity.
- Rehabilitation projects are those projects that are designed to lead to the rehabilitation of an activity that has suffered from some form of decline.
- Competing projects are those that involve the establishment of an activity in direct competition with another activity.

In addition it is also necessary to consider cases where there are institutional questions relating to the assumed behavior of other organizations without the project. Each case will be examined in turn.

Green Field Projects

Although green field projects are new activities they still involve the use of resources that may have other uses, and they may have an impact on people who without the project would otherwise be doing something else. It is therefore necessary to consider the alternative use of the resources involved and to make an assessment of what the people affected by the project would have been doing if the project did not take place.

In the case of projects that involve significant use of land, such as those in the agricultural sector or those involving road construction, the alternative use of the land must be considered. What would the land have produced without the project? It cannot be assumed that this will always be constant. In some cases technical progress might lead to increasing productivity of land even without the project. Where land is subject to environmental degradation the output from the land without the project might be assumed to decline. Similar issues have to be considered in relation to other natural resources such as minerals and fish.

The degree to which the without project situation has to be investigated also depends on the perspective from which the analysis is being undertaken. From a purely financial point of view what matters is only the situation for the owners of the project, that is, the alternative use of their own resources. When the analysis of a green field project does not contain any reference to the without project situation there is an implicit assumption that the value of the alternative use of the resources employed by the project is adequately represented by their price. This may be a reasonable assumption from the financial point of view of the owners, but from an economic point of view further investigation is required to account for the interests of all of the different people and organizations affected.

Expansion Projects

Expansion projects take place where an existing project has been successful or when a demand or need expands. Assessment of the without project situation in these cases therefore requires that careful attention be given to the question of demand. What would happen if the demand or need could not be satisfied? Would alternative means be found? In some cases demand might be satisfied by imports. In other cases prices might increase. In the case of infrastructure and social services it may be that a segment of the population would receive no service at all.

In the case of projects that expand the provision of support services to directly productive activities it is necessary to determine the nature of the relationship between the support service and the increase in production. For example, in the case of agricultural extension projects that are intended to lead to the diffusion of innovation, failure to expand provision of the service might lead to a slower rate of adoption. Assessment of the difference between the "with project" and the "without project" situations therefore depends on the specification of the relationship between service provision and diffusion of innovation. It is not enough to assume a certain impact. It is necessary to specify the process by which the intended impact is expected to be achieved for it to be possible to determine the difference between the "with project" and "without project" situations.

Rehabilitation Projects

The important question with rehabilitation projects is to determine what went wrong and why. In some cases failure may have been caused by an unfavorable policy environment.[1] In such cases, if the policy environment has not changed, there is no reason to believe that rehabilitation will not also fail. If the policy environment has changed, the project analyst must ask whether the project would continue to decline without the rehabilitation or whether some improvement would be recorded even without it.

Similar questions need to be asked for other causes of project failure. If bad management was the cause of the problem, what would happen if the management were replaced without a new project? If the alternative is assumed to be continued operation of the project under new management, there are usually some implications for investment even if full rehabilitation is not undertaken. Without a minimum of replacement investment or very heavy maintenance expenditure, it is unlikely that existing activities could continue.

It may be necessary to consider the possibility that the project would be forced to close without investment in rehabilitation. Assessment of whether the alternative to rehabilitation is continued operation at unsatisfactory levels of performance or whether it is complete closure is a particularly difficult issue. In some cases the without project situation might be assumed to be continued operation at diminishing performance levels for some years leading up to closure. In such cases the important factors to determine are the rate of decline and the length of time before closure might be expected to occur. It should be recognized that an assumption of indefinite continued operation of a failing activity may be unrealistic and may lead to exaggeration of the benefits of a project when these are defined as the difference between a positive "with project" situation and a negative "without project" situation.

Competing Projects

Projects can be in competition with each other and with ongoing activities for both markets and materials. In some cases there is also competition for labor. When examining the without project situation for competing projects we may discover that there will be a difference for the competitor between the situation without the project and the situation with the project. If there is competition for markets it may be that, without the project, the sales of the competitor would remain at existing levels but that with the project the sales of the competitor might decline. The value of sales could also decline if competition causes a reduction in prices. In such cases the situation for the consumer with and without the project would also have to be considered.

Similar factors have to be considered in relation to competition for materials and labor. In our tea factory example it is possible that the new project would lead to some farmers selling their green leaf to the new factory instead of to the old one. For the old factory it might be that without the project, processing of smallholder green leaf would continue as before but that with the project, the supply would be diverted to the new factory. If this were to happen, some of the tea processed at the new factory will not be additional tea produced; it will be tea diverted from one processor to another. It would therefore be wrong to assume that all the tea produced would be additional production. Similarly, competition for labor might lead to a difference in the level of production of competitors with and without the project or possibly a difference in the wages paid to workers.

To some extent all projects compete with each other for resources. For this reason it is important in the economic analysis of projects to establish what the alternative use of the resources might have been. The techniques that can be used to do this will be considered in more detail in Part 3 of this book.

Institutional Considerations

In establishing what might happen without the project some assumptions are being made about who will do what. The easiest assumption to make is that the existing institutional setup would stay as it is. For example, if lack of electricity generating capacity leads to power cuts, we might assume that the existing electricity supply company would continue to provide a sub-standard service without the project and that this would lead to production losses. However, we might also assume that some electricity consumers invest in generators and provide their own electricity. Similarly, if existing public health facilities are inadequate, we might assume that without the project the public would continue to receive inadequate health care. However, we might also assume that there would be an expansion in the provision of private medical facilities.

The latter case has been described as the *private-sector counter-factual*.[2] It has been argued that public investment is unnecessary in areas where the private sector would otherwise invest. In the extreme case where, without the project, there would be an exactly equivalent private invest-ment it could be argued that there is no additional benefit produced by the public investment. Indeed some would argue that if the private sector is a more efficient producer in some sectors, the additional benefit of the pub-lic-sector investment would actually be negative. An alternative version of the same argument suggests that public investment in areas where the pri-vate sector would be happy to invest would lead to higher taxation and that this would have a negative effect on incentives.

It should be recognized that such arguments rest on a number of assumptions and that these assumptions could be turned around. First of all it is assumed that private-sector funds are less scarce than public-sector funds and therefore that the private-sector funds diverted from the public-sector project would not be invested productively elsewhere. Second, it is assumed that the private-sector investment would give the same or greater benefit than the public-sector investment. While this may be true in most productive sector projects with commercial objectives, it is not necessarily true for other projects. In the case of the health-sector project it is unlikely that private investors would have the same priorities; therefore the impact would be likely to be both smaller and concentrated on particular groups, most probably the better-off sections of the community.

The institutional counterfactual argument can therefore be used in different ways to make assumptions about the without project situation. We should examine the likely response of other institutions without the project. We should also ask questions about the policies affecting the investment as a means of deciding whether an investment by the institution considering the project is justified.

In our tea factory example we were making the implicit assumption that the private sector would not be willing to invest in factory expansion for smallholders because of the high level of risk. Many would argue that the high level of risk was associated with a particular set of policies and that, if these policies were changed, the required investment might be forthcoming from the private sector. Such an argument might then lead to the suggestion that the appropriate role for the public sector would be to change the policies and leave the investment to the private sector. Would the private-sector investment be forthcoming? How well does the market system function in the country concerned? One of the reasons economic analysis of projects is done is that markets may not be working very well.

In the analysis of any project it is necessary to make an assessment of the without project situation. Such an assessment should lead to a thorough examination of all aspects of the environment within which the project operates. By asking what would happen without the project it is possible that a range of different alternatives might become apparent. In the process it is quite possible that the whole concept of the project could be changed. Such an examination really needs to take place before any attempt is made to make any of the detailed estimates of costs and benefits described in the rest of this chapter.

Basic Project Statements

Cost-benefit analysis involves the comparison of costs and benefits over the period of time that is defined as the project life. Costs and benefits are set out against the year in which they occur. There are two conventions commonly used for numbering the years of a project. Some project analysts describe the first project year as Year 0 while others describe the first year as Year 1. As long as the convention that is adopted is followed consistently it does not matter which convention is used. For convenience and for consistency with standard spreadsheet functions the convention of describing the first year of the project as Year 1 is followed in this book.[3]

Normally project costs and benefits are estimated in terms of constant prices with the base year being the year in which the project is planned. This procedure is intended to remove the distorting effect that fluctuations in the general level of inflation might have on the value of project costs and benefits.

Price changes occur for two reasons. First, there are changes in the general price level due to inflation and second, there are changes in relative prices because the prices of different things change at different rates. Project analysis conducted at constant prices will exclude changes in the general price level, but changes in relative prices must be taken into account.

In principle, where expected trends in prices are known, estimates of project costs and benefits should be adjusted for changes in relative prices. In practice, identification of differential price trends may be difficult and, unless there are good reasons to believe otherwise, it is customary to assume that relative prices are unchanged. Unfortunately the assumption of constant relative prices is not always a very good one for countries undergoing rapid structural change, so careful assessment may be required of the prices to be used in the analysis. The problem of price changes will be examined in more detail in Chapter 16 of the book.

For straightforward commercial projects there are four basic categories of costs and benefits: investment costs, operating costs, sales revenue (benefits), and working capital. For other types of projects the categorization of costs and benefits may differ slightly although they are likely to follow the same basic principles of distinguishing between capital and recurrent costs.

Investment Costs

The nature of investment costs varies considerably from sector to sector, but the categorization used in directly productive projects covers most of the items that are likely to be met in project analysis. Differences in categorization might occur where infrastructure projects do not involve the construction of buildings or where projects do not involve significant purchase of machinery and equipment and are unlikely to include installation as a separate item. The most important categories of investment cost for productive sector projects are land and site development, buildings and civil works, machinery and equipment, vehicles, plant installation, technical assistance, and training.

In CBA and CEA, all investment costs are entered into the analysis in full as and when they are expected to occur. Depreciation is an accounting convention used for the valuation of assets and the calculation of tax. It is not a real cost and is not normally used in any CBA statements, although it is used for the estimation of tax in the financial analysis of commercial projects.

Projects are assumed to have a project life. The project life is usually calculated on the basis of the expected life of major assets such as buildings or major items of equipment. For any medium- to large-scale projects, the project life is unlikely to be shorter than ten years and could be as long as fifty years. It is a mistake to use uncertainty about the future as an excuse for assuming a very short project life. Such a procedure can lead to the neglect of important long-term considerations, including the interests of future generations.

Investment costs usually involve the replacement of some assets, such as vehicles and some machinery and equipment, during the life of the project. These costs are entered when they occur. At the end of the life of a project there is usually a residual or *salvage value* for those assets whose life is not completely exhausted. This value is usually included as a benefit (or a negative cost) in the final year of operation of the project or in the year afterward. In this book the convention of recording the salvage value as a negative investment cost is adopted.

The principal of *sunk costs* is important in considering rehabilitation or expansion projects where the enterprise already exists and has some assets. Costs that have already been incurred and cannot be recovered are not included as costs in the analysis of subsequent investment. However, in the case of rehabilitation projects, one assumption that could be used for the without project situation is that the project would be liquidated. In this case the benefit without the project would be the value of the liquidated assets. This value would normally be very different from the initial cost of the project.

Investment costs are estimated with a certain margin of error. The earlier in the planning stage the estimation is made, the more likely it is that not all costs have been identified. Physical contingencies are sometimes added to investment costs where there are expected costs that have not been identified fully. This is particularly common for the estimation of building costs. Price contingencies are often used in financial planning to identify the likely effect of inflation on project costs. Price contingencies should not be used in any analysis that is conducted at constant prices.

Table 4.1 illustrates an investment cost schedule for a simplified project, which we shall assume to be a small cotton textile mill. There are five categories of investment cost. It is assumed that the value of the land purchased and the site development is maintained in real terms over the life of the project. The project life is assumed to be ten years from the commencement of operation in Year 2 and is defined by the operating life of the major items of machinery. The assumed life is adopted for simplicity and is considerably less than the life one might normally assume for such a project.

The cost of buildings includes a 10% physical contingency added to a base cost of $600,000. It is assumed that half the original value of the buildings remains at the end of the project life. For simplicity it is assumed

Table 4.1   Investment Costs by Year ($ '000)

	1	2	3	4	5	6	7	8	9	10	11	12
Land purchase	300											−300
Site development	600											−600
Buildings	6,600											−3,300
Machinery	12,500	12,500										
Vehicles		2,500					2,500					
Total investment cost	20,000	15,000					2,500					−4,200

Table 4.2   Production and Sales by Year ($ '000)

	1	2	3	4	5	6	7	8	9	10	11
Capacity ('000 units)	4,000										
Production ('000 units)		2,000	3,000	4,000	4,000	4,000	4,000	4,000	4,000	4,000	3,600
Total stocks ('000 units)		200	300	400	400	400	400	400	400	400	400
Incremental stock ('000 units)		200	100	100							−400
Sales ('000 units)		1,800	2,900	3,900	4,000	4,000	4,000	4,000	4,000	4,000	4,000
Unit price ($ per unit)	8.10										
Sales value ($ '000)		14,580	23,490	31,590	32,400	32,400	32,400	32,400	32,400	32,400	32,400

that there is negligible salvage value for the vehicles and machinery at the end of their lives. Vehicles are assumed to have a five-year life and so they are replaced at the beginning of Year 7.

Sales Revenue or Benefits

Sales revenue values are derived from estimates of the quantity to be produced, adjusted for changes in the level of stocks and assumptions about the expected price. In the early years of a project the quantity of sales is likely to be less than the level of production because of the need to build up stocks. It is extremely unlikely that in any project the maximum level of production will be reached in the first year of operation.

Projects in some sectors have benefits that are not sold directly. Nevertheless, the principle of setting out the value of benefits on a year-by-year basis is the same, and it is equally unlikely that the maximum level of benefits will be reached in the first year. To make a proper estimate of benefits it is necessary to have a very clear idea of what it is that causes the benefits to be achieved and the time scale over which the cause-effect relationship occurs.

Table 4.2 shows a schedule of production and sales revenue. The project has a capacity of 4,000,000 units per annum but does not reach full production until Year 4. It is assumed that stocks equivalent to 10% of annual production are kept. The quantity of sales is determined by deducting the annual increase in stocks from the total production. For convenience it is assumed that production is slightly lower in the final year of operation and that the lower level of production when added to the sale of stocks leads to a constant level of sales.

Operating Costs

Operating or recurrent costs are also recorded on a year-by-year basis. They are often divided into fixed costs (or overheads) and variable costs. Variable costs normally vary according to the quantity of sales. Some costs are variable but do not vary directly according to sales. These are sometimes described as semivariable costs. Note that, from an accounting point of view, variable costs should vary according to sales rather than production. There will be a difference between the volume of sales and the volume of production in the early years represented by an increase in stocks. The cost of building up stocks of finished goods is part of working capital (see below).

The logic behind operating cost estimation is important, as is the physical basis. Many production processes have recognized norms as to the quantity of inputs required to produce a given quantity of output. In most cases it is physically impossible to achieve an increase in output without an increase in at least some of the inputs. It is therefore important to think carefully about the process by which any assumed increase in sales is obtained and to ensure that it has been costed in full.

Table 4.3 shows the operating costs for the project. Unit costs are given for the variable cost items. These are multiplied by the quantity of sales to derive the direct operating costs. In addition there are some overhead costs that change over the life of the project but do not depend directly on the level of sales. Utilities are an example of a semivariable cost where part of the cost is an overhead and part is variable. For convenience in later analysis the variable and overhead parts of the cost of utilities have been recorded separately although this may not always be possible in practice.

Working Capital

Working capital for directly productive projects includes some or all of the following: stocks of material inputs, work in progress, stocks of output (finished goods), accounts receivable, accounts payable, and cash.

Stocks of material inputs are normally based on a certain number of weeks or months of supply for the input in question. The level of stocks usually depends on factors such as the perishability and availability of the item in question.

Work in progress and stocks of output are normally valued on the basis of the cost of production. Work in progress is only relevant for products where production takes a significant period of time. Valuation procedures vary, but a minimum estimate for stocks of output would be the direct cost of producing the item in question.[4] For work in progress the cost would be estimated on the basis of a proportion of the cost of production, normally half, representing the costs already incurred on products that are in the process of being produced.

The level of stocks of output held depends on the perishability of the product and on any seasonality in the production or marketing of the product. The more perishable a product is, the smaller the level of stock that will be held. Conversely the more seasonal the production or the marketing of a product, the higher the level of stocks required at peak periods.

Accounts receivable (debtors) is the value of credit advanced to purchasers of the product. The value of credit advanced will vary according to the nature of the product and the conditions prevailing in the market on which the product is sold.

Accounts payable (creditors) is the value of credit received from suppliers of goods and services to the enterprises. Such credit reduces the level

Table 4.3 Operating Costs by Year ($ '000)

		1	2	3	4	5	6	7	8	9	10	11
Variable costs												
Cotton lint	unit price	2.50										
	value		4,500	7,250	9,750	10,000	10,000	10,000	10,000	10,000	10,000	10,000
Chemicals	unit price	0.70										
	value		1,260	2,030	2,730	2,800	2,800	2,800	2,800	2,800	2,800	2,800
Labor	unit price	1.50										
	value		2,700	4,350	5,850	6,000	6,000	6,000	6,000	6,000	6,000	6,000
Utilities	unit price	0.50										
	value		900	1,450	1,950	2,000	2,000	2,000	2,000	2,000	2,000	2,000
Overheads												
Utilities			300	450	450	450	450	450	450	450	450	450
Maintenance			500	1,000	1,200	1,400	1,500	1,500	1,500	1,500	1,500	1,500
Management			1,500	2,250	2,250	2,250	2,250	2,250	2,250	2,250	2,250	2,250
Total operating costs			11,660	18,780	24,180	24,900	25,000	25,000	25,000	25,000	25,000	25,000

of working capital required by the enterprise. The value of accounts payable is deducted from the sum of all the other working capital items in order to determine working capital requirements.

A stock of cash may also be required for the day-to-day operations of the enterprise. There are various ways of taking account of the need for cash in project analysis. The easiest way is to specify a minimum cash balance and treat this as part of the financial requirement of the project.

Accounts receivable and accounts payable are often regarded as transfer payments from one enterprise to another because no real resource cost is involved. For this reason they are normally excluded from the economic analysis of projects. Since cash is simply one way in which the assets of the project can be held by the owners, it is not regarded as a resource cost, and it is also not included as a cost in economic analysis.

Only increases in working capital in each year are recorded in CBA statements. Estimation of the annual increase in the working capital requirement may be done by calculating each item on an incremental basis or by estimating the value of total working capital and deriving the incremental value from the increase in total working capital. In the last operating year of the project, working capital is run down so that at the end of the project life there are no stocks and no outstanding accounts. Incremental working capital in this final year is therefore negative.

Sometimes the level of working capital required fluctuates widely within the year due to seasonal factors. For a CBA conducted over the life of a project it is sufficient to calculate requirements on the basis of the average level of working capital in each year, but for detailed financial planning it is necessary to show how the peak requirements are to be financed.

Table 4.4 shows a working capital schedule for our project. The top half of the table shows the value of total working capital and the bottom half shows the increase from one year to the next. It is this incremental value that will be carried forward into the analysis of the project since this represents the additional resources required from one year to the next.

The project uses locally grown cotton as its main raw material. Stocks vary over the year because the supply is seasonal, but, on average, it is assumed that stocks are kept equivalent to one quarter of one year's requirements for production.

The value of stocks of output was derived from Tables 4.2 and 4.3. Stocks of output were valued on the basis of the variable cost of production. The quantity of stocks was multiplied by the sum of the unit costs for materials, labor, and utilities.

Accounts receivable and accounts payable are also given in this schedule. Whether or not they should be included at this stage depends partly on

Table 4.4   Working Capital by Year ($ '000)

	1	2	3	4	5	6	7	8	9	10	11
Stocks											
Cotton lint		1,250	1,875	2,500	2,500	2,500	2,500	2,500	2,500	2,500	
Chemicals		117	175	233	233	233	233	233	233	233	
Output		1,040	1,560	2,080	2,080	2,080	2,080	2,080	2,080	2,080	
Accounts receivable		1,215	1,958	2,633	2,700	2,700	2,700	2,700	2,700	2,700	
Accounts payable		642	963	1,271	1,271	1,271	1,271	1,271	1,271	1,271	
Total working capital		2,980	4,605	6,175	6,243	6,243	6,243	6,243	6,243	6,243	
Incremental stocks											
Cotton lint		1,250	625	625							−2,500
Chemicals		117	58	58							−233
Output		1,040	520	520							−2,080
Incremental accounts receivable		1,215	743	675	68						−2,700
Incremental accounts payable		642	321	308							−1,271
Incremental working capital		2,980	1,625	1,570	68						−6,243

whether the prime purpose of the analysis is to provide a basis for financial analysis or for economic analysis and partly on whether the credit is going to or coming from foreigners. At an early stage of the analysis of a project we are only trying to get a rough estimate of the overall costs and benefits of the project to determine whether it is likely that the project will turn out to be both desirable and feasible. Since these items have to be financed somehow, they have been left in at this stage. It is assumed that one month's credit is advanced to customers and that one month's credit is received from the suppliers of raw materials and utilities.

Other Categories of Costs and Benefits

Our example shows the costs and benefits for a commercial production project. Projects in other sectors may use different categories of costs and benefits, and the relative importance of different categories may differ. For example, in road improvement projects, the major benefit is often "savings in vehicle operating costs." The benefits of projects aimed at improving water supply may come from improvements in public health or from reduction in the cost of pollution. In some sectors measurement of benefits in terms of money may be very difficult, and nonmonetary indicators may need to be used.

Many projects are implemented with the idea that the project activity will help stimulate the activity of some other agents rather than the project organization itself. Such projects may involve more than one agent, some of which may be commercial in orientation and others not. In such projects it is necessary to set out the costs and benefits for each agent or group of agents separately. There may then be a summary table in which the costs and benefits to all agents are brought together.

In some projects the distinction between investment costs and operating costs may be blurred. Projects involving the improvement of extension services to small producers are improving what is essentially a recurrent activity. Costs that appear as project costs during the period of project implementation and so might be thought of as investment costs may later on be treated as recurrent costs and so might be categorized as operating costs.

A particularly important category of costs in the economic analysis of projects is that of external costs. These may result from such sources as increased pollution, increased pressure on public services, and reduced recreational amenities. There may also be external benefits from a project. In our tea project example there is an external benefit from the improvement of feeder roads that will be used by the local population. The treatment of external costs and benefits is discussed in Chapter 8.

Annual Statement of Project Costs and Benefits

Once the basic estimates of costs and benefits have been made it is necessary to draw them together in an Annual Statement of Project Costs and Benefits at Constant Market Prices.[5] This statement is sometimes referred to as a *resource flow* or even as a *cash flow*. The latter terminology is misleading because such statements are not always just about cash values and because the term *cash flow* has a very specific meaning for accountants.

A conventional annual statement will usually show the four basic categories of costs and benefits on a year-by-year basis over the project life, either in summary form or subdivided into the various items. The net revenue or net benefit is the difference between total project revenue or benefits and total project costs.

The annual statement will give an indication of the overall desirability of the project to all the capital involved at constant market prices. It may then be refined through an economic analysis to give a perspective of the value of the project to the economy, or it may be used to provide the basis for a financial analysis of the project from the point of view of the owners. If the basic supporting schedules are regarded as the roots of the project analysis tree, the annual statement can be regarded as the trunk from which the analysis can branch out into more detailed financial or economic analysis.

An example of an annual statement for our cotton textile project is given in Table 4.5. The net revenue or net benefit of the project in each year is defined by

$$NB_t = B_t - IC_t - WC_t - OC_t \qquad (4.1)$$

where NB_t is the value of net benefits in year t;
  B_t is the value of benefits in year t;
  IC_t is the value of investment costs in year t;
  WC_t is the value of incremental working capital in year t; and
  OC_t is the value of operating costs in year t.

Tables 4.1 to 4.5 assume that the project under consideration is a green field project and that the value of the resources used by the project is adequately represented by their price. For this reason no without project assumption is given.

If the project involves expansion or rehabilitation of an existing enterprise, it is necessary to deduct the assumed situation without the project. The assumption that the prices used provide an adequate estimate of the value of resources will be reconsidered in Part 3 of the book. A different view of the without project scenario will also be built up in which the alter-

Table 4.5   Annual Statement of Costs and Benefits by Year ($ '000)

	1	2	3	4	5	6	7	8	9	10	11	12
Investment costs	20,000	15,000					2,500					-4,200
Incremental working capital			1,625	1,570	68						-6,243	
Operating costs		11,660	18,780	24,180	24,900	25,000	25,000	25,000	25,000	25,000	25,000	
Sales revenue		14,580	23,490	31,590	32,400	32,400	32,400	32,400	32,400	32,400	32,400	
Net revenue	-20,000	-15,060	3,085	5,840	7,433	7,400	4,900	7,400	7,400	7,400	13,643	4,200

Net present value at 4% = 17,352; at 8% = 6,539; at 12% = -733. Internal rate of return = 11.5%.

native uses of the resources used by the project will be specified in greater detail to obtain a wider perspective of the impact of the project on the national economy.

The Issue of Time Preference

Projects involve the investment of resources in the expectation of future benefits. This means that the net benefits of projects are usually negative in the early years and positive in later years. To get a measure of the overall value of the project we have to be able to compare costs and benefits that take place at different periods of time. Most of the criteria used in CBA are concerned specifically with this issue. In particular there is a general assumption that benefits received in the future have a lower value than benefits received now. Why should this be?

The first and most obvious answer to the question is that funds used for investment have alternative uses. If the funds used to invest in the project could be used to earn a positive return in another project, then the project should earn at least as high a return as that of the alternative project. The return on the next best alternative project is called the opportunity cost of capital.

From the financial point of view, even if there is no alternative project, it would be possible to invest the funds in a bank and earn a positive return from the interest paid. This argument has to be used carefully because interest rates often contain an element of compensation for the loss of value of money caused by inflation. Normally an annual statement is prepared in constant prices and so the return earned by the project is a real return and should only be compared with real interest rates. The issue of inflation is considered in more detail in Part 4 of the book.

It could be argued that it is unnecessary to compare one project with another because it might be possible to increase investment without reducing investment elsewhere if we were to reduce consumption. Even if this is the case, there is still a reason to give a lower value to benefits in the future than to benefits now. As long as there is positive growth in real incomes, it can be assumed that people in the future will be richer than they are now. If we accept the principle that the richer we are, the less important an additional unit of income is to us, then we will put a lower value on benefits the further they occur into the future. This principle, known as the principle of diminishing marginal utility of consumption, provides the basis for arguments for a positive rate of social time preference.

One further argument is sometimes made for positive time preference. This is the argument that the future is inherently uncertain. If benefits in the future are uncertain they are less valuable than certain benefits now. This is a reasonable argument for an individual with limited resources who cannot afford to make a mistake. However, it can be argued that for a government, uncertainty can relate both to positive and negative variations and therefore that, as long as there is no bias in the estimation of costs and benefits, the favorable impact of uncertain events on some projects will match the unfavorable impact on others. Though there may be good reason to try to reduce the uncertainty surrounding individual projects, there is no particular reason why we should let this influence our view of time preference from a collective viewpoint. There are better ways of dealing with uncertainty. Some of these are considered in Chapter 15.

An argument for positive time preference can therefore be made both on the basis of the possible returns from alternative investments and on the assumption of greater prosperity in the future. The next step is to determine the nature of the relationship between the value of resources and the passage of time so that appropriate weights can be applied to costs and benefits occurring in different periods. The relationship can be established intuitively on the basis of two simple postulates:

- The absolute difference between the value to us of something in one year's time and the value of something in two years' time may be quite significant. The absolute difference between the value to us of something in forty-nine years' time and something in fifty years' time is unlikely to have the same degree of significance. Therefore the absolute value of the decline in the value of costs and benefits from one year to the next is likely to diminish the further we project into the future.
- The value of benefits in the future will always be positive however far into the future projections are made.

These two postulates determine the nature of the relationship. A linear relationship between the weight to be applied and time does not satisfy either of these two postulates but an exponential relationship does. The normal approach to estimating the weights to be attached to costs and benefits expected in the future is the approach of discounting. The process of discounting is the reverse of the process of estimating factors for compound growth. The weight or discount factor for any one year is given by

$$DF_t = \frac{1}{(1+r)^t} \qquad (4.2)$$

where DF_t is the discount factor for year t, and
      r is the rate of discount.

The discount factor estimated in this way is used as a weight to determine the present value of a cost or benefit item received or incurred at some specified time in the future. As long as agreement is possible on the appropriate rate of discount (r) to be applied, it should be possible to compare future benefits with present costs and therefore to make a judgment as to whether a particular investment is worthwhile or not.

Figure 4.2 shows the values of discount factors at three selected discount rates over a period of thirty years. It can be seen that the higher the discount rate, the steeper the rate of decline in the value of a unit over time. Therefore the higher the rate of discount, the less value we put on future benefits in relation to current costs.

Measures of Project Worth

If we are to make comparisons of project costs and benefits, we require measures of the value or worth of a project from which we can derive criteria for judging the acceptability or the desirability of a project.

Figure 4.2   Discount Factors at Selected Discount Rates

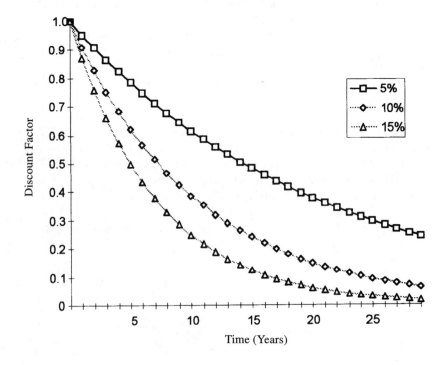

There are three main measures of project worth. Normally each measure leads to the same recommendation as to whether or not to go ahead with a project, but there are some special circumstances when they do not. The three main measures of project worth are the net present value (NPV), the benefit cost ratio (BCR), and the internal rate of return (IRR). All commonly used computer spreadsheet packages include special functions for calculating both the NPV and the IRR.

The Net Present Value

The NPV is a measure of the absolute value of the discounted net benefits of a project.[6] It can be defined as

$$NPV = \sum_{t=1}^{n} \frac{(B_t - C_t)}{(1 + r)^t}$$ (4.3)

where B_t is the value of project benefits in Year t;
      C_t is the value of project costs in Year t;
      r is the rate of discount; and
      n is the number of years in the project life.

The NPV is obtained by multiplying the net benefit in each year by the appropriate discount factor and summing the values.

The decision rule for using the NPV as an indicator of acceptability is that the NPV should be positive at the discount rate specified. The size of the NPV is an indicator of desirability. The higher the NPV, the better the project is.

Table 4.5 shows the NPV for our project at three different discount rates. At discount rates of 4% and 8% the NPV is positive, but at 12% discount rate the NPV is negative. This means that the project would be acceptable if either 4% or 8% were regarded as the appropriate target or test discount rate, but it would not be acceptable if 12% were chosen as the test rate.

The Benefit Cost Ratio

The benefit cost ratio is the ratio of discounted benefits to discounted costs. There are two different ways of measuring the BCR. The first approach (BCR_1) is to divide the discounted value of the benefits by the discounted value of the costs. The second approach (BCR_2) is to divide the discounted value of the benefits net of operating costs by the discounted value of the capital costs. The two approaches can be defined as

$$BCR_1 = \frac{\displaystyle\sum_{t=1}^{n} \frac{B_t}{(1+r)^t}}{\displaystyle\sum_{t=1}^{n} \frac{C_t}{(1+r)^t}} \tag{4.4}$$

$$BCR_2 = \frac{\displaystyle\sum_{t=1}^{n} \frac{(B_t - OC_t)}{(1+r)^t}}{\displaystyle\sum_{t=1}^{n} \frac{K_t}{(1+r)^t}} \tag{4.5}$$

where B_t, C_t, r, and n are as in equation (4.3);
OC_t is the value of operating costs in Year t; and
K_t is the value of capital costs in Year t.

The decision rule for using either of the BCR measures as an indicator of acceptability is that the BCR should be greater than one at the discount rate specified. As with the NPV the size of the BCR is an indicator of desirability. The higher the BCR, the better the project is. However, some problems arise in making comparisons. The different versions of the BCR measure give different results. For the cotton textile project the values for the BCR are

Discount Rate	4%	8%	12%
BCR_1	1.08	1.04	0.99
BCR_2	1.54	1.21	0.98

It can be seen that the second version of the BCR, sometimes described as the net benefit-investment ratio, gives more extreme values than the first version. The first version will be very sensitive to the capital intensity of the project. For relatively material-intensive projects such as cotton textiles, the ratio will always be close to 1.0 because the operating costs are a very large proportion of the value of the benefits. This would make comparison of the BCR values for capital-intensive projects with those of material-intensive projects quite difficult.

As an investment criterion it would appear that the net benefit-investment ratio is likely to be more useful because it focuses on the value of net benefits in relation to the proposed investment. However, there are practical difficulties. There may be problems in defining exactly what is a capital cost and what is an operating cost. It is not altogether obvious where working capital belongs in the estimate or whether replacement investments should be included in the definition of investment costs or treated as operating costs. As a result there may be inconsistencies in the way the ratio is calculated for different projects.

The great advantage of the BCR as a measure is that it is easily understood. However, this advantage is countered by the disadvantage that the potential for inconsistency in application could lead to misleading comparisons.

The Internal Rate of Return

The internal rate of return is defined as the rate of discount at which the present value of benefits is equal to the present value of costs, that is, the rate of discount at which the NPV is zero.[7] Thus $IRR = r$ where

$$NPV = \sum_{t=1}^{n} \frac{(B_t - C_t)}{(1 + r)^t} = 0 \tag{4.6}$$

The IRR is estimated by iteration. It is necessary to estimate the NPV for the project at a number of different discount rates. When two values for the NPV are found, one of which is positive and the other negative, at discount rates that are reasonably close together, the IRR can be estimated either graphically or by the formula

$$IRR = r_1 + \left(\frac{(r_2 - r_t) * NPV_1}{(NPV_1 + NPV_2)} \right) \tag{4.7}$$

where r_1 and r_2 are the lowest and the highest discount rates respectively;
NPV_1 and NPV_2 are the values for the NPV at discount rates r_1 and r_2.

The use of the above formula can be seen if the values from Table 4.5 are substituted into the formula. If values of 4% and 12% for r_1 and r_2 are substituted into the formula we have

$$IRR = .04 + \left(\frac{(.12 - .04) * 17352}{17352 - (-733)} \right) = .04 + \frac{1388}{18085} = 11.7\%$$

If values of 8% and 12% for r_1 and r_2 are substituted into the formula we have:

$$IRR = .08 + \left(\frac{(.12 - .08) * 6539}{6539 - (-733)} \right) = .08 + \frac{262}{7272} = 11.6\%$$

It can be seen that the second value is closer to the actual IRR than the first value. This is because the interval between the two discount rates is much smaller. The formula for the IRR therefore can only be used with any accuracy when the two discount rates chosen are reasonably close both to the actual IRR and to each other. The reason for this is demonstrated graphically in Figure 4.3. From Figure 4.3 it can be seen that the relationship between the NPV and the discount rate is not linear. The estimate of the IRR obtained from the formula assumes a linear relationship and therefore leads to a margin of error that increases with the difference between the two discount rates used. A difference of 8% between the two discount rates used in estimating the IRR is too great to give an accurate estimate. Figure 4.3 also shows that where the IRR is estimated from two NPV values of which one is negative and one is positive, the linear estimate derived from the formula will always be an overestimate. This leads to the convention of always rounding IRR estimates downward. The convention is unnecessary when using spreadsheet functions because the level of accuracy is much greater.

Figure 4.3   Graphical Estimation of the IRR

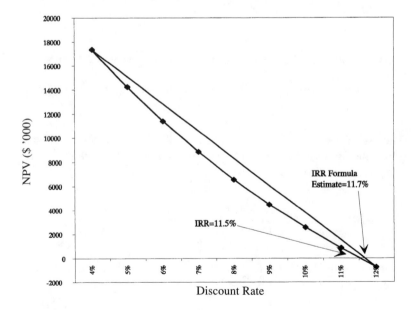

In theory there is a problem with the IRR as a measure of project worth in that there can be cases where there are two possible values. These cases can occur when the value of project net benefits goes from negative to positive and then back to negative. Such a situation could arise with projects experiencing heavy replacement costs or two investment phases separated by a period of normal operation. Normally for such projects it is obvious what the appropriate IRR should be. The most problematic case is when there is a heavy cost at the end of the project life. This can arise in the decommissioning of a nuclear power plant or in the rehabilitation of worked-out mining areas. In such cases it is better not to rely on the IRR alone as a guide to decisionmaking.

In most cases all three measures of project worth will lead to the same recommendation. However, there are cases where there could be conflicting recommendations. We have seen that there are some problems in the definition of the BCR and therefore that it does not provide a very reliable indicator for comparing projects. When deciding whether to use the NPV or the IRR it is as well to consider what each indicator is measuring and what assumptions are being made.

The NPV is a measure of the size of net benefits. It will give a reliable indicator of choice as long as the appropriate discount rate is known and there is no shortage of investment resources available for financing projects with positive NPVs at that discount rate. Unfortunately the discount rate is one of the most difficult values to specify and therefore there will usually be some uncertainty surrounding the choice of an appropriate rate.

The IRR is a measure of efficiency in the use of investment resources, as is the net benefit-investment ratio. The IRR will give a reliable indicator of choice as long as all projects are independent of each other and as long as there is a unique solution. However, where projects are mutually exclusive or where there are projects with two IRRs, the IRR can give misleading results.

Both measures tell us something about a project. It is therefore sensible to calculate both the NPV for a range of discount rates and the IRR for any project. The range of discount rates used should include a lowest estimate, a highest estimate, and an intermediate "best" estimate. This approach has been used in Table 4.5. It is only when there is a question of choice among alternatives or when investment resources are rationed that the relative merit of one measure over the other becomes an issue. A summary of the features of the various measures of project worth is indicated in Table 4.6.

Choice of Alternatives

Decisions about projects can involve straightforward questions about whether or not to go ahead, or they can involve more complex questions

Table 4.6   Summary of the Principal Features of Measures of Project Worth

Indicator	Measures	Correct ranking if . . .	Not useful if . . .
NPV	Size of discounted net benefits	Discount rate known	No idea what discount rate should be
IRR	Efficiency in use of capital costs	Discount rate unknown and projects are independent	Capital investment relatively unimportant
BCR_1	Efficiency in use of all costs	Not reliable for purposes of ranking	
BCR_2	Efficiency in use of capital costs	Not reliable for purposes of ranking	

about different alternatives. Choice among alternatives can relate both to different designs for the same project and to choices between different projects. Choices occur because projects may be mutually exclusive. That is, the choice of one project implies rejection of the other. Mutual exclusivity can be caused by one of a number of factors:

- Different versions of the same project are mutually exclusive because only one design of the same project can be implemented. This situation applies to questions of choices of location, technology, and scale.
- Projects can be mutually exclusive if they are competing for the same resource. This situation can arise because two different projects intend to use the same project site.
- If projects are competing for the same limited investment resources, a capital rationing problem arises. In such cases mutual exclusivity could be due to the shortage of capital rather than to any physical or technical reasons.
- Sometimes choices between projects involve questions of timing. When is the best time to invest in a project? Questions of timing can relate both to the question of appropriate timing of the project itself and to the timing of one project in relation to another.

In the first two cases the constrained resource is either the project opportunity itself or the physical location. The rational response is to maximize the return to the constrained resource. This implies seeking the largest possible net benefit for that resource. The correct criterion is therefore the NPV at the appropriate discount rate.

In cases of choice between two alternatives that differ in size it is also possible to use the IRR criterion by finding the IRR of the difference between the net benefit streams of the larger project and the smaller one.

Where there is some doubt as to which should be the appropriate discount rate it is possible to use the crossover discount rate as a guide to decisionmaking. The crossover discount rate is the discount rate at which the NPV of two alternatives is the same, or the IRR of the difference between the two net benefit streams.

The use of the crossover discount rate for the analysis of mutually exclusive projects can be illustrated by an example. Suppose there are two mutually exclusive projects, one being larger and more capital-intensive and the other being smaller and more labor-intensive. The net benefits for the two projects are

Year	1	2	3	4	5	6	7–20
Project A	−2,000	−5,000	−3,000	500	1,000	1,500	2,000
Project B	−1,000	−1,000	200	400	500	500	500
Difference (A–B)	−1,000	−4,000	−3,200	100	500	1,000	1,500

The NPV for the two projects can be calculated at various discount rates and the IRR estimated. The NPV and IRR for the difference between the two net benefit streams can also be estimated. The following results are obtained:

Discount Rate	4%	8%	12%	IRR
Project A	9,918	3,864	454	12.8%
Project B	3,614	1,923	923	19.0%
Difference (A–B)	6,304	1,941	468	11.0%

According to the NPV criterion, Project A would be chosen at discount rates of 4% and 8% but not at a discount rate of 12%. According to the IRR criterion Project B would be chosen. The crossover discount rate is 11%, the IRR of the difference between the two net benefit streams. The situation is illustrated in Figure 4.4.

The results indicate that Project A should be preferred at all discount rates up to 11% but that Project B should be preferred if the discount rate is higher than 11%. This information is useful if there is uncertainty about the exact value of the discount rate but there is certainty within a range. If it were known that the value of the discount rate should be in the range of (say) 6% to 10%, it would be possible to state clearly that Project A would be the better option.

Where a question arises as to the appropriate timing of a single project, the normal rule is to use the NPV criterion. An example of a situation where such an approach should be taken is the timing of road projects. If

Figure 4.4   Mutually Exclusive Projects and the Crossover Discount Rate

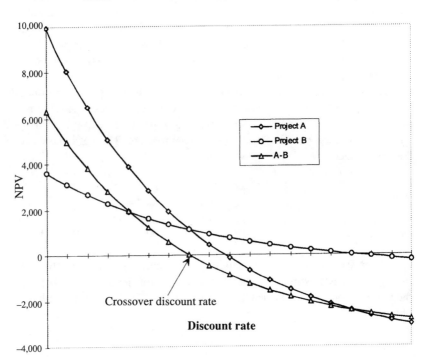

the main benefit of a road improvement project is in the form of cost savings to road users, and if the traffic using the existing road is increasing each year, the benefit stream will be larger the further into the future the project is postponed. If the IRR criterion were to be used, it would appear that the project should be postponed indefinitely. A more logical conclusion is obtained using the NPV criterion where the absolute size of the present value of the benefits may start to decline if the project is delayed for too long. The timing problem can be illustrated by a simple example.

Assume that a road improvement project can be implemented in one year and will cost $10 million. The improvement will generate cost savings for a period of twenty-five years. The cost savings in Year 2 would be $1 million but are expected to increase in line with traffic growth at 2% per annum. If the project is delayed by a year, the benefit stream will therefore be 2% greater but delayed by a year. The investment cost is the same but is delayed by a year. Assume further that the discount rate is 8%. The results obtained for different times for implementation of the project are ($'000, present values):

Year the project is implemented	1	2	3	4	5	6
NPV at 8% discount rate	2,476	2,510	2,529	2,536	2,531	2,516
Incremental NPV due to delay		+34	+19	+7	−5	−15
IRR		10.7%	11.0%	11.2%	11.5%	11.7%	12.0%

It can be seen that the IRR increases with the delay in the project, but the NPV starts to decline after a four-year delay. The best time to implement the road improvement is therefore after four years.

Not all questions of timing relate to the timing of a single project. The issue is more complex in situations such as the preparation of a public investment program where investment resources may be limited for a particular period although potentially expandable over the longer term. The straightforward single period capital rationing approach would suggest that projects should be selected according to their IRR. However, it may be that the cost of delay for some projects is greater than for others. In principle the problem could be solved by using a programming approach to maximize the NPV of a selection of projects to be implemented in a given investment period. For each project it would be necessary to prepare different variants assuming different implementation schedules. In practice such optimization is unlikely to be feasible and a simpler procedure may be required.[8]

Given the uncertainty surrounding the value of the discount rate in most countries, a more practical procedure might be to classify projects according to priority, using the IRR as an indicator to identify high-priority projects but using a wider variety of criteria to select among the medium-priority projects. Indicators such as the NPV and IRR are themselves subject to significant margins of error and so reliance on these indicators alone risks placing undue emphasis on uncertain results.

One approach that has been suggested for capital rationing situations is to use the ratio of the NPV to the capital cost in the period during which investment resources are being rationed. Maximizing this *NPV/K* ratio leads to the highest possible total NPV with a given investment resource. Though this is a convenient theoretical approach it does not address the issue that the cost of delay will be different for different projects. Only if all possible variants of all possible projects can be investigated can a perfect solution be found. In practice such a perfect solution is quite impossible.

Cost-Effectiveness Analysis

When using indicators such as the NPV or IRR it is assumed that the benefits of the project can be measured in monetary terms. This is not always possible. There are some sectors and some projects for which measurement of the benefits in money terms is impossible, the information required is difficult to determine, or the assumptions required are so debatable that any attempt to make a precise monetary measure of benefits would be open to considerable dispute. In these cases it is still possible to try to make sure that investment resources are used as effectively as possible. Cost-effectiveness analysis (CEA) is an important tool that can help to ensure efficient use of investment resources in sectors where benefits are difficult to value. There are two main ways of expressing cost-effectiveness criteria. These are (1) maximum output for a given input and (2) minimum input for a given output. There are two main circumstances when cost-effectiveness analysis can be used: (1) when benefits can be measured in money terms but they are the same for two different alternatives and so the objective is to choose the cheapest alternative, and (2) when benefits cannot be measured in money terms but can be measured in some nonmonetary terms. The most common example of the first case is that of choice of technology. The second case applies particularly to projects with nonmarketable outputs such as projects in the education, health, and social security sectors.

In the first case it is important to be sure that the benefits really are exactly the same before accepting the least-cost alternative. Often choice of technology involves some difference in the output as well as the cost. In such cases some adjustment would have to be made to take account of the difference. This would only be important if the quality or quantity of the output of the least-cost alternative were lower than the more expensive alternative. Ideally adjustments should be made on a quantifiable basis, but they might just involve asking in a qualitative way the question, "Is the extra benefit from the more expensive alternative worth the extra cost?"

In the second case the most important question is to define the objectives of the project in a way that will allow the measurement of effectiveness to be made.

Examples are given below to illustrate some of the ways in which cost-effectiveness analysis can be used:

Example 1: Cost-Effectiveness in the Choice of Technology

This is a case of determining the minimum cost for a given output. It is proposed to improve the boilers in a district heating system. There are three possible alternatives, each of which is assumed to have a life of twenty years.

Option A would involve the replacement of all the existing boilers with new wood-burning boilers. This option would have an investment cost of $6 million, annual fixed maintenance costs of $150,000, and annual fuel costs for wood chips of $300,000 for a heat requirement estimated at 60,000 gigacalories (Gcal).

Option B would involve extensive renovation of existing oil- and gas-fired boilers at a total investment cost of $3.25 million. Annual fixed maintenance costs would be $100,000, and fuel costs would be $600,000.

Option C would provide for essential repairs of existing boilers at a cost of $500,000. Annual fixed maintenance costs would be $300,000, and fuel costs would be $750,000.

Figure 4.5 shows how the discount rate can affect least-cost analysis. The capital cost of the wood-fired boiler option is the highest, but the operating cost is the lowest.

In Figure 4.5 the present value of the costs of the different options is shown. When the discount rate is low, the capital-intensive option is attractive, and Option A is chosen. As the discount rate increases, the decision changes and, at a discount rate of 6.5%, Option B becomes the cheapest option. If the discount rate increases further up to 11.2%, the choice changes again, and Option C is chosen. This is another illustration of the

Figure 4.5   Cost-Effectiveness Analysis for Boiler Rehabilitation

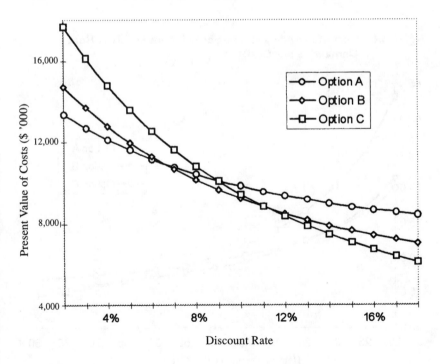

use of the crossover discount rate. The rate at which the decision changes can be compared with estimates for the cost of capital to decide which is the least-cost option.

Figure 4.6 shows a slightly different application. This time the discount rate is held constant at 8%, and different values are indicated for the total annual heat requirement. At low values for the heat requirement Option C is chosen because of its relatively low capital cost. At a heat demand of 32,000 Gcal the decision changes, and Option B is the cheapest. The decision changes again at 66,000 Gcal, when Option C is the cheapest option. The values for parameters like the level of heating demand when the decision changes are known as switching values, and they can be compared with the estimates for the most likely value for heating demand to determine the cheapest alternative.

Example 2: Use of Cost-Effectiveness
Analysis in the Design of a Health Program

In this example it is assumed that the health authorities in a particular region have as one of their objectives the reduction of infant and maternal mortality. The region has a population of 3 million and has a combined

Figure 4.6   Cost of Providing Heating at Different Levels of Heat Demand ($ per Gcal)

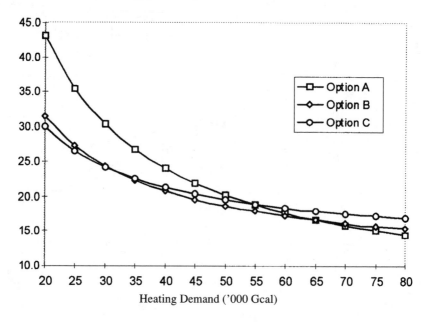

Heating Demand ('000 Gcal)

infant and maternal mortality of 3,960 per year. About 35% of these deaths could be avoided with the implementation of specific interventions. There are three programs proposed, each of which is assumed to have an operating life of ten years.

Program A would involve investment in the expansion of prenatal and delivery care at rural health centers. This program would have an investment cost of $1.6 million each year for three years and a recurrent cost rising to $1.5 million on completion. The number of deaths saved from this program would rise to 728 on completion.

Program B would involve expansion of prenatal and delivery care at district hospitals. This program would have an investment cost of $2 million each year for two years and a recurrent cost rising to $0.75 million on completion. The number of deaths saved from this program would rise to 432 on completion.

Program C would involve provision of additional equipment and staff training to allow better treatment of obstructed deliveries at district hospitals. This program would have an investment cost of $0.5 million each year for two years and a recurrent cost rising to $0.05 million on completion. The annual number of deaths saved from this program would rise to 179 on completion.

It is apparent that Program A is the most effective in terms of reducing mortality, but it is also the most expensive. How might we consider the problem in terms of cost-effectiveness? The most convenient way to approach the problem is to try to identify the cost per life saved. To do this it is necessary to compare the costs of the project with the annual number of lives saved. It is then possible either to compare a "discounted value of lives saved" with a present value of costs or to compare an annual equivalent value of costs with the annual number of lives saved. The latter approach is the easiest to interpret in cases where the operating lives of the programs being compared differ. Details of the three programs are set out in Table 4.7.

Table 4.7 shows that Program C is the most cost-effective in terms of lives saved and therefore, other things being equal, should be given highest priority. For Programs A and B the results are very similar, and choice depends on the discount rate. Program B is relatively more capital-intensive and would be preferred to Program A at low discount rates, while Program A is preferred at higher discount rates.

An annual equivalent of the costs for the three programs can be calculated by multiplying the present value of costs by a capital recovery factor for the project life at the given discount rate (in this case assumed to be 8%).[9] The annual equivalent of the investment cost can then be compared with an annual equivalent value of lives saved, calculated in a similar manner. Annualized figures can be useful when comparing programs with dif-

Table 4.7 Cost-Effectiveness of Health Programs by Year (costs in $ '000)

	1	2	3	4	5	6	7	8	9	10	11
Program A											
Investment costs	1,600	1,600	1,600								
Recurrent costs		500	1,000	1,500	1,500	1,500	1,500	1,500	1,500	1,500	1,500
Total costs	1,600	2,100	2,600	1,500	1,500	1,500	1,500	1,500	1,500	1,500	1,500
Lives saved		243	485	728	728	728	728	728	728	728	728
Program B											
Investment costs	2,000	2,000									
Recurrent costs		375	750	750	750	750	750	750	750	750	750
Total costs	2,000	2,375	750	750	750	750	750	750	750	750	750
Lives saved		216	432	432	432	432	432	432	432	432	432
Program C											
Investment costs	500	500									
Recurrent costs		25	50	50	50	50	50	50	50	50	50
Total costs	500	525	50	50	50	50	50	50	50	50	50
Lives saved		90	179	179	179	179	179	179	179	179	179
Discount rate	4%	8%	12%								
Present value of costs											
Program A	14,769	12,189	10,257								
Program B	9,275	7,905	6,865								
Program C	1,310	1,181	1,077								
Discounted lives saved											
Program A1	5,214	4,228	3,487								
Program B	3,296	2,699	2,248								
Program C	1,366	1,119	932								
Cost per life saved											
Program A	2,833	2,883	2,942								
Program B	2,814	2,929	3,054								
Program C	959	1,056	1,156								

ferent operating lives or when trying to relate costs to budgetary implications. The value of the total annual equivalent cost is given below along
with the annual equivalent lives saved:

	Annual Equivalent Cost ($'000)	Annual Equivalent Lives Saved
Program A	1,816	630
Program B	1,178	402
Program C	176	167

The fact that Program C is the most cost-effective does not necessarily
mean that the other programs should not be implemented. If funds were
available for all three projects, it would be possible to achieve the maximum reduction in mortality by implementing all three projects, but if funds
are limited, Program C should be chosen.

If the programs were completely independent and divisible, it would be
possible to determine the minimum cost for achieving a given output by
setting a target for the reduction of infant mortality. For example, with the
above assumption and using a discount rate of 8%, the cheapest way to
achieve an annual equivalent reduction in mortality of 1,000 would be to
implement Programs A and C in full and half of Program B. This would
have an annual equivalent cost of about $2.6 million.

It would also be possible to determine the maximum output for a given
input by indicating the level of funding available and determining the most
effective way of using the available funds in terms of reduction of avoid-
able deaths. For example, if the annual equivalent of funds available were
set at $2.5 million, the most effective way to use the funds would be to
implement Programs A and C in full and 43% of Program B.

The above examples are simplifications, and there are often more complex relationships that make such conclusions less clear-cut, especially
where there are interrelationships among project proposals or where projects
have additional benefits other than those specified in the main objective. For
example, in this example it is almost certain that the number of lives saved
by implementing both Program A and Program B would be less than the sum
of the lives saved by the programs individually. This is because hospitals
and rural health centers might to some extent be serving the same populations. On the other hand the combination of either A or B with C would
probably enhance the overall numbers of lives saved because greater access
to prenatal and delivery care would lead to more referrals of potential
obstructed deliveries. It is therefore necessary to be careful in interpreting
such results. Nevertheless, the approach of estimating the cost for achieving
a particular objective in different ways can have a considerable impact in
indicating ways of improving the effectiveness of expenditure in the social
sectors. These approaches are explored further in Chapter 9.

Viewpoints in Project Analysis

For each person or organization involved in a project there is a different viewpoint. Most project analysis techniques relate to the measurement of costs and benefits and their appraisal according to standard investment criteria. However, the question arises as to whose costs and benefits are being measured and whose viewpoints are being considered.

A distinction has been made between financial analysis and economic analysis. Financial analysis is undertaken from the viewpoint of the investor. Economic analysis is undertaken from the overall national point of view and includes the viewpoints of all agents affected by a project either directly or indirectly.

Financial analysis may be undertaken from more than one point of view for the same project. The most obvious example is the case of an agroindustrial project where farmers are supplying raw materials to a processing facility. The financial profitability of the project to both parties is important because neither will do what it is expected to do unless it is worthwhile. A similar situation could arise with a multipurpose project such as a dam. A dam project could potentially involve farmers in irrigation as well as agencies of water supply and electricity generation.

The interests of different agents in a project can be complementary or opposed. Often the relationship will be ambiguous. The existence of an agroprocessing facility may improve the income-earning opportunities of farmers and in this sense the interests of farmer and processor may be complementary. However, when it comes to the price to be paid for the farmers' product the interests are opposed. The more the farmer is paid, the lower the profit of the processor and vice versa. This issue is a distributional question. The overall benefits to the national economy are the same whatever the price to the farmer as long as the output of the project remains the same. The total value of benefits to the national economy is only altered if distributional questions start to affect the motivation of one or the other party and lead to a reduction in the overall output of the project.

The questions of desirability and feasibility are closely related when the viewpoints of individual agents are considered. If a project is not desirable from the point of view of a key agent, the project is unlikely to be feasible. For this reason it is essential that a thorough analysis of profitability to farmers should be done for any project where success depends on farmer behavior. A similar point could be made for projects involving other types of small-scale producer. Part 2 of the book looks at the financial analysis of projects for both large and small producers.

Appraisal of projects is not only concerned with financial and economic questions. The motivation behind a project may relate to social, political, or even aesthetic criteria. This does not mean that CBA and CEA have nothing to say. It only means that they do not provide the whole story.

Conventional project appraisal can provide information on financial and economic criteria, which can be assessed against other noneconomic criteria. Where multiple criteria are being used multicriteria analysis techniques may be used to help in decisionmaking. Some of these issues and techniques are discussed in Chapter 14.

Analysis of Projects with Changing Design

The techniques of CBA and CEA assume some degree of certainty in the estimates of costs and benefits. The less certain these estimates are, the less reliable the techniques are likely to be. This provides particular problems for process projects where the design of one phase may be dependent on the results of the previous phase. We might then ask whether these techniques have any value at all for process projects.

The first point to be made is that it may be possible to appraise each phase of a project separately. This would imply that a process project would go through a series of appraisals, each relating to a single phase. However, there are two problems with such an approach. First, it is quite likely that the rationale for the initial phase of the project depends on the expected results of subsequent phases, however loosely defined they may be. In other words, the justification for starting the project may depend on more than just the benefits of the first phase. The second problem is that the work of project appraisal might become excessive if each phase had to involve completely separate appraisals.

The problem can be resolved if the initial appraisal is used to set out the parameters for subsequent appraisals. The initial appraisal could be based on a crude estimate of the likely impact of the project including an initial assumption of what subsequent phases might involve. This would provide the basis for a provisional commitment to funding over a longer period. The appraisal would then be reviewed periodically with assumptions adjusted at the same time as the review of the design of subsequent phases. Standard project appraisal techniques would then be equally valid for process projects except that the appraisal assumptions would be subject to periodic review, a procedure that would probably benefit a large number of projects including many that might not be thought of as "process" projects.

Further Reading

Most books on cost-benefit analysis outline the use of basic techniques. Gittinger (1982) is a useful starting point. Snell (1997: chap. 2) is useful on the estimation of costs and benefits. Behrens and Hawranek (1991) give a comprehensive set of cost schedules for industrial projects. The Food and

Agriculture Organization (FAO) (1986: vols. 2, 3, and 4) is similarly useful for agricultural projects. Both Perkins (1994: chap. 5) and Curry and Weiss (2000: chap. 3) contain extended discussions of investment criteria. There are some useful examples of the application of cost-effectiveness analysis in Asian Development Bank (1997) and Belli et al. (1998).

Notes

1. A comprehensive discussion of the issues relating to rehabilitation projects can be found in Yaffey and Tribe (1992).

2. This concept is described in Devarajan et al. (1996).

3. The original reason for using Year 0 as the first year may have related to the fact that it reduced the number of discounting calculations by one since there was no need to discount Year 0. This advantage is of no significance when discounting calculations are done by spreadsheet functions. One argument for not using the Year 0 convention is that, if the present is Year 0, there is normally some gestation period between the preparation of a project and its implementation and so it is unlikely that work on the project will start until Year 1 at the earliest.

4. In ex-post accounting it is common to attribute a proportion of overheads in the valuation of stocks. This procedure will tend to increase the value of working capital and reduce the value of operating costs. The ex-post accounting procedure can be used in ex-ante project accounts, but it is slightly more complicated than valuing stocks on the basis of direct costs only.

5. The terminology adopted here is similar to that used in Overseas Development Administration (1988).

6. The spreadsheet functions =NPV (Microsoft Excel) or @NPV (Lotus 1-2-3) can be used for calculating the NPV.

7. The spreadsheet functions =IRR (Microsoft Excel) or @IRR (Lotus 1-2-3) can be used for calculating the IRR.

8. Not the least of the problems is the fact that some of the potential projects that might be considered for the later years of the program may not yet have been prepared or even identified. Optimization in these circumstances is logically impossible.

9. The capital recovery factor gives the annual value of a single capital payment at a specified rate of discount. It is obtained by taking the reciprocal of the annuity factor for the period in question. The annuity factor is the sum of the discount factors for a given period. The capital recovery factor can be estimated on the following basis:

$$CRF_n = \frac{r}{1 - (1 + r)^{-n}}$$

where CRF_n is the capital recovery factor for a repayment term of n years and r is the rate of interest on the loan.

The spreadsheet functions =PMT (Microsoft Excel) or @PMT (Lotus 1-2-3) can be used in calculations involving capital recovery factors.

PART 2
Financial Analysis

5

Financial Analysis
for Commercial Projects

All projects require some form of financial analysis because they involve
the expenditure of money, which must be both planned and justified. The
main purposes of the financial analysis of projects are

- To provide an adequate financing plan for the proposed investment
- To determine the profitability of a project from the point of view of
  the owners or the project beneficiaries
- To assist in planning the operation and control of the project, by
  providing management information to both internal and external
  users.

In the financial analysis of projects the two most important concepts
are those of *liquidity* and *profitability*. Financial analysis statements also
provide performance indicators on a number of other issues for management information.

The concept of liquidity is concerned with the availability of funds for
the continued implementation and operation of the project. The liquidity
status of a project is determined primarily from the *cash flow*. This statement is also described by some people as the sources and applications of
funds statement or as the funds flow statement. Liquidity is an important
issue for all projects.

The concept of profitability is concerned with the question of whether
the project is worthwhile from the point of view of the investor. Accountants' measures of profitability are determined primarily from the *profit and
loss account,* which is also known as the income statement, particularly in
U.S. practice. Discounted measures of the value of a project to the owners
can be derived from the cash flow. Measures of profitability to the project
owners are only relevant to those projects with an output that is sold com-
mercially.

Performance indicators of the financial status of an enterprise are derived from both the profit and loss account and the *balance sheet,* which together with the cash flow make up the three main statements for financial analysis. However, these statements cannot be derived without the supporting statements described in the next section.

Many different layouts and approaches for the various statements can be found in the literature. To make matters worse, the terminology used by economists when writing about financial analysis may not be very precise from the point of view of accountants. This is due in part to differences in perspectives and objectives. Figure 5.1 shows some of the connections between the various schedules included in a financial analysis and the annual statement of costs and benefits. The construction of the balance sheet is shown separately in Figure 5.2. The numerical example of the cotton textile project used in Chapter 4 is extended in this chapter to cover the main financial statements through Tables 5.1 to 5.5.

Supporting Statements

The five main supporting statements required for the financial analysis of a project are

- fixed assets schedule
- depreciation schedule
- trading account
- working capital schedule (current assets and current liabilities)
- loan payment schedules

The Fixed Assets Schedule (Investment Cost Schedule)

This schedule includes details of investment costs (fixed assets), the timing of investments and replacements, and the terminal (salvage) value at the end of the project life. These details were provided in Table 4.1 in Chapter 4.

The Depreciation Schedule

Depreciation is a means of charging the cost of an asset against profit over a number of years. The term *depreciation* is used both to refer to the physical deterioration of assets over time and to refer to a charge used in the calculation of tax liability.

The former use of the term relates to the measure of depreciation that might be made by a company for internal accounting purposes to determine

Figure 5.1   Financial Analysis (Commercial Project)

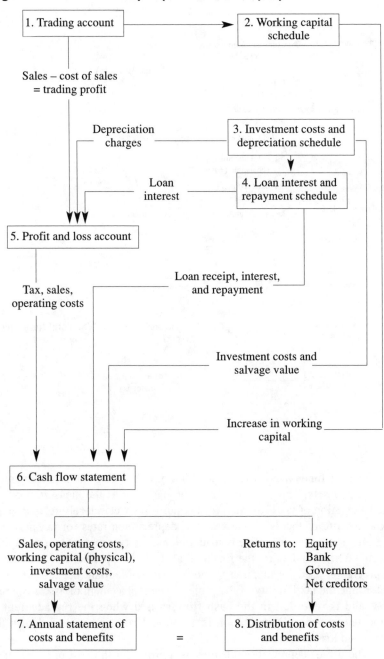

Figure 5.2   Construction of a Balance Sheet

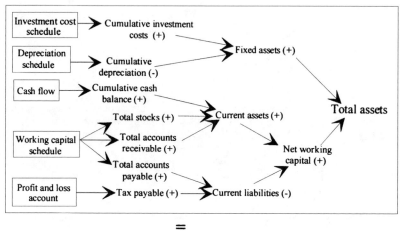

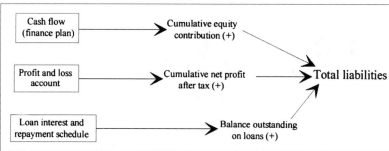

the level of funds needed to be set aside for financing the replacement of worn-out assets. This measure might be the same as the measure used for the calculation of tax if the rate for tax purposes were closely related to the expected life of the asset. However, if depreciation rates for tax purposes are affected by tax incentive considerations, the two measures may be different. When conducting the financial analysis of a project it is the rate of depreciation used for taxation purposes that is important because this will determine the tax liability of the project. The replacement of assets is a real cost and is recorded in the cash flow as and when the replacement is expected to occur. Depreciation is a notional cost and is recorded in the profit and loss account.

The use of depreciation charges as a proxy for the cost of using fixed assets is based on the principle that the full cost of an asset cannot be charged against one year's profit when the benefit of the use of the asset is expected to last for a number of years. By making a depreciation charge, the capital cost of the asset can be charged against the profits earned over its expected life.

The depreciation schedule illustrated in Table 5.1 shows the annual amount of depreciation for all of the project assets set out in Table 4.1. The total value of depreciation charges is then entered as a cost in the profit and loss account.

There are several methods employed to calculate depreciation, the most common being the *straight line method* and the *reducing balance method*. Table 5.1 illustrates the use of the straight line method. The precise rates of depreciation allowed for taxation purposes in any country are normally governed by the tax authorities, although it is quite common for individual rates to be negotiated for specific items where appropriate.

The value of depreciation using the straight line method can be calculated on the following basis:

$$D_i = \frac{K_i - S_i}{n} \qquad (5.1)$$

where D_i is the value of depreciation for asset i;
K_i is the original cost of asset i;
S_i is the expected salvage value of asset i at the end of its life; and
n is the number of years of the life of the asset.

For example, if the original cost of an asset is $1,000 and the expected salvage value after a ten-year operating life is $200, the annual value of depreciation using the straight line method is $(1,000–200)/10 = $80.

In Table 5.1 the salvage values of the machinery and vehicles have been assumed for simplicity to be zero. For the buildings the value of S_i is assumed to be 50% of the original cost.

With the reducing balance method a certain percentage of the value of an asset is depreciated each year. Since the remaining balance of the value of the asset after the deduction of depreciation is reduced in each year, the depreciation amount will fall every year. In principle the value of the asset will never fall to zero, but in practice the residual value of the asset will be written off at some stage, either when it is disposed of or when the value is negligible. The value of depreciation using the reducing balance method is given by

$$D_{it} = K_{it} \cdot P_i \qquad (5.2)$$

where D_{it} is the value of depreciation for asset i in Year t;
K_{it} is the remaining value of asset i in Year t; and
P_i is the annual percentage of the remaining balance of asset i to be depreciated.

The value of K_{it} can be determined by

$$K_{it} = K_i(1-P_i)^n \tag{5.3}$$

where n is the age in years of the asset i in Year t.

For example, if the original cost of an asset is $1,000 and the annual rate of depreciation is 20%, the value of depreciation in the first year of operation is $1,000*0.2 = $200. At the end of this year the remaining value of the asset is $1,000 − $200 = $800. The value of depreciation in the second year is then $800*0.2 = $160, and the remaining value of the asset is $800–$160 = $640 and so on.

Depreciation allowances can be used as tax incentives when companies are allowed to write off a higher proportion of the value of an asset than would be justified by physical wear and tear and technical obsolescence early in the life of the asset. This procedure increases the nominal value of costs in the profit and loss account and therefore reduces tax liability in the early years of a project. This can be helpful because it is usually the early years of a project when financial problems are most acute.

Investment allowances are a form of tax incentive that might be recorded in the same schedule as the depreciation allowances. This incentive allows the company to write off more than 100% of the value of the asset with the percentage above 100% being the investment allowance. Investment allowances are usually given at the beginning of the life of an asset and have to be recorded separately from depreciation allowances because they will be treated differently in the balance sheet.

The Trading Account

The trading account is often included with the profit and loss account. It sets out the value of sales and the cost of sales. The trading profit is the difference between the two. The necessary information for drawing up a trading account is provided in Tables 4.2 and 4.3. In principal a separate trading account can be drawn up for each different product that an enterprise might produce. In calculating the trading profit only the direct costs attributable to each product are included. The term *gross margin* or *gross profit* can also be used for trading profit.

Table 5.1 Depreciation Schedule by Year ($ '000)

	1	2	3	4	5	6	7	8	9	10	11
Buildings		330	330	330	330	330	330	330	330	330	330
Machinery		2,500	2,500	2,500	2,500	2,500	2,500	2,500	2,500	2,500	2,500
Vehicles		500	500	500	500	500	500	500	500	500	500
Total depreciation		3,330	3,330	3,330	3,330	3,330	3,330	3,330	3,330	3,330	3,330

Table 5.2 Loan Interest and Repayment Schedule by Year ($ '000)

	1	2	3	4	5	6	7	8	9	10	11
Interest rate	8.0%										
Loan principal	10,000	12,000									
Total payment				4,285	4,285	4,285	4,285	4,285	4,285	4,285	4,285
Unpaid interest		800	1,824								
Interest paid				1,970	1,785	1,585	1,369	1,135	883	611	317
Loan repayment				2,315	2,500	2,700	2,916	3,150	3,402	3,674	3,968
Balance outstanding	10,000	22,800	24,624	22,309	19,809	17,109	14,192	11,043	7,641	3,968	0

Working Capital Schedule (Current Assets/Liabilities)

The working capital schedule was set out in Table 4.4. The items included in this schedule are sometimes described as *current assets* and *current liabilities*. Current assets include stocks (inventories) of materials and output, work in progress, accounts receivable (debtors), and cash. Current liabilities include accounts payable (creditors) and tax payable (where there is a delay in paying taxes due), and they are deducted from current assets.

Loan Interest and Repayment Schedule

This schedule sets out the annual value of receipts and payments associated with a loan. The period when the loan is being received is known as the *disbursement period,* while the period when the loan is being repaid is known as the *repayment period.* Loans are normally subject to a written agreement in which the terms agreed by the borrower and the lender are stipulated.

The terms covering the disbursement period will normally define

- The maximum amount of the loan
- The currency in which the loan is to be taken out
- The period over which the loan is to be disbursed
- The basis for any interest charges accruing during the disbursement period
- The nature of any other fees associated with the loan

Loans may be taken out in a single installment, but project loans are more often taken out in a number of drawdowns during the investment period. Usually interest is charged from the moment each installment of the loan is taken out. Interest may be paid during the disbursement period, but, more often, interest during the drawdown period is accumulated into the sum to be repaid. If a part of the loan is committed but not yet taken out, there may also be a commitment fee for the part of the loan that has not yet been taken out. Some lenders also demand a front-end fee to cover the administrative expense of making the loan. When governments guarantee foreign currency loans for investors there is usually a loan guarantee charge.

The loan agreement will include the terms on which the loan is to be repaid. These will include the term of the loan (the number of years over which the loan has to be repaid), the grace period, if any, and the method and currency of repayment. Grace periods can help borrowers to get their project started by providing a period during which interest and principal repayment does not have to be paid. This period can be critical in the establishment of a project.

There are three main methods of calculating loan repayments. The method illustrated in Table 5.2 is the equal annual installments method using a capital recovery factor.[1] This is the most common method employed in project analysis and the most helpful from the point of view of the investor. The capital recovery factor method keeps the total payments the same over the life of the loan. When repayments start, most of the expenditure goes on interest and only a small proportion goes into the repayment of the loan. As the loan is paid off the interest portion declines and the part that goes into loan repayment increases. Since interest is tax deductible this method reduces tax liability in the early years of the project.

The total payment (*TP*), starting in Year *t*, on the loan is determined by

$$TP = OB_{t-1} * CRF_n \tag{5.4}$$

where OB_{t-1} is the outstanding balance on the loan at the end of year *t*–1 and CRF_n is the capital recovery factor for n years where n is the number of years over which the loan has to be repaid.

Interest payment (I_t) in Year *t* is estimated by

$$I_t = OB_{t-1} * r \tag{5.5}$$

where *r* is the rate of interest on the loan.

Loan repayment R_t in Year *t* is estimated by

$$R_t = TP - I_t \tag{5.6}$$

The main alternatives to the capital recovery method of loan repayment are the equal annual repayments method and the lump sum repayment method. The former method involves equal installments of repayment of the principal sum. This method implies that the greatest total value of repayment and interest will take place in the first year of the repayment period. Such a payment schedule may lead to difficulties for projects with insufficient funds at the beginning of their operating lives. The latter method leads to the need to finance a single large payment at the end of the term of the loan. Repayment of a single large sum in one year may be disruptive to the operation of an enterprise unless plans to set aside funds for the loan repayment are adhered to strictly.

There are a number of other issues associated with assessing the real cost of loan finance, particularly where loans are offered at an apparently concessionary rate either by development finance agencies or by equipment suppliers through suppliers' credit. These issues are discussed in Chapter 16.

The Profit and Loss Account (Income Statement)

The format of this statement varies depending on who is preparing it and for what purpose and on the type of activity under consideration. An example of the profit and loss account is given in Table 5.3.

Net profit is calculated in the profit and loss account by deducting fixed or overhead costs (including depreciation and loan interest) from gross profit. Loan interest may include interest paid and also the unpaid interest, which is accumulated into the principal sum during the grace period of a loan. Company taxes are usually payable on the basis of a percentage of net profit. The final retained earnings figure (net profit after tax) is found by deducting tax and interest charges from net profit. Normally losses recorded early in the project life can be carried forward into the later years of the project life for the purposes of calculating tax liability. This means that tax is not paid until the cumulative taxable profit is positive.

The profit and loss account may also include an appropriation account, which shows how the retained earnings are appropriated by the different shareholders and how much is transferred to building up project reserves. This part of the statement is not often used in project analysis because the information is unlikely to be known in advance of project implementation.

The fundamental principle behind the profit and loss account is the *accruals concept,* which matches sales made in an accounting period with the cost of making those sales. Accordingly sales revenue is made up of all sales, including those for which payment has not yet been received in that accounting period. Similarly cost of sales will account for materials that have been received and used but not paid for. The cost of sales will not include the cost of materials that are used in manufacturing stocks of finished goods or work in progress. These costs are included in working capital.

The Cash Flow

The main function of the cash flow is to analyze the liquidity position of the project, to identify potential periods of cash shortage, and to plan appropriate responses designed to remove such shortages. Table 5.4 shows the cash flow for the cotton textile project. The cumulative cash flow, also known as the balance carried forward, must always be positive. A negative amount signals that the project will run out of money and therefore that the financial plan is not feasible and will have to be changed. Preparation of the cash flow can therefore be an iterative process. It can be seen that, although the net cash flow in Year 2 is negative, the positive cash balance carried forward from Year 1 is enough to cover the shortfall in Year 2. The liquidity position of the project therefore appears to be feasible.

Table 5.3 Profit and Loss Account by Year ($ '000)

	1	2	3	4	5	6	7	8	9	10	11
Sales revenue		14,580	23,490	31,590	32,400	32,400	32,400	32,400	32,400	32,400	32,400
Less variable costs		9,360	15,080	20,280	20,800	20,800	20,800	20,800	20,800	20,800	20,800
Gross or trading profit		5,220	8,410	11,310	11,600	11,600	11,600	11,600	11,600	11,600	11,600
Less overheads		2,300	3,700	3,900	4,100	4,200	4,200	4,200	4,200	4,200	4,200
Less depreciation		3,330	3,330	3,330	3,330	3,330	3,330	3,330	3,330	3,330	3,330
Less loan interest		800	1,824	1,970	1,785	1,585	1,369	1,135	883	611	317
Net pretax profit		-1,210	-444	2,110	2,385	2,485	2,701	2,935	3,187	3,459	3,753
Cumulative taxable profit		-1,210	-1,654	456	2,841	5,327	8,028	10,963	14,149	17,608	21,360
Tax @ 30%				137	716	746	810	880	956	1,038	1,126
Net profit after tax		-1,210	-444	1,973	1,670	1,740	1,891	2,054	2,231	2,421	2,627
Cumulative net profit after tax		-1,210	-1654	319	1,989	3,729	5,620	7,674	9,904	12,326	14,952

Table 5.4 Cash Flow for Financial Planning by Year ($ '000)

	1	2	3	4	5	6	7	8	9	10	11	12
Cash inflow												
Equity capital	15,000	12,000										
Loan	10,000											
Sales		14,580	23,490	31,590	32,400	32,400	32,400	32,400	32,400	32,400	32,400	32,400
Total annual cash inflow	25,000	26,580	23,490	31,590	32,400	32,400	32,400	32,400	32,400	32,400	32,400	32,400
Cash outflow												
Investment	20,000	15,000					2,500					-4,200
Incremental working capital		2,980	1,625	1,570	68						-6,243	
Operating costs		11,660	18,780	24,180	24,900	25,000	25,000	25,000	25,000	25,000	25,000	
Loan interest				1,970	1,785	1,585	1,369	1,135	883	611	317	
Loan repayment				2,315	2,500	2,700	2,916	3,150	3,402	3,674	3,968	
Tax					137	716	746	810	880	956	1,038	1,126
Total annual cash outflow	20,000	29,640	20,405	30,035	29,389	30,001	32,531	30,095	30,165	30,241	24,080	-3,074
Annual net cash flow	5,000	-3,060	3,085	1,555	3,011	2,399	-131	2,305	2,235	2,159	8,320	3,074
Cumulative balance C/F	5,000	1,940	5,025	6,580	9,591	11,990	11,860	14,164	16,399	18,558	26,878	29,952
Return to equity	-10,000	-3,060	3,085	1,555	3,011	2,399	-131	2,305	2,235	2,159	8,320	3,074

NPV to equity at 4% = 7,936
NPV to equity at 8% = 3,346
NPV to equity at 12% = 294
IRR = 12.5%

The cash flow records cash inflows and outflows when they are expected to occur. It is not based on the accruals concept, and it does not give an indication of profitability from an accounting viewpoint. It simply indicates the amount of cash available to the organization at any one point in time. For this reason it is likely that, in the absence of a pay-as-you-earn tax scheme, the line showing the amount of tax paid in any one year will be in arrears of the tax due calculated in the profit and loss account (see Tables 5.3 and 5.4). This is because the amount of tax payable can only be determined after the accounts for the period in question have been completed. The amount of the arrears will vary depending on the frequency with which accounts are produced. In our case it is assumed that tax is paid one year in arrears.

The cash flow schedule can be used to derive the internal rate of return to equity capital. The net cash return to equity is calculated by deducting the value of the additional equity capital provided by the shareholders in each year from the net cash flow line. The IRR to equity is then obtained by discounting the resulting net cash return to equity stream.

In principle the internal rate of return to equity capital can be compared with commercial rates of interest to decide whether the project is worthwhile from the viewpoint of the owners. It can be seen that the IRR to equity capital for our project is 12.5%, and the NPV is positive at all the discount rates shown. The IRR is significantly above the cost of borrowing of 8%. The project would therefore appear to be a reasonable investment from the point of view of the owners unless they have more profitable alternatives for investing their money.

However, it is important to be aware of the difference between real and nominal rates of return when making these comparisons. Strictly speaking the cash flow is about money inflows and money outflows. The value of these is affected by the rate of inflation, which can also have an indirect effect on the rate of interest. In principle, therefore, it is important to adjust the financial analysis of projects for the expected rate of inflation. Inflation and related exchange-rate changes lead to some significant complications that are often ignored and can lead to serious financial problems. The effects of inflation and rate changes are considered in more detail in Chapter 16.

The Balance Sheet

The balance sheet is used to obtain an understanding of the financial position of a project or an enterprise. It is a statement comparing the assets and liabilities and gives the net worth of an enterprise at a specific point in time. It is usually prepared on an annual basis for project analysis, but, during the operation of an enterprise, half-year or monthly balance sheets may also be prepared for management information. Unlike the trading and profit and loss account, which measures the performance of a business over a period of time, the balance sheet is a measure of what the business is worth at a particular point in time. This valuation is made by comparing project assets (what the project owns) with project liabilities (what the project owes).

Where a project involves an enterprise that already exists (e.g., an expansion or rehabilitation project), funding agencies may be interested both in the most recent actual balance sheet for an enterprise and in the projected balance sheet with implementation of the proposed project. The most recent actual balance sheet will give an indication of the current financial status while the projected future balance sheet gives an indication of the assumed future financial status.

A number of different formats may be used in the presentation of the balance sheets. In the past, the standard UK practice was to list the liabilities on the left and assets on the right. The standard U.S. practice was the reverse. It is now more common to use a vertical presentation, with assets listed above liabilities. This presentation is more helpful for project analysis in which the balance sheet is actually a projection over a number of years rather than a record for a single year. The various categories of assets and liabilities are listed in Table 5.5 and discussed below.

Fixed Assets

These are assets held by an enterprise for use over a period of time in the production process. They are acquired with the intention of being used on a continuing basis and not intended for sale in the ordinary course of business. The value of fixed assets is obtained by deducting the cumulative value of depreciation charges from the cumulative value of fixed investment. The necessary information is provided in the investment cost (fixed assets) schedule (Table 4.1) and the depreciation schedule (Table 5.1).

Current Assets

Current assets are items of value normally realizable within one year from the date of the balance sheet. These items can be described as cash or near cash and include such items as stocks of raw materials and finished goods, debtors, and cash. In Table 5.5 the value of current assets is obtained by adding the value of stocks and accounts receivable taken from Table 4.4 to the cumulative cash flow (cash balance) taken from Table 5.4.

Table 5.5 Projected Balance Sheet by Year ($ '000)

	1	2	3	4	5	6	7	8	9	10	11	12
Employment of funds (assets)												
Fixed assets												
(net of depreciation)	20,000	31,670	28,340	25,010	21,680	18,350	17,520	14,190	10,860	7,530	4,200	
Current assets												
Cash balance	5,000	1,940	5,025	6,580	9,591	11,990	11,860	14,164	16,399	18,558	26,878	29,952
Current assets		3,622	5,568	7,446	7,513	7,513	7,513	7,513	7,513	7,513		
Total current assets	5,000	5,562	10,593	14,026	17,104	19,504	19,373	21,678	23,912	26,072	26,878	29,952
Current liabilities												
Accounts payable		642	963	1,271	1,271	1,271	1,271	1,271	1,271	1,271		
Tax payable				137	716	746	810	880	956	1,038	1,126	
Total current liabilities		642	963	1,408	1,986	2,016	2,081	2,151	2,227	2,308	1,126	
Net working capital	5,000	4,920	9,630	12,618	15,118	17,487	17,292	19,527	21,686	23,763	25,752	29,952
Total assets	25,000	36,590	37,970	37,628	36,798	35,837	34,812	33,717	32,546	31,293	29,952	29,952
Funds employed (liabilities)												
Equity capital	15,000	15,000	15,000	15,000	15,000	15,000	15,000	15,000	15,000	15,000	15,000	15,000
Accumulated profits		-1,210	-1,654	319	1,989	3,729	5,620	7,674	9,904	12,326	14,952	14,952
Loans	10,000	22,800	24,624	22,309	19,809	17,109	14,192	11,043	7,641	3,968		
Total liabilities	25,000	36,590	37,970	37,628	36,798	35,837	34,812	33,717	32,546	31,293	29,952	29,952

Liabilities

These are normally divided into two types. Current liabilities such as creditors and overdrafts are items that the business has to pay within one year. Current liabilities may include the tax payable recorded in the profit and loss account but shown one year in arrears in the cash flow. In some presentations, including the one used in Table 5.5, current liabilities are shown as negative items in the assets side of the balance sheet and are deducted from current assets to give a value for net working capital.

Long-term liabilities are divided between those that are owed to the owner (accumulated profits and owners' equity) and those owed to outsiders (long-term loans). The cumulative value of owners' equity is derived from the cash flow (Table 5.4) while the value of accumulated profits is obtained from the profit and loss account (Table 5.3). The outstanding balance on long-term loans is taken from the loan interest and repayment schedule (Table 5.2).

Figure 5.2 indicates the sources of information used in constructing a balance sheet. For the balance sheet to balance, total assets must match total liabilities.

From the point of view of the project economist the most important financial information is contained in the cash flow. This will give an indication of the adequacy of the finance plan in ensuring that payments can be met and can also be used to show the internal rate of return on the net cash flow to the owners of the project. The profit and loss account and the balance sheet are required respectively for tax calculations and as a check on consistency, but they will probably not be used for anything else. For the financial analyst these statements can also be used to generate ratios that may give some indication of the potential future health of the enterprise.

Financial Ratios and Financial Criteria

The profit and loss account and the balance sheet can be used to estimate a number of financial ratios (Table 5.6). Normally such financial ratios are used during the operation of an enterprise to provide management information for monitoring performance and financial status. They are less important in the planning stage of a project because many of them depend on information about the use of cash balances that is unlikely to be known in advance. Nevertheless there are some financial ratios that can be used in project appraisal, particularly by financing agencies, to assess the acceptability of a financial plan. The most important of these are described below.

Profitability Ratios

Two main profitability ratios are sometimes used. These relate to the annual rate of return on total capital (RK_t) and the annual rate of return to equity capital (RE_t). For any year t:

$$RK_t = \frac{NP_t + I_t}{K_t} \tag{5.7}$$

where NP_t is the net profit after tax, I_t is the value of interest charged on long-term debt, and K_t is the total capital employed.

$$RE_t = \frac{NP_t}{E_t} \tag{5.8}$$

where E_t is the total equity capital invested.

Shareholders in a project may also be interested in the return on total net worth. The net worth is defined as the sum of the equity capital invested and the value of accumulated profits and is an indicator of the size of the shareholders' stake in the enterprise.

Profitability can also be related to sales value. The ratio of gross profit to sales indicates the extent to which the sales value is absorbed by direct costs and also gives an indication of the margin from which the other expenses of the enterprise have to be met. The ratio of net profit after tax to sales indicates the margin after all expenses have been met. Both of these ratios could be regarded as efficiency ratios in that they give an idea of the overall efficiency of the enterprise in converting costs into profit.

The problem with using any of these ratios as indicators of project profitability is that the values will vary considerably from year to year, and in the early years of a project they are likely to be negative. In the case of the cotton textile project the ratios change every year. It is only if there is something like a typical year that such indicators have much meaning. Their main use in project analysis is for relatively simple projects where a "typical" year can be defined. It should be noted that profitability ratios are primarily of interest where profitability is an important objective. They are of less interest where service delivery is the main objective and cost recovery is regarded as a constraint, although they may be used as indicators in determining price regulation of monopolies.

Debt-Equity Ratios

Debt-equity ratios are used to assess the financial risk of a project, particularly from the point of view of the providers of debt finance. The most useful ratio in this respect is the ratio of the value of long-term debt to the net worth of the enterprise or project. The information needed to calculate this ratio is obtained from the liabilities part of the balance sheet. In the early years of the project life the net worth of the enterprise can be less than the value of the equity invested because accumulated profits may be negative. If there is a grace period with unpaid interest accumulated, the value of the long-term debt may also be increasing in the early years of the project life so that the debt-equity ratio will increase. In the case of our cotton textile project the value of long-term debt increases until Year 3 and the net worth of the project declines until the same year. The ratio of debt to equity reaches a maximum of 1.85 or 65:35 in Year 3. This is probably close to the maximum that would be tolerable to a bank for a medium-risk project. The debt-equity ratio declines fairly rapidly thereafter.

Debt-equity ratios are also indicators of the *gearing* or *leverage* of the investors. High debt-equity ratios allow the shareholders to control the project with a relatively small stake. Such ratios can be attractive to shareholders for profitable projects because the earnings per share after loan service has been accounted for will be very high. However, such ratios are also potentially risky if the project does not meet its expectations because the margin left after loan service could become very low or even negative, and there may be a risk of bankruptcy. Most banks therefore have a maximum acceptable debt-equity ratio and pay particular attention to projected balance sheets to ensure that this is not exceeded.

Debt Service Coverage

Where a project relies quite heavily on borrowed funds, a useful ratio to calculate is the ratio of uncommitted funds to debt service requirements. In this case the value of uncommitted funds is the sum of the net profit after tax, interest on long-term debt, and depreciation. The debt service requirement is the sum of loan interest and principal repayment. This ratio gives an idea of safety margin over and above debt service requirements in the projected funds available. The ratio must be greater than one or the project will be unable to service the debts it has accumulated. How much greater than one the ratio must be will depend on the potential risk of adverse changes to the value of uncommitted funds. In the case of the cotton textile project the debt service coverage ratio is never lower than 1.46.

Liquidity Ratios

One of the critical issues for financial analysis is the liquidity of the project. Comparison of the assets and liabilities of an enterprise allows an assessment of whether the enterprise will be in a position to pay its debts. Two ratios are commonly used.

The current ratio is the ratio of current assets to current liabilities. This is a measure of short-term liquidity. It could be argued that the inclusion of stocks in the estimation of such a ratio is misleading if the stocks cannot be converted readily into cash. An alternative ratio, the quick ratio, is the ratio of current assets minus stocks to current liabilities.

Behrens and Hawranek (1991: 299) suggest that generally acceptable values for the current ratio should be in the range 2.0 to 1.2, while acceptable values for the quick ratio are in the range 1.2 to 1.0. In practice these indicators can be difficult to use in project analysis beyond the first few years because the value of the cash balance in current assets will depend on the policy of the management of the enterprise on how this balance should be used. Project analysts do not usually speculate on such policy and so cash balances are assumed to accumulate in the absence of information to the contrary, whereas in practice such balances are likely to be distributed as dividends or used for further investment.

In practice the use of most financial ratios in the appraisal of any but the simplest projects is often of limited value. However, they can be useful for quick assessment of small-scale projects involving little fixed investment. They can also be useful for monitoring project performance and for assessing the status of existing enterprises when they are applying for loans for further investment. Financial ratios point to particular concerns that are important for the financial health of enterprises and might sometimes be overlooked in the overall judgments based on the information provided in the cash flow.

Pricing and Tariff Design for Public Utilities

So far it has been assumed that the prices charged by the enterprise are externally determined in a competitive market and that the enterprise seeks to maximize profits, hence the focus on indicators of profitability. However, while liquidity is always an issue for any activity that has to be financed, financial profitability is not always the only objective for commercial enterprises. Public utilities are often monopolies providing basic needs. In the absence of regulation, monopolies can set their own prices, but monopoly pricing to maximize profits is unlikely to be acceptable.[2] Public utilities must therefore have a basis for determining their prices or

Table 5.6 Financial Ratios by Year

	1	2	3	4	5	6	7	8	9	10	11
Profitability ratios											
Return on assets		-1.1%	3.6%	10.8%	11.3%	11.4%	11.7%	12.1%	12.5%	13.0%	13.6%
Shareholders' return		-8.8%	-3.3%	12.9%	9.8%	9.3%	9.2%	9.1%	9.0%	8.9%	8.8%
Gross profit		35.8%	35.8%	35.8%	35.8%	35.8%	35.8%	35.8%	35.8%	35.8%	35.8%
Markup		55.8%	55.8%	55.8%	55.8%	55.8%	55.8%	55.8%	55.8%	55.8%	55.8%
Net profit											
Before tax		-8.3%	-1.9%	6.7%	7.4%	7.7%	8.3%	9.1%	9.8%	10.7%	11.6%
After tax		-8.3%	-1.9%	6.2%	5.2%	5.4%	5.8%	6.3%	6.9%	7.5%	8.1%
Liquidity ratios											
Current ratio		8.7	11.0	10.0	8.6	9.7	9.3	10.1	10.7	11.3	
Quick ratio		4.9	7.3	6.5	6.2	7.3	7.0	7.8	8.6	9.2	
Efficiency ratios											
Stock turnover		3.9	4.2	4.2	4.3	4.3	4.3	4.3	4.3	4.3	
Fixed assets turnover		0.5	0.8	1.3	1.5	1.8	1.8	2.3	3.0	4.3	7.7
Trade debtor collection period		30.4	30.4	30.4	30.4	30.4	30.4	30.4	30.4	30.4	
Trade creditor collection period		30.4	30.4	30.4	30.4	30.4	30.4	30.4	30.4	30.4	
Investment ratios											
Capital gearing		62.3%	64.9%	59.3%	53.8%	47.7%	40.8%	32.8%	23.5%	12.7%	

tariffs. Publicly owned utilities may be required to cover their costs but not necessarily to maximize their profits. Where public utilities are privately owned, prices are usually controlled by a regulatory body. How can the tariff be set to maintain a proper balance between the interests of the producers and those of the consumers?

The Purpose of a Tariff

The first step is to establish the purposes of the tariff. There can be a number of purposes for a tariff for a public utility. The most important are

- To ensure the most efficient use of resources. Tariffs should ensure that the benefit derived from any additional supply is at least equal to the additional cost of providing the supply.
- There may be redistributional aims in setting a tariff related to the provision of basic needs. Tariffs may be set to ensure affordability to poor consumers.
- There are financial aims related to the financial sustainability of the enterprise. An enterprise that makes consistent losses is unlikely to work effectively and will be a continuous drain on public resources.

Marginal Cost Pricing

Economic theory would suggest that the most appropriate tariff would be that which equates marginal cost with the price consumers are willing to pay. This is illustrated for a hypothetical water enterprise in Figure 5.3 at point C, where there is demand of about 1,700 m^3 and a price of about 0.45 per m^3. This position contrasts with the position at point A, which would equate marginal revenue with marginal cost. At point A the monopoly enterprise maximizes its profits and restricts supply to about 400 m^3 at a price of 2.36 per m^3.

The problem with the most appropriate tariff from an economic point of view is that it may not always cover the full cost of supplying the utility, particularly for a capital-intensive enterprise like urban water supply. In fact, at point C the enterprise makes a loss of about 0.65 per m^3.

Part of the problem is related to the difference between *short-run marginal cost* (SRMC), in which the existing capacity may be assumed to be fixed, and *long-run marginal cost* (LRMC), in which it is possible to increase the capacity through further investment. An economic tariff should be based on LRMC and therefore should allow for the cost of investment in replacement of equipment and establishment of additional capacity where consumer demand is rising.

Figure 5.3   Tariff Determination

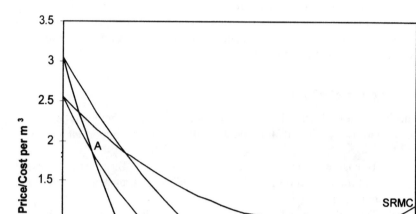

Making Marginal Cost Pricing Operational—
Average Incremental Cost (AIC)

One of the problems in operationalizing marginal cost pricing is that investment tends to be lumpy and so LRMC may be dependent on the particular time reached in the investment expansion cycle. A way of resolving the problem is by calculating the *average incremental cost* (AIC). This is defined as the ratio of the present value of the capital and operating costs of an expansion in capacity to the present value of the output measured in physical terms (e.g., m³ or kwh). This can be expressed as

$$AIC = \frac{\displaystyle\sum_{t=1}^{T} \frac{(K_t - OC_t)}{(1+r)^t}}{\displaystyle\sum_{t=1}^{T} \frac{(Y_t)}{(1+r)^t}} \tag{5.9}$$

where K_t is the capital cost in Year t;

OC_t is the operating cost in Year t;

Y_t is the physical level of output in Year t; and

r is the discount rate.

In principle an AIC calculation should be made each time there is a significant increase in capacity and should relate to the useful life of the capacity addition.

Income Distributional Questions

There are practical problems in charging each consumer a tariff related to the marginal cost of supply. Obviously it is cheaper to supply water to a large-scale user in a valley than to supply water to small-scale users on hillsides. If the same charge is adopted, cross-subsidization will take place. However, if there are too many different rates the tariff system becomes too complicated. It can also be expensive to provide individual meters for small-scale users.

If public utilities are regarded as basic needs, there may be grounds for altering tariffs for distributional reasons. A lower tariff could be charged for users up to a certain level of consumption. This is common for electricity tariffs as well as for water users. For example,

Consumption Range (m³ per month)	Tariff per m³ in Consumption Range ($)
0–10	0.10
10–40	0.30
40–90	0.50
90+	0.80

Financial Self-Sufficiency

Financial self-sufficiency is often an objective for a public utility. If the long-run average cost (LRAC) is above the LRMC for a given demand, as in Figure 5.3, revenue will be insufficient for full cost recovery. On the other hand, if LRAC < LRMC, there will be a financial surplus. In principle a subsidy could be justified to cover the difference between LRAC and LRMC, however the government may not have sufficient funds to provide such a subsidy. It may therefore be necessary to compromise between different potentially conflicting objectives.

Compromise Tariffs

In principle an ideal tariff would satisfy economic, distributional, and financial conditions. In practice there are likely to be conflicts between the objectives and a compromise may be required. One way around the problem is to have a mixture of fixed and variable charges and to vary the fixed charge according to income or some proxy for income. The fixed charge might cover consumption up to a defined minimum need ("lifeline allowance"), while the variable charge would cover the AIC on all consumption above the minimum. If households could be defined in three categories according to some estimate of property value, we might have:

Consumer Category	Lifeline Allowance	Basic Charge per m^3	Excess Unit Rate per m^3
Low income	10 m^3 /month	$1.0	$0.30
Middle income	10 m^3 /month	$4.0	$0.30
High income	10 m^3 /month	$8.0	$0.30

Electricity Tariffs

There are some specific issues related to the setting of electricity tariffs. These relate to the type and nature of electricity costs:

- The cost of a unit of electricity varies according to voltage and according to the time of day and season of the year.
- Electricity cannot be stored except through expensive pump storage schemes. Capacity must therefore be sufficient to meet peak demand.
- Some costs relate to capacity (kw), some relate to energy use (kwh), and some relate to consumer costs (connection, billing, and meter reading).

It is therefore normal to include both a fixed charge and a variable charge in electricity tariffs. It is also common to distinguish between different types of consumers (e.g., heavy industrial, light industry and commercial, agricultural, domestic).

Electricity charges can also be divided between generation costs and distribution costs. Where electricity is privatized these functions are sometimes undertaken by different enterprises.

Electricity generation costs may be estimated on the concept of *average marginal generating costs*. This estimate relates to the costs of the generating units that are able to supply the marginal units of output. The supply available from different units may vary at different times of day, and so the average marginal generating cost will be based on a weighted average of the marginal generating costs of combinations of different units. Any generating capacity that is fully utilized at all times of day will be irrelevant to this calculation.

Further Reading

Behrens and Hawranek (1991) provide a systematic description of financial accounts for industrial enterprises. The most comprehensive source on the financial analysis of projects is Yaffey (1992). Gittinger (1982) and Selvavinayagam (1991) are useful for those involved in agricultural projects.

There is a great deal of literature on the setting of tariffs. Much of the recent literature relates to the issue of regulation of the prices of privatized public utilities. Useful introductions to the subject can be found in Curry and Weiss (2000: chap. 8) and Asian Development Bank (1997: app. 22).

Notes

1. There are some additional complications involved in recording the timing of loan payments. These are associated with the question of the time within the year when the loan is taken out and the period during which the loan interest accrues. These issues are considered in more detail in Part 4 of the book.

2. Economic theory suggests that profit maximization for an unregulated monopoly involves restricting supply and raising prices to the consumer. This leads to monopoly profits, losses to consumers, and production below the economically optimal level. Monopoly pricing is therefore undesirable both on distributional and efficiency grounds.

6

Analysis of Incentive and Response for Small-Scale Producers

Projects That Generate Benefits for Small Producers

The period since the mid-1980s has seen a decline in public investment in directly productive projects, mainly due to the predominance of the view that investment in these sectors should be done by the private sector. Public investment has shifted toward projects providing the infrastructure and services intended to induce a positive response from producers. In developing countries such projects are usually oriented toward small producers, partly because of concerns with the income distribution effect of public investment. Since the justification of such projects depends on the producer response, it is necessary to investigate the potential costs and benefits to small producers and to use this information to assess the likely scale and timing of the response.

There are also many organizations whose purpose is to promote the activities of small-scale producers by providing support, often in the form of advice and/or loans. Such organizations may have to judge the merits of applications for loan finance without the benefit of the kind of full-scale financial analysis described in Chapter 5. If a different type of analysis is required, it is necessary to establish the common features of such small-scale producers before determining the most appropriate form for the analysis. Among the most common features are

- Small-scale producers are often based on households or small groups and may not have conventional accounts.
- Producers may be involved in a number of different production activities. Often a project may be concerned with only one of these

activities, but changes in one activity may have significant implications for the others.

- Many of the workers employed may be family members who are not paid wages but who have entitlements to a share of the household income. The distinction between work for financial gain and work for the maintenance of the household therefore may not be very clear. There may also be a division of labor according to gender and age such that the available labor cannot be regarded as homogeneous.
- In many cases fixed investment costs are of less significance than working capital. Requests for loans are therefore often for seasonal loans within a year rather than for long-term loans over a period of years.
- Constraints on productive activity may not always be easily defined in straightforward financial terms. The conventional objective function to maximize financial gain may therefore need to be adapted to take account of such constraints.

The implications of these features for the type of analysis adopted are

- The form of accounting adopted for the individual producer must be relatively simple.
- While the analysis may concentrate on one particular productive activity, adequate account should be taken of the likely effect on other activities.
- Analysis of the activity should cover more than just the associated cash transactions. Availability of labor of different types and at different times may be an important issue.
- Analysis of the activity within the year may be more important than analysis from year to year. The conventional cash flow on a year-by-year basis may therefore be replaced with a month-by-month or quarterly analysis for one or two years.
- In many cases the absence or relative insignificance of fixed investment costs reduces the relevance of time-based indicators like the standard measures of project worth.
- Nonfinancial constraints may need to be included explicitly in the analysis. These are likely to include labor of different kinds, land, cash at different times of year, subsistence requirements, and any major social factors that have implications for productive activities.

A further factor to consider in projects involving small producers is that a single project may affect a large number of producers. Estimation of the overall costs and benefits of the project involves assumptions about the timing of adoption of assumed changes by different producers and also involves the aggregation of costs and benefits to large numbers of producers. For this exercise to be manageable it is necessary to construct models of *typical producers,* and the number of different models used will depend on some form of categorization of those producers.

For project analysis there are therefore two reasons for requiring a relatively simple way to assess profitability for small producers. One of these is to allow the analyst to make a quick judgment of small project proposals. The other reason is to allow the aggregation of project costs and benefits for relatively large projects affecting large numbers of small producers. The issues and approaches involved will be illustrated in this chapter through the analysis of small farms. However, many of the approaches outlined can be adapted quite readily to the analysis of small-scale producers of processed goods and services.

Activity Budgets

The simplest form of analysis of a production activity is the preparation of an activity budget. This involves setting out the production of the activity concerned, the value of what is produced, and the direct cost of producing it. Some of the costs may be costs in kind, such as family labor or use of animal traction. Activity budgets are usually prepared in relation to a standard unit. In the case of a crop, the most likely unit to be used is a unit of land. For small-scale manufacturing, the standard unit might be a unit of processing equipment. It may also be useful to build up a budget for a single item of output. This can then be compared directly with the sales price. The gross margin per unit of sales can then be used to provide an estimate of the break-even sales quantity required to cover the cost of any equipment used or the servicing of short- and long-term loans.

Table 6.1 shows an example of activity budgets for two different categories of farmer in the project area affected by the proposed cotton textile project. The activities are based on one hectare of each of the crops grown by the farmers. In this case, farmers are categorized as those who cultivate by hand and those who use ox ploughs. The crops they grow are the same, but, due to different factor endowments, the yields and costs are different. The yields of the ox cultivators are assumed to be higher, partly because of better cultivation, partly because of use of animal manure, and partly because of better knowledge. At this stage it is assumed that all labor is provided from within the household and therefore that labor costs are not financial costs. It is further assumed that the major difference between the situation with the project and the situation without the project is that the farmers receive a better price for their cotton because of the demand derived from the project. This is indicated in Table 6.1.

Table 6.1 Hectare Budgets for Major Crops ($/Ha)

	Hand Cultivation				Ox Cultivation			
	Cotton	Maize	Sorghum	Groundnuts	Cotton	Maize	Sorghum	Groundnuts
Yield (kg/ha)	600	750	600	200	900	900	750	300
Unit price without ($/kg)	5.70	3.00	2.50	15.00	5.70	3.00	2.50	15.00
Unit price with ($/kg)	6.00				6.00			
Gross revenue without	3,420	2,250	1,500	3,000	5,130	2,700	1,875	4,500
Gross revenue with	3,600				5,400			
Costs								
Seed	75	75	56	300	75	75	56	300
Pesticide	210				210			
Bags/cloth	250	75	60	120	250	75	60	120
Tools, etc.	40	40	40	40	325	375	375	295
Total costs	575	190	156	460	860	525	491	715
Gross margin without	2,845	2,060	1,344	2,540	4,270	2,175	1,384	3,785
Gross margin with	3,025				4,540			
Labor (days)	140.0	84.0	132.0	102.0	115.0	57.0	75.0	72.0
Return/day without	20.3	24.5	10.2	24.9	37.1	38.2	18.5	52.6
Return/day with	21.6				39.5			
Return/unit cost without	5.9	11.8	9.6	6.5	6.0	5.1	3.8	6.3
Return/unit cost with	6.3				6.3			

Activity budgets like those in Table 6.1 can give a number of indicators of the profitability of each activity. The most obvious indicator is the gross margin per unit. In this case, since the unit is a unit of land, the gross margin is an indicator of the profitability of each crop in the use of land.

If land were the only consideration, it would be possible to inspect the gross margin and select the crop with the highest gross margin. In our example this would lead the farmers to grow only cotton. However, there may be some other considerations. Cotton is the most labor-intensive crop, and the gross margin analysis has not costed labor. It is assumed to come from within the household. Would all the labor required be available if the farmers were to grow only cotton?

If labor availability is constrained, it is possible to look at another indicator. This is the gross margin per unit of labor. According to this indicator, the most profitable crop is groundnuts.

For poorer farmers another issue might be significant. In general, cultivation of crops requires that farmers invest in seeds, agrichemicals, tools, and other materials in advance of the receipt of the revenue from the crop. The availability of cash for such expenditure might be a constraint. A third indicator might therefore be the gross margin per unit of cash costs. In this case the best crop for the hand cultivators is maize, and the best crop for the ox cultivators is groundnuts.

Activity budgets can therefore be used to give several indicators of profitability, but none of them are definitive. Furthermore the situation may be further complicated by a number of other issues:

- Agriculture is seasonal. Labor in one month cannot usually be substituted with labor in another month. Labor availability therefore needs to be considered on a monthly basis. Seasonality is also an important issue for many small-scale processing enterprises.
- Labor is not homogeneous. Sometimes it is possible to define labor availability in terms of adult equivalents, but this is not the case in all cultures. Division of labor by gender is common in many cultures and therefore it may be necessary to consider male and female labor as separate resources.
- Food security is an important issue for poor people. Farmers may therefore be unwilling to change their cropping patterns in such a way that their basic food requirements are not covered. In our example it is assumed that farmers maintain a minimum area of maize and sorghum for food security. Although sorghum is not the most profitable crop under any of the criteria put forward, it is drought resistant and therefore contributes to the food security objective.
- Risk is also important. Even if farmers were not concerned about

food security, they would be unlikely to put the entire area under one crop because of the risks associated with price changes and natural events such as pest attack and drought.

- Environmental conditions cannot be ignored. Cultivation of one crop to the exclusion of all others is unlikely to be sustainable in the long term due to the potential effect on soil fertility.

It can be seen therefore that, although activity budgets can be used to provide indicators of profitability, they cannot be used on their own to determine whether a particular course of action is justified. It is necessary to give adequate consideration to the other factors defining the constraints and opportunities facing small producers. One of the ways in which this can be done is through the use of labor profiles.

Labor Profiles

The seasonal pattern of labor use can be investigated by setting out for each activity the amount of labor required per unit in each month. Table 6.2 shows labor profiles for each of the crops for both categories of farmer. The labor required per unit can then be multiplied by the number of units for each activity to give the total labor requirement for all activities. This can then be compared with an estimate of labor availability, which is usually determined by the number of adult equivalent workers in a household multiplied by the number of working days assumed in a month and adjusted for noncommercial activities like household maintenance. Such activities can be very significant in terms of overall labor use, particularly where households have to travel some distance to collect water or firewood.

Table 6.3 shows labor availability and use for hand cultivators with an assumed pattern of cultivation. It is assumed that these farmers are either unwilling or unable to hire labor and therefore that household labor availability acts as a binding constraint on the cropping pattern. It can be seen that labor is entirely used up in November because of the heavy labor requirements for cotton and maize. Assuming that all available land is used, and that a minimum of 1 hectare of maize is required for subsistence, farmers cannot increase their income by changing their cropping pattern because the most profitable crop per unit of land is cotton, which is also the crop that uses the most labor in November. The cropping pattern indicated in Table 6.3 therefore balances the objective of maximizing income with the constraints of available land and labor and subsistence requirements. It should be noted that the farmers have some surplus labor in every month except November. This labor is potentially available for hire. The lowest level of availability is in January when 77% of available labor is used.

121

Table 6.2 Crop Labor Profiles (Days)

Days/ha	Hand Cultivation				Ox Cultivation			
	Cotton	Maize	Sorghum	Groundnuts	Cotton	Maize	Sorghum	Groundnuts
January	21.0	10.0	24.0	10.0	16.0	13.0	10.0	10.0
February	11.0	12.0		12.0	11.0	9.0	8.0	12.0
March	3.0				6.0		10.0	
April	8.0	20.0	20.0	6.0	6.0		20.0	6.0
May	4.0		40.0	18.0	6.0	10.0	14.0	16.0
June	18.0		18.0	6.0	17.0	8.0		6.0
July	14.0				18.0			
August	15.0				12.0			
September	9.0				6.0			
October	3.0	14.0		14.0	1.0	7.0		
November	20.0	22.0	30.0	30.0	8.0	5.0	8.0	16.0
December	14.0	6.0		6.0	8.0	5.0	5.0	6.0
Total	140.0	84.0	132.0	102.0	115.0	57.0	75.0	72.0

Table 6.3 Labor Availability and Use—Hand Cultivation (Days)

	Cotton	Maize	Sorghum	Groundnuts	Other Tasks	Total Use	Availability	Unused
Area	1.10	1.00	0.40	0.20		2.70	2.70	
Days used								
January	23.1	10.0	9.6	2.0	14.0	58.7	76.0	17.3
February	12.1	12.0		2.4	14.0	40.5	76.0	35.5
March	3.3				14.0	17.3	66.0	48.7
April	8.8		8.0		14.0	30.8	66.0	35.2
May	4.4	20.0	16.0	1.2	14.0	55.6	76.0	20.4
June	19.8		7.2	3.6	14.0	44.6	86.0	41.4
July	15.4			1.2	14.0	30.6	86.0	55.4
August	16.5				14.0	30.5	86.0	55.5
September	9.9				14.0	23.9	86.0	62.1
October	3.3	14.0		2.8	14.0	34.1	86.0	51.9
November	22.0	22.0	12.0	6.0	14.0	76.0	76.0	
December	15.4	6.0		1.2	14.0	36.6	66.0	29.4
Total	154.0	84.0	52.8	20.4	168.0	479.2	932.0	

Table 6.4 shows a slightly different use of the same idea. It is assumed that ox cultivators are rich enough to be able to hire labor if necessary. Labor availability can therefore be compared with the labor requirement to determine when hired labor is required and when family labor is available. Table 6.4 also indicates the daily rate for hired labor, which varies between seasons. For most of the year labor is likely to be available locally because the hand cultivators have excess labor. However, in January the demand for hired labor is high and the local availability is relatively low. As a result the wage paid is higher, and it is possible that some labor is brought in from outside the area. In November there is no labor available locally and so any additional labor required has to be brought in from outside the area. The cost of labor is therefore highest at this time. Table 6.4 shows that ox cultivators have to hire about 9% of their total labor requirement. The approach indicated in Table 6.4 can in principle be applied to any kind of enterprise with multiple activities that uses household labor and has seasonal labor requirements.

Table 6.4 applies to the "without project" situation. A slightly different situation is illustrated in Table 6.5, which applies to the "with project" situation. The assumed price increase for raw cotton improves the profitability of cotton relative to other crops and causes farmers to increase the area under cotton and to reduce the area under groundnuts. This increases the hired labor requirement slightly but reduces the labor constraint in November and leads to a slight improvement in overall net farm income, as will be seen when the overall profitability of the enterprise is considered.

Working Capital and the Monthly Cash Flow

In principle the same seasonal approach can be taken to the assessment of working capital needs. A similar table to Table 6.2 could be drawn up indicating the timing of expenditure on each activity, and this could be compared with availability. No attempt has been made to do this for our project because to do so would increase the complexity of the overall model without adding any new concepts.

An alternative approach is to add a percentage to the cost of any materials that are assumed to be bought on credit to account for the cost of short-term loans. Such an approach would probably suffice for the analysis of small farms, but it is not adequate for any processing enterprise with significant material costs because these costs are likely to be a higher proportion of overall costs.

For processing enterprises the short-term liquidity position is fundamentally important, and the most important financial question may be whether the enterprise is able to meet payments on short-term loans. For

Table 6.4 Labor Availability and Use—Ox Cultivation Without the Project (Days)

	Cotton	Maize	Sorghum	Groundnuts	Livestock	Total Use	Availability	Hired Labor	Daily Rate ($)
Area	5.0	2.0	1.0	1.0		9.0	9.0		
Days used									
January	80.0	26.0	10.0	10.0	20.0	146.0	94.0	52.0	40.0
February	55.0	18.0	8.0	12.0	20.0	113.0	94.0	19.0	30.0
March	30.0		10.0		20.0	60.0	80.0		15.0
April	30.0		20.0	6.0	20.0	76.0	80.0		15.0
May	30.0	20.0	14.0	16.0	20.0	100.0	94.0		20.0
June	85.0	16.0		6.0	20.0	127.0	108.0	6.0	30.0
July	90.0				20.0	110.0	108.0	19.0	20.0
August	60.0				20.0	80.0	108.0	2.0	15.0
September	30.0				20.0	50.0	108.0		15.0
October	5.0	14.0			20.0	39.0	108.0		15.0
November	40.0	10.0	8.0	16.0	20.0	94.0	94.0		50.0
December	40.0	10.0	5.0	6.0	20.0	81.0	80.0	1.0	20.0
Total	575.0	114.0	75.0	72.0	240.0	1,076.0	1,156.0	99.0	

Table 6.5 Labor Availability and Use—Ox Cultivation With the Project (Days)

	Cotton	Maize	Sorghum	Groundnuts	Livestock	Total Use	Availability	Hired Labor	Daily Rate ($)
Area	5.5	2.0	1.0	0.5		9.0	9.0	9.0	
Days used									
January	88.0	26.0	10.0	5.0	20.0	149.0	94.0	55.0	40.0
February	60.5	18.0	8.0	6.0	20.0	112.5	94.0	18.5	30.0
March	33.0		10.0		20.0	63.0	80.0		15.0
April	33.0		20.0	3.0	20.0	76.0	80.0		15.0
May	33.0	20.0	14.0	8.0	20.0	95.0	94.0	1.0	20.0
June	93.5	16.0		3.0	20.0	132.5	108.0	24.5	30.0
July	99.0				20.0	119.0	108.0	11.0	20.0
August	66.0				20.0	86.0	108.0		15.0
September	33.0				20.0	53.0	108.0		15.0
October	5.5	14.0			20.0	39.5	108.0		15.0
November	44.0	10.0	8.0	8.0	20.0	90.0	94.0		50.0
December	44.0	10.0	5.0	3.0	20.0	82.0	80.0	2.0	20.0
Total	632.5	114.0	75.0	36.0	240.0	1,097.5	1,156.0	112.0	

this reason it may be advisable to prepare a cash flow on a month-by-month basis. Assuming that the schedule for the fixed investment costs involved in such enterprises will be relatively simple, it may be reasonable to set out on a month-by-month basis the cash flow in the initial year and a similar cash flow for the first full operating year. If the life of the fixed assets is known, the project can then be appraised on the assumption that subsequent operating years will be similar for the life of the project. Working capital requirements can be traced on a month-by-month basis, and short-term loan requirements can be determined accordingly. Provision of loan finance would be justified if the cash flow indicated that all short- and long-term financing requirements could be met. An example of a month-by-month cash flow showing repayment of a seasonal loan is given in Table 6.6.

The project illustrated is a small-scale maize mill employing three people and a supervisor. The main activity of the maize mill is to provide a service for local farmers who are assumed to bring their maize for milling and pay a charge for the service. In addition it is proposed that the maize mill will purchase some maize from farmers and sell maize flour to local schools. A market equivalent to 200 bags of maize is assumed. The mill will have to buy its maize during the five-month period following the harvest when maize is relatively cheap. Some maize will have to be stored in order to ensure a regular supply of maize flour. To finance the stock of maize it is proposed to take seasonal loans in each of the five buying months to cover half of the cost of purchasing the maize. The seasonal loan would then be repaid over the following seven months. The enterprise takes out a long-term loan over five years to cover the cost of the equipment and installation. Equity capital is provided by the owner in the form of the building and cash to cover some other small items. It is assumed that the long-term loan has a three-month grace period during which interest is accumulated into the principal sum.

The main operating costs for the enterprise are the purchase of maize and the electricity used to power the mill. There are also some transport costs for collecting the purchased maize and delivering the maize flour to the schools. It is assumed that the owner pays herself a salary for supervision of the work and negotiation with customers. Other costs include labor costs, periodic maintenance, insurance, and office expenses.

Table 6.6 shows that the enterprise is able to meet its expenses in each month of the year; however, the liquidity position in the first four months is fairly tight, particularly when the first payments on the long-term loan fall due. It might be advisable for the owner to negotiate an extra month of grace period to ease the liquidity position. It can be concluded that the liquidity of the project is reasonably sound and could be improved with a slight relaxation of the long-term conditions, but is the project profitable?

Table 6.6 Cash Flow for Financial Planning for the First Year of the Maize Mill Project ($)

	Pre-Op	June	July	Aug.	Sep.	Oct.	Nov.	Dec.	Jan.	Feb.	March	April	May
Cash inflow													
Equity	320,000												
Long-term loan	320,000												
Short-term loan		55,000	96,250	75,625	61,875	41,250							
Sales revenue		90,952	90,952	90,952	90,952	88,952	86,952	86,952	86,952	84,952	84,952	82,952	86,952
Total cash inflow	640,000	145,952	187,202	166,577	152,827	130,202	86,952	86,952	86,952	84,952	84,952	82,952	86,952
Cash outflow													
Investment	595,000												
Increase in working capital		87,892	137,500	96,250	68,750	28,250	−54,250	−55,000	−55,000	−54,250	−55,000	−54,250	−56,500
Direct costs		66,000	66,000	66,000	66,000	65,000	64,000	64,000	64,000	63,000	63,000	62,000	64,000
Overhead costs		7,500	3,000	10,500	3,000	3,000	3,000	3,000	3,000	10,500	3,000	3,000	3,000
Short-term loan service							50,657	50,657	50,657	50,657	50,657	50,657	50,657
Long-term loan service					8,002	8,002	8,002	8,002	8,002	8,002	8,002	8,002	8,002
Tax paid													
Total cash outflow	595,000	161,392	206,500	172,750	145,752	104,252	71,409	70,659	70,659	77,909	69,659	69,409	69,159
Net cash flow	45,000	−15,440	−19,298	−6,173	7,075	25,950	15,543	16,293	16,293	7,043	15,293	13,543	17,793
Cumulative cash flow	45,000	29,560	10,262	4,089	11,164	37,114	52,657	68,950	85,242	92,285	107,578	121,121	138,913

Annual Profitability Indicators

Discounted measures of project worth may not be very helpful for small-scale enterprises where the capital investment may not be the most important expenditure. In the maize mill case, the annual value of maize purchases is greater than the total investment costs, and so operational efficiency in converting maize into maize flour is the most important consideration.

Judgments on the profitability of the maize mill project can be made by looking at the profit and loss account for the first year. For simplicity it is assumed that the financial year corresponds with the agricultural year so that stocks at the end of the year are zero. The profit and loss account is shown in Table 6.7. It can be seen that the project makes a gross profit of over 26% of sales, but that the net profit before tax is only just over 7% of

Table 6.7   Maize Mill Project—First-Year Profit and Loss Account ($)

Sales	1,053,424
Less direct costs	
Maize purchase	660,000
Electricity	75,750
Labor	25,250
Transport	12,000
Total direct costs	773,000
Gross profit	280,424
Less overheads	
Salaries	24,000
Other expenses	12,000
Maintenance	15,000
Insurance	4,500
Depreciation	77,750
Total overheads before interest	133,250
Net profit before interest and tax	147,174
Interest on long-term loan	44,531
Interest on short-term loans	24,602
Total overheads	202,383
Net profit before tax	78,041
Tax provision @ 30%	23,412
Net profit after tax	54,629
Ratios	
Gross profit: sales	26.6%
Net profits before tax: sales	7.4%
Net profit after tax: sales	5.2%
Net profit before interest and tax: total investment	24.7%
Net profit before tax: equity	24.4%
Net profit after tax: equity	17.1%

sales value. The relatively low profitability in relation to sales is due to the high value of maize purchases and is common for simple agroprocessing activities. The net profit before interest and tax is over 24% of the investment costs, and net profit after interest and tax is just over 17% of equity capital—slightly higher than the 15% interest rate. Overall the project would appear to be fairly profitable as long as the assumptions are well founded, but there is not much room for error.

Marketing, Sales, and Prices

When a small producer produces the same product as many other producers the sales price is likely to be given by the market, and it is unlikely that a single producer will have any significant influence over the total supply. In such circumstances the main issue is the production efficiency of the producer in relation to scarce resources. Marketing channels are important, but it is unlikely that the producer will be constrained by the size of the market.

Where a small producer produces a differentiated product with a restricted market, marketing is likely to be extremely important. There is likely to be an inverse relationship between sales and price, and the producer must make strategic decisions about production volume and sales price. The quality of the product may also be an issue, particularly in activities such as handicrafts. There may be a choice between a high-volume, low-quality market with low prices and a low-volume, high-quality market with high prices. Marketing is therefore likely to be a critical factor for projects involving specialized producers and differentiated products. It is therefore important that any projection of sales should be based on a careful assessment of the market and that the choice of strategy achieves an acceptable balance between risk and profitability. Any projection of production and sales is based on assumptions, and if these assumptions are seriously wrong an apparently profitable enterprise can easily fail. Failure rates for small enterprises are notoriously high and incorrect assumptions about the market are a common cause.

Consolidated Enterprise Budgets

Once an overall plan for production and sales has been determined it is possible to draw up a consolidated budget for the enterprise encompassing all activities. This simply involves multiplying the activity budgets already defined by the number of units of each activity included in the production plan. The process is an iterative one because the plan is likely to be modified in order to arrive at the best possible feasible plan. A process for determining an optimum production plan is described below, but it cannot be followed without establishing a consolidated budget, starting with dummy values for the number of units (number of hectares in our example) or with the existing values where the enterprise already exists.

Consolidated farm budgets are provided for both farmer categories in Tables 6.8 to 6.10. For the hand cultivators the only difference between the with and without project situation is that the revenue changes because of the assumed price increase for raw cotton. These farmers are already cultivating as much cotton as their resources allow and cannot expand their production without some change in technology. Since the project does not include any component promoting such a change there is no reason to assume that the technology will change and certainly no reason to ascribe such a change to the project. It is important that any assumed changes in behavior can be related to some project-related activity, otherwise an inaccurate impression of project benefits will be obtained.

For the ox cultivators the overall farm model changes with the project because the profitability of cotton improves in relation to groundnuts. As a result, half a hectare of groundnuts is transferred to cotton production, and the net farm income is increased by $1,430 (about 4%). There are also changes in the family labor requirement.

The importance attached to changes in family labor use affects the perspective taken on the relevance of the value of net farm income. Is the objective to maximize net farm income irrespective of the family labor required to earn that income, or does family labor have some opportunity cost? If it is believed that family labor does have an opportunity cost, it is necessary to impute a value for any changes in family labor use.

Overall there is a slight increase in the amount of labor required but a reduction in the requirement in the peak month of November when labor is most valuable. It is possible to impute a cost for this change in labor requirement using the monthly labor cost values given in Tables 6.4 and 6.5. If the imputed labor cost is deducted, an estimate of the overall net farm benefit is obtained. The increase in net farm benefit of $1,442 is similar to the increase in net farm income, but this represents about 10% of net farm benefit. Of course this estimate assumes that the monthly cost of hired labor is a reasonable indicator of the opportunity cost of labor to these farmers, a debatable assumption given their relative affluence, but one that makes little effect on the overall analysis in this case. In other cases where changes in labor use are more substantial the assumption about the opportunity cost of family labor can be of significant importance.

Optimization of Returns to Scarce Resources

Once the scarce resources for an enterprise have been defined, as well as any other constraints assumed to affect producer behavior, it is possible to

Table 6.8   Consolidated Farm Budget—Hand Cultivation ($)

	Cotton	Maize	Sorghum	Groundnuts	Total
Area (ha)	1.1	1.0	0.4	0.2	2.7
Production (kg)	660	750	240	40	
Gross revenue with	3,762	2,250	600	600	7,212
Gross revenue without	3,960	2,250	600	600	7,410
Costs					
Seed	83	75	22	60	240
Pesticide	231				231
Bags/cloth	275	75	24	24	398
Tools, etc.	44	40	16	8	108
Total costs	633	190	62	92	977
Gross margin without	3,130	2,060	538	508	6,235
Gross margin with	3,328	2,060	538	508	6,433
Labor (days)	154	84	53	20	311

Table 6.9   Consolidated Farm Budget—Ox Cultivation Without the Project ($)

	Cotton	Maize	Sorghum	Groundnuts	Total
Area (ha)	5.0	2.0	1.0	1.0	9.0
Production (kg)	4,500	1,800	750	300	
Gross revenue without	25,650	5,400	1,875	4,500	37,425
Costs					
Seed	375	150	56	300	881
Pesticide	1,050				1,050
Bags/cloth	1,250	150	60	120	1,580
Tools, etc.	1,625	750	375	295	3,045
Total costs	4,300	1,050	491	715	6,556
Gross margin without	25,018	5,210	1,813	4,408	36,448
Labor (days)	575	114	75	72	
Hired labor					3,400
Net farm income					33,048
Imputed family labor cost					19,035
Net farm benefit					14,013

try to identify an optimum plan. To do this it is necessary first of all to determine whether the objective is to maximize net farm income or whether it is to maximize net farm benefit.[1] In our case the distinction makes little difference, but this will not always be the case. There are two ways of approaching the optimization problem.

The first approach is to optimize manually by iteration. In this approach the following steps might be followed:

Table 6.10 Consolidated Farm Budget—Ox Cultivation With the Project ($)

	Cotton	Maize	Sorghum	Groundnuts	Total
Area (ha)	5.5	2.0	1.0	0.5	9.0
Production (kg)	4,950	1,800	750	150	
Gross revenue without	29,700	5,400	1,875	2,250	39,225
Costs					
Seed	413	150	56	150	769
Pesticide	1,155				1,155
Bags/cloth	1,375	150	60	60	1,645
Tools, etc.	1,788	750	375	148	3,060
Total costs	4,730	1,050	491	358	6,629
Gross margin with	29,068	5,210	1,813	2,158	38,248
Labor (days)	633	114	75	36	858
Hired labor					3,770
Net farm income					34,478
Imputed family labor cost					19,023
Net farm benefit					15,456

- First of all decide what is to be maximized (net farm income or net farm benefit).
- Next define the constraints, such as the minimum area under food crops, the maximum area of cultivable land, the maximum availability of family labor in each month, the maximum availability of cash in each month, etc.
- Next try to maximize the return to each binding constraint until the availability of the resource is exhausted. We might start by considering the return to land. The highest return to land is for cotton. We might then try to maximize the area under cotton until one of the labor constraints is reached. The next step would be to investigate the crop with the highest return to labor in the month in which family labor was exhausted. If land is not exhausted, it should then be possible to increase net farm income by substituting more than one unit of this crop for one unit of cotton. The process could be repeated with each binding constraint until a maximum value is reached.

The same result can be obtained more quickly and more accurately through linear programming. This is no longer as difficult as it used to be because it can be undertaken using spreadsheet facilities (for example the Solver tool in Microsoft Excel). As long as both the objective function and the constraints are specified correctly the solution can be reached quite easily. This approach has the attraction of being very precise and consistent; however, it should be used with care.

The problem with precise solutions to small farm plans is that they assume that all farmers are the same. In fact each farm household is different, as is each farm. Also, most constraints are not absolute. If the reward is large enough, family labor availability can be increased through longer working hours, and working capital constraints can be overcome by borrowing. It is very difficult to model all the constraints realistically into a farm model, and simple models tend to give simple and unrealistic solutions. The sensible approach is therefore to use optimization tools as a guide to supplement judgment, not to replace it.

Categorization and Aggregation

Models of small producers are based on categorization because any project involving large numbers of small producers cannot hope to model the situation of each producer individually. It is therefore necessary to have some means to categorize producers. The following are among the possible approaches:

Categorization by Product

The nature of the activities of small-scale industrial producers is usually determined by the type of product since the product will determine the nature of the costs. Usually projects promoting small-scale industries cover a number of different types of activity. Estimation of the costs and benefits of such projects therefore requires a categorization to group together producers with similar products and costs. Inevitably there is a trade-off between accuracy and complexity in such categorizations. What is important is that any such categorization should be usable and meaningful.

Categorization by Ecological Zone/Farming System

The intended beneficiaries of projects designed to improve smallholder agricultural production (e.g., extension projects, small-scale irrigation, rural access roads, etc.) can be categorized in different ways. Where a project covers more than one ecological zone it is logical to base the categorization on the farming system that relates to that zone because the nature of the costs and benefits will be similar for all farmers in each zone. Such an approach is reasonable where differentiation of the rural population within the zone is not marked, but it will not be sufficient when farm sizes or household sizes or both are highly differentiated.

Categorization by Enterprise Size

Categorization by size can be important where enterprise sizes vary significantly. In the agricultural sector this might be because of the size of landholding or the mode of cultivation, hence the distinction in our example between those with ox ploughs and those cultivating by hand.

For small industries a distinction is often made between small enterprises and microenterprises based on the number and type of employees. Where categorization by size is undertaken it is necessary to obtain information on the target population to determine significant breaks in the population and the relative numbers of each category.

Categorization by Type of Household

The size of the enterprise is not the only way in which producers may be differentiated. The size of the household can be equally important as the gender of the head of household or the head of the enterprise. In many countries female heads of household and female entrepreneurs face different constraints than those faced by their male counterparts. In such cases it may be useful to use household characteristics to define categories.

In all of the above cases the fundamental basis for any categorization must be a good knowledge of the target population. Without such knowledge it is extremely difficult to say anything meaningful about the likely response to any stimulus provided by a project. Knowledge of the target population is particularly important for interventions intended to make a significant contribution to poverty reduction. It is likely to be crucial for identifying the characteristics that define the poorest groups.

Once the basis for categorizing beneficiaries has been established, the next stage is to assess the basis for determining how the project is likely to affect the different groups and over what period. This requires a realistic assessment of the process by which the project achieves its impact. The more indirect the process, the longer the impact is likely to take. Innovation in agriculture usually takes a long time because most farmers are more influenced by their neighbors than they are by intervention agents. Again a good knowledge of the target population is important to be able to make a reasonable assessment of attitudes to change.

Usually the process of aggregation requires specification of two aspects of change. These are: (1) The stages involved between commencing the process of change and reaching the assumed final state. It is unusual for producers to reach the final state within one year. Usually there are intermediate stages associated with risk avoidance, the process of trial and testing, and the process of knowledge diffusion. (2) The proportion of the target population commencing on the process of change in each year. It is unusual for the entire target population to start changing at the same time. Some people are more risk averse than others and will wait to see what happens to the innovators before changing themselves. In cases where extension agents are involved it is unlikely that they can reach the whole target population at one time.

The process of aggregation therefore involves setting out for each category of producer the different stages of change and the number of producers reaching each stage in different years. Estimation of aggregate costs and benefits therefore involves multiplying and adding together different numbers of producers from different categories at different stages of change. It can easily be seen that such a process can become quite complex as soon as reasonably realistic assumptions are made.[2] The length of time involved in reaching the final state can also be very long. Processes of change lasting for more than ten years should not be surprising in the agricultural sector. It is also quite likely that in the early years of a project the incremental benefits may only be a very small proportion of the final value.[3]

In our example a very simple process is assumed to take place because what is involved is not a change in technology but a change in cropping pattern induced by a change in the relative prices of different crops. This change only applies to the ox cultivators. Farmers are assumed to change half of the eventual area in Year 2 and the rest in Year 3. It is assumed that all farmers change at the same time and at the same speed (or that variations between farmers cancel each other out!). These assumptions are made to simplify the model for illustrative purposes and should not be regarded as normal. In reality we should expect the process to take significantly longer for any reasonably large project.

Table 6.11 shows the aggregated costs and benefits for the hand cultivators. This is relatively simple because the only change assumed to occur with the project is an increase in the price of raw cotton from Year 2 onward.

Table 6.12 shows similar information for the ox cultivators. These farmers are relatively affluent and only make up 20% of the total population. Nevertheless their total net revenue is higher than that of the hand cultivators. Although the average household size is larger, and the hand cultivators may supplement their income from other sources, the per capita income of the ox cultivators is probably more than twice that of the hand cultivators. Aggregation of this group is slightly more complicated because there are two stages and because there are also changes in family labor use.

The two groups are brought together in Table 6.13, which shows aggregate incremental costs and revenue for the two groups combined. The incremental value was obtained by deducting the Year 1 value, which was assumed to represent the without project situation. It should be noted that this procedure implicitly assumes that the without project situation remains

Table 6.11 Aggregated Farmer Costs and Revenue by Year—Hand Cultivation

	1	2	3	4	5	6	7	8	9	10	11
Number of farmers	3,200	3,200	3,200	3,200	3,200	3,200	3,200	3,200	3,200	3,200	3,200
Production (tons)											
Cotton	2,112	2,112	2,112	2,112	2,112	2,112	2,112	2,112	2,112	2,112	2,112
Maize	2,400	2,400	2,400	2,400	2,400	2,400	2,400	2,400	2,400	2,400	2,400
Sorghum	768	768	768	768	768	768	768	768	768	768	768
Groundnuts	128	128	128	128	128	128	128	128	128	128	128
Revenue ($ '000)											
Cotton	12,038	12,672	12,672	12,672	12,672	12,672	12,672	12,672	12,672	12,672	12,672
Maize	7,200	7,200	7,200	7,200	7,200	7,200	7,200	7,200	7,200	7,200	7,200
Sorghum	1,920	1,920	1,920	1,920	1,920	1,920	1,920	1,920	1,920	1,920	1,920
Groundnuts	1,920	1,920	1,920	1,920	1,920	1,920	1,920	1,920	1,920	1,920	1,920
Total revenue	23,078	23,712	23,712	23,712	23,712	23,712	23,712	23,712	23,712	23,712	23,712
Costs ($ '000)											
Seed	768	768	768	768	768	768	768	768	768	768	768
Pesticide	739	739	739	739	739	739	739	739	739	739	739
Bags/cloth	1,274	1,274	1,274	1,274	1,274	1,274	1,274	1,274	1,274	1,274	1,274
Tools, etc.	346	346	346	346	346	346	346	346	346	346	346
Total costs	3,126	3,126	3,126	3,126	3,126	3,126	3,126	3,126	3,126	3,126	3,126
Net revenue	19,952	20,586	20,586	20,586	20,586	20,586	20,586	20,586	20,586	20,586	20,586

Table 6.12 Aggregated Farmer Costs and Revenue by Year—Ox Cultivation

	1	2	3	4	5	6	7	8	9	10	11
Number of farmers	800	800	800	800	800	800	800	800	800	800	800
Production (tons)											
Cotton	3,600	3,780	3,960	3,960	3,960	3,960	3,960	3,960	3,960	3,960	3,960
Maize	1,440	1,440	1,440	1,440	1,440	1,440	1,440	1,440	1,440	1,440	1,440
Sorghum	600	600	600	600	600	600	600	600	600	600	600
Groundnuts (with)	240	180	120	120	120	120	120	120	120	120	120
Revenue ($ '000)											
Cotton	20,520	22,680	23,760	23,760	23,760	23,760	23,760	23,760	23,760	23,760	23,760
Maize	4,320	4,320	4,320	4,320	4,320	4,320	4,320	4,320	4,320	4,320	4,320
Sorghum	1,500	1,500	1,500	1,500	1,500	1,500	1,500	1,500	1,500	1,500	1,500
Groundnuts	3,600	2,700	1,800	1,800	1,800	1,800	1,800	1,800	1,800	1,800	1,800
Total revenue	29,940	31,200	31,380	31,380	31,380	31,380	31,380	31,380	31,380	31,380	31,380
Costs ($ '000)											
Seed	705	660	615	615	615	615	615	615	615	615	615
Pesticide	840	882	924	924	924	924	924	924	924	924	924
Bags/cloth	1,264	1,290	1,316	1,316	1,316	1,316	1,316	1,316	1,316	1,316	1,316
Tools, etc.	2,436	2,442	2,448	2,448	2,448	2,448	2,448	2,448	2,448	2,448	2,448
Hired labor	2,720	2,868	3,016	3,016	3,016	3,016	3,016	3,016	3,016	3,016	3,016
Total costs	7,965	8,142	8,319	8,319	8,319	8,319	8,319	8,319	8,319	8,319	8,319
Net revenue	21,975	23,058	23,061	23,061	23,061	23,061	23,061	23,061	23,061	23,061	23,061
Labor days ('000)	782	785	788	788	788	788	788	788	788	788	788

Table 6.13   Aggregate Incremental Farmer Costs and Revenue by Year

	1	2	3	4	5	6	7	8	9	10	11
Production											
Cotton		180	360	360	360	360	360	360	360	360	360
Groundnuts		-60	-120	-120	-120	-120	-120	-120	-120	-120	-120
Revenue											
Cotton		2,794	3,874	3,874	3,874	3,874	3,874	3,874	3,874	3,874	3,874
Groundnuts		-900	-1,800	-1,800	-1,800	-1,800	-1,800	-1,800	-1,800	-1,800	-1,800
Incremental revenue		1,894	2,074	2,074	2,074	2,074	2,074	2,074	2,074	2,074	2,074
Costs											
Seed		-45	-90	-90	-90	-90	-90	-90	-90	-90	-90
Pesticide		42	84	84	84	84	84	84	84	84	84
Bags/cloth		26	52	52	52	52	52	52	52	52	52
Tools, etc.		6	12	12	12	12	12	12	12	12	12
Hired labor		148	296	296	296	296	296	296	296	296	296
Incremental costs		177	354	354	354	354	354	354	354	354	354
Net incrementasl revenue		1,717	1,720	1,720	1,720	1,720	1,720	1,720	1,720	1,720	1,720
Hand cultivators		634	634	634	634	634	634	634	634	634	634
Ox plough cultivators		1,083	1,086	1,086	1,086	1,086	1,086	1,086	1,086	1,086	1,086
Family labor cost		-5	-10	-10	-10	-10	-10	-10	-10	-10	-10
Net incremental benefit		1,722	1,730	1,730	1,730	1,730	1,730	1,730	1,730	1,730	1,730
Ox plough cultivators		1,088	1,096	1,096	1,096	1,096	1,096	1,096	1,096	1,096	1,096

	Hand	Oxcult	Fam lab	Total
NPV at 4% =	4,941	8,467	73	13,482
NPV at 8% =	3,937	6,745	58	10,739
NPV at 12% =	3,196	5,476	46	8,719

unchanged throughout the period of the project life. This is not necessarily a good assumption and should not be adopted without question.

In Table 6.13 an estimate of net incremental benefit is obtained by deducting an imputed family labor cost. Although there is a slight increase in the family labor requirement, the imputed cost actually falls because there is an increase in labor requirements in off-peak periods and a reduction in the peak month. The project improves the timing of family labor requirements, and this is recorded as a benefit (negative cost). Table 6.13 also shows a breakdown of the net present value of the incremental benefits between the hand cultivators and the ox cultivators. It can be seen that the hand cultivators, who are 80% of the population, receive less than 40% of the benefits. This result should not be surprising. It simply reflects the existing distribution of resources between the two groups, which allows the wealthier group to respond more quickly to the opportunities presented by improved cotton prices.

The costs and benefits for the farmers are brought together in a single statement because the values of different resource costs and benefits will be required for the economic analysis of the project, which is the subject of Part 3. It is important to recognize the links among different aspects of the analysis of a project when setting out cost and benefit estimates. Failure to do so can lead to inconsistent results.

Further Reading

The literature on farm planning tends to be separate from the literature on small and micro-enterprises. For issues and techniques related to farm planning Brown (1979), FAO (1986), Upton (1987), and Ellis (1988) are useful. Ideas on planning for small enterprises can be found in the literature on business plans. The NatWest business handbooks are useful although they are oriented to UK conditions. Some relevant ideas are given in Yaffey (1992: chap. 14). The Intermediate Technology Development Group also has some useful publications on analysis of small enterprises.

Notes

1. The perception of the objective function of the peasant household assumed in any optimization model is of course highly simplified. A good review of some of the issues and potential complexities is given in Ellis (1988).

2. As a result of the number of different calculations the memory requirements of spreadsheet models involving large numbers of small producers can be quite demanding. Realistic models therefore have to be designed quite efficiently.

3. The nature of the aggregation process and related assumptions is discussed in FAO (1991) and Potts (1994a).

PART 3

Economic and Social Analysis

7

Economic Analysis: An Overview

General Principles

The use of the word *economic* implies that the viewpoint from which the analysis is undertaken is that of the nation or the economy as a whole. Economic analysis is therefore cost-benefit analysis from the national point of view. Initial analysis of a project is usually undertaken from the point of view of the sponsors of the project. Economic analysis of a project involves steadily expanding the boundaries of the project until they encompass the impact of the project on the entire economy.

What Are the Objectives of Economic Analysis?

Economic analysis of projects has two main objectives: to provide information for making decisions on the acceptability of projects from the national point of view and to provide information of value for project design and planning, macroeconomic planning, and economic research.

The second objective is often neglected in favor of the first, although it could be argued that the second objective might be more important in practice. Project analysis need not be just about making yes or no decisions. It can also be used to help improve the design of projects by taking account of their likely impact on affected groups and ensuring that they have a reasonable chance of being implemented successfully. The relative neglect of the information role of economic analysis is reflected in the neglect of presentational issues in much of the academic literature.[1]

How Does Economic
Analysis Achieve Those Objectives?

Economic analysis broadens the perspective on the project. Attention is no longer confined solely to the project itself. To investigate the impact of the project on the national economy a number of procedures are undertaken involving various steps. The presentational approach adopted and the order in which the steps take place vary with different methodologies. However, most approaches have the following steps in common:

- Identifying and eliminating *transfer payments*. This process may involve several stages, since some transfer payments may be more obvious than others. It can be helpful to record which group makes the transfer payment and which group receives the payment. The treatment of transfer payments in economic analysis is discussed further below.
- Extending the definition or boundary of the project to include all *linkage effects* and *externalities*. Sometimes these may be relatively easily quantifiable, while at other times identification and quantification of such effects may be more difficult. Among the most important external effects for many projects are *environmental effects*.
- Identifying and valuing the effect of the project on *nontraded costs and benefits* and in particular assessing the benefits of projects in the social and infrastructure sectors.
- Identifying the effect of the project on the use or production of *traded goods*. This can show the effect of the project on the availability of *foreign exchange,* an important resource that may be in scarce supply. Foreign exchange may then be valued according to its scarcity value or *opportunity cost*. It may also be possible to estimate the effect of the project on the *balance of payments*.
- Identifying the effect of the project on the *employment* of labor, in particular those categories of labor that are in excess supply. In most cases this involves the identification of the payment of wages to *unskilled workers* and the estimation of the opportunity cost of their employment.

These steps relate to the following important government economic objectives:

- Elimination of transfer payments, identification of all the linkage and external effects of the project, valuation of nontraded sector costs and benefits, and valuation of foreign exchange and labor resources in terms of their opportunity cost should provide a measure of the impact of the project on the overall level of GNP and welfare.

- Identification and valuation of foreign exchange effects according to their opportunity cost should take account of possible *balance of payments* constraints.
- Identification and valuation of wage costs according to their opportunity cost might help to take account of problems of *unemployment* and *underemployment*.

Efficiency Analysis and Distribution Analysis

In addition to the five steps outlined above, there are two other steps that have been included in some approaches: (6) Consider the effect of the project on the level of *investment*. This is usually taken to be the same thing as the effect on savings. Estimation of this effect requires some knowledge of the effect of the project on the distribution of income. (7) Once the distribution of income has been specified, it is also possible to consider the effect of the project on the *distribution of consumption* among different income groups.

These steps are related to government objectives in the following way: (1) Identification of savings effects may focus attention on the way these savings may influence the *rate of growth of GNP*, and (2) identification of income distribution effects may show the contribution of the project toward objectives related to *poverty reduction* and *maldistribution of income*.

Since the mid-1970s many contributions to the literature on project analysis have made a distinction between *economic analysis* and *social analysis.*[2] More recently the approach adopted in using project analysis to influence the distribution of income has changed, partly on the grounds of practicality. This change, along with moves to widen the disciplinary background of those involved in project analysis, has led to use of the term *social analysis* in the broader context of examining the social impact of projects. Because of the potential confusion in understanding the meaning of the term *social analysis*, the term *distribution analysis* will be used when referring to the estimation and assessment of distribution effects. Since distributional questions are also economic questions, what is sometimes referred to as economic analysis will be referred to as *efficiency analysis*. The term *efficiency* implies that the analysis is concerned with economic efficiency regardless of the distribution of the costs and benefits.

Steps one to five outlined above are all concerned with the impact of the project on GNP irrespective of distribution and are included in efficiency analysis. Steps six and seven are concerned with the distribution of income between savings and the consumption of different income groups and are considered in distribution analysis. A carefully constructed efficiency analysis can provide all the most important information for the conduct of a distribution analysis, but it is unusual in practice for any attempt to be made to put different weights on income to different groups, as originally proposed in the literature. Figures 7.1 and 7.2 show the structure and steps involved in efficiency analysis and distribution analysis. Figures 7.1 and 7.2 follow directly from Figure 5.1.

Stages of Economic Analysis

Normally economic analysis will be done in at least two stages, the first stage involving the identification of linkages and external effects and the second involving the adjustment of the prices of goods and services to take account of their relative scarcity. The first stage is likely to be conducted initially in constant market prices while the second involves the estimation and application of economic, or "shadow," prices. It should be noted that, in many respects, the application of efficiency shadow prices is merely a way of taking account of those secondary linkages that are not included at the first stage.

Figure 7.1 outlines the stages in the analysis and indicates that, at each stage, any change identified in resource costs and benefits in principle can be attributed as a change in the income or welfare of some person, group, or organization. A difference between the net benefits at one stage of the analysis and the net benefits at the next stage indicates the existence of an income transfer involving a loss or a gain to a group that was not identified in earlier versions of the analysis.

Transfer Payments and the Transition from Financial Analysis to Economic Analysis

The concept of a transfer payment is important in economic analysis. This concept was introduced in Chapter 4 in relation to accounts receivable and accounts payable. A transfer payment is a payment made by one group to another without any equivalent transfer of resources. The most obvious example is a tax. If a project pays a tax there is an income gain to the government but there is no equivalent transfer of resources to the project. Of course governments do provide services, but the service provided to the project is not related to the tax paid by the project. The overall level of resources available to the economy is unchanged by the tax; only the distri-

Figure 7.1   Efficiency Analysis

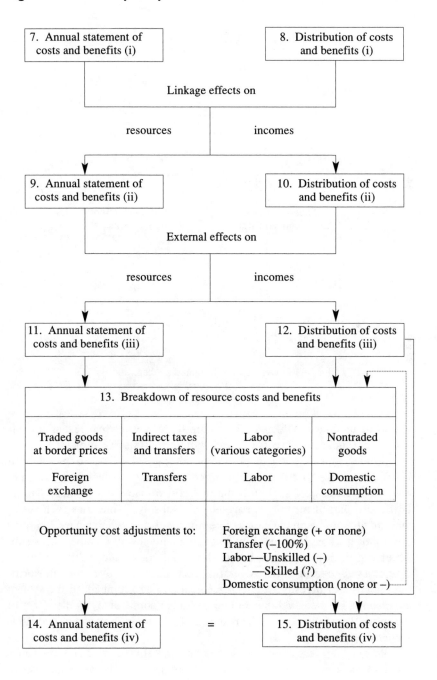

Figure 7.2   Distributional Analysis

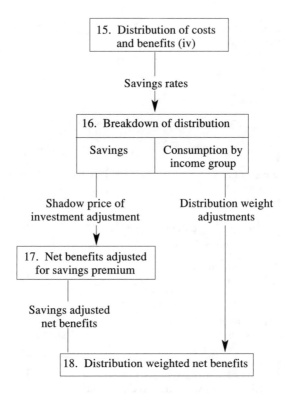

bution of income is affected.[3] Taxes are therefore not real resource costs and are not included as costs in the economic analysis of a project.

Similar considerations apply in considering subsidies. For example, it is often the case that the tariff charged for water or electricity does not cover the full cost of supply. If the real cost of supply is greater than the tariff, then part of the cost is covered by a subsidy. Sometimes such subsidies are obvious, as in the case of a fertilizer subsidy, where an explicit proportion of the cost is covered by a government subsidy. In other cases subsidies can be less obvious. A typical example of a hidden subsidy is the case of a public utility where operating costs might be covered by the tariff, but the costs of investment in replacement and development of the system are covered by the development budget. In economic analysis the effect of the subsidy is removed, and the real cost of providing the good or service is included.

Where there are transactions between different agents involved in a project these can also be regarded as transfer payments because the costs to one agent become the benefits to the other. This will be seen more clearly in Chapter 8 when the costs and benefits to the farmers are introduced as well as those to the ginnery that undertakes the primary processing of the farmers' cotton.

Where there is a transfer payment we can identify a gainer and a loser. The gain to one group will be equal to the loss by the other group. This situation can be illustrated in the transition from the financial analysis of a project to economic analysis. Before any of the complications of externalities or shadow pricing are introduced it is possible to move from the narrower perspective of the return to the project sponsor to the return to all the parties identified in the financial analysis. Some financial flows can be identified as transfer payments:

Financial Flow	Gainer	Loser
Company taxes	Government	Project
Loan principal	Project	Bank
Loan interest and repayment	Bank	Project
Accounts receivable	Debtors	Project
Accounts payable	Project	Creditors

Normally all of the above financial flows would be excluded from an economic analysis of the project, leaving only the resource costs and benefits included in the annual statement of costs and benefits (sometimes described as a resource flow or resource statement). Figure 5.1 showed that the distribution of the net benefits from this statement could also be derived by adding the cash flows to the various parties affected by the project.[4] Table 7.1 shows a statement of the distribution of costs and benefits for the example project used in Chapters 4 and 5. Note that the line "Net Benefits (1)" is identical to the bottom line of Table 4.5. The line "Net Benefits (2)" includes adjustments for the transfer payments involved in accounts receivable and payable. It could be described as the starting point for an economic analysis because it allows for the removal of all obvious transfer payments.

There are, however, a few exceptions to the standard approach to dealing with financial flows in economic analysis:

- Where accounts receivable is the delay in payment by an overseas buyer for an export, the cost is not a transfer payment within the economy but a foreign exchange cost to the economy (the gainer from the transfer is a foreigner).
- Where accounts payable is the delay in payment to an overseas supplier for an import, the benefit is a foreign exchange benefit to the economy (the loser is a foreigner).

Table 7.1 Distribution of Benefits by Year ($ '000 Constant Market Prices)

	1	2	3	4	5	6	7	8	9	10	11	12
Shareholders (equity)	-10,000	-3,060	3,085	1,555	3,011	2,399	-131	2,305	2,235	2,159	8,320	3,074
Bank (loan)	-10,000	-12,000		4,285	4,285	4,285	4,285	4,285	4,285	4,285	4,285	
Government tax					137	716	746	810	880	956	1,038	1,126
Net benefits (1)	-20,000	-15,060	3,085	5,840	7,433	7,400	4,900	7,400	7,400	7,400	13,643	4,200
Income to debtors		1,215	743	675	68						-2,700	
Income to creditors		-642	-321	-308							1,271	
Net benefits (2)	-20,000	-14,487	3,507	6,207	7,500	7,400	4,900	7,400	7,400	7,400	12,213	4,200

	NPV at		
	4%	8%	12%
Equity	7,936	3,346	294
Bank	4,937	0	-3,344
Government (taxes)	4,478	3,192	2,317
NPV (1)	17,352	6,539	-733
Debtors	662	1,015	1,188
Creditors	-317	-486	-571
NPV (2)	17,697	7,067	-115

- Where a foreign exchange loan is obtained that is specific to a project and would not be available for an alternative project the loan receipt can be regarded as a foreign exchange benefit and the loan interest and repayment as foreign exchange costs. It should be noted that most multilateral and bilateral aid donors do not regard their funds as being tied to a particular project.
- Where a project involves foreign direct investment that would not otherwise be available to the economy, the stream of costs and benefits that accrue to the foreign investor would not be regarded as part of the national costs and benefits. In such cases the foreign investment inflow would be regarded as a foreign exchange benefit, and that part of the return to the project owners that accrues to the foreign investor would be regarded as a foreign exchange outflow. This case does not necessarily apply to all investment by foreign-owned companies. A foreign investor already established within a country might use locally generated funds for investment, and these funds might be regarded as potentially available for other projects.

Once the most obvious transfer payments have been identified and removed it is possible to consider further adjustments in the process of undertaking an economic efficiency analysis. These adjustments are the subject of the next two chapters.

Further Reading

Introductions to economic analysis can be found in all the major texts. Curry and Weiss (2000: chap. 2), Little and Mirrlees (1974: chap. 1), Perkins (1994: chap. 1), Snell (1997 chap. 1), Squire and van der Tak (1975: chap. 1–2), and UNIDO (1972: part I) are all worth looking at for different ways of explaining similar ideas.

Notes

1. This neglect may explain some of the problems involved in the implementation of economic analysis in a systematic way. If the analysis does not tell the client anything more useful than whether or not the project should be accepted, it is not surprising if the client does not pay much attention to the analysis.

2. The introduction of this distinction between economic and social analysis is closely associated with Squire and van der Tak (1975).

3. There are of course transaction costs involved in such payments, but these are usually ignored in economic analysis either because they are relatively small or

because they are regarded as fixed costs that do not vary with the implementation of the project.

4. This idea is described by Yaffey (1989: 22) as an application of what he calls the "flow equality principle."

8

Linkages, Multipliers, and Externalities

Linkages and Multiagent Projects

Financial analysis confines its attention to a single entity, but sometimes projects have effects on other producers. These can be taken into account in two ways: (1) extending the boundaries by which the project is defined and (2) shadow pricing of nontraded goods.

The first approach can be described as a *linkage* approach. The second approach is discussed in Chapters 10 and 11. There are two types of linkage: (1) *forward linkage,* for example, from a forestry project to a sawmill; and (2) *backward linkage*, for example, from a tea factory to a tea farmer.

The linkage approach is particularly important for agroindustries and multiagent projects. In most other cases it is easier to take linkages into account through shadow pricing.

There is an important rule for establishing the existence of a linkage effect: Only take account of the effect if it is a *necessary consequence* of the project under consideration.

Sometimes there may be a connection but no necessary linkage. For example, an orange juice factory may require orange production. Does the factory *cause* an increase in orange production, or does it divert oranges from the fresh market? If the effect of the project is simply to divert the production from another end use, then we should not attribute the production of the raw material to the implementation of the project. Where linkages *are* particularly important is in projects where the raw product is perishable or bulky and has little or no value without processing (e.g., green leaf tea, sugarcane, etc.). In these cases it is reasonable to assume that the production of the raw material would not take place without the project.

Where a necessary linkage can be established the boundaries of the project are redefined so that project net benefits = factory net benefits + farmers' net benefits.

In the process of adding up the costs and benefits to both parties the price between the factory and the farmers becomes a transfer payment. The total benefits of the project are the same irrespective of the price paid by the factory to the farmers, although, strictly speaking, the level of price obviously does have some implications for incentives and therefore may affect production levels.

The benefits of *enabling*-type projects are also a form of linkage. For example a new rural road may lead to increased economic activity in the area served by the road. Similar benefits can arise from rural electrification, port improvement projects, and industrial estates. Tourism projects are often justified on the basis of their effect on economic activity in the surrounding area. Such effects are better described as *externalities* because there is no direct transaction between the project and the affected activities.

It is sometimes possible to analyze a cluster of closely related projects together rather than individually. This approach is seen in some multipurpose rural development projects. In these projects the objective of raising rural welfare is not achieved by a road on its own or an agricultural extension project on its own, but through a combination of roads, extension, credit, and water supplies. Such projects are usually analyzed as a whole so that there may be no need to trace the linkage effects although, whenever possible, it is advisable to appraise each of the different components of the project individually to ensure that they make a positive contribution.

Linkage effects are more likely to be important in large and/or relatively closed economies and less likely to be important in small and/or relatively open economies where the economic value of many items is likely to be defined by the possibility of trade.

Linkage effects are included in Figure 7.1. On the resource side, including the linkage effect will change the values of resource costs and benefits. On the income side, analysis of the linkage will probably indicate income effects on some group or groups. The sum of these income effects will be equivalent to the net resource cost or benefit of the linkage.

The introduction of linkage effects is illustrated in our cotton textile project example by the inclusion of the costs and benefits to the farmers and the costs and benefits to the ginnery that processes the seed cotton. The project net benefits can be redefined as project net benefits = factory net benefits + ginnery net benefits + farmer net benefits.

It will be seen, however, that the only real linkage effect is from the additional cotton production induced by price changes.[1] Most of the cotton purchased by the new factory is diverted from existing exports for which the economic value is derived from the alternative export value (see Chapter 10). However, it has been assumed that the factory will pay a higher price than the exporters in order to ensure a regular supply of good-quality lint and that, as a result, the ginnery is able to pay a higher average price to the farmers. This higher price induces some extra production and it is this extra production that can be described as a linkage effect.

Table 8.1 shows the ginnery costs and benefits.[2] The ginnery eventually benefits from the project, but this depends on the quantity of cotton lint it is able to sell to the factory at the higher price. In Years 2 and 3, when the factory production is lower, the ginnery loses money, but incremental revenue is positive thereafter.

The IRR to the ginnery is very high, but this is a reflection of the fact that no extra investment is involved, only price changes through higher throughput. The size of the NPV to the ginnery is small relative to the value of sales. This is a case where the use of different indicators of project worth is important. The IRR is not a very relevant criterion in this case because it suggests a very high rate of return when in fact the benefit to the ginnery is marginal.

The value of the purchase of seed cotton from the farmers is exactly the same as the sum of the sales of seed cotton by farmers shown in Tables 5.9 and 5.10. The seed cotton is processed into cotton lint and cotton seed. The cotton seed is sold to local seed crushers for oil extraction, but the cotton lint is sold partly to the factory and partly for export. Assuming that the lint export quantity in Year 1 represents the without project situation, it can be seen that the main effect of the project is to reduce cotton lint exports.[3] Only 360 tonnes of seed cotton (equivalent to 120 tonnes of cotton lint) are additional to what would have been produced without the project. However, the quantity of lint sales to the factory (given by the sum of the cotton lint included in factory operating costs, the raw material stock, and the stocks of finished goods) is 400 tonnes in a normal year (1 tonne per 10,000 units produced). It can be deduced that 280 tonnes (70%) of the cotton purchased by the factory would otherwise have been exported.

The remaining 120 tonnes of extra cotton lint produced can be regarded as a backward linkage to the ginnery and then to the farmers, induced by price changes. The inclusion of this linkage in the overall analysis of the project will be shown later in the chapter after examination of a potential external cost.

In principle a forward linkage could also be identified from the sale of the additional cotton seed to the seed crushers. It is assumed here that there is either insufficient information for the value of this forward linkage to be traced or that the cotton seed substitutes for some other local oilseed production. It is often the case that the project analyst has to determine how far it is practically possible to trace the linkage effects of a project.

Table 8.1 Ginnery Costs and Benefits by Year

	1	2	3	4	5	6	7	8	9	10	11
Purchases and production (tonnes)											
Purchases of seed cotton	5,712	5,892	6,072	6,072	6,072	6,072	6,072	6,072	6,072	6,072	6,072
Cotton lint production	1,904	1,964	2,024	2,024	2,024	2,024	2,024	2,024	2,024	2,024	2,024
Cotton seed production	3,656	3,771	3,886	3,886	3,886	3,886	3,886	3,886	3,886	3,886	3,886
Lint exports	1,904	1,714	1,699	1,599	1,624	1,624	1,624	1,624	1,624	1,624	1,764
Lint sales to factory		250	325	425	400	400	400	400	400	400	260
Production costs ($ '000)											
Purchases of seed cotton	32,558	35,352	36,432	36,432	36,432	36,432	36,432	36,432	36,432	36,432	36,432
Transport to ginnery	6,854	7,070	7,286	7,286	7,286	7,286	7,286	7,286	7,286	7,286	7,286
Ginning costs	4,570	4,714	4,858	4,858	4,858	4,858	4,858	4,858	4,858	4,858	4,858
Transport of lint to port	5,712	5,142	5,097	4,797	4,872	4,872	4,872	4,872	4,872	4,872	5,292
Transport of lint to factory		313	406	531	500	500	500	500	500	500	325
Total costs to ginnery	49,694	52,591	54,079	53,904	53,948	53,948	53,948	53,948	53,948	53,948	54,193
Sales revenue ($ '000)											
Sale of cotton seed	12,795	13,198	13,601	13,601	13,601	13,601	13,601	13,601	13,601	13,601	13,601
Sale of cotton lint											
Exporters	42,840	38,565	38,228	35,978	36,540	36,540	36,540	36,540	36,540	36,540	39,690
Factory		6,250	8,125	10,625	10,000	10,000	10,000	10,000	10,000	10,000	6,500
Total sales revenue	55,635	58,013	59,954	60,204	60,141	60,141	60,141	60,141	60,141	60,141	59,791
Net revenue to ginnery	5,940	5,423	5,875	6,300	6,193	6,193	6,193	6,193	6,193	6,193	5,598
Incremental ginnery revenue		−518	−66	359	253	253	253	253	253	253	−342

NPV at 4% = 680
NPV at 8% = 480
NPV at 12% = 331
IRR = 30.5%

Multipliers

It is sometimes claimed that projects generate additional benefits through the multiplier effect that expenditure on the project has on the level of economic activity in the economy. To claim such additional benefits it is necessary to show that the project generates additional income that would not have been derived from expenditure elsewhere on some alternative activity.

The condition for such a claim to be accepted is that there should be excess capacity or unused resources utilized that would otherwise be underutilized. Such a situation might occur because of the existence of underemployment of labor or because of additional use of underutilized production capacity.

Rather than claim a questionable multiplier effect, it is better to use shadow prices to take account of underutilized labor or excess production capacity for nontraded goods. Where the effect on capacity utilization is very specific to the project it may be better to include this effect as a linkage or an intended externality and therefore to redefine the boundaries of the project to include the underutilized facility or to measure the external effect.

Externalities

Externalities can be defined as effects that are imposed by a project on another group of people without proper compensation being made.[4] They can include both *external costs* and *external benefits* and both effects that are *quantifiable* and can be valued as well as effects that are *intangible*.

An important concept in the discussion of externalities is that of *potential compensation*. In welfare economics a general improvement in welfare is said to occur when somebody can be made better off without making anybody else worse off.[5] This is a very restrictive condition for project analysis because projects may result in both gainers and losers. A less restrictive condition is implied by the Hicks-Kaldor compensation principle, which states that a potential welfare improvement can take place if the gainers could potentially compensate the losers.

The general rule for externalities in project analysis is that, where possible, they should be *internalized* (i.e., brought into the analysis of the project). This is easier for some kinds of effects than for others, but, in principle, it means that all costs and benefits both internal and external are included in the analysis of the project and added together.

When the economic costs and benefits of a project are added together it is the potential compensation principle that is being used. The value of one unit of loss to one group affected by the project is given the same weight as the value of one unit of gain by another group. This is the standard approach used in economic efficiency analysis, although an alternative approach can be taken when differential weights are used in distribution analysis.

Sometimes externalities can be internalized only in the analysis of the project. However, increasing attention is now being given to the possibility of actual internalization of externalities through project redesign or through the imposition of user charges for public goods and taxes on resource use.

In conceptualizing the effects of externalities it is sometimes helpful to use the concepts of *consumer surplus* and *producer surplus*. Figure 8.1 illustrates these two concepts. In principle any external effect can influence either the supply conditions or the demand conditions for a particular item or both. This in turn will affect the surplus obtained by consumers and producers.

In Figure 8.1 the line DD_1 represents the demand curve for an item indicating the willingness of consumers to pay for different quantities of that item. The line SS_1 represents the supply curve for producers indicating the marginal cost of production. At point A supply is equal to demand with Q units being bought at price P. The area DAP represents the consumer surplus (i.e., the extent to which consumers would have been willing to pay more for some of the items they purchase). The area SAP represents the

Figure 8.1   Consumer and Producer Surplus

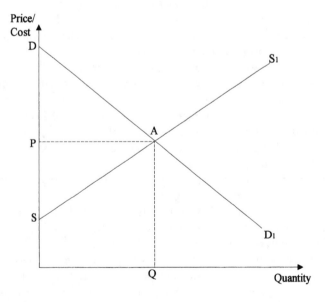

producer surplus (i.e., the extent to which the price received exceeds the marginal cost of supply). The extent to which different groups are affected by an externality will depend on the effect of the change on demand and supply conditions and the slope of the demand and supply curves (i.e., the elasticities of demand and supply for the affected activities).

Externalities can be categorized in different ways. Cook and Mosley (1989) use the common distinction between *technological* (or "real") *externalities* and *pecuniary externalities*.

Technological Externalities

Technological externalities occur when the welfare of one group is affected directly by the activities of a project without any payment or compensation being involved. For example river pollution has a negative impact on the incomes of fishermen, while a rural road should have a positive effect on the incomes of local farmers. In terms of the concepts used in Figure 8.1, river pollution would shift the supply curve to the left, while a rural road would shift the supply curve for agricultural products to the right. Projects that enhance the skill level of workers or lead to the adoption of new technology also give rise to technological externalities, again shifting the supply curve to the right. If demand is less than perfectly elastic these changes will also have an effect on prices and so there will be changes in consumer welfare. In none of these cases is the recipient likely to make a direct payment for the resulting benefit or receive direct compensation for the resulting loss.

Another approach used in the estimation of technological externalities is the *human capital approach*. The human capital approach looks at the effect of an activity on human productivity, normally assuming that the level of wage or salary paid to people provides an indication of their productivity. This approach can be used in health and transport projects to value benefits from savings in time and loss of life and also to estimate the benefits of training and education.

In some sectors the main benefits are in the form of technological externalities. The benefits of road projects normally accrue to road users in the form of reduced costs. Roads can also divert traffic from other areas, leading to benefits from the relief of congestion but also to reduced income to traders if business is diverted away from the area that is bypassed. The benefits of health and education projects are also normally in the form of technological externalities, although some of the benefits may be internalized by user charges. The valuation of the benefits of projects in the social and infrastructure sectors is discussed in more detail in Chapter 9.

Pecuniary Externalities

Pecuniary externalities occur where the activities of a project affect the prices paid by other groups. For example competition between a new project and an existing project for labor or raw materials can affect the price or the quantity available to the existing project. Linkages are sometimes regarded as pecuniary externalities because the existence of additional demand for a product from a project may affect the price that the producers receive, as in the case of our textile project. These effects are best estimated by tracing the links and measuring the costs and benefits to the parties affected.

For straightforward linkages it is relatively easy to extend the boundaries of the project to include directly affected agents. For competition effects it is slightly more complicated. The tea project described in Chapter 3 illustrates the point.

The proposed tea factory will result in some increase in the production of tea but also some diversion of green leaf from an existing factory. Valuation of the benefits from additional tea is straightforward. If tea is exported, the economic value of the additional tea is the export price received. If the scope of the project analysis were to be restricted simply to the new factory, an impression might be given of significant net benefits because all the tea produced would be assumed to be additional.

However, the additional benefit to the economy from tea diverted from one factory to the other could be very small, possibly even negative. For the tea that is diverted there are a series of changes, which are tabulated in Table 8.2, assuming that that the price paid to farmers is fixed through a national producer price policy. A more complex set of changes occurs if the fixed producer price assumption is dropped.

Table 8.2   Effects of Diverting Green Leaf to a New Tea Factory

Cost/Revenue Item	Effect on New Factory	Effect on Old Factory	Effect on Farmers	Net Change to Economy
Made tea sales	+	–	Nil	Nil unless there is change in quality/ processing efficiency
Green leaf sales/purchase	–	+	Nil unless the price changes	Nil
Processing costs	–	+	Nil	Nil unless there is difference in processing costs
Net benefit	+	–	Nil unless the price changes	Probably small

The situation arising from the fixed producer price assumption can also be shown graphically (Figure 8.2). At the fixed producer price P, farmers are willing to supply Q_2 tonnes of green leaf, but the existing factory is only willing to buy Q_1 tonnes. Farmers lose a producer surplus equivalent to the area ABC. When the new project is implemented both the supply curve for green leaf and the demand curve from the factories shift outward (from S_1S_1 to S_2S_2 and from D_1D_1 to D_2D_2 respectively). Assuming an unchanged producer price, the farmers would be willing to supply Q_3 tonnes of green leaf, but the factories would like to buy Q_4 tonnes. Assuming that the farmers have a marginal preference for sending their green leaf to the new factory, there will be a shortfall in green leaf deliveries to the original factory of $Q_4 - Q_3$ tonnes and this will impose a loss equivalent to the area DEF on the existing factory. The financial analysis of the new project will show additional tea production for $Q_4 - Q_1$ tonnes of green leaf, but the actual additional production will only come from $Q_3 - Q_1$ tonnes with $Q_4 - Q_3$ tonnes of the production being diverted from the existing factory.

If the assumption of fixed producer prices is relaxed, competition for green leaf supplies raises the price to farmers. This situation is illustrated in Figure 8.3. The overall producer surplus to farmers increases from SCP_1 to SFP_2. The income to existing farmers is increased by P_1P_2CD, partly because of price changes on existing production and partly because of the

Figure 8.2   Impact of the Tea Project with Fixed Producer Prices

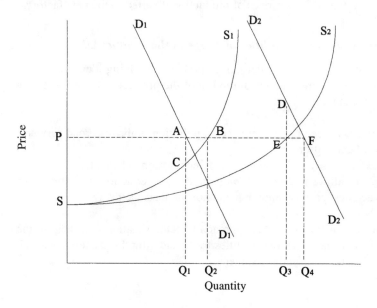

Figure 8.3   Price Changes and the Tea Project

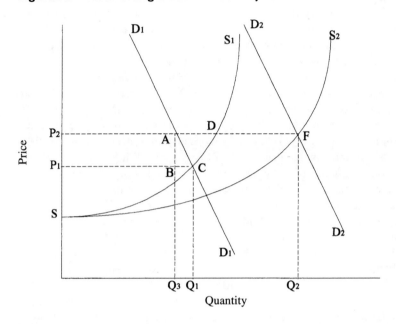

surplus on additional production generated by the improved price. There is also a producer surplus to the new farmers of $SFP_2 - SDP_2$. The income of the existing factory is reduced by P_1P_2CA. This includes a transfer of income to farmers through increased prices of P_1P_2BA and a loss of profit of ABC from the $Q_1 - Q_3$ tonnes of production diverted to the new factory.

Categorization of Externalities by Stage in the Product Life

Perkins (1994) suggests an alternative approach involving identification of externalities at different stages in the life of the product of the project. She defines three stages:

- Externalities in *production* (e.g., pollution, improved road services, skill generation)
- Externalities in *distribution* (e.g., congestion, accidents)
- Externalities in *consumption* (e.g., disease reduction from the use of vaccines, passive smoking, alcohol-induced accidents)

The main reason for using this approach to categorization is to help in the identification of potential externalities by considering the process by which a product reaches the final consumer.

Sometimes quantification of externalities is impossible. In such cases it is useful at least to mention the existence of the externality and to provide any relevant information to provide the basis on which a decision could be made.

Environmental and social impact effects are often very difficult to quantify, but they should not be ignored if they are known to be significant. Decisions are not made on the basis of numbers alone, and relevant qualitative information can be of equal or even greater importance.

Methods that can supplement or substitute for cost-benefit analysis are being developed, and there is a body of literature on *multicriteria analysis* where attempts are made to trade off criteria that may be formulated in different ways. These approaches are discussed in Part 4.

Project Analysis and the Environment

There are many definitions of the environment. Among the simplest is "the natural and social conditions encompassing all . . . mankind and including future generations" (World Bank 1991). The major implication of this definition is that environmental assessment is concerned with both biophysical and socioeconomic changes. Although a great deal of attention has been focused on effects related to the physical environment, social and cultural impacts are also important although they may be more difficult to measure.

The valuation of environmental effects in project analysis has a fairly long history in cost-benefit analysis in Western Europe as the classic case of an externality. A famous early example is the study conducted on the environmental impact of the proposed Third London Airport (Roskill 1971). Many more studies of environmental impact have been undertaken since then, and methods of valuing environmental effects have become increasingly sophisticated.

Recent concerns with global warming and depletion of the ozone layer as well as man-made disasters such as Chernobyl have led to greater awareness of environmental problems in all countries. Environmental externalities are seen to transcend national boundaries. All major bilateral and multilateral aid agencies now require some kind of environmental screening in project analysis. The problem, as always, is how to measure the effects, or at the very least how to assess them.

Development of approaches to take account of the impact of projects on the social environment has been more recent, and their valuation is more problematic. Nevertheless there is increasing concern about the social and cultural impact of projects, particularly the impact on groups who may be vulnerable for reasons of ethnic diversity, social class, or gender.

Stages of Environmental Assessment

There are different stages in the process of environmental assessment that to some extent mirror the conventional project sequence. Environmental screening can be seen as a necessary part of the project identification process, while environmental impact assessment can be seen as a part of the project preparation and appraisal process that may be required if environmental impact is expected to be significant.

Environmental Screening

Not all projects will require a full-scale *environmental impact assessment* (EIA), but it is important to be aware of the potential environmental effects of a project. Some projects may only need an initial screening to show that environmental effects are insignificant. Environmental screening for some projects may just involve satisfying a checklist of the most important factors to be considered in the environmental analysis of projects. The most obvious factors to consider are size of the project, location of the project, and nature of the project (e.g., sectoral origin). Large projects in environmentally sensitive locations investing in resource extraction are likely to have a greater need for environmental assessment than smaller and less sensitive projects. There are a number of useful checklists produced by different organizations that can help determine the likely level of assessment required.[6]

The result of the environmental screening process will be a recommendation either that there is nothing to be concerned about or that further assessment is required. The United Nations Environment Programme (UNEP) (1988) describe this stage as a *preliminary assessment* that will (1) identify the various impacts of the project on the local environment, (2) describe and predict the extent of each impact, and (3) assess their importance to decisionmakers. This process will narrow down the alternatives by eliminating some projects as being unacceptable and clearing others. It will also lead to a recommendation for a full EIA in some cases.

It can be useful to distinguish among those projects for which environmental benefit is the main objective, those with nonenvironmental objectives but significant environmental effects, and those for which environmental effects are relatively minor. Clearly it is the first two categories for which environmental assessment is most important.

Curry and Weiss (2000: 240) point out that there is a relationship between the policy environment and the extent to which additional environmental impact assessment is necessary. Where environmental policy enforces appropriate standards it is likely that more rigorous assessment can be restricted to the first two categories. Where policy is weak the need for environmental impact assessment may apply to a higher proportion of projects.

Environmental Impact Assessment

Where an EIA study is required it will need to consider

- What will happen as a result of the project—what the impacts are, how big they are, and what causes them. It is also necessary to make a judgment on what would have happened without the project, to ensure that the additional impact caused by the project is properly assessed.
- How big the changes resulting from the project will be. This implies the use of some form of measurement or classification scale.
- Whether the changes resulting from the project matter.
- If there is some negative impact, what measures can be taken in mitigation.

Many of the questions that will need to be asked will be technical in nature and as such are beyond the scope of this book. However, questions relating to whether the changes matter and what can be done in mitigation are questions that must concern a project analyst. In particular they may require methods of valuing environmental effects using some of the concepts of environmental economics. These concepts can help in establishing an analytical framework. They are derived from the idea of sustainable development.

Sustainable Development
and Environmental Capital

There are many definitions of sustainable development of which the most famous is the Brundtland Commission statement that sustainable development should "meet the needs of the present without compromising the ability of future generations to meet their own needs" (World Commission on Environment and Development 1987).

The above statement leads to the idea of maintaining environmental capital. We should hand on to future generations an environmental capital stock at least as valuable as that which we inherited. This proposition immediately raises the problem of defining the economic value of a capital stock. This is difficult enough for man-made capital, and it is even more difficult for a nonrenewable resource. To resolve the problem to a sufficient extent to provide guidance, a distinction is made between

- *man-made capital,* which is potentially expandable
- *critical natural capital,* which is priceless
- *other natural capital,* which may be renewable or nonrenewable but is substitutable

The implications of the above categorization are that:

- We should maintain the value of the stock of man-made capital and, if possible, increase it.
- We should avoid damage to critical natural capital at all costs.
- We should limit exploitation of renewable natural capital to sustainable levels.
- We should "internalize" the cost of depleting nonrenewable resources through some form of compensation measures leading to additions to the stock of man-made capital.

The issue of compensation for environmental damage is central to the valuation of the environmental effects of projects. The idea of compensating for the depletion of nonrenewable resources through addition to the stock of man-made capital leads to the concept of substitutability. In principle compensation for the use of noncritical natural capital can be achieved by investing in substitutes. For example, compensation for the use of nonrenewable energy resources might be made in the form of investment in renewable energy. Compensation for degradation of the landscape might be made in the form of landscape enhancement measures.

Environmental Valuation Techniques

Valuation of environmental effects involves the measurement of environmental costs and benefits. Environmental benefits can be defined by:

- User benefits—these can include direct use values from goods extracted and consumed as well as indirect use values from services provided such as recreation and maintenance of resource quality (World Bank 1998).
- *Option value,* that is, the potential future user benefit made available if a resource is maintained.
- *Existence value,* that is, the value that people put on the existence of something even if they do not intend to use it (e.g., the value that people place on the continued existence of rare species of animals).

The ease with which such benefits can be measured varies considerably and obviously; putting a value on the existence of an endangered species is particularly difficult. Economic analysis cannot easily answer moral or aesthetic questions although it may be able to point out the cost of making decisions.

There are various methods available for estimating environmental costs and benefits. They have been categorized in different ways by different authors, and there are different views on their applicability, but there is some common agreement on the range of methods. Dixon et al. (1994) distinguish between approaches based on *objective valuation* (OVA) and those based on *subjective valuation* (SVA). OVA approaches are based on physical relationships describing cause and effect where an attempt is made to value the physical effect. SVA methods are based on subjective assessment derived from information either on surrogate real markets (e.g., property values and wages) or on hypothetical markets constructed from survey data.

Valuation techniques can also be divided between those that attempt to value both costs and benefits and those that concentrate only on the cost side. The former allow the inclusion of environmental considerations in cost-benefit analysis, while the latter might be used either in cost effectiveness analysis or in some form of multicriteria analysis. The main valuation techniques are discussed in turn below:

Effect on Production (OVA)

This approach involves the estimation of the effect of an environmental change on production in the affected area. It is also called the *changes in productivity* approach. It has particular application in projects affecting natural resources such as soil, forests, and fisheries. These could include both projects with negative effects (e.g., water pollution, destruction of wetlands and forests) as well as projects having positive effects (e.g., soil conservation and afforestation). In principle it is the most straightforward approach since all that is required is (1) determination of the physical effects of the project on the environment (e.g., the quantity of fish lost to fishermen due to river pollution or the positive effect of soil conservation on crop yields) and (2) estimation of the value of the effect (the quantity of fish lost or of crops gained multiplied by the market price of the fish or the crops, taking account of any quality changes).

The main problem is to define the physical effects. This requires careful study of the project environment in order to define the likely with and without project scenarios. Particular care needs to be taken in defining the without project scenario in order to avoid introducing bias into the analysis.

Loss of Earnings (OVA)

This approach covers the *human capital* approach to the valuation of human life and the *cost of illness* approach to the valuation of sickness and injury costs.

Some environmental effects have significant effects on human health. This applies particularly to forms of pollution that affect health directly, for example, through contamination of water or air. A common approach to measurement is the *loss of earnings* approach where the cost of pollution is measured by the present value of the earnings lost through sickness or premature death.

It is likely that this approach will understate the cost of damage to health. Other nonincome effects may be ignored, and there is a major conceptual problem in valuing human life. Valuation of human life on the basis of earnings makes very strong assumptions about the working of the labor market and disregards the value placed on a person's life by other people, such as close relatives. In principle it might appear that the lives of people who do not work for wages have no value at all. Alternative approaches can be used using life insurance premiums or surrogate earnings to value the contribution of household members who are not formally employed, but these approaches are not very reliable. The loss of earnings approach can also be supplemented with estimates of the cost of additional health care (or reduced health care costs for environmental improvement projects).

There are significant problems with the use of the loss of earnings approach as a measure of human life and such measures cannot be regarded as accurate. However, given the alternative of not valuing life at all, it may sometimes be necessary to accept the loss of earnings approach as a crude estimate in the knowledge that the margin of error may be very large. It is likely, however, that alternative cost-effectiveness approaches would be used in cases where the saving of human lives is one of the major objectives of the project.

Replacement Cost and
Compensating (Shadow) Project (OVA)

In this approach the idea is that the costs of environmental damage can be measured by the cost of replacing or restoring the damaged asset. The assumption is that the cost of restoration is less than the value of the resources destroyed. If this were not the case, it would be necessary to measure the value of the damaged asset directly. An obvious example of this approach is the inclusion of land restoration costs in mining and quarrying projects. However, in these cases, restoration usually only takes place after some years, and the restored environment is not the same as the one destroyed. Where there is a time lag between environmental damage and restoration, full compensation for environmental damage would imply restoration of the environment to a state that is better than the original to compensate for the period before the restoration.

A more general application of this approach is the compensating, or *shadow*, project approach. Here a compensating project is devised to restore the environment at the end of the project to an acceptable level or to provide compensating benefits when a project is implemented (e.g., provision of recreational facilities to compensate for the use of recreational land for a factory). In these cases the costs of the compensating project are included in the project cost.

In principle the costs of the damage to the environment and the benefits of the compensating project should also be included. In practice the cost of the compensating project is often taken as a proxy for all three items because the costs of environmental damage and the benefits of the compensating project may be difficult to measure and are implicitly assumed to cancel each other out. In effect it is assumed that the damage to the environment is equal to the benefit of the compensating project on the basis of "willingness to accept." This approach may miss out on some effects or undervalue them. There is nothing quite like the original state of the environment, and anticipation of the impact of a project may affect public perception of what is acceptable.

Preventive Expenditure

In this approach the expenditures people make to avoid the effects of environmental damage are used as an indicator of what people would be willing to pay for environmental improvement. For example, if people spend money on purchasing clean water from elsewhere or on boiling and filtering their water, then these costs can be taken as a measure of the value of improving a polluted water supply. This measure may give an underestimate where individuals' expenditure is constrained by low income or by imperfect information or where there are other external costs, such as increased public health costs, that are not borne by the individual.

Hedonic Methods (SVA)

The methods described as *hedonic* are based on the principle that the value of a particular environmental state can be derived from surrogate markets.[7] Two particular markets are used, those of housing (the *property value* approach) and labor (the *wage differential* approach).

In the property value approach, estimates of environmental impact are derived from changes in property values. This approach is sometimes used for measuring the cost of such effects as air or noise pollution. If there is a difference in the price of similar houses where one is affected by noise and the other is not, the value of noise avoidance can be derived from the price difference. A problem with this approach is that it is biased in favor of those with the most valuable properties.

The wage differential approach is used to estimate the costs associated with the risk of ill health or death at work. These costs can be estimated by measuring the extra wages required to induce workers to environmentally hazardous occupations or locations. This approach could be used in assessing the potential cost of environmental risks or in estimating the value of human life.

Both hedonic methods require strong assumptions about the efficiency of the working of the market mechanism that are unlikely to be valid in many developing country contexts. They also require quite extensive data collection.

Travel Cost Method

This approach is used for valuing public recreation sites. It assumes that the travel cost must at least equal the benefit of the visit. This is a consumer surplus approach similar to the approach used to measure the benefits of urban roads.

The approach makes strong assumptions about the motives for visits, but it can be useful for getting an idea of orders of magnitude. It is not useful for locations where very little travel is involved (e.g., urban recreational areas), but it could be used if a project involved the use of land that was part of a national park or affected land of significant natural beauty. It has been used to try to assess the economic value of wildlife, but, from the national economic point of view, much of the consumer surplus may be captured by foreigners. This raises the question of who should pay for wildlife protection. The travel cost approach can also be used in the estimation of the willingness of foreign tourists to pay for admission to national parks. This provides useful information for setting tariffs.

Contingent Valuation Method (SVA)

In this approach market research techniques are used to establish *willingness to pay* for environmental improvement or *willingness to accept* compensation for environmental damage. Those affected are asked about their reactions to certain situations, and inferences are made about the demand curve for a particular environmental good and therefore the consumer surplus derived from its availability or nonavailability.

The *contingent valuation* approach may have a role in compensatory environmental improvement projects, but there are problems of bias, defini-tion of the population, and the ability of people to understand the questions they may be asked. It may be difficult for people to take seriously questions about hypothetical payments that they will not actually have to make. Contingent valuation has also been used to try to determine willingness to pay for public utilities.

The advantage of the contingent valuation approach is that it can be used to value almost any environmental benefit and can be targeted to the specific changes expected from a project. It does require extensive testing of questionnaires to avoid bias. Sometimes it is possible to use contingent valuation alongside other approaches to provide a consistency check. Contingent valuation has been used alongside the travel cost method to measure the consumer surplus of tourists to game parks.

Opportunity Cost Approach

This approach is based on the opportunity cost principle[8] of the foregone alternative. If a resource is to be used for a project, what is its value in its alternative use? Sometimes it is difficult to measure the value of resources that are not priced (e.g., the leisure value of forests or the existence value of a natural feature). To get around the problem an alternative project is defined in which the resource in question is preserved. The difference between the net benefits of the two versions of the project defines the opportunity cost of preservation. It is then possible to make a decision on whether the extra cost of preservation of the resource is worthwhile without having to give a precise estimate of the value of the resource. Such infor-mation could also be used in multicriteria analysis. This approach can be very useful because it may show that the incremental cost of preservation is relatively small, and this might facilitate the search for funds to pay for conservation.

Cost-Effectiveness Analysis

The cost-effectiveness techniques outlined in Chapter 4 can also be used in environmental analysis, either to determine the cheapest way to achieve an environmental goal or to determine the maximum achievement for a given level of expenditure. This approach can be particularly useful where a deci-sion has been taken to achieve a particular standard for parameters such as the levels of water or air pollution. Where particular standards have been defined by the political process the need for valuation of the benefits of pollution reduction is removed. The only question is then how to achieve the standard defined.

Cost-effectiveness measures can also be used in conjunction with other nonquantified criteria in multicriteria analysis. This approach is discussed in Chapter 14.

Distributional Issues and the Environment

Environmental debates have revived some of the issues surrounding the valuation of income to different groups and the comparison of benefits between present and future generations. The major problems are:

- Methods that take the valuation of environmental effects from the observation of existing market values will have a bias toward those things that are valued by people with the highest incomes. This applies particularly to the use of property value–based approaches to the cost of negative environmental effects.
- There may be circumstances where the benefits from environmental damage accrue primarily to the rich, and the costs are felt primarily by the poor. For example the main beneficiary from the use of publicly owned forests for timber concessions may be the high-income concessionaire, but the main losers may be relatively low-income people losing forest products.
- The use of high rates of discount in economic analysis may discriminate against future generations. This does not necessarily mean that the discounting technique should not be used, but it may have some implications for policies that lead to high real interest rates. Other things being equal, higher rates of discount discriminate against projects with long gestation periods such as those involving soil conservation and planting trees. On the other hand low discount rates encourage investment, which can lead to a higher rate of depletion of resources.

Treatment of the distribution of costs and benefits in project analysis is discussed in Chapter 12, and the issues surrounding the choice of discount rate are discussed in Chapter 11.

Illustration—Environmental
Externalities and the Textile Project

Estimation of environmental costs can be illustrated with the cotton textile project example. Textile projects involve the use of dyes and other chemicals and can therefore be responsible for some groundwater pollution. It is assumed here that the villages immediately surrounding the factory are likely to be affected by such pollution. As a result it is necessary to sink twenty new tubewells at a cost of $30,000 each over a period of two years in order to ensure continuation of the same quality of water supply as before. It is also necessary to operate and maintain these wells.

Investment in and operation of the new tubewells can be regarded as a compensating project. However, it begs the question as to who pays for the wells. Ideally, payment should be made by the polluter, but this will be affected by the bargaining positions of the parties involved. It is quite likely that many of the inhabitants of the village will be cotton farmers who might want the textile factory to go ahead so that they can get a better price for their crop. It is possible that environmental protection legislation could be too weak to enforce compensation from the factory. It will be assumed for the moment that the cost of restoring the water supply will be borne by the community but that, should the project be approved in principle, this might be one of the main areas subject to negotiation.

Table 8.3 brings all the linkages and externality effects of the project together and sets out the incremental resource costs and benefits of the project. The table is divided into four sections. These are

- The incremental costs and benefits to farmers. This includes the incremental revenue from the sale at a higher price.
- The incremental costs and benefits to the ginnery. The revenue to the farmers is a cost to the ginnery, and so when these are added together they will cancel out. The incremental revenue to the ginnery consists of the export sales, which decline, and sales to the factory.
- The incremental costs associated with restoration of the village water supply.
- The costs and benefits associated with the factory. These have been categorized according to types of resource cost so that the costs associated with stocks of materials and final goods have been included together with operating costs of the same type. This approach simplifies the application of shadow prices in subsequent stages of the economic analysis and also clarifies the transfers between the factory and the ginnery. The sales of cotton lint by the ginnery to the factory are exactly matched by the costs to the factory and therefore cancel out when added together.

The resultant NPV has now increased substantially, and the IRR is 17.4%. It seems that taking account of the linkage effects considerably improves the apparent economic desirability of the project despite the negative environmental effect.

Table 8.3 is supplemented by Table 8.4, which shows the distribution of benefits to the various agents affected by the project. It can be seen that the farmers, in particular the ox cultivators, are the major beneficiaries

Table 8.3 Annual Statement of Costs and Benefits Including External and Linkage Effects by Year ($ '000)

	1	2	3	4	5	6	7	8	9	10	11	12
Incremental farm costs and benefits												
Sale of seed cotton		2,794	3,874	3,874	3,874	3,874	3,874	3,874	3,874	3,874	3,874	
Groundnuts		−900	−1,800	−1,800	−1,800	−1,800	−1,800	−1,800	−1,800	−1,800	−1,800	
Seed		45	90	90	90	90	90	90	90	90	90	
Pesticide		−42	−84	−84	−84	−84	−84	−84	−84	−84	−84	
Bags/cloth		−26	−52	−52	−52	−52	−52	−52	−52	−52	−52	
Tools, etc.		−6	−12	−12	−12	−12	−12	−12	−12	−12	−12	
Hired labor		−148	−296	−296	−296	−296	−296	−296	−296	−296	−296	
Family labor cost		5	10	10	10	10	10	10	10	10	10	
Incremental ginnery costs and benefits												
Purchases of seed cotton		−2,794	−3,874	−3,874	−3,874	−3,874	−3,874	−3,874	−3,874	−3,874	−3,874	
Ginning costs		−144	−288	−288	−288	−288	−288	−288	−288	−288	−288	
Transport costs		42	−223	−48	92	−92	−92	−92	−92	−92	−337	
Sales of cotton seed		403	806	806	806	806	806	806	806	806	806	
Exports of cotton lint		−4,275	−4,613	−6,863	−6,300	−6,300	−6,300	−6,300	−6,300	−6,300	−3,150	
Local sales of cotton lint		6,250	8,125	10,625	10,000	10,000	10,000	10,000	10,000	10,000	6,500	

	1	2	3	4	5	6	7	8	9	10	11	12
External costs												
Tubewells	−300	−300										
Diesel		−15	−30	−30	−30	−30	−30	−30	−30	−30	−30	
Spare parts		−6	−12	−12	−12	−12	−12	−12	−12	−12	−12	
Factory costs and benefits												
Land purchase	−300											300
Site development	−600											600
Buildings	−6,600											3,300
Machinery	−12,500	−12,500										
Vehicles		−2,500					−2,500					
Cotton lint		−6,250	−8,125	−10,625	−10,000	−10,000	−10,000	−10,000	−10,000	−10,000	−6,500	
Chemicals		−1,517	−2,158	−2,858	−2,800	−2,800	−2,800	−2,800	−2,800	−2,800	−2,287	
Unskilled factory labor		−3,000	−4,500	−6,000	−6,000	−6,000	−6,000	−6,000	−6,000	−6,000	−5,400	
Utilities		−1,300	−1,950	−2,450	−2,450	−2,450	−2,450	−2,450	−2,450	−2,450	−2,250	
Maintenance		−500	−1,000	−1,200	−1,400	−1,500	−1,500	−1,500	−1,500	−1,500	−1,500	
Management		−1,500	−2,250	−2,250	−2,250	−2,250	−2,250	−2,250	−2,250	−2,250	−2,250	
Sales		14,580	23,490	31,590	32,400	32,400	32,400	32,400	32,400	32,400	32,400	
Total Net Benefits	−20,300	−13,604	5,128	8,253	9,440	9,340	6,840	9,340	9,340	9,340	13,559	4,200

NPV at 4% = 30,985
NPV at 8% = 17,509
NPV at 12% = 8,232
IRR = 17.4%

Table 8.4 Distribution of Incremental Costs and Benefits by Year ($ '000)

	1	2	3	4	5	6	7	8	9	10	11	12
Shareholders (equity)	-10,000	-3,060	3,085	1,555	3,011	2,399	-131	2,305	2,235	2,159	8,320	3,074
Bank (loan)	-10,000	-12,000		4,285	4,285	4,285	4,285	4,285	4,285	4,285	4,285	
Government tax					137	716	746	810	880	956	1,038	1,126
Debtors		1,215	743	675	68						-2,700	
Creditors		-642	-321	-308							1,271	
Hand cultivators		634	634	634	634	634	634	634	634	634	634	
Ox cultivators		1,088	1,096	1,096	1,096	1,096	1,096	1,096	1,096	1,096	1,096	
Ginnery		-518	-66	359	253	253	253	253	253	253	-342	
Villages	-300	-321	-42	-42	-42	-42	-42	-42	-42	-42	-42	
Total net benefits	-20,300	-13,604	5,128	8,253	9,440	9,340	6,840	9,340	9,340	9,340	13,559	4,200

	NPV at		
	4%	8%	12%
Equity	7,936	3,346	294
Bank	4,937	0	-3,344
Government Tax	4,478	3,192	2,317
Debtors	662	1,015	1,188
Creditors	-317	-486	-571
Hand Cultivators	4,941	3,937	3,196
Ox Cultivators	8,540	6,803	5,523
Ginnery	680	480	331
Villages	-874	-778	-702
Total NPV	30,985	17,509	8,232

from the project. Such a table can be useful in determining possible pricing and compensation issues. As we have seen, the compensation issue could be important in this case.

Further Reading

Literature on linkages and multipliers is not extensive, and most of it is relatively old. Some ideas can be found in Little and Mirrlees (1974: chap. 16), Squire and van der Tak (1975: chap. 2), and Overseas Development Administration (1988: chap. 3). General expositions on externalities can also be found in these sources as well as in Perkins (1994: chap. 11) and Dinwiddy and Teal (1996: chaps. 12 and 14). Cook and Mosley (1989) is a useful source on externalities. There is a rapidly expanding literature on environmental assessment of projects. Two very useful texts on environmental valuation are those by Dixon et al. (1994) and Winpenny (1991). A good summary of the state of the art can be found in World Bank (1998). Other valuable sources include Asian Development Bank (1996), Hanley and Spash (1993), Abelson (1996), a collection of papers edited by Weiss (1994), and a number of publications by Pearce with various collaborators (including the Blueprint series).

Notes

1. Such price effects are also described as pecuniary externalities.
2. Table 8.1 is a simplification and ignores the implications of the changes in prices and quantities of seed cotton and cotton lint for working capital requirements. This is done to limit the size of the model. A proper financial analysis for the ginnery would require careful assessment of working capital requirements.
3. This assumption is made for convenience only to avoid the introduction of additional complications into the example. It should not be perceived as a justification for automatically assuming that the without project situation will remain unchanged.
4. Dinwiddy and Teal (1996: 200) provide the following definition: "An externality is said to exist when goods enter the utility functions of consumers or the profit functions of producers directly, rather than through the workings of the price mechanism." This is a rather restrictive definition because it excludes pecuniary externalities where the price mechanism is involved, and there may be distributional changes that would not be captured in the financial analysis of a single entity.
5. Such an improvement is often called a Pareto improvement because it relates to the concept of optimality defined by Pareto.
6. See, for example, Overseas Development Administration (1989).
7. The word *hedonic* is derived from the Greek word for pleasure. Thus the pleasure or utility derived by people from a difference in their environment is measured by the difference in price.
8. The opportunity cost concept is discussed in more detail in Chapter 10.

9

Benefit Estimation in the Social and Infrastructure Sectors

General Principles

In the infrastructure and social sectors there are many cases where the economic benefits of projects are not adequately defined by the projected financial value of sales. This could be because the service provided is not sold or because it is a natural monopoly with a controlled price. There are four main ways in which such benefits can be measured. These are

- the consumer surplus approach (willingness to pay)
- the producer surplus approach
- the human capital approach
- the cost saving approach (in principle this could be considered a variant of either the consumer or the producer surplus approach)

In the consumer surplus approach the benefits of a project are defined in terms of the value to users of the good or service provided over and above what they would have been willing to pay. This can be illustrated in Figure 9.1. If a project causes the price or user cost of a good or service to be reduced from P_1 to P_2, there is an increase in the demand for the activity from Q_1 to Q_2. The benefits (B) resulting from the project can be defined by

$$B = P_1P_2AE + ABE \tag{9.1}$$

where P_1P_2AE is the saving to existing consumers of the activity, and ABE is the net benefit to additional consumers.

In the producer surplus approach, the benefits are derived from the increased activity caused by a change in the price of either inputs or outputs or both. This is shown in Figure 9.2. If the marginal cost curve of an activi-

Figure 9.1   Estimation of Consumer Surplus

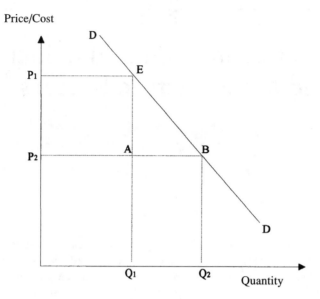

ty shifts from MC_1 to MC_2, the quantity produced will shift from Q_1 to Q_2 and a benefit equivalent to the area $ABGC$ will be derived. If in addition the sales price of the activity is increased (e.g., because of reduced transport costs to the market) from P_1 to P_2, there is an additional benefit of P_1P_2FG of which P_1P_2CE is due to the change in price and $CEFG$ is due to the combination of price and cost changes. The example given in Figure 9.2 relates to a rural road project, but could equally be applied to any similar project leading to a change in producer costs.

Note that this example assumes that the increase in production does not affect the consumer price. It is assumed either to be of marginal significance in relation to the intended market or is in the form of traded goods where demand is assumed to be infinitely elastic. If the production increase is nonmarginal and demand is not perfectly elastic, some of the benefits P_1P_2FG will go to consumers. Some of the reduced transport costs may also be captured by the transport operators.

The human capital approach looks at the effect of an activity on human productivity, normally assuming that the level of wage or salary paid to people provides an indication of their productivity.

The cost saving approach looks at benefits from the point of view of the next best alternative saved, essentially an opportunity cost approach. A pure cost saving approach assumes that the overall supply of the good or service

Figure 9.2 Producer's Surplus—Benefit Estimation for a Rural Road

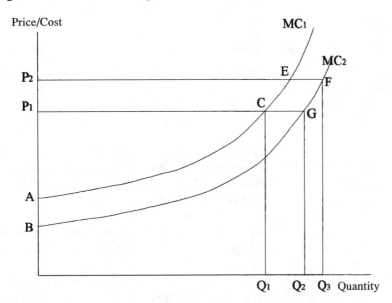

is unchanged. Where a change in the volume of supply of the good or service in question is assumed to take place, the cost saving approach may have to be supplemented with one or more of the other approaches because of the effect of possible price changes on consumers and producers.

The various approaches to benefit valuation will be illustrated by outlining in turn the main methods adopted for a number of different social and infrastructure sectors.

Transport Projects

The discussion of transport projects that follows concentrates on the issues surrounding road transport. The approaches used will also be related, where relevant, to other modes of transport (i.e., railways, ports, and airports).

Road transport projects can be divided conceptually between those that provide commercial transport services (freight and passenger transport) and those that provide physical infrastructure for which no direct user charges are made (most roads). The benefits from road construction projects tend to be pure externalities whereas the users of railways, ports, and airports are normally charged for the service. Nevertheless there may also be significant externalities arising from some commercial transport services, especially when prices are controlled and objectives are not entirely commercial.

Commercial Transport Services

The benefits of commercial transport projects are derived from the willingness of users to pay for the service provided. Where this is a competitive activity, such as road freight or car hire, it is reasonable to assume that the market price paid provides an adequate indicator of the benefit to the user.

Where prices are controlled and significant externalities are involved, such as in some urban transport networks, it may be necessary to consider the valuation of benefits more carefully. In principle the value of the service to consumers can be determined by estimating willingness to pay and using the consumer surplus approach in cases where there is a significant change in supply conditions. If the price of the service is controlled, it can be assumed that any addition to the service will help to reduce the level of excess demand. An indication of willingness to pay can sometimes be derived from considering the price paid for close substitutes. For example the value of benefits from an improved urban transport system might be estimated using information on the cost of using alternative transport systems not subject to price control, such as minibuses.

Sometimes willingness to pay may be difficult to determine, especially if users have little or no alternative but to use a service. Other approaches may then be used. In cases where significant savings in time are involved the loss of earnings approach can be used to value time savings. Urban transport projects may also have significant environmental externalities, particularly where they relieve congestion or reduce the level of pollution from exhaust fumes. The latter source of benefits applies particularly to urban railways. The value of relief from traffic congestion can be measured in terms of time savings and savings in vehicle operating costs (VOC). The value of reduced air pollution is likely to be reflected in health benefits from reduced sickness and mortality. Such benefits apply to improvements in urban public transport both by road and rail.

Where ports compete with each other it is reasonable to assume that charges reflect the willingness to pay of port users. Often these charges are made to foreign users and so can be regarded as direct foreign exchange earnings. However, port and airport improvement projects also tend to have additional benefits derived from generated traffic and the development of related industries. In principle these generated benefits can be estimated in a similar way to those related to the benefits from generated traffic on new or improved roads (see below).

Benefits from Road Construction and Improvement Projects

The main benefits from road construction and improvement projects are savings in vehicle operating costs, benefits from generated traffic, time savings, and reduced accident costs.

Savings in vehicle operating costs typically form the major benefit from road improvement projects and from efficiency improvements on railway networks. Efforts are made to estimate the costs of operation with and without the project and to forecast the number of vehicles that would use the facility over the period of the project life. In calculating savings in vehicle operating costs it is therefore important to have the following information:

- An estimate of the average number of vehicles (N) using the stretch of road per year by vehicle type (v) without the project.
- An estimate of the rate of growth (g) of traffic by vehicle type without the project.
- An estimate of the cost per kilometer of operating different types of vehicle on the stretch of road being improved for each year without the project ($VOCwo_{vt}$) and with the project ($VOCw_{vt}$).[1]
- The average number of kilometers traveled in each journey with and without the project (Kw_{vt} and Kwo_{vt} respectively). It should be noted that not all vehicles travel the full stretch of the road being improved and that road improvements often lead to new alignments that shorten the distance traveled.

Vehicle operating cost savings ($VOCS$) can then be estimated for each time period (t) on the following basis:

$$VOCS_t = \sum_v N_v (1 + g_v)^t (VOCwo_{vt} \cdot Kwo_{vt} - VOCw_{vt} \cdot Kw_{vt}) \quad (9.2)$$

A distinction is made between *existing traffic* (i.e., traffic that would have used the facility even without the project) and *generated traffic* (i.e., new users that are generated because of the cost reduction). Generated traffic leads to an *increase* in vehicle operating costs, which is more than compensated by an increase in either consumer or producer benefits. In Figure 9.1 the benefits from generated traffic could be represented by the incremental benefits to users (Q_1Q_2BE) minus the incremental vehicle operating costs (Q_1Q_2BA). Benefits from generated traffic can also be important in port improvement and airport projects although the majority of the beneficiaries from any consumer surplus may be foreigners for international traffic. More significant national benefits in the cases of ports and airports are likely to come from induced investment in other activities.

In the case of generated traffic using a trunk road the benefits will depend on

- The number of additional journeys generated per vehicle category. This may be estimated as a proportion of the projected traffic (P) using the existing road.
- The average benefit from the additional journeys. This is conventionally estimated at half the sum of the VOC with and without the project.
- The additional VOC incurred as a result of the extra journeys. This will be equal to the VOC for each vehicle type with the project.

The benefit from generated traffic (BGT) can be estimated on the following basis:

$$BGT_t = \sum_v N_v (1 + g_v)^t P_{vt}(VOCwo_{vt} \cdot Kwo_{vt} + VOCw_{vt} \cdot Kw_{vt})/2 \qquad (9.3)$$

and the cost of additional vehicle operating cost for generated traffic ($VOCGT$) is:

$$VOCGT_t = \sum_v N_v (1 + g_v)^t (VOCwo_{vt} \cdot Kwo_{vt}) \qquad (9.4)$$

An example of the estimation of savings in vehicle operating costs and of benefits from generated traffic is given in Tables 9.1 and 9.2. Table 9.1 outlines the basic data required to estimate the values set out in Table 9.2. Table 9.2 shows the projection of existing traffic and the estimation of generated traffic as a percentage of existing traffic affected by the state of completion of the road improvement.

Projections of savings in VOC for existing traffic and the additional VOC and benefits for generated traffic are given for ten years for illustration purposes. In practice such projections should be made for a much longer period because road improvements are usually expected to last more or less indefinitely if the road is maintained properly. It should be noted that in this case the net benefit from generated traffic is only 5.2% of the total benefits after ten years. Benefits from generated traffic are sometimes a relatively small proportion of the total benefits for improvements to existing trunk roads, but this may not be the case when roads are upgraded substantially or where new roads are developed.

Almost all the benefits from development of rural feeder roads are derived from generated activity, but estimation of the benefits for these projects may be made directly on the basis of the earnings expected from the new economic activities made possible, rather than indirectly through

Table 9.1 Basic Assumptions for Estimating Benefits for a Trunk Road Improvement Project

		Buses	Trucks	Cars
Existing average daily traffic		20	98	67
Estimated annual traffic growth rates		4.5%	4.0%	4.5%
Road length (km)				
With the project	68			
Without the project	75			
Average journey length (km)				
With the project		41	55	41
Without the project		45	60	45
Vehicle operating costs (D$ per km)				
With the project		27.50	20.00	12.50
Without the project		35.00	26.00	17.50
Vehicle operating costs per journey (D$)				
With the project		1,127.50	1,100.00	512.50
Without the project		1,575.00	1,560.00	787.50
Vehicle operating cost saving (D$)		447.50	460.00	275.00
Percentage of road improvement completed				
Year 2	15%			
Year 3	45%			
Year 4	75%			
Generated traffic as % of normal traffic				
Year 3		1.5%	2.0%	3.0%
Year 4		3.0%	2.0%	6.0%
Year 5		4.5%	6.0%	9.0%
Year 6		6.0%	8.0%	12.0%
Year 7		7.5%	10.0%	15.0%

differences in vehicle operating costs. This is because in such cases road transport without the project may be minimal or even nonexistent and therefore does not provide a reliable indicator for measuring the benefits of generated activity. For rural roads the farm or small enterprise planning approach to benefit estimation outlined in Chapter 6 is likely to be more appropriate. This could be described as a producer's surplus approach. It is mainly used where a new facility is introduced that makes possible an increase in economic activity that otherwise would not have occurred. It should also be noted that benefits from improvements in rural roads can also come from cost saving in the form of reductions in labor costs in situations where without the road most things have to be carried on foot.

Improvements in roads can reduce the number of accidents. To some extent the cost of accidents can be measured by damage to vehicles. However, at least as important is the saving of human life and the saving in

Table 9.2 Annual Traffic Projections (Vehicles) and Estimation of Benefits (D$ '000) of Road Improvement Project by Year

	1	2	3	4	5	6	7	8	9	10
Annual number of vehicles—existing traffic										
Buses	7,629	7,972	8,331	8,706	9,098	9,507	9,935	10,382	10,849	11,337
Trucks	37,201	38,689	40,237	41,846	43,520	45,261	47,071	48,954	50,912	52,948
Cars	25,555	26,705	27,907	29,163	30,475	31,846	33,279	34,777	36,342	37,977
Annual number of vehicles—generated traffic										
Buses			125	261	409	570	745	779	814	850
Trucks			805	1,674	2,611	3,621	4,707	4,895	5,091	5,295
Cars			837	1,750	2,743	3,822	4,992	5,217	5,451	5,697
Savings in vehicle operating costs										
Buses		535	1,678	2,922	4,071	4,254	4,446	4,646	4,855	5,073
Trucks		2,670	8,329	14,437	20,019	20,820	21,653	22,519	23,420	24,356
Cars		1,102	3,453	6,015	8,381	8,758	9,152	9,564	9,994	10,444
Total savings in vehicle operating costs		4,306	13,460	23,374	32,471	33,832	35,250	36,728	38,268	39,873
Additional VOC from generated traffic										
Buses			141	294	461	643	840	878	918	958
Trucks			886	1,841	2,872	3,983	5,178	5,385	5,600	5,825
Cars			429	897	1,406	1,959	2,558	2,674	2,794	2,920
Total additional vehicle operating costs			1,455	3,033	4,739	6,585	8,576	8,937	9,312	9,703
Net vehicle operating cost savings										
Buses		535	1,537	2,628	3,610	3,612	3,606	3,768	3,937	4,115
Trucks		2,670	7,444	12,595	17,147	16,837	16,475	17,134	17,819	18,532
Cars		1,102	3,025	5,118	6,975	6,799	6,593	6,890	7,200	7,524
Total		4,306	12,005	20,341	27,732	27,248	26,674	27,792	28,957	30,170
Benefits from generated traffic										
Buses			169	353	553	770	1,007	1,053	1,100	1,149
Trucks			1,071	2,226	3,473	4,816	6,260	6,510	6,771	7,042
Cars			544	1,138	1,783	2,484	3,245	3,391	3,543	3,703
Total benefits from generated traffic			1,784	3,717	5,808	8,070	10,512	10,954	11,414	11,894
Total benefits		4,306	13,788	24,058	33,540	35,318	37,186	38,746	40,371	42,064

the costs of hospitalization and lost output from invalidity. Estimation of these benefits requires estimation of the value of human life and the value of lost work time. These kinds of benefits are particularly important for projects investing in safety improvements. As discussed in Chapter 8, estimation of the value of human life is controversial, and it is sometimes better to adopt a cost-effectiveness approach where additional costs are incurred for safety measures. It is easier to estimate the incremental cost per life saved than it is to put a direct value on human life. It is then possible to ask whether the benefit justifies the cost when compared to other measures intended to save lives.

Sometimes the main benefit of a transport project is the saving in time for the users of the facility. Once again the human capital approach is required in order to place a value on people's time on the basis of their notional earnings. This kind of benefit is important in urban road improvement projects and commuter railways.

Energy Projects

Estimation of the benefits from power projects depends to some extent on whether the project is introducing a new service or providing the same (or similar) service at a reduced cost. Where energy projects are concerned with providing energy at lower cost the benefits will depend in part on whether the reduced cost is all retained by the energy supplier or whether some of the cost reduction is passed on to the consumer.

If none of the benefits are passed on to the consumer, the benefit of an energy project is simply the cost savings to the energy supplier. If some of the benefits are passed on to the consumer, there will be a change in the demand for energy and a gain to consumers in the form of consumer surplus both for existing demand levels and for the increased demand generated (see Figure 9.1). Estimation of the value of this benefit will depend on the demand curve for energy. This can be difficult to establish in a situation of unstable prices. Demand for energy will also be affected by the rate of growth of the population served and the rate of growth of their income.

In many cases energy projects involve the substitution of one form of energy for another. The direct costs saved in this way may be relatively easy to estimate, but energy projects often involve environmental issues where part of the benefit of a project may come in the form of reduced environmental pollution. If environmental taxes correspond reasonably well to environmental costs, then the taxes can be used as a proxy for environmental costs. Where there are no environmental taxes or where they do not correspond well with environmental costs it will be necessary to obtain independent estimates of the cost of pollution.

In projects involving energy substitution important issues include the estimation of energy requirements and the assumed energy efficiency and energy losses associated with each energy source. The district heating example used in the discussion of cost-effectiveness analysis illustrates the point. The benefits of the wood chip boiler project could be defined in terms of the savings from not using existing oil- and gas-fired boilers. The value of these savings will depend on assumptions about existing energy efficiency and energy losses.

When electricity is provided to an area that previously had no supply the benefits will be derived from three sources:

Energy Substitution

Where households are using an existing energy source (for example, kerosene lamps for lighting or charcoal for cooking), part of the benefit is derived from savings in the cost of the alternative energy source. These savings can accrue to the household itself in the form of income or labor savings and also to the wider society through the environmental benefit from reduced deforestation caused by less charcoal use.

Consumer Surplus

For household consumption of electricity leading to new or increased energy use, the value of electricity can be measured by consumer willingness to pay. If a demand curve for energy use can be constructed, the consumer surplus can be measured as the difference between the price actually paid and willingness to pay. An example of the estimation of consumer willingness to pay is provided below for an urban water project. The principles are similar for energy projects.

Producer Surplus

Where electricity is used by producers to increase their economic activity the producer surplus approach can be used in a similar way to the case of rural road improvement but benefits are likely to be in the form of output from small-scale industrial activities rather than agricultural output.

Water Supply and Sanitation Projects

For some water and sanitation projects the most important effect may be in the form of health benefits. The higher the quality of water provided and the better the standard of sanitation, the better the health status of the population is likely to be. The problem is that it may be quite difficult to estimate the impact of improved water and sanitation services on the health status of the population. The relative importance of health benefits is likely to depend on the quality of water and sanitation provided without the project.

In some countries the availability of water may have other benefits in the form of increased agricultural output due to the use of water for irrigation and reduced time spent in water collection. For these benefits a producer surplus approach would be used. Time savings can be very important where water has to be collected from some distance away. In many societies time savings from water projects are particularly important for women, and the effect on women's time can affect both the productivity of the affected women and the health of both the women and their children.

The value of health benefits can in part be measured in terms of the reduction in loss of earnings from sickness and premature death. There are also savings in the cost of health care. However, earnings-based estimates of health benefits would give no value to the improved health of the unemployed, young people, and those who are retired. Such estimates therefore underestimate the value of improvements in health.

Attempts can also be made to measure directly the willingness of people to pay for water services. This is likely to be more important in urban water projects. However, indicators of willingness to pay are heavily influenced by past policies on charging for water and hence may not be very reliable. Sometimes indicators can be obtained by reference to the cost of other sources of supply such as water vendors or wells. Contingent valuation approaches can also be used to estimate willingness to pay.

Water and sanitation improvement projects may also have significant environmental benefits, both in terms of production (e.g., increased value of fishing) and in terms of recreational benefits and preservation or restoration of natural habitats.

As with energy and transport projects the estimation of demand for water over time is also important. Demand for water tends to increase with population and also with income level and so an analysis of water consumption that fails to take these factors into account will always underestimate requirements.

Table 9.3 outlines the kind of basic data required for estimation of the benefits of an urban water supply project designed to provide household connections to an area currently being served by a mixture of water vendors, wells, and standpipes.

Information on the existing supply can be used to give an indication of the likely demand for piped water at the proposed price of $ 0.10 per m^3. The cheaper the supply, the higher the demand is likely to be. However, it is important to take into account the ease of access and hence the opportu-

Table 9.3 Basic Data for Estimation of Benefits of an Urban Water Project by Source of Supply

	Vendors	Wells	Standpipe	Mains
Estimated consumption per household (m³)	100	125	160	200
Distribution of households supplied				
Without the project	45%	30%	25%	
With the project				
Year 2	36%	24%	20%	20%
Year 3	27%	18%	15%	40%
Year 4	18%	12%	10%	60%
Year 5	9%	6%	5%	80%
Year 6				100%
Cost of water supply (D$/m³)				
Purchase price	4.50	2.00	0.50	1.00
Labor cost for fetching water	0.40	0.60	0.80	
Total cost of water to consumer	4.90	2.60	1.30	1.00
Value of incremental water to consumers				
(D$/m³)	2.08	1.52	1.15	

Note: Initial population is 30,000 households; population growth rate is 3.0%.

nity cost of the household labor used to secure the water supply. The purchase price of the water is only part of the cost of supply.

Given the demand curve shown in Figure 9.3 it is possible to estimate the value of the additional water likely to be purchased by consumers. The value of the additional water is given by the area under the demand curve for the relevant range. Thus for consumers who currently purchase from water vendors, the first 25 m³ of extra water has a value of $(4.90 + 2.60)*25/2 = $93.75. The next 35 m³ of water has a value of $(2.60 + 1.30)*35/2 = $68.25. The final 40 m³ of extra water has a value of $(1.30 + 1.00)*40/2 = $46.00. The total value of the additional 100 m³ of water is therefore $208, an average of about $2.08 per m³. The consumer surplus obtained is the difference between the value of the water and the tariff paid of $1.00 per m³. Similar calculations can be made for other classes of consumers. It should be noted that these estimates are average values, and there may be considerable differences among consumers, particularly if there are significant variations in income levels. It is also assumed that the water supplied can be accurately metered. Clearly this is not always the case.

The next factors to consider are the effects of the growth of population and the phasing of the introduction of household connections on the demand for water. These are illustrated for a ten-year period in Table 9.4 with an assumption of population growth of 3% per annum and a five-year

Figure 9.3   Demand Curve for Urban Water Supply

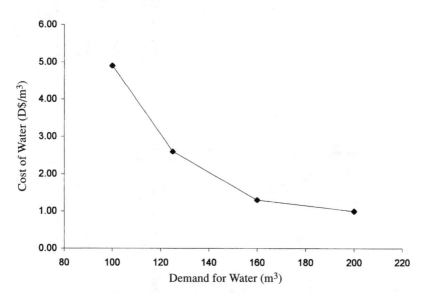

period of implementation of household connections, which impacts evenly on the reduction of the water supply from other sources. In this case it is assumed that the price of water from household connections is set at a level that is competitive with all other sources when the opportunity cost of labor is taken into account. This will not always be the case, and it cannot be automatically assumed that all other sources of supply will cease.

Table 9.4 can be used to estimate the benefits of the water supply project shown in Table 9.5. The main benefit is the saving in costs to consumers from alternative sources of supply. These benefits may be exaggerated if the existing suppliers of water are gaining some producer surplus from their activities. To the extent that the water consumers gain at the expense of income losses to water suppliers, part of the gain may simply be a distributional change. This could be a significant source of conflict if the project threatens the livelihoods of existing suppliers, and measures may be required to compensate these people in some way.

The second main source of benefit is the consumer benefit from additional water. This is derived from the measures of consumer benefit outlined in Table 9.3 and the quantity of additional water outlined in Table 9.4.

The third source of benefit is the labor saving to the households who no longer have to carry water significant distances. This benefit is not a direct financial benefit and may be perceived in different ways by different members of the household depending on who carries the water and who

Table 9.4 Estimation of Water Demand for Urban Water Project by Year ('000 m³)

Year	1	2	3	4	5	6	7	8	9	10
Population ('000 Households)	30.9	31.8	32.8	33.8	34.8	35.8	36.9	38.0	39.1	40.3
Water supply without the project										
Vendors	1,391	1,432	1,475	1,519	1,565	1,612	1,660	1,710	1,761	1,814
Wells	1,159	1,194	1,229	1,266	1,304	1,343	1,384	1,425	1,468	1,512
Standpipes	1,236	1,273	1,311	1,351	1,391	1,433	1,476	1,520	1,566	1,613
Total	3,785	3,899	4,016	4,136	4,260	4,388	4,520	4,655	4,795	4,939
Water supply with the project										
Vendors	1,391	1,146	885	608	313					
Wells	1,159	955	738	506	261					
Standpipes	1,236	1,018	787	540	278					
Mains		1,273	2,623	4,052	5,565	7,164	7,379	7,601	7,829	8,063
Total	3,785	4,392	5,032	5,706	6,417	7,164	7,379	7,601	7,829	8,063
Incremental water supply										
Vendors		−286	−590	−912	−1,252	−1,612	−1,660	−1,710	−1,761	−1,814
Wells		−239	−492	−760	−1,043	−1,343	−1,384	−1,425	−1,468	−1,512
Standpipes		−255	−525	−810	−1,113	−1,433	−1,476	−1,520	−1,566	−1,613
Mains		1,273	2,623	4,052	5,565	7,164	7,379	7,601	7,829	8,063
Additional Consumption		493	1,016	1,570	2,156	2,776	2,859	2,945	3,034	3,125
Previously supplied by vendors		286	590	912	1,252	1,612	1,660	1,710	1,761	1,814
Previously supplied by wells		143	295	456	626	806	830	855	881	907
Previously supplied by standpipes		64	131	203	278	358	369	380	391	403

Table 9.5 Estimation of Benefits of Urban Water Project by Year (D$'000)

	1	2	3	4	5	6	7	8	9	10
Cost savings										
Previously supplied by vendors		1,289	2,655	4,102	5,634	7,254	7,471	7,696	7,926	8,164
Previously supplied by wells		477	983	1,519	2,087	2,687	2,767	2,850	2,936	3,024
Previously supplied by standpipes		127	262	405	556	716	738	760	783	806
Total cost savings		1,894	3,901	6,027	8,277	10,657	10,977	11,306	11,645	11,994
Family Labor Saving										
Previously supplied by vendors		115	236	365	501	645	664	684	705	726
Previously supplied by wells		143	295	456	626	806	830	855	881	907
Previously supplied by standpipes		204	420	648	890	1,146	1,181	1,216	1,253	1,290
Total family labor saving		461	951	1,469	2,017	2,597	2,675	2,755	2,838	2,923
Consumer benefits from additional water										
Previously supplied by vendors		596	1,227	1,896	2,604	3,353	3,453	3,557	3,664	3,774
Previously supplied by wells		218	449	694	954	1,228	1,265	1,303	1,342	1,382
Previously supplied by standpipes		73	151	233	320	412	424	437	450	464
Total consumer benefits from additional water		887	1,828	2,824	3,878	4,993	5,142	5,297	5,456	5,619
Revenue to water project		1,273	2,623	4,052	5,565	7,164	7,379	7,601	7,829	8,063
Net benefits to consumers		1,969	4,057	6,268	8,608	11,082	11,415	11,757	12,110	12,473
Total benefits		3,242	6,679	10,320	14,172	18,247	18,794	19,358	19,939	20,537

controls the income from which the water bills are paid. The assumption that a household can be treated as a unit is not always valid where there are conflicts of interest within the household.

The benefits are divided up between the consumers and the water project, and the division of the benefits depends on the tariff charged. In this case about 60% of the benefits accrue to the consumers and 40% to the water project. However, the water project will have to pay for the costs and so the overwhelming majority of the net benefits accrue to the consumers.

Estimation of benefits using the approach outlined above assumes that the quality of the water supplied is broadly comparable between different sources. If this is not the case, there may be additional benefits in health improvements from cleaner water. The measurement of health benefits is discussed below.

Health Projects

Since health projects are usually intended to have a direct effect on health the estimation of their impact may be slightly easier than for water and sanitation projects where the effect may be more indirect. In principle it should be possible to measure the benefits of health projects in terms of reduced mortality rates and reduced morbidity (sickness) rates. These could then be valued according to the loss of earnings caused by premature death or sickness. There may also be cost savings from reduced expenditure on health care in some cases, such as immunization programs.

The approaches used in valuing human life were discussed in Chapter 8 along with the problems with using such approaches.

If estimates of the value of an average human life of a particular age group are regarded as *minimum* estimates of the benefits, such approaches could be used to justify some projects on the grounds that the real value of the benefits would certainly not be less than those estimated. In other words, if a project could be justified using such an approach, it is unlikely that there would be any reason to reject it.

Although a number of cost-benefit studies of health projects have been undertaken they are comparatively rare. In practice cost-effectiveness indicators are more likely to be used. The example used in Chapter 4 made comparisons in terms of lives saved. This could be regarded as a simple variant of the years of life gained (YLG) approach. The YLG measure is useful for assessing cost effectiveness where mortality is significant, but it has the disadvantage that it takes no account of the quality of life and puts no value on the reduction of sickness.

A particular issue for health projects is how to compare the effects of health interventions with different or multiple outcomes. In principle economic rationalization of expenditure on health services requires the comparison of different activities with different combinations of reduction in morbidity and mortality. To make such comparisons a standard measure is required.

Recent approaches have tried to measure health impact in terms of healthy years of life gained (HYLG) and gains in disability adjusted life years (DALYs). The HYLG measure uses weights to compare morbidity effects with mortality effects. A year of life with some degree of morbidity has a lower value than a healthy year, and the weight given is lower the higher the degree of morbidity or disability. It can be argued that such a measure has the advantage of being able to combine medical judgments (in determining the weights) with the economic logic of measuring the costs.

The DALY measure is similar but also takes into account the age of the population affected, with the highest weight attached to years of high productivity. In this respect it is controversial since years of life gained by young adults are given a higher value than those of old people and children.

More general approaches such as the HYLG and DALY approaches are useful in making comparisons between different health activities, but they can also be more demanding in data requirements than simpler measures. Whatever the measure, there is always likely to be a high level of uncertainty as to whether the proposed intervention will actually achieve the impact expected. In this respect health projects are no different than any other projects although the degree of uncertainty and therefore the potential for disagreement may be higher.

Education Projects

The advantages and limitations of the human capital approach can also be seen in the valuation of education benefits. In principle the value of education and training projects can be determined by estimating the present value of the difference in earnings between a person with a certain level of education or training and a similar person without such education or training.

In practice there are considerable difficulties in using this approach. The major ones are

- Many people value education for its own sake. They do not necessarily perceive education as just a means of earning more money. This would suggest that human capital approaches underestimate the value of education.
- Differences in education may be reflections of other differences

such as in social background or intelligence. It may be very difficult to make true comparisons that eliminate the effect of other influences. This might suggest that human capital approaches could overestimate the value of education.
- The approach requires a lot of data on earnings profiles over a long period of time. Such data are not usually available. The approach also assumes that the past is a good guide to what will happen in the future. This might not be the case.

In undertaking cost-benefit analysis of education projects it is important to consider both private and social costs and benefits. The benefits of education projects accrue primarily to the individual, although there are also clear external benefits derived from improved literacy and social education. In most countries a large part of the cost of education is borne by the state. This is justified partly on the grounds of educational externalities but more fundamentally on distributional grounds. It is argued that children have a right to education irrespective of the wealth of their parents. Most education projects therefore involve public expenditure leading to largely private benefit. Attempts to introduce school fees and to make people pay for uniforms and books introduce an element of private cost, while foregone income opportunities are important as children get older. All these factors need to be taken into account in conducting any cost-benefit analysis of education projects.

As with health projects, human capital approaches to benefit estimation can be used as an indication of order of magnitude so long as the size of the margin of error in such estimates is recognized. Cost-benefit analysis is most likely to be of use for vocational training and higher education where the connection between training or education levels and earnings is clearest and most valid.

It is likely that other considerations will always be important in general primary and secondary education and that cost-effectiveness approaches will be at least as useful as attempts to measure benefits in money terms for such projects. In these cases it is more likely that general policy objectives such as universal primary education will be important and that the role of the project or program analyst will be restricted to the question of the most cost-effective way of achieving a given educational outcome. Nevertheless it is worth examining how such outcomes are defined. Measurement of numbers of years spent in school says nothing about how much the children have learned. More appropriate indicators would include some indicator of achievement such as measures of literacy and numeracy. Even these indiators can be open to dispute because they focus on narrow aspects of learning and ignore the synthesis of different skills and the importance of wider knowledge.

Further Reading

Useful general discussions of the issues raised in this chapter can be found in Curry and Weiss (2000: chap. 7), Belli et al. (1998: chaps. 8–11 and 13), Perkins (1994: chaps. 11 and 12), and Snell (1997: chap. 4). Winpenny (1983: chaps. 4–13) is useful for checklists.

Adler (1987), Dickey and Miller (1984), and Transport and Road Research Laboratory (1988) are useful sources on road project appraisal. Foster and Knowles (1982) is useful on appraisal of railway projects. Asian Development Bank (1998a) is useful for appraisal of telecommunications projects.

Ali (1991) provides a relatively recent source on energy projects. A case study of an energy project is in Londero (1996a: chap. 10). Turvey and Anderson (1977) is a useful but dated source.

Asian Development Bank (1998b) and Asian Development Bank (1999) are useful sources on water and sanitation projects, as is Commission of the European Communities (1998). Cummings et al. (1996) and Klumper (1996) are also useful, as are Overseas Development Administration (1984) and Whittinton and Swarna (1994).

Adhikari et al. (1999) and Asian Development Bank (2000) are useful recent contributions on health sector projects. Birley (1995) provides a comprehensive discussion of the health impact assessment of projects. A useful but older text on economic analysis of health care is Carrin (1984). Anand and Hanson (1998) discuss use of the DALY measure. Hammer (1993) and Kim and Benton (1995) provide case studies of the analysis of specific health interventions. A number of useful articles on the use of cost effectiveness in the health sector in a developing country context have been published in the journal *Health Policy and Planning*.

Some of the most important work on the analysis of investment in education can be seen in the various works by Psachoropoulos. Bennell (1995) gives a useful critique of the use of rates of return in education. Johnes (1993) is a general text on the economics of education.

Notes

1. A number of engineering models are available for computing vehicle operating costs according to the expected condition of the road surface. The World Bank's highway design model (HDM) is a frequently used example.

10

Opportunity Cost and the Basis for Economic Valuation

Opportunity Cost and Economic Analysis

The principle of opportunity cost underlies all estimation of values in economic efficiency analysis. This principle states that the economic value of a resource is determined by its next best alternative use. The idea that the value of a project is determined by the difference between the assumed situation with and without project is an application of the opportunity cost principle. When we define the without project situation we try to establish the next best alternative outcome to the one defined by the project. In principle we can apply the with and without project approach to the valuation of all of the costs of a project, and we can follow a similar logic in defining the economic value of the benefits. The economic value of each cost or benefit item can be determined by examining the indirect effects of purchasing or creating the item with and without the project, or it can be done by investigating the prices of the costs and benefits to determine whether those prices reflect opportunity costs.[1]

Whenever the opportunity cost of an item is not equal to its market price there is an argument for using *shadow prices*. Shadow prices are prices that reflect the opportunity cost of resources and therefore they measure the economic cost or benefit of the item concerned. They can also be called economic prices.[2]

The use of the opportunity cost principle in economic analysis can be explained by investigating how it is applied to the basic resource categories that are sometimes described as *primary factors*. These will be considered in turn.

The Opportunity Cost of Land

The opportunity cost of land can be investigated by asking what the alternative uses of the land might be. *Urban land* can be used for houses, offices, shops, and factories. *Rural land* is normally used for crops, pasture, and forestry. The opportunity cost of rural land is likely to be very important in the economic assessment of any agricultural or agroindustrial project, and it can also be important in road projects where roads take up large areas of land.

Although the financial analysis of a project might enter the cost of land as a single capital item (land purchase), the opportunity cost is the value of the surplus produced by that land in its next most profitable use. This surplus could be estimated on the basis of a land rent or on the basis of the surplus earned from the next most profitable activity. The land rent approach is usually taken for urban land because of the diversity of uses to which urban land could be put. In the case of rural land it is normal to try to estimate the surplus in the next best use indirectly through the without project situation.

For example, a proposed sugar mill may induce farmers to change from growing bananas (the next best alternative crop) to growing sugarcane. The opportunity cost of the land used for growing sugarcane is the expected surplus (or gross margin) earned from bananas. This surplus may be valued in terms of the lost production of bananas net of the cost of producing them. In doing this, the opportunity cost of land is taken into account through the specification of the without project situation. We would record the foregone banana production as a cost (foregone revenue) and the costs of growing the bananas as a benefit (costs avoided).

The opportunity cost of land is the surplus foregone in altering land use. It is usually assumed that this value remains constant over the life of a project. However, it is important to recognize that if, without the project, this surplus is expected either to increase or decrease due to factors such as exogenous technological change or deteriorating soil fertility, account should be taken of the expected increase or decrease in the opportunity cost of land over the lifetime of the project.

The Opportunity Cost of Labor

The opportunity cost of labor usually varies significantly among occupational groups and often among regions. Most project appraisals distinguish between *skilled* and *unskilled labor,* the most common assumption being that skilled labor is in scarce supply and has an opportunity cost equal to or greater than its market price, while unskilled labor is in excess supply and has an opportunity cost below its market price.

The first assumption implies that skilled workers are able to obtain the same salary whether they work on the project in question or on another project. Such an assumption is probably reasonable for many countries, and the basis for making any other assumption can be difficult to establish.

However, there are some countries where certain categories of skilled workers are in excess supply in relation to existing economic conditions. In such cases the next best alternative job may command a lower salary than that offered by the project. In other countries, particularly those undergoing very rapid structural change, there may be a shortage of skilled labor. This does not usually mean that skilled workers would earn less on the project under consideration than in their alternative occupations; after all in such a situation it is unlikely that they would move. However, it may mean that their employment imposes losses on the alternative activities that lose their services, and it is possible that such losses could be greater than the saving in salaries. Such a situation could arise because the replacement of a skilled worker might lead to additional training costs or other cost increases caused by the employment of a less experienced replacement with a lower level of productivity.

The opportunity cost of urban unskilled labor depends on alternative employment possibilities. Where unemployment is high and workers do not have access to land as an alternative source of income, the opportunity cost of labor may be very low. This may be the case in highly urbanized societies or where population density is high. Even in these cases it is unlikely that the opportunity cost will be zero. There are some additional costs involved in working, such as the transport cost involved in going to work, and unemployed workers may also have some alternative sources of income at certain times of year (for example periods of peak labor demand in the rural areas). To the workers themselves the opportunity cost of going to work is also affected by any taxes they have to pay, even though, from a national point of view, these would be regarded as transfer payments.

Ideas about the opportunity cost of formal-sector unskilled labor usually stem from models of migration.[3] Unskilled workers migrate from the rural areas and the *informal sector* to the urban areas and the *formal sector* in search of higher earnings. This has happened in the course of the development of almost every country in the world and occurs most readily when there is a significant gap between urban, or formal, sector and rural, or informal, sector wage levels. Such a gap might exist due to factors such as minimum wage legislation or trade union power, either of which could keep the formal-sector wage for unskilled labor at a level above the supply price. It should be noted that the gap between formal-sector and informal-sector wages is not just caused by the strong bargaining power of formal-sector workers. It is also likely to be related to the relatively weak bargaining power of the rural and urban poor who may have very limited access to land and capital. The observation that the opportunity cost of labor is less than the value of formal-sector wages is the result of a combination of economic factors and does not necessarily provide a justification for reducing formal-sector wages or for constraining the rights of trade unions.

Differences between prices and opportunity costs can have policy implications, but they are the result of the complex interaction of diverse economic factors and therefore need to be interpreted carefully.

It is usually supposed that the opportunity cost of unskilled labor in the formal sector is the value of alternative earnings in rural areas, either as a small farmer or as a casual laborer. The most common form of estimate would be the casual daily wage rate multiplied by the number of days worked in a year. Such estimates can be very crude, or they can be the result of a detailed survey of unskilled laborers and migrants from the rural areas. A comprehensive survey should take account of a number of factors including seasonal and regional variations, variations according to gender and age, and consideration of the wage level that might be regarded as the minimum acceptable to justify the effort of working.[4]

The opportunity cost of informal-sector unskilled rural labor (e.g., casual agricultural laborers) is usually assumed to be equal to the market wage if there are no institutional regulations preventing the equalization of the supply price of labor and the market wage. Whether this is the case or not depends on how the labor market works in the rural areas. Even if the market wage is relatively freely determined, there may be circumstances when it is necessary to pay close attention to the value of the commodities produced by laborers, particularly if the opportunity cost of those commodities does not correspond very closely to their market price due to factors such as discriminatory taxes and subsidies.

There may also be a difference between the opportunity costs of unskilled labor in the formal sector in rural areas and in urban areas. The assumption that the ultimate source of recruitment of additional unskilled labor is the agricultural sector may not be valid in the cases of relatively industrialized countries or for urban employment in countries with relatively high levels of urbanization and urban underemployment. Excess labor may exist in the urban areas where the opportunity cost might be defined by informal-sector earnings or earnings from part-time work. Where there is partial migration from the rural areas and partial recruitment from the urban informal sector the opportunity cost may be defined as a weighted average of rural and urban informal-sector earnings with weights determined by the migration patterns of entrants into the formal-sector workforce.

In some countries it can be helpful to distinguish between skilled and semiskilled workers. This is likely to be important in the case of transitional economies undergoing industrial restructuring where there may be significant underemployment of urban-based, semiskilled workers. In these situations it may be advisable to define a category of semiskilled labor whose opportunity cost is determined primarily by earnings in urban occupations in sectors in decline.

In large countries there may be a significant variation in the opportunity cost of labor from one region to another. In such countries it is advisable to categorize unskilled labor by region. Such regions are usually defined by administrative boundaries, but they could also be defined by ecological zone in countries where excess labor is primarily located in the agricultural sector and where the composition of agricultural production varies significantly from one zone to another.

Traded Goods and Foreign Exchange

Traded goods are those goods that are imported or exported. The opportunity cost of traded goods to an economy is the *border price,* cost insurance and freight (CIF) for imports and free on board (FOB) for exports.[5] For example, a country may be able to produce sugar to satisfy the local market. The next best alternative is to import the sugar. The value of the sugar produced is then the CIF price that has been saved. Similarly, a textile project may use locally produced cotton lint as a raw material, the alternative being to export the cotton lint. The opportunity cost of using the cotton lint for the textile project is the export price (FOB) foregone.

The above cases referred to import substitution and export replacement. Of course some projects also purchase imports directly and produce outputs that are directly exported. The economic cost or value of these is also determined by their border price.

For some commodities the relevant world price may be hard to identify. This is the case for commodities where the world market is the small residual that lies outside commodity agreements, particularly if the world price has a tendency to be unstable. It is also the case for specialized products where product differentiation makes the definition of a single world price difficult. These are measurement problems and are best dealt with through careful analysis of the market for the relevant product, including the use of sensitivity analysis where appropriate (see Chapter 15). They do not affect the general principle that the opportunity cost of a traded good is its border price.

Some commodities may be *tradable* but not traded. Such a situation can occur when the import of commodities that are produced locally is restricted. Should trade be regarded as an opportunity cost in this case? This really depends on whether there is any likelihood that the government will change its policies. If it will not, there is no point in regarding trade as a possible opportunity, since the government has excluded the possibility of trade. With the widespread liberalization of trade such cases are increasingly rare. A more likely case could occur when the local price is higher than any conceivable export price and lower than any conceivable import price. In such cases the good is effectively nontraded and can be valued on the basis of willingness to pay or on the basis of long-run marginal cost of production (see below).

In some cases a traded good may be imported in some years and exported in others. In such cases the most sensible approach is to take a weighted average of the values determined by the import price and the export price with the weights being determined by the expected future levels of exports and imports. Such an approach may be based on past import and export data, but it is supposed to be a forecast and so it should take account of any significant trends over time.

Some goods are not traded, but their economic value is derived from a traded good. Such cases can be found in the agricultural sector where perishable products have to undergo primary processing before they can be exported. Examples of such products, which can be described as indirectly traded goods, include green leaf tea, sugarcane, and fresh milk. Usually it is not important to estimate the economic value of such products in their unprocessed form. The benefits of projects aimed at increasing the production of indirectly traded products are estimated on the basis of the value of the processed product, and the costs of the processor are also taken into account. The price paid to the farmer is recorded as a benefit to the farmer and a cost to the processor and therefore disappears from the analysis. However, there are times when estimates are required for global average values of agricultural production including indirectly traded products. In such cases the economic value of the indirectly traded good is obtained by subtracting processing and marketing costs from the border price of the processed product.

All commonly used methods of economic analysis use border prices in the valuation of traded goods. This does not imply acceptance of the justice of the existing international economic order or a commitment to free trade. It is merely a recognition that trade is an alternative opportunity to local production or local use. As in the case of the opportunity cost of labor, it is possible to make recommendations on trade policy based on observations about the difference between market prices and opportunity costs, but such recommendations rest on judgments about the efficiency and desirability of different degrees of trade liberalization. Such judgments should take account of wider issues and should not depend on the situation of a single project.

The economic value of traded goods is determined by the border price, which is a foreign exchange value. The opportunity cost valuation of traded goods therefore also depends on the opportunity cost of foreign exchange. If an extra unit of foreign exchange is used for purchasing inputs for a project, what is its opportunity cost? This will be determined by the next best alternative use of the foreign exchange either for purchasing additional imports or for using goods that otherwise would be exported. These considerations are important for determining the economic value of a unit of foreign exchange in terms of local values.

Nontraded Goods

Some goods may be nontraded because of government policies. Others may be nontraded because trade is either impossible or pointless. Internal transport and construction are nontraded by definition because they occur within the country. For many countries public utilities such as water supply and electricity are nontraded, although there are also countries where these are traded, at least in some regions. The production of many building materials is also nontraded in many countries because the cost of transport means that the local price is always below the import price and above the export price. Similar considerations apply to a number of perishable or low-value agricultural products. What is the opportunity cost of using these items?

The answer to the question really depends on whether use of the item in question will cause more units of that item to be produced or whether it will deprive another person of its use. If more items are produced, the opportunity cost is the cost of producing the extra items. Since projects are reasonably long-term activities, the relevant cost is usually defined as the long-run marginal cost of production.

If an alternative user is deprived of the use of that item, the opportunity cost is the price that the alternative user would have been willing to pay. Such estimates would be based on the local market price, but they might have to be adjusted if the item concerned were subject to rationing because the existence of excess demand would indicate that willingness to pay is greater than the market price. Situations of excess demand do sometimes occur for public utilities in the short run, but it is usually assumed that, over the life of a project, the production of most nontraded goods can be expanded to meet additional demand.

A different approach may need to be taken for the valuation of nontraded outputs. In such cases the benefit is likely to be defined by the willingness of consumers to pay for the product. Here the opportunity cost is defined by the value of the goods consumers would have been willing to sacrifice in order to obtain the benefit of the good or service produced, that is, their willingness to pay. If the extra production of the nontraded good leads to a change in price or if something is made available that was previously unavailable, some of the additional consumers may have been willing to pay more than the project price. In such a case they would have gained some *consumer surplus*. Valuation of the nontraded output would then be based on the market price plus an element of consumer surplus (see Chapter 9).

For some nontraded outputs the market price may provide a reasonable estimate of value. This applies particularly to goods and services in competitive supply with many substitutes. The most obvious example is perishable low-value agricultural products where local market prices are not controlled. In these cases the local market prices reflect willingness to pay, and therefore the market price is likely to be a reasonable indicator of the economic value of additional production.

The Opportunity Cost of Capital (Investment Funds)

The opportunity cost of capital for an individual, a company, or an economy is the rate of return available on the next best alternative project. For an individual or a company, commercial rates of interest may give a reasonable guide. The alternative to investing in a project is to lend money to a bank or to another organization offering a rate of interest. However, market interest rates are influenced by the rate of inflation and cannot be used in any constant price analysis unless they are first adjusted for expected future inflation to give an estimated real rate of interest.

For an economy, estimation of the opportunity cost of capital may be difficult. It is necessary to have an idea of the likely rates of return on alternative investment projects. One way would be to rank all possible projects according to their economic IRR and to draw a cutoff line at the point where investment funds are exhausted. In practice it is unlikely that projects can be listed in this way very easily, particularly when investment funds are being used in sectors where benefits are hard to enumerate or when it is difficult to transfer investment from one sector to another. It is also unlikely that there will be complete consistency in the way projects are prepared and in the parameters that are used. Furthermore it is not obvious what time scale should be used in considering which projects define the opportunity cost of capital. The value obtained by considering only the projects proposed for one particular year is unlikely to be very stable.

Estimation of the opportunity cost of capital from the national point of view is also affected by some other considerations. There may be a difference between private and collective views of time preference. It may be possible to borrow funds from abroad or to lend them abroad. It may also be possible to transfer resources from consumption to investment or vice versa. All these factors can influence the selection of a discount rate for economic analysis. They are described in more detail in Chapter 12.

Disaggregation of Market
Price Values into Primary Factors

The economic values of the cost and benefit categories used in project analysis can be estimated using the following steps: (1) Identify the opportunity cost of the relevant item; (2) disaggregate (break down or decompose) the market price value into primary factors; and (3) revalue each component according to the opportunity cost values of the primary factors. For such disaggregation a typical list of primary factors might be:

Foreign Exchange	(F)
Skilled Labor	(SL)
Unskilled Labor	(UL)
Domestic Resources[6]	(D)
Taxes and Transfers	(T)

In principle, some of these categories could be broken down further into various types of skilled or unskilled labor or, in the case of taxes and transfers, into taxes and subsidies (which affect government income) and other income transfers (such as excess or subnormal profits of enterprises).

The first step in the disaggregation of cost or benefit items is to define the basis for valuation. For traded goods the basis for valuation is the appropriate border price, while for nontraded inputs it is likely to be the long-run marginal cost of production. Disaggregation of the values of traded and nontraded goods is discussed in turn:

Traded Goods

In the case of traded goods it is necessary to relate the project price to the border price, taking account of any intermediate costs or cost savings. To do this it is sometimes helpful to draw a simple sketch map (Figure 10.1) to derive a border parity price at the project. Figure 10.1 can be used to illustrate a number of scenarios:

Scenario A. The project is located at the farm and is producing an exported crop. The value of the crop to the economy is determined by the FOB price (X), but, in order to realize the export price, it is necessary to incur transport costs (Tr_D), port handling costs (P), and an export tax (T_x). The project price (P_x) is therefore given by:

$$P_x = X - Tr_D - P - T_x \tag{10.1}$$

where X is a foreign exchange benefit; Tr_D and P are local costs; and T_x is a transfer payment.

Scenario B. The project is located at the farm and requires an imported input. The cost to the economy is determined by the CIF price, but, to get the imported product to the project, additional costs are incurred for import

Figure 10.1   Mapping Border Parity Prices for the Disaggregation of Traded Goods

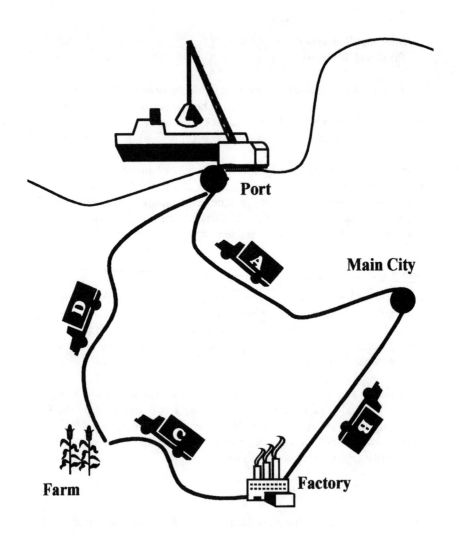

duties (T_m), port handling costs (P), and transport to the project (Tr_D). The price paid by the project (P_m) will be given by:

$$P_m = M + T_m + P + Tr_D \qquad (10.2)$$

where M is a foreign exchange cost; Tr_D and P are local costs; and T_m is a transfer payment.

Scenario C. The project is located at the farm and is producing an import substitute for which the market is in the main city. The value of the crop to the economy is determined by the CIF price (M), but additional costs for import duties (T_m), port handling costs (P), and transport to the market (Tr_A) are incurred when the product is imported. When the product is produced locally, additional transport costs to the market (Tr_B+Tr_C) are incurred. The project price (P_m) will therefore be given by:

$$P_m = M + T_m + P + (Tr_A - Tr_B - Tr_C) \qquad (10.3)$$

where M is a foreign exchange cost; Tr_A, Tr_B, Tr_C and P are local costs; and T_m is a transfer payment. $Tr_A - Tr_B - Tr_C$ could be either positive or negative depending on the relative value of transport costs from the project to the market and from the port to the market.

Scenario D. The project is located at the factory and processes produce from the farm that otherwise would have been exported. The cost to the economy is determined by the FOB price of the foregone export, but, in order to realize the export price, it is necessary to incur transport costs (Tr_D), port handling costs (P), and an export tax (T_x). In order to transport the produce from the farm to the factory it is necessary to incur some transport costs (Tr_C). The price to the project (P_x) will therefore be given by:

$$P_x = X - (Tr_D - Tr_C) - P - T_x \qquad (10.4)$$

where X is a foreign exchange benefit; Tr_D, Tr_C and P are local costs; and T_x is a transfer payment. Again the net transport cost could be positive or negative depending on the relative value of transport costs from the farm to the factory and from the farm to the port.

Scenario E. The project is located at the farm and is producing an import substitute for which the main market is in the main city. However, the output of the project is unprocessed and the imported product is processed. Therefore, to be able to compare the project output with the imported alternative, it is necessary to consider the processing costs at the factory and the ratio between the quantity of the raw material and the quantity of processed product. The value of the crop to the economy is determined by the CIF price (M), but additional costs for import duties (T_m), port handling costs (P), and transport to the market (Tr_A) are incurred when the product is imported. When the product is produced locally, additional transport costs from the factory to the market (Tr_B) are incurred as well as the cost of transporting the crop from the farm to the factory (Tr_C) and processing it (Pr). Processing the product locally also gives rise to a by-product (B), which is sold locally. The rate at which the crop is converted to the processed product is R. The project price (P_m) will therefore be given by:

$$P_m = ((M + T_m + P + (Tr_A - Tr_B) - Pr + B)/R) - Tr_C \qquad (10.5)$$

where M is a foreign exchange cost; Tr_A, Tr_B, Tr_C, P, and Pr are local costs; B is a local benefit; and T_m is a transfer payment. Again net transport costs could be positive or negative. It is assumed in this example that the values of processing costs and by-products are defined per unit of the processed product, not per unit of raw material.

Scenario F. The project is located at the farm and is producing an export, but the crop has to be processed before it can be exported. The value of the crop to the economy is determined by the FOB price (X), but, in order to realize the export price, it is necessary to incur transport costs from the factory to the port $(Tr_B + Tr_A)$, port handling costs (P), an export tax (T_x), processing costs (Pr), and transport from the farm to the factory (Tr_C). Processing the product locally also gives rise to a by-product (B), which is sold locally. The rate at which the crop is converted to the processed product is R. The project price (P_x) will therefore be given by:

$$P_x = ((X - (Tr_B + Tr_A) - P - T_x - Pr + B)/R) - Tr_C \qquad (10.6)$$

where X is a foreign exchange benefit; Tr_A, Tr_B, Tr_C, P, and Pr are local costs; B is a local benefit; and T_x is a transfer payment.

In all of the above cases some of the local costs could be disaggregated further if the relevant information were available. Some numerical examples are outlined below to illustrate both simple and more sophisticated approaches to the disaggregation of the market prices of traded goods.

Example 1 (Export). A project is established to produce coffee for export. The project is paid D$16.50 for each kilo of coffee. The FOB price for the coffee is D$20.50 per kilo.[7] Transport costs are D$0.75 per kilo, and other local costs are D$1.50 per kilo. The government charges D$1.50 per kilo export duty, and the marketing board makes D$0.25 per kilo excess profits. The basic breakdown for coffee is shown in Table 10.1.

Table 10.1   Disaggregation of the Project Price for Exported Coffee

	Price/Cost (D$)	Foreign Exchange (F)	Domestic Resources (D)	Taxes and Transfers (T)
FOB price	20.50	20.50		
Export tax	−1.50			−1.50
Transport	−0.75		−0.75	
Other local costs	−1.50		−1.50	
Excess profits	−0.25			−0.25
Project price (D$)	16.50	20.50	−2.25	−1.75
(%)		124.2%	−13.6%	−10.6%

The composition in terms of primary factors of the local price of coffee is 124.2% foreign exchange, −10.6% import duties and other transfers, and −13.6% local resources. Transfer payments could in turn be broken down into taxes and excess profits. If sufficient information were available, the local costs (D) (i.e., the nontraded costs such as transport and handling) could be broken down further into the main primary factors. As is usually the case for exports, the foreign exchange content is over 100% because the FOB price exceeds the price paid to the project. The other items represent the additional costs that cause the FOB price to exceed the price to the project. They appear as negative values because they are additional costs.

Example 2 (Import Substitute).   A project is proposed to provide support services to farmers growing wheat. The project is expected to result in an increase in the quantity of wheat available for sale to other regions. The project area normally sells its surplus wheat to the urban areas, which would otherwise rely on imported wheat. The following information is available:

- Farmers sell their wheat at D$2,400 per ton, but it can be imported at a CIF price of $150 (D$1,500) per ton.
- Transport costs from the project area to the wholesale market are D$300 per ton.
- Transport of imported wheat from the port to the wholesale market costs D$600 per ton.
- The government charges 20% duty on imported wheat (D$300 per ton).
- Port charges for imported wheat are D$100 per ton.
- Locally purchased wheat has an administrative and marketing cost of D$200, while for imported wheat it is D$300.
- The wheat marketing board makes a loss of D$50 per ton when it buys locally produced wheat.

- Transport costs are estimated to have a foreign exchange component of 60% and a tax component of 10%. All other costs other than import duties are assumed to be local.

The process of estimating the breakdown of the price paid to farmers is illustrated in Table 10.2.

The composition in terms of primary factors of the local price of wheat is 70.0% foreign exchange, 17.9% import duties and other transfers, and 12.1% local resources. For every D$1,000 worth of local wheat production, D$700 worth of foreign exchange is saved while D$179 of the price paid represents duties and excess profits lost by the government and the marketing board. A total of D$121 worth of net local resource costs is saved by producing the wheat locally. A similar process of estimation could have been undertaken if the project had been a tea project leading to replacement of wheat with vegetables. In this case the wheat is a foregone output (a cost). The designation of with the project and without the project would be reversed but the breakdown into primary factors would be the same.

The above case shows both the primary breakdown into cost components and also a secondary breakdown of the cost components themselves into basic resource categories. In principle it would be possible to do further iterations until the local cost element is reduced to those items whose values are determined entirely in the domestic economy. In practice it is

Table 10.2 Disaggregation of the Project Price for an Import Substitute

	Cost	F	D	T
With the project				
Price to farmers	2,400			
Transport from farm to market	300	180	90	30
Administrative and handling costs	200		200	
Cost of wheat to market	2,900	−180	−290	−30
Without the project				
CIF price	1,500	1,500		
Import duty	300			300
Port handling charges	100		100	
Transport from port to market	600	360	180	60
Administrative and handling costs	300		300	
Cost of wheat to market	2,800	1,860	580	360
Net loss to marketing board	100			100
Breakdown of farm gate price (%)	2,400	1,680	290	430
		70.0%	12.1%	17.9%

usually unnecessary to undertake more than two or three iterations to get a fairly accurate breakdown. A more detailed example of how a breakdown of transport costs can be determined is illustrated below in the nontraded goods example.

Nontraded Goods

The basic principle behind breaking down the value of nontraded goods is that of long-run marginal cost estimation. For the variable inputs the procedure is fairly straightforward as long as data are available. For overheads the procedure can be more complicated.

If the activity concerned is one where there are a number of different producers, it can be assumed that overheads are included as part of long-run marginal cost because changes in the demand for the product could lead to a change in the number of producers rather than a change in the output of a single producer. Where there is only one producer and/or there is excess capacity in the sector over the medium to long term it can be reasonable to exclude some overhead costs in the estimation of long-run marginal cost because a change in the demand for the product would have no change on the level of overheads.

Sometimes it is difficult to decide on the extent to which overheads might be variable in the long run. It may be difficult to distinguish between those overhead costs that can be treated as variable in the long run and those for which excess capacity can be assumed over the foreseeable future for the likely changes in demand. The electricity sector provides an example. Maintenance of power lines is an important activity, and the cost may be fairly constant over a relatively large range of power supply. On the other hand, purchase of turbine spares can be regarded as a variable cost in long-run cost estimation because the amount of spares required will depend at least in part on the level of demand for power. Data are not usually available in a form that allows such judgments to be made in a clear-cut way, and so inevitably this introduces some margin of error in any estimates. However, where the level of public infrastructure provision is well below the desired long-term level, all elements of cost can be treated as potentially variable.

Further problems are introduced by trying to reconcile accounting measures of the cost of capital used with the economic concept of the annualized cost of capital assets. Accounting measures of depreciation are usually based on historic cost, and they do not take account of the return that capital should earn. They therefore invariably understate the economic cost of capital. The problem of using historic cost depreciation measures is more serious the higher the rate of inflation and the longer the time period before the last asset revaluation was undertaken. The problem of taking into account the return that capital should earn is more significant the longer the life of the asset and the higher the assumed rate of discount.

In principle all depreciation values should be revalued to try to obtain as closely as possible the current replacement values. Assumptions have to be made about the average life of the assets, and an adjustment factor can then be applied. This factor is based on the principle that an economic measure of the cost of capital should use a capital recovery factor for the period of the life of the asset rather than division of the value of the asset by its life as in straight line depreciation. The depreciation adjustment factor for a nontraded sector i (DAF_i) is given by:

$$DAF_i = CRF_i \times AL_i \tag{10.7}$$

where CRF_i is the capital recovery factor for the assumed life, AL_i, of the asset in question. In calculating the capital recovery factor a value for the discount rate must be assumed. Using this economic definition of the cost of capital it is quite possible for a subsector to have a positive profit from an accounting standpoint but a negative operating surplus from an economic viewpoint. Such a situation would indicate that the level of profit was insufficient to allow for the long-term replacement of assets.

Another issue that occurs in trying to break down the value of nontraded goods is that it may be difficult to obtain consistent data on *both* the cost and the revenue for a particular activity. Since it is the value of the *output* that is being broken down, it is important that cost data can be related to a particular output value. In ensuring that cost data are related to output values it is sometimes necessary to use a factor that relates the value of some part of costs to the value of revenue. This is particularly relevant where adjustments are made to accounting values of capital costs and where a number of different data sources are being used. In this respect a useful ratio that can be used is the ratio of revenue to noncapital costs. This may be used where there are reasonably reliable sources of information on the overall value of variable operating costs and revenue, but where the data may not be broken down into convenient categories and may not be reliable for the estimation of capital costs. If an alternative source of information on the broken-down value of costs is available but without revenue data, the breakdown for the output value of the subsector can be defined in the following manner:

$$R_i = RC_i \times \sum_{f=1}^{n} C_{fi} \tag{10.8}$$

$$A_{fi} = \frac{C_{fi}}{\displaystyle\sum_{f=1}^{n} C_{fi}} \times RC_i \tag{10.9}$$

$$C_{gi} = AC_{gi} \times DAF_{gi} \tag{10.10}$$

$$A_{gi} = \frac{C_{gi}}{\displaystyle\sum_{f=1}^{n} C_{fi}} \times RC_i \tag{10.11}$$

where R_i is the value of revenue for subsector i;
RC_i is the ratio of revenue to noncapital costs for subsector i;
C_{fi} is the cost of input f into subsector i;
A_{fi} is the value breakdown coefficient of operating cost item f for subsector i;
C_{gi} is the economic cost of capital input g into subsector i;
AC_{gi} is the accounting cost (depreciation) of capital input g into subsector i;
DAF_{gi} is the depreciation adjustment factor for capital input g into subsector i; and
A_{gi} is the value breakdown coefficient of capital cost item g for subsector i.

In the above set of equations it is assumed that Equation 10.8 might be derived from one aggregated information source, and Equations 10.9, 10.10, and 10.11 might be derived from more disaggregated sources such as cost studies. Obviously it is important when mixing information sources to try to ensure that data relate to the same period or have at least been updated to take account of any significant changes. The operating surplus can be obtained as a residual after deducting operating costs and annualized capital costs from revenue.

Example 3 (Nontraded Good). Most projects involve some road transport costs. It is therefore worthwhile to have some centrally available estimate of the breakdown of road transport costs. An estimate of a breakdown for road transport costs is shown in Table 10.3 (based on annual values [D\$] per truck).

The first step is to collect data on the cost composition of the activity concerned. The annual equivalent of the cost of the truck was calculated using the capital recovery factor approach outlined above. In the case of

Table 10.3   Disaggregation of the Cost of a Nontraded Good

	F	SL	UL	D	T
Diesel and lubricants	48,500	31,100		8,200	9,200
Tires	45,500	35,500		900	9,100
Maintenance and spares	34,400	20,800	7,500	3,500	300	2,300
Labor	20,500		8,000	12,500	
Other expenses	3,000			3,000	
Insurance	9,400			9,400	
Road tax	3,000				3,000
Annualized value of capital costs	84,000	63,000		800	20,200
Total costs	248,300	150,400	15,500	16,000	22,600	43,800
Revenue	250,000				
Excess profit to owners	1,700				1,700
Allocated road maintenance costs	38,500	20,400	4,200	1,800	9,800	2,300
Government expenditure on roads	−38,500				−38,500
Total breakdown	250,000	170,800	19,700	17,800	32,400	9,300
		68.3%	7.9%	7.1%	13.0%	3.7%

transport costs an additional complication occurs because vehicles make use of roads for which they do not pay directly. In principle the breakdown of the economic value of transport costs should include an estimate for the additional cost of road maintenance incurred when extra vehicles use the roads. This item would not appear in the cost structure of transport enterprises, and so a balancing item would have to be included under the transfer payments category to account for the extra government expenditure caused by extra road use.

Other nontraded items for which such data might be collected centrally include construction, water supply and sewage disposal, electricity, local wholesale trade, port costs, and rail transport.

Labor

Usually the different categories of labor are treated as primary factors into which other costs are broken down. However, in order to estimate the economic value of labor, it may be necessary to break the opportunity cost of labor down in the same way as for other nontraded goods. This is because the opportunity cost of labor consists of a set of products, and the value of each of these products can also be broken down. Breaking down the opportunity cost of labor can also be helpful in tracing the distributional impact of projects. An example will illustrate the point:

A survey of unskilled laborers in a certain country has revealed that 80% of recruits for formal-sector unskilled jobs were recruited from the rural areas, and 20% were recruited from the urban informal sector. The foregone earnings in the rural areas are D$750 and are assumed to be in the form of agricultural products. The foregone earnings of informal-sector workers in the urban area are D$960, consisting mainly of handicrafts and other services. It is estimated that the additional costs involved in moving to a formal-sector job are D$80 for workers recruited from the rural areas and D$40 for workers recruited from the urban areas. The minimum wage for formal-sector unskilled laborers is D$1,200.

Agricultural output is partly nontraded and partly traded with exports more important than imports. An overall breakdown for agriculture indicates 50% domestic resources, 55% foreign exchange, and −5% transfers (mainly taxes on export). The market wage for labor (MW_L) is broken down in the following way:

$$MW_L = a(OC_r + Z_r + T_r) + b(OC_u + Z_u + T_u) \qquad (10.11)$$

where a is the proportion of unskilled workers recruited from the rural areas;

OC is the opportunity cost of labor;
Z is the additional cost involved in taking up a formal-sector occupation;
T is the additional income gained by becoming a formal-sector worker;
subscript r refers to workers recruited from the rural areas; and
subscript u refers to workers recruited from the urban areas.

The breakdown of unskilled labor costs into primary factors is shown in Table 10.4.

It can be seen that, in principle, labor costs can be broken down into two primary factors (foreign exchange and domestic resources) and transfer payments, in this case taxes (T_G) and additional income to labor (T_L).

Table 10.4 Disaggregation of the Cost of Unskilled Labor

	F	D	T_G	T_L
Rural output foregone	600	330	300	−30
Urban output foregone	192		192	
Additional costs to rural recruits	64		64	
Additional costs to urban recruits	8		8	
Additional income to workers	336				336
Total breakdown	1,200	330	564	−30	336
		27.5%	47.0%	−2.5%	28.0%

Disaggregation of the transfer payments allows the identification of income effects. A similar process could be applied to skilled labor.

Semi-Input-Output Analysis

In recent years the kind of information required for disaggregating costs and benefits has been generated in a number of countries through the use of *semi-input-output* (SIO) analysis in which an economy is divided into a number of traded and nontraded sectors. Primary data are collected to disaggregate the value of the output of each sector into primary factors and inputs from other sectors. Input-output analysis techniques are then used to derive the final breakdown into primary factors. This technique is particularly useful in generating general sets of shadow prices for economies (see below). All the iterative calculations required are obtained through inverting the SIO matrix. Although this approach has the advantage of being comprehensive, as with all techniques, it is only as accurate as the data used in drawing up the SIO matrix. A simplified illustration of this approach is provided in the appendix to Chapter 11.

Further Reading

The issues discussed in this chapter are discussed in most texts dealing with the economic analysis of projects. Authors explain the issue of economic valuation from different perspectives although the practical implications of these differences are not usually as great as the differences in the explanation. Useful sources include Curry and Weiss (2000: chap. 4), Perkins (1994: chap. 10), Powers (1981: chap. 2), Overseas Development Administration (1988: chap. 3), Little and Mirrlees (chaps. 3, 9, and 12), UNIDO (1972: chaps. 5 and 8), UNIDO (1980: chap. 2), and Squire and van der Tak (chap. 3).

Notes

1. An alternative approach to the use of shadow prices is the *effects method,* an approach developed in France and used in some francophone countries. This approach, which is adopted in the most recent *EU Manual on Financial and Economic Analysis* but has been criticized heavily by proponents of shadow pricing approaches, is described in more detail in the appendix to Chapter 13.

2. Another term often used is *accounting price.* This term will be avoided because it can lead to confusion with concepts of accounting that have nothing to do with economics.

3. The most well-known of these models in relation to estimation of the

opportunity cost of labor in developing countries is that put forward by Harris and Todaro (1970).

4. This level is sometimes described as the "reservation wage" and covers the disutility of extra effort and the additional costs involved in working.

5. The terms *CIF* (cost, insurance, and freight) and *FOB* (free on board) were devised in the context of trade by sea where it is assumed that freight and insurance are a foreign exchange cost. Obviously the concept of a border price has to be modified to some extent to take account of differences when freight is by road or rail and may be paid locally and when insurance is a local cost.

6. In such disaggregation the *domestic resources* category is a residual item, which is normally assumed to have an equivalent value to a unit of domestic consumption. The definition of these categories is discussed further in Chapter 11.

7. In this and subsequent chapters the designation D$ will be used for local currency and $ for foreign exchange. The initial exchange rate is assumed to be D$10 per $1.

11

Shadow Prices and Shadow Pricing Systems

Shadow Prices and the Numeraire

Once the information is available to disaggregate the costs and benefits of a project into primary factors, the next step is to value the primary factors according to their opportunity costs. To do this it is necessary to have a unit in which the costs and benefits will be measured. The obvious unit to choose is a unit of the local currency at prices of the base year. This is what is normally used in any constant price analysis of a project. However, for economic analysis this definition is not sufficiently specific. The reason for disaggregating cost and benefit items into primary factors is that the different primary factors do not have the same scarcity value. Transfer payments are not real costs and so they have an economic value of zero. We have seen that the economic value of labor costs can be defined in terms of other primary factors. The remaining primary factors are foreign exchange and domestic resources.[1] One of these must therefore provide the unit in relation to which the values of all other categories are defined. This unit of account is described as the *numeraire*.[2]

When economists first started using shadow prices the most obvious procedure appeared to be to use domestic resources as the unit account and to estimate the scarcity value of foreign exchange through the use of a *shadow exchange rate*. This procedure corresponded to what is now described as the use of a *domestic price numeraire* and is most closely associated with a series of publications by the United Nations Industrial Organization (UNIDO 1972, 1978, and 1980).

The alternative approach, which is associated with the work of Little and Mirrlees and a later publication by Squire and van der Tak, is to use a unit of foreign exchange, still expressed in local currency units, as the numeraire. This procedure, which was adopted by many international agencies from the 1970s onward, is described as the use of a *world price numeraire*. These approaches will be outlined in greater detail below, and it will be shown that as long as common assumptions are used, the two approaches give exactly equivalent results. To use either approach, what is needed is

- A choice of numeraire
- A means of estimating the value of the other main primary factors in terms of units of the numeraire
- A method by which shadow prices can be calculated on the basis of disaggregation into primary factors and revaluation of those factors
- A method for applying shadow prices in project analysis

Conversion Factors and the Application of Shadow Prices

The simplest and most widely used approach for converting market price values into shadow price values is the *conversion factor* approach. A conversion factor (CF) can be defined as

$$CF = \frac{\text{shadow price}}{\text{market price}^3}$$

If such a ratio can be estimated for each cost and benefit item, the economic values of costs and benefits are obtained simply by multiplying the market price values by the relevant conversion factors. The first step is to determine the conversion factors for the primary factors. In the first instance a domestic price numeraire will be used to illustrate the estimation and application of shadow prices. The world price numeraire approach will then be illustrated.

Transfer Payments

These are the easiest to deal with as they have a shadow price of zero. In economic analysis, taxes and transfer payments, once identified, are eliminated. Since the shadow price is zero the conversion factor is also zero, whatever the numeraire.

Domestic Resources

Where a unit of domestic resources has been defined as the numeraire, the value of domestic resources remains unchanged and has a conversion factor of one.

Foreign Exchange (the Shadow Exchange Rate)

Shortage of foreign exchange is a significant constraint in many countries. Where this is so, it may be argued that the official exchange rate understates the value of foreign exchange and that a *shadow exchange rate* (SER) should be used in project analysis. Use of an SER should encourage those projects that either save or earn foreign exchange and discourage those projects that use foreign exchange.

Shadow exchange rates are usually expressed as conversion factors to be applied to the official exchange rate rather than as a specific rate of (say) D$12 to the US$.[4] The reason is that economic analysis of projects is concerned with the value of foreign exchange as a whole rather than the value of particular currencies. The only exception is that a different SER might be used for currencies that are not freely convertible and may therefore be less valuable than freely convertible foreign exchange. Since nearly all trade is done in convertible currencies such cases are relatively unimportant for most countries.

The most commonly used method of estimating shadow exchange rates is to measure the extent to which the local prices of traded goods exceed the world prices of such goods. This difference between local prices and world prices is usually reflected in the levels of import duties and export subsidies.

The SER should really be an estimate of the opportunity cost of foreign exchange. This can be interpreted as the relationship between the local value of traded goods no longer available for domestic use and the amount of foreign exchange spent on those goods. For example, a project may require an imported machine costing D$1 million CIF at the official exchange rate. Ultimately that D$1 million of additional foreign exchange expenditure must be covered either by decreased imports or by increased exports or by a combination of the two.

Suppose that imports are reduced by D$600,000 and exports increased by D$400,000 and that import duties are charged at a rate of 20% while exports are taxed at 5%. Assuming that transport and distribution costs are either insignificant or directly proportional to market price values, the local market price of the imports would be D$720,000, 20% higher than the import price because of the import duty. The local market price of the exports would be D$380,000, 5% lower than the export price, because exports are subject to an export tax. Expenditure of an additional D$1,000,000 in foreign exchange has reduced the value of goods available on the domestic market by D$1,100,000. The government has lost D$120,000 in import duties and gained D$20,000 in export taxes. The ratio of the value of traded goods at domestic prices (D$1,100,000) to their value at world prices (D$1,000,000) is 1.10. The SER (CF_F) is therefore 1.10. Two equations are often given for the SER. These are:

(i) $$CF_F = \frac{(M + T_m + X - T_x + S_x)}{M + X}$$ (11.1)

where M is the total value of imports;
T_m is the total value of import duties;
X is the total value of exports;
T_x is the total value of export taxes; and
S_x is the total value of export subsidies.

This equation assumes that additional foreign exchange expenditure affects the level of imports and exports in proportion to their value in total trade.

(ii) $$CF_F = \frac{(M + T_m)}{M}$$ (11.2)

This equation assumes that additional foreign exchange expenditure only affects the level of imports.

Equation 11.2 usually gives a higher value for the SER than Equation 11.1 because, in most countries, the average rate of import duty is much higher than the rate of net export subsidy. This can be seen by an example:

M = 100;
X = 60 (there is a deficit on the balance of trade);
T_m = 25 (average 25% rate of duty);
T_x = 6 (average 10% rate of duty);
S_x = 3 (average 5% rate of subsidy).

Under Equation 11.1 $$CF_F = \frac{100 + 25 + 60 - 6 + 3}{100 + 60} = 1.14.$$

Under Equation 11.2 $$CF_F = \frac{100 + 25}{100} = 1.25.$$

Other more complex formulas for the SER can be derived if data are available to indicate the types of imports or exports that change with a change in the availability of foreign exchange. Such formulas attempt to use the elasticity of demand for imports and exports with respect to changes in foreign exchange availability to provide weights for different import and export categories. It is usually quite difficult to obtain reliable information on these elasticities, and so the more simple formulations are more commonly used. Where semi-input-output models are available the weighted average of the conversion factors for traded goods can also be used. It is also possible to try to take account of nontariff trade restrictions such as import quotas, which may have the same effect as import duties in raising local prices.[5]

The question as to which formula is appropriate is essentially an empirical question. The appropriate value will, in most cases, lie between the values given by Equations 11.1 and 11.2 and will probably be nearer to Equation 11.2 if account is taken of any quantitative trade restrictions. It is also important, wherever possible, to consider more than one year when estimating the SER. It is possible that one single year could be unrepresentative and also that there may be changes in the real exchange rate over time.[6] An illustration of the application of SER formulas to some data based on a real case is shown in Table 11.1. These data would suggest an SER value somewhere between 1.15 and 1.25 with some evidence of a declining trend. Use of an initial estimate of 1.15 or 1.20 might be reasonable.

In cases where quantitative restrictions are very significant the value of the SER may be well above the estimate given by either equation. Under such circumstances estimation of the SER becomes very difficult, and the only approaches readily available are either direct comparison of local and world prices or projection from an earlier period when quantitative restrictions were not so important. In the latter case, movements in local prices, world prices, and exchange rates can be used to make the projection.[7] Quantitative restrictions on trade have become less important in most countries due to the widespread trade liberalization that has occurred since the mid-1980s. As a result the standard SER formulas are probably more applicable than they were in the 1970s and 1980s when many developing countries had more extensive import controls.

Estimation of the SER is particularly difficult in a country undergoing rapid economic change. This is because the exchange rate is likely to be at

Table 11.1 Estimation of Shadow Exchange Rate (values in D$ million)

	1991	1992	1993	1994	1995	1996	Average
Imports	3,912	3,213	4,691	5,906	6,487	7,064	4,842
Exports	952	969	1,227	1,770	2,729	2,579	1,529
Total trade	4,864	4,182	5,918	7,676	9,216	9,643	6,371
Taxes on imports	754	1,044	894	1,686	1,008	1,087	1,077
Net export taxes	36	35	67	92	137	129	73
SER (1)	1.19	1.32	1.19	1.29	1.16	1.15	1.22
SER (2)	1.15	1.24	1.14	1.21	1.09	1.10	1.16

a real level that is significantly different from the likely level in the long run. In such a situation a sensitivity analysis approach might be appropriate, and this might imply use of the *domestic resource cost of foreign exchange* measure (see below and Chapter 13). In the example given in Table 11.1 it might be worthwhile to do sensitivity tests using an SER of 1.10.

Labor

In most countries unskilled labor is likely to have an opportunity cost below the market wage. In urbanized societies this is reflected in the level of unemployment. For countries with a large agricultural sector the opportunity cost of unskilled labor is likely to be derived mainly from rural incomes. In rural areas it was suggested that the opportunity cost might be estimated on the basis of the average daily wage rates of casual laborers working in agriculture and the number of days worked by such laborers in a year.

In principle the shadow wage rate determined by the opportunity cost of labor may also be adjusted for any difference between the shadow price and market price of the commodities produced by workers in their alternative occupations. This can be important when the shadow value of output in the rural areas is either considerably above or below the market value. In many countries, such workers (i.e., small farmers) produce crops whose value in domestic prices is considerably below their value at border prices. In such cases a further adjustment should be made to the shadow wage to reflect the extent to which domestic prices undervalue the output of farmers. Table 10.4 provides the kind of information needed to make such an adjustment. The shadow wage rate can be estimated using the following procedure:

- Determine the opportunity cost of labor by finding out the market price value (m) of the alternative daily earnings for labor of the category under consideration and the average number of days worked (n).
- Estimate any additional costs (z), such as transport and the extra cost of purchased food, associated with the transfer to work on the project from the alternative occupation.
- Estimate the conversion factors (c) for the output of the worker in the alternative occupation without the project and (d) for the additional costs associated with the new job.

The shadow wage rate (SWR) is then given by

$$SWR = mnc + zd \tag{11.3}$$

Where there is more than one alternative occupation (i) as there is in Table 10.4, Equation 11.3 can be adapted using weights a_i to derive a weighted average of the opportunity cost for labor derived from different sources:

$$SWR = \sum_i a_i m_i n_i c_i + \sum_i a_i z_i d_i \tag{11.4}$$

If we take the example from Table 10.4, the opportunity cost of rural labor might be derived from a daily casual wage rate (m) of D\$5 with workers able to obtain 150 days (n) of work in a year. Similarly the opportunity cost of urban labor might be derived from a daily casual wage rate of D\$6 with workers able to obtain 160 days (n) of work in a year.

Assuming a value for the SER of 1.20, the additional costs (z) used in the example of D\$80 for workers recruited from the rural areas and D\$40 for workers recruited from the urban areas, and a conversion factor of 1.0 for the additional costs, we can derive the shadow wage rate in the following way:

	Rural Labor	Urban Labor
Weight (a_i)	0.8	0.2
Daily opportunity cost (m_i)	5	6
Number of days worked (n_i)	150	160
Conversion factor for output (c_i)	[(330 × 1.2) + 300]/600 = 1.16	1.0
Additional costs (z_i)	80	40
Conversion factor for additional costs (d_i)	1.0	1.0
Total economic cost	760	200

The SWR is therefore 760 + 200 = D\$960, and the conversion factor for unskilled labor (CF_L) is 960/1,200 = 0.80. When, as in this case, the SWR is below the market wage rate, use of the SWR for project selection will encourage projects that employ unskilled labor. We could have achieved the same answer for the conversion factor from the breakdown given in Table 10.4. For each unit of expenditure on labor there is a loss of 0.275 units of foreign exchange and 0.47 units of domestic resources. The rest of the cost of labor consists of income transfers, which are not resource costs. Each unit of foreign exchange is worth 1.2 units of domestic resources so $CF_L = (0.275 \times 1.2) + 0.47 = 0.80$.

The above example has assumed that it is possible to estimate the additional costs involved in taking up a formal-sector job. Such costs could be felt by the worker in the form of increased expenditure on food and travel or reduced time for leisure, but they could also be costs to the economy through the environmental cost of greater congestion in urban areas. Such costs are quite difficult to measure, and in practice they tend to be ignored. It is therefore likely that there is some tendency to underestimate the economic cost of employing additional formal-sector labor.

Although it is useful to have an average national estimate of the SWR, it is also likely that there may be considerable regional variations so that the SWR will be at least regionally specific and possibly even specific to a particular project. There may also be different categories of surplus labor (e.g., unskilled labor and semiskilled labor).

The conversion factor for unskilled labor may also be project specific because market wages may differ. For example,

SWR = D$960 per year;
Market wage for workers in Project A = D$1,200;
Market wage for workers in Project B = D$1,500;

$$CF\ (A) = \frac{960}{1,200} = 0.80;\ \text{and}$$

$$CF\ (B) = \frac{960}{1,500} = 0.64$$

Although the shadow wage itself is the same, the CFs are different.

The conventional approach to the estimation of the shadow wage rate and its associated conversion factors assumes that the various parameters used in the calculation are reasonably easy to identify and measure and that the underlying relationships are reasonably stable. This may not be the case in economies where rapid changes are taking place, and so an alternative approach may be useful in which labor costs of different categories are separated out and sensitivity analysis is conducted on the SWR.

In Chapter 10, I suggested that skilled labor was often assumed to have an opportunity cost equal to the domestic market wage. When this is the case, no adjustment is usually made to skilled labor costs. The assumption that skilled labor has an opportunity cost equal to the market wage does not always hold. In some countries the opportunity cost of some categories of skilled labor may be below the market wage. In other countries the opportunity cost of skilled labor could be above the market price due to factors such as training costs. It may also be that most skilled labor is employed in sectors in which the economic value of the output is different from the market price value. In such cases it would be necessary to follow a similar approach to the estimation of the SWR for unskilled labor. However, in the case of skilled labor, it is likely that any income transfers due to the difference between the opportunity cost of skilled labor and the market price would affect the incomes of employers (e.g., through training costs or reduced output) rather than the skilled workers themselves. In the illustrative example used here it will be assumed that the opportunity cost of skilled labor is equal to the market wage.

Conversion Factors for Individual Cost and Benefit Items

To obtain the conversion factor for unskilled labor used in our example it was necessary to calculate a conversion factor for agricultural output. This value was obtained by breaking down the value of agricultural output into primary factors and multiplying the broken-down components by the relevant conversion factors for the primary factors. A similar process can be undertaken for all cost and benefit items for which such breakdown information is available. Formally the conversion factor (CF_i) for any cost or benefit item i can be defined as:

$$CF_i = \sum_i a_{ij} CF_j \qquad (11.5)$$

where a_{ij} is the proportion a of primary factor j contained in item i, and CF_j is the conversion factor for primary factor j.

Assuming a value for the SER of 1.20 and a value for the SWR of 0.80, conversion factors can be estimated for the traded and nontraded goods illustrated in Tables 10.1, 10.2, and 10.3:

> For exported coffee (Table 10.1) the conversion factor (CF) is $(1.20 \times 1.242) - 0.136 = 1.35$;
> For imported wheat (Table 10.2) the CF is $(1.20 \times 0.70) + 0.121 = 0.96$;
> For transport (Table 10.3) the CF is $(1.20 \times 0.683) + 0.079 + (0.80 \times 0.071) + 0.13 = 1.09$

The process of estimating conversion factors is shown in Table 11.2, which relates to the textile project example described in Chapters 4 to 8. In Table 11.2 the conversion factors for the primary factors are set out at the top, the breakdowns of the various cost and benefit items are given, and the conversion factors using a domestic price numeraire are given under column CF(d). The second row of figures and the column headed CF(w) relate to the

Table 11.2 Cost Breakdowns and Conversion Factors

	F 1.20 20% 1.00	D 1.00 0.83	SL 1.00 0.83	UL 0.80 -20% 0.67	T 0.00 -100% 0.00	CF(d)	CF(w)
Groundnuts	125.0%	-12.5%			-12.5%	1.38	1.15
Other agricultural costs		100.0%				1.00	0.83
Agricultural labor (hired and family)	55.0%	50.0%			-5.0%	1.16	0.97
Ginning costs		100.0%				1.00	0.83
Transport costs	68.3%	13.0%	7.9%	7.1%	3.7%	1.09	0.90
Cotton seed		100.0%				1.00	0.83
Land opportunity cost (urban)		100.0%				1.00	0.83
Site development	56.0%	20.0%	8.0%	10.0%	6.0%	1.03	0.86
Buildings	18.0%	30.0%	10.0%	26.0%	16.0%	0.82	0.69
Machinery (including purchase of tubewells)	80.0%	4.0%			16.0%	1.00	0.83
Vehicles	64.0%	4.0%			32.0%	0.81	0.67
Exported cotton lint	115.0	-3.5%			-11.5%	1.35	1.12
Chemicals (and pesticides)	87.0%	4.3%			8.7%	1.09	0.91
Labor				100.0%		0.80	0.67
Utilities	72.0%	15.0%	10.0%	20.0%	-17.0%	1.27	1.06
Maintenance (including tubewell operation)	55.0%	25.0%		20.0%	20.0%	0.91	0.76
Management			100.0%			1.00	0.83
Sales	75.8%	5.3%	18.9%			0.96	0.80

Note: The first line below the primary factor headings gives conversion factors using a domestic proce numeraire. The second line presents the same information as adjustment factors (see p. 238). The third line shows the conversion factors for primary factors using a world price numeraire (see p. 235).

use of a world price numeraire and can be ignored for the time being. *It should be noted that Table 11.2 gives values for conversion factors using both numeraires for purposes of comparison only to demonstrate the equivalence of different approaches. In practice it is necessary to decide on which numeraire to use and to use that numeraire on a consistent basis.* In any practical work such a table should therefore include only one column for the chosen numeraire, which would normally be determined by the agency responsible for shadow price estimation where such an agency exists.

The breakdowns given in Table 11.2 are mostly quite straightforward. Site development, buildings, and utilities are nontraded items estimated in the same way as the transport example in Table 10.3. Machinery and vehicles are imports, and sales are import substitutes. These are similar to Table 10.2. Groundnuts, production of which is reduced when seed cotton production is increased, are diverted exports similar to Table 10.1. Cotton lint, which is used by the project but which would otherwise have been exported, is also a diverted export. Chemicals and pesticides are imported. Maintenance is a mixture of local costs and imported parts. In Table 11.2 the conversion factor for unskilled labor is given, and no breakdown is indicated at this stage. The conversion factor for informal sector agricultural labor is the same as the conversion factor for general agriculture, which can be derived from the first line of Table 10.4. The capital cost of factory land is assumed to be a transfer payment and is replaced by an annual value for the foregone rent. All other costs are relatively minor and are assumed to be domestic resource costs in the absence of more detailed information. Note that all physical working capital costs have already been allocated to specific resource categories in Table 8.4.

Applying the Conversion Factors

All that now remains to be done to complete the economic analysis of the project is to multiply the market price values of the costs and benefits by the relevant conversion factors, to recalculate the net benefits, and to discount at whatever discount rate is chosen. Application of the conversion factors, recalculation of the net benefits, and estimation of the economic NPV at selected discount rates and the IRR are shown in Table 11.3. The opportunity cost of land in this example is assumed to be an annual value of 8% of the capital cost.

The project NPV is negative at 8% and 12% discount rates, and the IRR is only 7.1%. It appears that the project is quite marginal from the economic point of view and considerably less desirable than the market price values in Table 8.4 indicate. Why might this be?

There are three main reasons. First, most of the materials used are diverted exports bought at a price below the world price, mainly because of

Table 11.3 Economic Analysis Using Conversion Factors by Year (D$ '000 domestic price numeraire)

	1	2	3	4	5	6	7	8	9	10	11	12
Groundnuts		-1,238	-2,475	-2,475	-2,475	-2,475	-2,475	-2,475	-2,475	-2,475	-2,475	
Pesticide		-46	-91	-91	-91	-91	-91	-91	-91	-91	-91	
Other agricultural costs		13	26	26	26	26	26	26	26	26	26	
Hired agricultural and family labor		-166	-332	-332	-332	-332	-332	-332	-332	-332	-332	
Ginning costs		-144	-288	-288	-288	-288	-288	-288	-288	-288	-288	
Transport costs		45	-242	-52	-100	-100	-100	-100	-100	-100	-366	
Cotton seed		403	806	806	806	806	806	806	806	806	806	
Exports of cotton lint		-5,750	-6,204	-9,230	-8,474	-8,474	-8,474	-8,474	-8,474	-8,474	-4,237	
Tubewells	-300	-300										
Tubewell operating costs		-19	-38	-38	-38	-38	-38	-38	-38	-38	-38	
Land opportunity cost	-24	-24	-24	-24	-24	-24	-24	-24	-24	-24	-24	
Site development	-619											600
Buildings	-5,438											3,300
Machinery	-12,500	-12,500										
Vehicles		-2,020					-2,020					
Chemicals		-1,649	-2,346	-3,107	-3,044	-3,044	-3,044	-3,044	-3,044	-3,044	-2,486	
Unskilled factory labor		-2,400	-3,600	-4,800	-4,800	-4,800	-4,800	-4,800	-4,800	-4,800	-4,320	
Utilities		-1,656	-2,484	-3,121	-3,121	-3,121	-3,121	-3,121	-3,121	-3,121	-2,867	
Maintenance		-455	-910	-1,092	-1,274	-1,365	-1,365	-1,365	-1,365	-1,365	-1,365	
Management		-1,500	-2,250	-2,250	-2,250	-2,250	-2,250	-2,250	-2,250	-2,250	-2,250	
Sales		14,035	22,611	30,409	31,188	31,188	31,188	31,188	31,188	31,188	31,188	
Net benefits	-18,882	-15,370	2,159	4,340	5,710	5,619	3,599	5,619	5,619	5,619	10,883	3,900

NPV at 4% = 6,488
NPV at 8% = -1,563
NPV at 12% = -6,867
IRR = 7.1%

a 10% export tax. The conversion factor for diverted cotton lint is therefore quite high. Second, the price paid for utilities is below the long-run marginal cost of production. This leads to a high conversion factor for utilities. Both these conversion factors also feed into the economic cost of the stocks of output. The third reason is that the project is producing an import substitute with a sales price above the import price because of the protection provided by import duties. Although the sales save quite a lot of valuable foreign exchange, the conversion factor is reduced by the removal of the effect of import duties.

There are some other effects of shadow pricing. The economic cost of heavily taxed imports is reduced, as is the value of unskilled labor costs and construction where profit levels are high. However, in this case, none of these effects is sufficiently important to counteract the major factors relating to the impact of removing taxes on trade and hidden utility subsidies from the analysis.

Economic Analysis Systems
Using a World Price Numeraire

Two of the most influential expositions on the economic analysis of projects have been those by Little and Mirrlees (1974), whose approach is referred to as *LM,* and Squire and van der Tak (1975), referred to as *SVT.* These works were commissioned by the Organisation for Economic Cooperation and Development (OECD) and the World Bank respectively and put forward a method that has been used by many funding agencies, including the World Bank and the bilateral aid agencies of the UK, the United States, and Germany. The two works can be regarded as different expositions of the same method, and they share in common the use of a world price numeraire.

In economic analysis costs and benefits must be measured in units of something. When we calculated the shadow exchange rate (SER), in effect we stated that D$1.00 worth of foreign exchange was worth more than D$1.00 of domestic resources and that the SER measured the value of a unit of foreign exchange in terms of domestic resources. Units of domestic resources were left unchanged in the analysis while units of foreign exchange were multiplied by the SER. Costs and benefits were therefore measured in units of domestic resources, which could be called the numeraire of the system.

The world price numeraire system leaves units of foreign exchange unchanged and adjusts the value of domestic resources. Cost and benefits are therefore counted in terms of units of foreign exchange at the official exchange rate. A unit of foreign exchange at the official exchange rate is therefore the numeraire of the system. This means that, other than transport and handling cost adjustments, world prices for traded goods can be used as shadow prices unadjusted by the SER. This is why these systems are said to have a world price numeraire.

The Standard Conversion Factor (SCF) and the SER

In the world price system the standard conversion factor (SCF) can be defined as the average value of a unit of domestic resources in relation to a unit of foreign exchange. It is the inverse of the SER. Domestic resource costs and benefits (when not further broken down) are therefore multiplied by the SCF. An example can show how this might work:

Assume that the SER is calculated by the formula that assumes that changes in foreign exchange availability only affect imports. Using the average figures from Table 11.1:

$$SER = \frac{(M + T_m)}{M} = \frac{4,842 + 1,077}{4,842} = 1.22 \qquad (11.6)$$

Using a world price numeraire we would not use an SER to adjust foreign exchange costs and benefits. Instead we would use an SCF to adjust domestic resource costs.

$$SCF = \frac{1}{SER} = \frac{M}{(M + T_m)} = \frac{4,842}{4,842 + 1,077} = 0.82 \qquad (11.7)$$

In our example we assumed an SER of 1.20. This is equivalent to an SCF of 0.83.[8] The conversion factors obtained from Tables 10.1, 10.2, 10.3, and 10.4 can be reworked using the world price numeraire:

For exported coffee (Table 10.1) the conversion factor is 1.242 – (0.136 × 0.83) = 1.13;
For imported wheat (Table 10.2) the conversion factor is 0.70 + (0.121 × 0.83) = 0.80;
For labor (Table 10.4) the conversion factor is 0.275 + (0.47 × 0.83) = 0.67;
For transport (Table 10.3) the conversion factor is 0.683 + (0.079 × 0.83) + (0.67 × 0.071) + (0.13 × 0.83) = 0.90.

In each case the conversion factor is 20% smaller using a world price numeraire because the numeraire is 20% more valuable.

Composite Conversion Factors

The use of specific composite conversion factors for individual cost and benefit items is a distinguishing feature of the published versions of the world price numeraire approach. Little and Mirrlees argued that such conversion factors should be available centrally for commonly used cost categories. The task of the project analyst would then be to apply the centrally available conversion factors for all items other than those that were very specific to the project. This would make economic analysis both easier and potentially more consistent for the comparison of different projects.

Procedures

The distinguishing features of the world price numeraire approach are (1) the world price numeraire and (2) the use of composite conversion factors.

Once the CFs have been calculated, the procedure is simply to multiply the market price values for each item by the relevant conversion factor. A new annual statement at shadow prices is then drawn up and discounted at the discount rate based on the opportunity cost of capital. This discount rate is also described in some of the literature as the *accounting rate of interest* (ARI).

In Table 11.2 the third row shows the conversion factors for the primary factors to be applied in our example using the world price numeraire approach. The conversion factors for the individual cost and benefit items are shown in the column headed CF(w). These conversion factors are then applied in Table 11.4. It can be seen that the IRR is exactly the same as for the domestic price numeraire and that the NPV using the domestic price numeraire is 20% bigger at all discount rates. The results are therefore exactly equivalent.

Advantages of the World Price Approach

The main advantage of the world price approach is that, once the CFs for different items are known, all that is required is simple multiplication. If the CFs are provided centrally, all the project analyst has to do is the multiplication. This advantage is related to the use of centrally calculated conversion factors and not to the choice of numeraire. It therefore applies equally to the use of a domestic price numeraire approach using composite conversion factors as illustrated in Table 11.3.

A second advantage is that world prices can be used unadjusted as shadow prices—a rough estimate for a CF is obtained simply by dividing the world price by the market price although, to be strictly correct, local transport and handling costs should be taken into account. The method does not require estimation of an SER although the inverse, the SCF, is required.

It has sometimes been contended that, when most inputs and outputs

Table 11.4 Economic Analysis Using Conversion Factors by Year (D$ '000 world price numeraire)

	1	2	3	4	5	6	7	8	9	10	11	12
Groundnuts		-1,031	-2,063	-2,063	-2,063	-2,063	-2,063	-2,063	-2,063	-2,063	-2,063	
Pesticide		-38	-76	-76	-76	-76	-76	-76	-76	-76	-76	
Other agricultural costs		11	22	22	22	22	22	22	22	22	22	
Hired agricultural and family labor		-138	-276	-276	-276	-276	-276	-276	-276	-276	-276	
Ginning costs		-120	-240	-240	-240	-240	-240	-240	-240	-240	-240	
Transport costs		38	-202	-44	-83	-83	-83	-83	-83	-83	-305	
Cotton seed		336	672	672	672	672	672	672	672	672	672	
Exports of cotton lint		-4,792	-5,170	-7,692	-7,061	-7,061	-7,061	-7,061	-7,061	-7,061	-3,531	
Tubewells	-250	-250										
Tubewell operating costs		-16	-32	-32	-32	-32	-32	-32	-32	-32	-32	
Land opportunity cost	-20	-20	-20	-20	-20	-20	-20	-20	-20	-20	-20	
Site development	-516											500
Buildings	-4,532											2,750
Machinery	-10,417	-10,417										
Vehicles		-1,683					-1,683					
Chemicals		-1,374	-1,955	-2,589	-2,536	-2,536	-2,536	-2,536	-2,536	-2,536	-2,071	
Unskilled factory labor		-2,000	-3,000	-4,000	-4,000	-4,000	-4,000	-4,000	-4,000	-4,000	-3,600	
Utilities		-1,380	-2,070	-2,601	-2,601	-2,601	-2,601	-2,601	-2,601	-2,601	-2,389	
Maintenance		-379	-758	-910	-1,062	-1,138	-1,138	-1,138	-1,138	-1,138	-1,138	
Management		-1,250	-1,875	-1,875	-1,875	-1,875	-1,875	-1,875	-1,875	-1,875	-1,875	
Sales		11,696	18,843	25,340	25,990	25,990	25,990	25,990	25,990	25,990	25,990	
Net benefits	-15,735	-12,808	1,799	3,617	4,758	4,683	2,999	4,683	4,683	4,683	9,069	3,250

NPV at 4% = 5,406
NPV at 8% = -1,303
NPV at 12% -5,723
IRR = 7.1%

are traded, using the wrong SCF is not as serious as using the wrong SER. From a strictly arithmetic point of view, this argument is false since the domestic price and world price numeraire methods give equivalent results with equivalent assumptions. A more valid argument is that the original proponents of the domestic price numeraire approach did not develop some of the more detailed aspects of shadow pricing to the same extent in practice.[9]

It was probably also true that, when these methods were being developed, the value of the SCF did not have the same political sensitivity as the value of the SER since public use of an SER might have been construed to have implications for exchange rate policy. The widespread adoption of more liberalized trade policies has reduced the significance of this argument.

Disadvantages of the World Price Numeraire Approach

There are a number of arguments that might be used against the world price approach.

It can be argued that the concept of a shadow exchange rate is easier to understand than a standard conversion factor. It is logically easier to understand the idea of adjusting foreign exchange values upward to take account of a foreign exchange shortage rather than adjusting domestic resource costs downward.

Central determination of composite CFs means that project analysts can apply shadow pricing without understanding what they are doing. This might be the cause of serious mistakes. This argument of course applies to any centrally produced set of conversion factors whatever the numeraire.

Composite CFs do not allow ready access to information on distribution effects or the impact on foreign exchange, tax revenue, and employment. They also make it difficult to conduct sensitivity analysis on key parameters such as the relative value of foreign exchange and domestic resources. This is a more serious argument and will be explored further below and in Chapter 13.

Use of the world price numeraire did initially lead to some misunderstanding—particularly the mistaken view that the method necessarily means advocacy of free trade. All that the method actually implies is the recognition of the opportunity cost represented by trade opportunities.

Domestic Price Systems and Procedures

Use of an SER rather than an SCF implies the use of a domestic price numeraire. Costs and benefits are measured in terms of average domestic prices. The approach outlined in 11.2 is therefore one version of the domestic price numeraire approach.

The most well-known expositions of the domestic price numeraire approach are three publications commissioned by UNIDO: the original *Guidelines for Project Evaluation,* the subsequent *Guide to Practical Project Appraisal,* and a book of case studies of application of the method to projects in Pakistan (UNIDO 1980). The second publication is, in most respects, a condensed version of the *Guidelines,* and it is the *Guide* approach that is outlined here. Only the differences between the *Guide* procedures and those already indicated will be dealt with. Many of the features of the domestic price numeraire system are common to both the *Guide* and the method described earlier.

The Integrated Documentation System

The *Guide* was the first major work on economic analysis to pay much attention to the relationship between economic analysis and financial analysis. The book uses what it calls an "integrated documentation system" in which there is a "net cash flow real" concerned with resource costs and benefits, which is balanced by a "net cash flow financial," which shows the financing of the project and the distribution of benefits. Shadow pricing adjustments are made to the resource costs and benefits included in the net cash flow real. The equality between the two statements is similar to the equality between the statement of resource costs and benefits and the statement of the distribution of costs and benefits, which was shown in Chapters 7 and 8 and illustrated in Tables 4.5, 7.1, 8.3, and 8.4.

The Use of Present Values

All costs and benefits in the *Guide* are presented in terms of present values at selected discount rates. It suggests using 0%, 10%, and 20% if the discount rate is unknown. Discounting is therefore the first step in the analysis before the application of shadow pricing. This approach, which was also adopted in the original *Guidelines,* reduces the amount of multiplication in later stages of the analysis at the expense of a lot of discounting in the early stages.

The Use of Adjustment Factors

The *Guide* approach uses adjustment factors (AFs) rather than CFs. An adjustment factor (or "premium" in the original *Guidelines)* is simply the difference between the CF and one. In the *Guide* AFs are expressed as percentages. Thus

$$AF = (CF - 1) * 100\%$$

The value of each adjustment is estimated by multiplying the market price PV of the item concerned by the AF. The total value of each adjustment is obtained by adding up the values of the individual adjustments and then adding the adjustment to the NPV of the net cash flow real at the previous stage of the analysis. In principle, in the economic analysis stage, each adjustment can be associated with a change in income to a particular group (e.g., changes in taxes affect government revenue).

The Use of Different Stages in the Analysis

The *Guide* approach works in stages. The first stage is the NPV at market prices after taking account of linkages and externalities.

Stage two of the analysis involves adjusting for "market price distortions." Traded goods are valued at border prices thereby eliminating tariffs and other transfer payments. Labor is valued using an opportunity cost shadow wage adjustment. This is achieved by breaking down the market price values for different costs and benefits into primary factors (foreign exchange, domestic resources, skilled and unskilled labor, and transfer payments) using breakdowns like those given in Table 11.2. The relevant adjustment factors for the labor categories and transfer payments are then applied.

Stage three involves the shadow exchange rate adjustment. The AF for foreign exchange is applied to the foreign exchange component of each cost and benefit item. In practice, stages two and three are likely to be done at the same time although the adjustments are shown separately.

Stages four and five concern "social analysis," where distribution adjustments are introduced. These stages are discussed in Chapter 13.

The procedure is additive. The final economic NPV of the project is the stage one NPV plus the transfer payment and labor adjustment plus the foreign exchange adjustment. The procedure is illustrated for the example project in Table 11.5.

Switching Values and Sensitivity Analysis

The *Guide* emphasizes the uncertainty surrounding shadow price estimates and therefore recommends the use of sensitivity analysis for some of the key parameters. In this way switching values can be estimated. The most obvious switching value is the IRR, which gives the rate of discount at which the NPV changes from positive to negative. It can be seen from Table 11.5 that it would be relatively easy to test for the effect of different values for the AFs of different primary factors.

Table 11.5   Economic Analysis—UNIDO Guidelines Approach

A. Present Values at Market Prices (D$ '000)

	4.0%	8.0%	12.0%
Groundnuts	−13,206	−10,412	−8,363
Pesticide	−616	−486	−390
Other agricultural costs	191	150	121
Hired agricultural and family labor	−2,098	−1,654	−1,329
Ginning costs	−2,113	−1,666	−1,338
Transport costs	−833	−634	−494
Cotton seed	5,916	4,665	3,747
Exports of cotton lint	−44,196	−35,129	−28,419
Tubewells	−566	−535	−507
Tubewell operating costs	−308	−243	−195
Land purchase	−101	−159	−191
Site development	−577	−556	−536
Buildings	−6,346	−6,111	−5,893
Buildings and site salvage value	2,436	1,549	1,001
Machinery	−23,576	−22,291	−21,126
Vehicles	−4,211	−3,602	−3,124
Chemicals	−19,796	−15,610	−12,535
Unskilled factory labor	−42,297	−33,258	−26,637
Utilities	−17,470	−13,753	−11,030
Maintenance	−9,991	−7,777	−6,167
Management	−16,854	−13,336	−10,753
Sales	227,597	178,356	142,390
NPV at market prices	30,985	17,509	8,232
Land opportunity cost	−210	−171	−143
NPV adjusted for land	30,876	17,496	8,281

B. Present Values of Primary Factors

	4.0%	8.0%	12.0%
F	43,987	30,145	20,376
D	11,096	7,839	5,580
SL	−19,348	−15,417	−12,527
L	−47,557	−37,698	−30,464
T	42,697	32,628	25,316
NPV (1)	30,876	17,496	8,281

C. Stage 2—Application of Economic Analysis Premiums

	4.0%	8.0%	12.0%
F (+0.2)	8,797	6,029	4,075
L (−0.2)	9,511	7,540	6,093
T (−1.00)	−42,697	−32,628	−25,316
NPV (2)	6,488	−1,563	−6,867

A second switching value might be the CF for foreign exchange at which the NPV is zero. Calculation of this value gives the *domestic resource cost of foreign exchange* criterion, sometimes called the *Bruno Test* (after an economist called Bruno). This test is useful if the discount rate is known and projects are to be ranked according to the efficiency with which they earn foreign exchange. It is also used in the assessment of the competitiveness of different industries and has therefore been used quite widely in formulating specific recommendations for structural adjustment programs. The use of this indicator will be illustrated in Chapter 13.

Advantages of Using the UNIDO Guide Approach

The main advantages are

- The approach is flexible and can be taken to whatever degree of complexity is felt advisable.
- The approach shows the link between financial and economic analysis, although it could be argued that the "integrated documentation system" set out in the *Guide* is not as clear as it might be.
- The procedures are designed to allow easy use of sensitivity analysis where shadow price estimates are uncertain. This may be particularly valuable for economies in a stage of rapid transition.
- The approach can be adjusted to show clearly the income distribution effects of the project as well as the effects on foreign exchange, employment, and tax revenue.
- The approach relates more closely to the sort of approximate shadow pricing that has been used in some countries for many years and can be introduced relatively quickly (i.e., with rough adjustment of foreign exchange, labor, and taxes).

Disadvantages of Using the Guide Approach

Disadvantages include

- The use of present values obscures information on the timing of different effects. The use of present values, however, is not an essential part of the approach. It is quite possible to break down the costs and benefits into primary factors on a year-by-year basis and to discount the adjusted net benefits at the end of the procedure. This involves additional multiplication but provides additional information (see Chapter 13).
- The *Guide* contains some methodological errors. These do not affect the economic analysis and were resolved in UNIDO (1980: 5–9).

- The *Guide* approach has not been so extensively used as the LM/SVT approach and is not backed up by so many published case studies. It is also not currently used by major international donor agencies, although its use would probably be acceptable to most of these agencies.

Further Reading

The estimation of shadow prices for primary factors is covered in all the major texts on economic analysis. Curry and Weiss (2000: chaps. 5 and 6), Asian Development Bank (1997: apps. 10–12 and 15–16), Belli et al. (1998: chap. 6), Perkins (1994: chaps. 9 and 10), Overseas Development Administration (1988: chap. 3), and Powers (chaps. 2 and 3) are particularly useful. The classic expositions of the world price numeraire system are Little and Mirrlees (1974) and Squire and van der Tak (1975). Case studies of this approach can be found in Little and Scott (1976) and Scott, MacArthur, and Newbery (1976). The UNIDO approach is described fully in UNIDO (1972), UNIDO (1978), and UNIDO (1980). Comparisons of the two approaches can be found in Lal (1974) and in articles by Dasgupta, Joshi, and Stewart and Streeten in a special issue of the Bulletin of the Oxford University Institute of Economics and Statistics (1972: vol. 3).

Appendix 11.1: Estimating Shadow Prices Using Semi-Input-Output Analysis

In principle all shadow prices are interdependent because their value depends on the value of inputs from other sectors. To take account of all the interdependencies, conversion factors could be derived for an economy by solving a series of simultaneous equations using an input-output approach. In principle such an approach, which has been described as *semi-input-output (SIO) analysis*, can take account of all the interrelationships that occur among sectors. The SIO approach is particularly useful for the nontraded sectors where each sector may appear as an input into another. In using the SIO approach the following steps are involved:

1. The economy must be divided into a number of sectors and subsectors. The basis for the division into sectors is usually determined on a pragmatic basis by (a) data sources—the categorizations used in data already available, (b) the sectors for which shadow prices are likely to be needed in practice, and (c) the need to investigate in more detail those sectors where a significant divergence between market prices and shadow prices could be expected.

2. The value of the output of each sector identified must be broken down into inputs from other sectors and primary factors. For the nontraded sectors estimation of the breakdown requires that a discount rate should already have been specified so that the cost of capital inputs can be computed (see Chapter 10 for the procedure required for estimating the contribution of capital inputs).

3. The opportunity cost of labor must be estimated at market prices, and the sectors from which the foregone output of labor is derived must be defined.

4. A semi-input-output table is then drawn up. A conventional SIO table might have the dimensions $(N+L+PF) \times (N)$, where N is the number of sectors into which the economy is divided, L is the number of categories of labor, and PF is the number of categories of other primary factors (foreign exchange, domestic resources, taxes, and operating surplus).

5. An alternative approach, which is useful for identifying indirect distributional effects, is to draw up an extended SIO table with the dimensions $(N+L+PF+TR) \times (N+L)$, where TR is the number of categories of income transfers relating to labor.

6. The inputs into each sector of each other sector and of the primary factors are recorded in the columns of the table. The inputs are specified as coefficients (percentages of the total value of the output of the sector). The matrix with dimension $N \times N$ is what is commonly described as the "A matrix" in the SIO literature. The matrix with the dimension $(L+PF) \times N$ is usually described as the "F matrix" (see Figure 11.1).

Figure 11.1 Conventional Semi-Input-Output Table (conventional structure shaded)

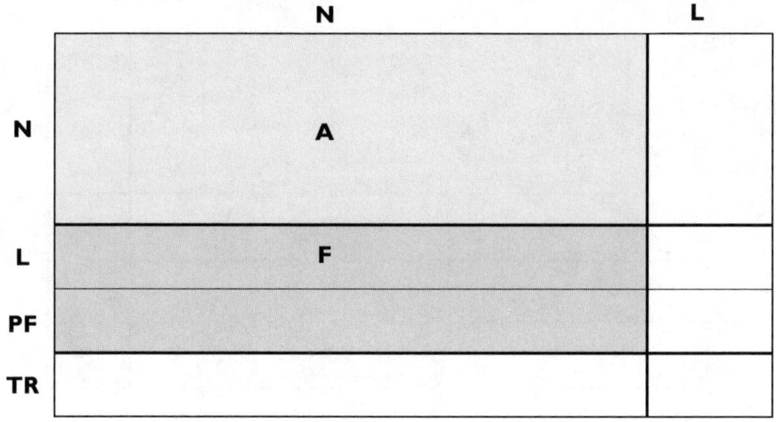

7. By inverting the A matrix and multiplying by the F matrix the value of the output of each sector is broken down into primary factors. Conversion factors are then derived by an iterative process.

8. The alternative *extended SIO* matrix has the dimensions $(N+L) \times (N+L)$. This matrix (the A^* matrix) is multiplied by the matrix with the dimensions $(PF+TR) \times (N+L)$ (the F^* matrix; see Figure 11.2). The extended SIO approach breaks down the output of each sector, and each labor category into foreign exchange, domestic resources, and transfer payments.[10] The conversion factors can then be derived without iteration. The same result is derived, but more information is provided on income effects.

The process of estimating shadow prices using SIO is illustrated using a simplified sixteen-sector model in Tables 11.6 to 11.14. The figures are based on actual figures for a real economy but aggregated into a smaller number of sectors than in the original model. In Table 11.6 the A matrix is defined by the rows and columns from EA to ACF. The F matrix is defined by rows SL to T3. The conventional SIO approach does not require columns SL to D until later and does not require rows IULF and IULR.

The next step is to draw up an identity matrix (I) with the same dimensions as the A matrix, to subtract the identity matrix from the A matrix, and then to invert the I–A matrix (i.e., the Leontief inverse of the A matrix, Table 11.7). Matrix inversion can be done using the Microsoft Excel function MINVERSE.

The F matrix is then multiplied by the inverted matrix to give the T matrix (Table 11.8). The T matrix gives a breakdown of the value of the

Figure 11.2   Extended Semi-Input-Output Table (extended structure shaded)

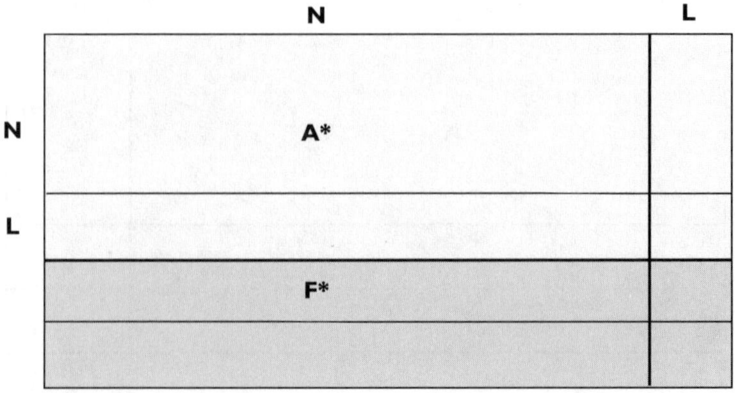

output of each sector into primary factors including the different categories of labor. The procedure can be summarized as:

$$(I-A)^{-1} \cdot F = T \tag{11.8}$$

The columns SL to ULR by rows EA to ACF from Table 11.6 form the L matrix and the columns SL to ULR by row D form the L_d vector. These are shown in Table 11.9 and are used in the procedure outlined below.

The estimation of conversion factors is undertaken by defining a vector (S, the first line of Table 11.10) with seed values for each of the labor categories, the SCF, and the value of foreign exchange (this is assumed to be 1.0 when a world price numeraire is used). The first estimate of the conversion factors is obtained by multiplying the vector S by the T matrix. This gives the first value for the vector of sector conversion factors (P_n, Table 11.11):

$$S \cdot T = P_n \tag{11.9}$$

A second vector of primary factors (P_f, the second line of Table 11.10) is defined with foreign exchange given the value of 1.0 and transfer payments given the value of 0.0.

In defining P_f, the conversion factors for the labor categories (P_{fl}) are determined by multiplying the P_n vector by the matrix of sector breakdowns for the labor categories (the L matrix = primary factor columns ULUF to ULR by sector rows EA to ACF in Table 11.9). The product of the seed value for the SCF (D) and the vector showing the domestic resource composition of the opportunity cost of labor (L_d, the bottom row of Table 11.9) are then added. Thus:

$$P_n \cdot L + D \cdot L_d = P_f \tag{11.10}$$

The value of domestic resources (the SCF) is then determined by multiplying the vector D_t (the right-hand column of Table 11.9) by the P_n vector. This procedure assumes that the SCF is estimated as a trade weighted average of the conversion factors for traded goods, since the values in the vector D_t are weights for the traded sectors of the economy. The effect is similar to that of using a standard SCF formula including both imports and exports. Alternative procedures might be simply to assume that the SCF is determined exogenously or to assume that the SCF is equal to the average conversion factor (ACF). Thus:

$$P_n \cdot D_t = D \tag{11.11}$$

Table 11.6 Semi-Input-Output Table (Coefficients) (A and F Matrices)

		EA	DAI	DAN	AI	IT	IM	CM	F
Export agriculture	EA								
Domestic agriculture (imp. sub.)	DAI								
Domestic agriculture nontraded	DAN								
Agroindustries	AI								
Manufacturing—traded	MT				−0.009				
Imported manufactures	IM							0.413	
Construction materials	CM							0.057	
Fuel	F							0.103	
Electricity	E							0.034	
Water and sewerage	W							0.020	
Transport and communications	TC	−0.098	0.086		0.007	0.019	0.032	0.013	0.118
Construction	C							0.100	
Distribution and finance	DF	−0.014	0.019		−0.004			0.023	0.068
Other services	OS								
Agriculture	A								
Manufacturing	M								
Average conversion factor	ACF	−0.053	0.056					0.003	
Skilled Labor	SL	−0.002			−0.001			0.033	
Unskilled labor—urban formal	ULUF		0.002		−0.001			0.027	
Unskilled labor—rural formal	ULRF	−0.008						0.002	
Unskilled labor—rural informal	ULR	−0.006							
Domestic resources	D			1.000					
Foreign exchange	F	1.258	0.710		0.941	0.717	0.806		0.618
Taxes and subsidies	T1	−0.049	0.060		0.108	0.264	0.162	0.092	0.149
Operating surplus (public)	T2	−0.001	0.067		−0.041			0.025	0.005
Operating surplus (private)	T3	−0.027						0.055	0.042
Income to unskilled labor—UF	IULF								
Income to unskilled labor—RF	IULR								

Table 11.7 Inverted Matrix (I-A)$^{-1}$

		EA	DAI	DAN	AI
Export agriculture	EA	0.985	0.016	0.000	0.000
Domestic agriculture (imp. sub.)	DAI	−0.009	1.009	0.000	0.000
Domestic agriculture nontraded	DAN	−0.013	0.014	1.000	0.000
Agroindustries	AI	−0.003	0.003	0.000	1.000
Manufacturing—traded	MT	−0.021	0.019	0.000	−0.008
Imported manufactures	IM	−0.054	0.049	0.000	0.003
Construction materials	CM	−0.002	0.003	0.000	0.000
Fuel	F	−0.022	0.020	0.000	0.001
Electricity	E	−0.001	0.001	0.000	0.000
Water and sewerage	W	0.000	0.000	0.000	0.000
Transport and communications	TC	−0.106	0.094	0.000	0.007
Construction	C	−0.007	0.008	0.000	−0.001
Distribution and finance	DF	−0.042	0.049	0.000	−0.005
Other services	OS	−0.012	0.013	0.000	0.000
Agriculture	A	−0.037	0.039	0.000	−0.001
Manufacturing	M	−0.005	0.005	0.000	0.000
Average conversion factor	ACF	−0.069	0.074	0.000	−0.001

Table 11.6 continued

E	W	TC	C	DF	OS	A	M	ACF	SL	ULUF	ULRF	ULR	D
				0.416									0.207
				0.234									0.095
				0.350									0.000
			0.006		0.594								0.068
	0.133	0.185	0.008		0.283								0.136
0.841	0.396	0.467	0.215	0.036									0.362
0.307	0.365		0.189			0.123							0.000
0.076	0.216	0.204	0.038										0.132
	0.092			0.002				0.005					
				0.002				0.004					
0.014	0.067		0.011	0.020				0.043					
0.474	1.042		0.244	0.058				0.028					
		0.034	0.007	0.290				0.154					
				0.006				0.172					
								0.528	0.040	0.143	0.582	0.953	
								0.066	0.210				
0.156	0.110	0.035	0.075	0.290									
0.135	0.246	0.053	0.045	0.068									
0.075	0.168	0.019	0.078	0.020									
			0.035										
					1.000			0.750	0.561	0.029	0.047		
0.154	0.351		0.045										
			0.097										
−1.232	−2.186		0.009	0.032									
		0.003	0.009	0.065									
										0.296			
											0.389		

Table 11.7 continued

IT	IM	CM	F	E	W	TC	C	DF	OS	A	M	ACF
0.000	0.000	0.011	0.008	0.054	0.067	0.014	0.028	0.099	0.000	0.413	0.001	0.236
0.000	0.000	0.006	0.005	0.031	0.037	0.008	0.016	0.056	0.000	0.233	0.001	0.133
0.000	0.000	0.009	0.007	0.046	0.056	0.011	0.023	0.083	0.000	0.348	0.001	0.198
0.000	0.000	0.002	0.002	0.010	0.013	0.003	0.005	0.027	0.000	0.000	0.594	0.043
1.004	0.006	0.015	0.025	0.026	0.179	0.196	0.013	0.031	0.000	−0.004	0.281	0.031
0.009	1.016	0.583	0.068	1.271	1.261	0.497	0.453	0.137	0.000	−0.011	0.076	0.066
0.000	0.000	1.126	0.003	0.485	0.756	0.003	0.285	0.038	0.000	0.000	0.138	0.028
0.004	0.007	0.144	1.027	0.178	0.409	0.215	0.095	0.023	0.000	−0.005	0.020	0.017
0.000	0.000	0.041	0.001	1.019	0.121	0.001	0.011	0.007	0.000	0.000	0.005	0.007
0.000	0.000	0.023	0.000	0.011	1.017	0.000	0.006	0.006	0.000	0.000	0.003	0.005
0.020	0.034	0.058	0.128	0.102	0.202	1.049	0.051	0.055	0.000	−0.022	0.017	0.046
0.000	0.000	0.213	0.011	0.735	1.600	0.010	1.385	0.150	0.000	−0.001	0.026	0.074
0.002	0.003	0.066	0.113	0.098	0.155	0.084	0.062	1.513	0.000	−0.006	0.005	0.237
0.000	0.000	0.009	0.007	0.043	0.053	0.011	0.022	0.087	1.000	−0.002	0.001	0.186
0.001	0.001	0.026	0.020	0.131	0.160	0.033	0.067	0.239	0.000	0.994	0.003	0.566
0.000	0.000	0.003	0.003	0.016	0.020	0.004	0.008	0.030	0.000	−0.001	1.000	0.071
0.001	0.002	0.049	0.038	0.248	0.303	0.062	0.126	0.452	0.000	−0.011	0.006	1.073

Table 11.8 Breakdown into Primary Factors (F·(I-A)⁻¹) = T Matrix

		EA	DAI	DAN	AI
Skilled labor	SL	−0.011	0.009	0.000	−0.001
Unskilled labor—urban formal	ULUF	−0.004	0.006	0.000	−0.001
Unskilled labor—rural formal	ULRF	−0.008	0.000	0.000	0.000
Unskilled labor—rural informal	ULR	−0.006	0.000	0.000	0.000
Domestic resources	D	−0.025	0.027	1.000	−0.001
Foreign exchange	F	1.157	0.806	0.000	0.938
Taxes and subsidies	T1	−0.071	0.081	0.000	0.106
Operating surplus (public)	T2	−0.001	0.068	0.000	−0.041
Operating surplus (private)	T3	−0.031	0.004	0.000	0.000

Table 11.9 Breakdown of Primary Factors (L Matrix, L_d and D_t Vectors)

		SL	ULUF	ULRF	ULR	D
Export agriculture	EA	0.000	0.000	0.000	0.000	0.207
Domestic agriculture (imp. sub.)	DAI	0.000	0.000	0.000	0.000	0.095
Domestic agriculture nontraded	DAN	0.000	0.000	0.000	0.000	0.000
Agroindustries	AI	0.000	0.000	0.000	0.000	0.068
Manufacturing—traded	MT	0.000	0.000	0.000	0.000	0.136
Imported manufactures	IM	0.000	0.000	0.000	0.000	0.362
Construction materials	CM	0.000	0.000	0.000	0.000	0.000
Fuel	F	0.000	0.000	0.000	0.000	0.132
Electricity	E	0.000	0.000	0.000	0.000	0.000
Water and sewerage	W	0.000	0.000	0.000	0.000	0.000
Transport and communications	TC	0.000	0.000	0.000	0.000	0.000
Construction	C	0.000	0.000	0.000	0.000	0.000
Distribution and finance	DF	0.000	0.000	0.000	0.000	0.000
Other services	OS	0.000	0.000	0.000	0.000	0.000
Agriculture	A	0.040	0.143	0.582	0.953	0.000
Manufacturing	M	0.210	0.000	0.000	0.000	0.000
Average conversion factor	ACF	0.000	0.000	0.000	0.000	0.000
Domestic resources	D	0.750	0.561	0.029	0.047	

Table 11.10 Seed Values and Vector of CFs for Primary Factors (S and P_f Vectors)

Primary Factors	PF	SL	ULUF	ULRF	ULR	D	F	T1	T2	T3
Seed value	S	0.873	0.628	0.587	0.961	0.874	1.000	0.000	0.000	0.000
Conversion factor (WP)	CFw	0.873	0.628	0.587	0.961	0.874	1.000			
Conversion factor (DP)	CFd	0.999	0.719	0.672	1.100	1.000	1.144			

Table 11.11 Vector of Final Results (P_n)

		EA	DAI	DAN	AI
Conversion factor (WP)	CFw	1.113	0.841	0.874	0.936
Conversion factor (DP)	CFd	1.274	0.962	1.000	1.071

Table 11.8 continued

IT	IM	CM	F	E	W	TC	C	DF	OS	A	M	ACF
0.001	0.002	0.065	0.015	0.201	0.384	0.062	0.082	0.116	0.000	-0.002	0.008	0.025
0.000	0.001	0.056	0.006	0.153	0.332	0.023	0.120	0.046	0.000	0.000	0.006	0.014
0.000	0.000	0.010	0.000	0.026	0.057	0.000	0.049	0.005	0.000	-0.003	0.001	0.001
0.000	0.000	0.000	0.000	0.000	0.000	0.000	0.000	-0.001	0.000	-0.002	0.000	-0.001
0.000	0.001	0.018	0.014	0.089	0.109	0.023	0.045	0.170	1.000	0.346	0.002	0.384
0.730	0.828	0.614	0.724	1.446	1.967	0.700	0.550	0.346	0.000	0.670	0.839	0.523
0.267	0.168	0.230	0.182	0.294	0.397	0.173	0.123	0.185	0.000	-0.011	0.167	0.048
0.000	0.000	-0.067	0.007	-1.255	-2.329	0.003	-0.005	0.032	0.000	0.015	-0.033	-0.005
0.000	0.001	0.074	0.051	0.046	0.082	0.018	0.036	0.100	0.000	-0.012	0.009	0.012

The values for the primary factors defined in P_f are entered into the S vector until the values of the S vector and the P_f vector converge. Convergence can usually be achieved in no more than two iterations as long as reasonably sensible initial seed values are used.

The SIO procedure normally produces results based on a world price numeraire because the value of foreign exchange is the only value determined outside the system. It is, however, very easy to convert the results to a domestic price numeraire system by dividing all the conversion factors by the SCF. This is shown in Tables 11.10 and 11.11.

The extended SIO procedure can be used to define the conversion factors more simply. In the extended SIO procedure the labor categories are treated as sectors, and a similar treatment can also be given to domestic resources. The extended SIO matrix is then inverted and multiplied with a modified F matrix consisting of foreign exchange and various income transfers. The resulting matrix consists of only foreign exchange (value 1.0 in the world price system) and various income transfers (value 0.0). The foreign exchange line then gives the conversion factor without any need for iteration. The disadvantage of this approach is that it apparently shows a foreign exchange content for goods whose value is determined entirely by the internal market. In our example a slightly modified version of the extended procedure has been followed with two primary factors remaining—those of foreign exchange and domestic resources. This allows more ready conversion of the results into the domestic price numeraire approach

Table 11.11 continued

IT	IM	CM	F	E	W	TC	C	DF	OS	A	M	ACF
0.732	0.831	0.728	0.754	1.811	2.640	0.788	0.765	0.627	0.874	0.966	0.853	0.888
0.838	0.951	0.833	0.862	2.072	3.022	0.902	0.875	0.717	1.000	1.105	0.976	1.016

Table 11.12 Inverted Extended SIO Matrix (I − A*)⁻¹

		EA	DAI	DAN	AI	IT	IM	CM	F
Export agriculture	EA	0.980	0.017	0.000	0.000	0.000	0.001	0.017	0.009
Domestic agriculture (imp. sub.)	DAI	−0.011	1.009	0.000	0.000	0.000	0.000	0.010	0.005
Domestic agriculture nontraded	DAN	−0.017	0.014	1.000	0.000	0.000	0.000	0.015	0.008
Agroindustries	AI	−0.004	0.004	0.000	1.000	0.000	0.000	0.010	0.004
Manufacturing—traded	MT	−0.022	0.020	0.000	−0.008	1.004	0.006	0.019	0.026
Imported manufactures	IM	−0.054	0.049	0.000	0.003	0.009	1.016	0.584	0.068
Construction materials	CM	−0.003	0.003	0.000	0.000	0.000	0.000	1.128	0.003
Fuel	F	−0.022	0.020	0.000	0.001	0.004	0.007	0.144	1.027
Electricity	E	−0.001	0.001	0.000	0.000	0.000	0.000	0.041	0.001
Water and sewerage	W	0.000	0.000	0.000	0.000	0.000	0.000	0.023	0.000
Transport and communications	TC	−0.106	0.094	0.000	0.007	0.020	0.034	0.058	0.128
Construction	C	−0.007	0.008	0.000	−0.001	0.000	0.000	0.213	0.011
Distribution and finance	DF	−0.042	0.049	0.000	−0.005	0.002	0.003	0.066	0.113
Other services	OS	−0.012	0.013	0.000	0.000	0.000	0.000	0.009	0.007
Agriculture	A	−0.048	0.040	0.000	−0.001	0.001	0.001	0.042	0.022
Manufacturing	M	−0.007	0.007	0.000	0.000	0.000	0.001	0.017	0.006
Average conversion factor	ACF	−0.069	0.074	0.000	−0.001	0.001	0.002	0.049	0.038
Skilled labor	SL	−0.011	0.009	0.000	−0.001	0.001	0.002	0.065	0.015
Unskilled labor—urban formal	ULUF	−0.004	0.006	0.000	−0.001	0.000	0.001	0.056	0.006
Unskilled labor—rural formal	ULRF	−0.008	0.000	0.000	0.000	0.000	0.000	0.010	0.000
Unskilled labor—rural informal	ULR	−0.006	0.000	0.000	0.000	0.000	0.000	0.000	0.000

Table 11.13 Breakdown into Primary Factors (F* · (I − A*)⁻¹ = T* Matrix

		EA	DAI	DAN	AI	IT	IM	CM	F
Domestic resources	D	−0.040	0.037	1.000	−0.002	0.002	0.003	0.104	0.029
Foreign exchange	F	1.147	0.808	0.000	0.938	0.731	0.829	0.636	0.728
Taxes and subsidies	T1	−0.071	0.081	0.000	0.106	0.267	0.168	0.232	0.183
Operating surplus (public)	T2	−0.002	0.068	0.000	−0.041	0.000	0.000	−0.067	0.007
Operating surplus (private)	T3	−0.031	0.004	0.000	0.000	0.000	0.001	0.074	0.051
Income to unskilled labor—UF	IULF	−0.001	0.002	0.000	0.000	0.000	0.000	0.017	0.002
Income to unskilled labor—RF	IULR	−0.003	0.000	0.000	0.000	0.000	0.000	0.004	0.000

Table 11.14 Seed Value and Vector of Final Results (Pₙ*)

		EA	DAI	DAN	AI	IT	IM	CM	F
Conversion factor (WP)	CF$_w$	1.113	0.841	0.874	0.936	0.732	0.831	0.728	0.754
Conversion factor (DP)	CF$_d$	1.273	0.962	1.000	1.071	0.838	0.951	0.833	0.862
Seed values (SCF, FE)	S*	0.874	1.000						
SCF	CF	0.874							
SER	CF	1.144							

Table 11.12 continued

E	W	TC	C	DF	OS	A	M	ACF	SL	ULUF	ULRF	ULR
0.073	0.106	0.016	0.048	0.105	0.000	0.412	0.002	0.236	0.017	0.059	0.240	0.392
0.041	0.060	0.009	0.027	0.059	0.000	0.232	0.001	0.133	0.009	0.033	0.135	0.221
0.061	0.089	0.013	0.040	0.088	0.000	0.346	0.002	0.199	0.014	0.050	0.202	0.330
0.035	0.061	0.011	0.015	0.041	0.000	-0.001	0.595	0.047	0.125	0.000	0.000	-0.001
0.037	0.202	0.200	0.018	0.038	0.000	-0.004	0.282	0.032	0.059	-0.001	-0.003	-0.004
1.273	1.266	0.498	0.454	0.138	0.000	-0.011	0.076	0.066	0.016	-0.002	-0.006	-0.011
0.491	0.767	0.005	0.287	0.042	0.000	0.000	0.139	0.029	0.029	0.000	0.000	0.000
0.179	0.410	0.215	0.095	0.023	0.000	-0.005	0.020	0.017	0.004	-0.001	-0.003	-0.004
1.019	0.121	0.001	0.011	0.007	0.000	0.000	0.005	0.007	0.001	0.000	0.000	0.000
0.011	1.017	0.001	0.006	0.006	0.000	0.000	0.003	0.005	0.001	0.000	0.000	0.000
0.101	0.201	1.049	0.050	0.055	0.000	-0.022	0.017	0.046	0.003	-0.003	-0.013	-0.021
0.736	1.602	0.011	1.386	0.151	0.000	-0.001	0.026	0.074	0.005	0.000	-0.001	-0.001
0.098	0.154	0.084	0.061	1.513	0.000	-0.006	0.005	0.237	0.001	-0.001	-0.003	-0.006
0.043	0.053	0.011	0.022	0.087	1.000	-0.002	0.001	0.186	0.000	0.000	-0.001	-0.002
0.175	0.255	0.038	0.115	0.252	0.000	0.990	0.005	0.568	0.041	0.142	0.576	0.943
0.059	0.101	0.017	0.025	0.054	0.000	-0.001	1.002	0.076	0.210	0.000	-0.001	-0.001
0.247	0.303	0.062	0.126	0.452	0.000	-0.011	0.006	1.073	0.001	-0.002	-0.007	-0.011
0.201	0.385	0.062	0.082	0.116	0.000	-0.002	0.008	0.025	1.002	0.000	-0.001	-0.002
0.153	0.333	0.023	0.120	0.046	0.000	0.000	0.006	0.014	0.001	1.000	0.000	0.000
0.026	0.057	0.000	0.049	0.005	0.000	-0.003	0.001	0.001	0.000	0.000	0.998	-0.003
0.000	-0.001	0.000	0.000	-0.001	0.000	-0.002	0.000	-0.001	0.000	0.000	-0.001	0.998

Table 11.13 continued

E	W	TC	C	DF	OS	A	M	ACF	SL	ULUF	ULRF	ULR
0.342	0.619	0.084	0.192	0.288	1.000	0.342	0.012	0.411	0.766	0.610	0.228	0.373
1.512	2.099	0.715	0.597	0.375	0.000	0.666	0.842	0.529	0.203	0.095	0.388	0.635
0.300	0.410	0.175	0.126	0.189	0.000	-0.011	0.167	0.049	0.035	-0.002	-0.006	-0.010
-1.255	-2.331	0.002	-0.004	0.032	0.000	0.015	-0.033	-0.005	-0.006	0.002	0.009	0.014
0.046	0.082	0.018	0.035	0.100	0.000	-0.012	0.009	0.012	0.001	-0.002	-0.007	-0.011
0.045	0.098	0.007	0.036	0.014	0.000	0.000	0.002	0.004	0.000	0.296	0.000	0.000
0.010	0.022	0.000	0.019	0.002	0.000	-0.001	0.000	0.000	0.000	0.000	0.388	-0.001

Table 11.14 continued

E	W	TC	C	DF	OS	A	M	ACF	SL	ULUF	ULRF	ULR
1.811	2.640	0.788	0.765	0.627	0.874	0.966	0.853	0.888	0.873	0.628	0.587	0.961
2.072	3.022	0.902	0.876	0.717	1.000	1.105	0.976	1.016	0.999	0.719	0.672	1.100

and a clearer specification of income distribution effects. The following procedure was used: The I-A^* matrix was constructed by subtracting the A^* matrix (this time, sector rows EA to ULR by sector columns EA to ULR) from the identity matrix. The extended matrix was then inverted over the specified range of the I-A^* matrix (Table 11.12). The F^* matrix (primary factor rows D to IULR by sector columns EA to ULR) was multiplied by the I-A^* matrix to derive the T^* matrix (Table 11.13). The T^* matrix gives a breakdown of the value of the output of each sector into domestic resources, foreign exchange, and various income transfers.

The estimation of the conversion factors is undertaken by defining a vector (S^*) with seed values for the SCF and the value of foreign exchange (assumed to be 1.0 with a world price numeraire). The first estimate of the conversion factors is obtained by multiplying the vector S^* by the T^* matrix. This gives the first value for the vector of sector conversion factors (P_n^*, the first line in Table 11.14).

A second vector of primary factors (P_f^*) is defined with foreign exchange given the value of 1.0 and the SCF derived by multiplying the P_n^* vector by the vector of sector breakdowns for the SCF (D_t vector = primary factor column D by sector rows EA to ULR). The values for the SCF defined in P_f^* are entered into the S^* vector until the values for the SCF in the S^* vector and the P_f^* vector converge. As with the conventional SIO approach, results in the domestic price numeraire system can be obtained by dividing by the SCF.

The big advantage of the extended SIO approach is that it allows the identification of indirect income effects. Table 11.13 consists only of two primary factors (foreign exchange and domestic resources) and transfer payments (income changes). If the domestic price numeraire approach is used an additional income change can be identified, arising from the difference between the shadow exchange rate and one, and applied to all foreign exchange effects. The issue of income distribution effects is explored further in Chapter 13.

At first sight the SIO approach seems to have many attractions. There is no doubt that it can be useful in providing global estimates of shadow prices for an economy. However, it is necessary to consider the limitations of the approach. First of all, SIO suffers from all of the limitations of any other form of input-output analysis. Inevitably it is likely to be highly aggregated. A sixty-sector model is quite possible if the data are available, but even a sixty-sector model provides a fairly aggregated picture of a complex modern economy. Within each sector there will be differences, and there will also be differences between different locations.

The results of SIO studies also become out of date quite quickly when there are rapid policy changes. It is therefore advisable to use the results carefully, and in general they should not be used for the most important

items of project costs and benefits. For such items a project-specific estimate is likely to be more reliable although the SIO estimates may be of use
as inputs into the calculation of project-specific estimates. If used carefully
and intelligently SIO estimates of national shadow prices can be very useful. If used without proper thought they are unlikely to be of any value.

Further Reading

A helpful introduction to the SIO approach is given in Weiss (1988). The
first application of the SIO approach was tried out in Kenya and is
described in Scott, MacArthur, and Newbery (1976). An explanation of the
SIO method backed up by case studies is given in Powers (1981). Applications of the SIO methodology in particular countries are described by
Saerbeck (1988) for Botswana and by Potts (1996a) for Lithuania. Potts
(1999) describes how SIO methods can be used to derive indirect income
effects (see chapter 13). Londero (1994) shows how the SIO approach can
be used to estimate the shadow exchange rate.

Notes

1. Strictly speaking the domestic resources category relates to values that are
determined by domestic willingness to pay and therefore might be defined as average domestic consumption. The relationship between the two main primary factors
is then defined by the relationship between average consumer willingness to pay
and border price values. In practice the domestic resources category is also used for
residual items where further disaggregation is either impossible because of data
limitations or of little value because the size of the item is small.

2. The term *numeraire* was first used in this context by Little and Mirrlees
(1969 and 1974).

3. Conversion factors are also sometimes described as *accounting price
ratios*. The use of this term has similar potential for causing interdisciplinary confusion as the use of the term *accounting price*.

4. The acronym SER is therefore used here to mean the shadow exchange
rate conversion factor rather than a particular rate.

5. An example of the estimation of the shadow exchange rate for the
Philippines is given in Asian Development Bank (1997: app. 16). This estimate
includes the effect of quantitative restrictions on trade and attempts to take account
of expected changes in the real exchange rate.

6. The real exchange rate concept is discussed in more detail in Chapter 16.
The issue of the long-term sustainability of the official exchange rate is discussed in
Asian Development Bank (1997) in relation to the Philippines example mentioned
above. The issue is also discussed in Curry and Weiss (2000: 141–142).

7. An example of the application of this approach can be seen in Potts
(1990).

8. Strictly speaking the equivalent SCF to an SER is 0.833 recurring. This is

the value that has been used because the purpose is to show the equivalence of the two systems and the values are determined by formulas in a spreadsheet. In practice it is neither necessary nor credible to go beyond the use of two decimal places in using conversion factors.

    9. See Irvin (1976: chap. 5) for some of the arguments used during the 1970s.

    10. The *extended SIO* approach was first used by Tan Tok Shiong and is described in Tan Tok Shiong and MacArthur (1995).

12

The Rate of Discount and the Value of Investment

All the measures of project worth outlined in Chapter 4 require that a discount rate is specified. In the case of the NPV and the various versions of the benefit-cost ratio the discount rate must be specified before the calculations can be made. Estimation of the IRR does not require prior specification of the discount rate, but without an idea of what the discount rate should be it is difficult to make judgments on the implications of the result. As long as investment resources are regarded as an important constraint there will always be a need to specify the discount rate(s) to be applied to the appraisal of investment projects.

There are two main approaches to estimating the discount rate for the economic analysis of projects. The first is based on the estimation of the opportunity cost of capital and requires assumptions about the alternative uses of the resources used for investing in a project. The second approach is based on the idea of social time preference and considers the economic logic underlying the preference for present as opposed to future consumption. These approaches are discussed in turn.

The Opportunity Cost of Capital Approach

The conventional approach to estimating the discount rate for economic efficiency analysis is to try to measure the economic opportunity cost of capital. The implicit assumption is usually that use of investment funds for any one project precludes the use of those funds for another project. In principle the economic opportunity cost of capital should be estimated at shadow prices, although there is an element of circularity involved because knowledge of the discount rate is required for the estimation of the shadow prices for some nontraded goods.[1]

There are four possible approaches to estimating the economic opportunity cost of capital, as described below.

Evaluation Studies

A number of projects could be evaluated at shadow prices to find out their economic rate of return. A rough estimate of the opportunity cost of capital might be obtained by using the lower end of the range of rates of return. The implicit assumption here is that the range of economic internal rate of return (EIRR) values for past projects gives a reasonable indication of the possible range for future projects. Various approaches can be used.

The simplest approach is to use the EIRR values for projects already appraised for the most recent public investment program or medium-term economic plan. The disadvantages of this approach include the following: (1) Usually a PIP will include some projects for which a full-scale project appraisal has been done and others, particularly in the social sectors, where such an appraisal has not been done. It is difficult to be sure that the subset for which full appraisals have been done is representative. Often it is also difficult to ensure that projects have been appraised on a consistent basis. (2) The PIP only covers the public sector and in some cases a small number of private-sector projects with implications for the availability of public investment funds (e.g., where there is a loan guarantee). In principle it can be argued that the marginal public-sector investment should have an EIRR that is similar to that of marginal private-sector investments. Otherwise a welfare improvement could be obtained by shifting resources between the private sector and the public sector in favor of the sector for which the EIRR is highest.

An alternative approach is to undertake an expost evaluation of a representative sample of projects implemented in recent years, if necessary including both the public and the private sectors, and to ensure that the evaluations are conducted in a consistent manner. If it were felt that the marginal unit of public investment would be displacing marginal private investment, then the analysis could be restricted to the private sector.

The expost evaluation approach has the disadvantage that it is potentially expensive and that there may be a significant difference between expost evaluation results and those of exante appraisals.[2] It could be argued that a discount rate to be used for project appraisal purposes should relate to project appraisal practice rather than evaluation results. The cost of the expost evaluation approach could be reduced by using existing evaluation studies, but it is unlikely that these would be consistent in their approach or in their use of economic parameters.

Using Macroeconomic Data

In principle it is possible to estimate the total amount of value added in the economy and the value of the capital stock used to produce it from national accounts data and input-output tables.[3] Some of the value added will represent a return to various types of labor and land. Both the value added and the returns to labor and land should be measured in shadow prices. The remaining value added is then assumed to be the return to capital, and the ratio of this value added to the value of the capital stock gives an estimate of the opportunity cost of capital. Such estimates are almost invariably overestimates for a number of reasons:

1. The estimate obtained in this way is an average figure while the opportunity cost of capital is a marginal concept—the lowest acceptable rate of return before investment funds are exhausted. The average rate of return will always be above the marginal rate.
2. Use of the shadow wage rate understates the contribution of labor. It may be possible to use unskilled workers on an additional project at a relatively low opportunity cost in terms of foregone production, but it would not be possible to transfer all workers at such a low cost in production.
3. Historic cost data on the value of the capital stock understate its value. It is extremely difficult to get a reasonably accurate measure of the value of the capital stock expressed in current prices.
4. The residual method of apportioning returns to capital tends to lead to overstatement because all technical progress is assumed to be a return to capital.

Macroeconomic approaches to the estimation of the opportunity cost of capital are therefore not very reliable unless conducted very carefully and with full recognition of the nature of the assumptions used.

The Real Cost of Borrowing

Many countries borrow money from abroad to finance at least part of their investment requirements. If borrowing money from abroad is a possible option and if a country is considering this option, then the economic rate of return on the project should be at least equal to the real cost of borrowing. This is usually defined in relation to an international rate such as the London Inter-Bank Offer Rate (LIBOR). In practice this approach is quite common, and, partly for this reason, discount rates for most countries tend to lie in the range of 5% to 15%, although the higher end of this range cannot be justified by any historical levels of *real* interest rates.[4] However, such an approach cannot be used very easily for the poorest developing countries, which are often unable or unwilling to borrow on commercial markets. For such countries the cost of foreign commercial borrowing is not a relevant opportunity cost.

Trial and Error

The discount rate can be treated as an unknown. An initial figure might be selected on the basis of experience elsewhere or an estimate based on the limited data available. Most countries seem to choose about 10% as a starting estimate, although this figure is probably rather high if it is compared to the *actual* rates of return on marginal projects. The initial figure could then be adjusted in the light of experience. If too many projects are accepted, the discount rate could be raised; if not enough are acceptable, a lower discount rate could be used.

There are two main problems with the trial and error approach. First of all there is a risk that those preparing projects will overestimate the benefits and underestimate the costs if they think that there is a chance that the discount rate will be increased. This problem is common to all capital rationing approaches to the discount rate. A second problem, also associated with capital rationing approaches, is that the investment budget is assumed to be fixed. The possibility is not considered that overall welfare could be improved by increasing or reducing the proportion of income invested with a corresponding effect on present consumption. Finally, it is not obvious which period should be used in determining how to ration capital. In most cases the starting date for the implementation of projects can be delayed, and so the relevant capital constraint may be availability over a medium-term period, not a single year.

There is no completely reliable way to calculate the opportunity cost of capital. In practice therefore it is common for those attempting to make such estimates to use a variety of approaches and then to make a judgment as to which approach reflects best the situation of the country concerned. Whatever rate is eventually chosen is sure to be subject to a significant margin of error. There is therefore good reason to estimate the NPV of projects at discount rates above and below the official rate to determine the sensitivity of the project to the choice of discount rate.

Even if it were possible to obtain a reliable estimate of the opportunity cost of capital using the above approaches, problems would still remain because each of the above approaches makes assumptions about the nature of the capital market and the extent to which resources can be switched between different uses.

Those approaches that concentrate on the opportunity cost of public investment assume that there is no possibility for substitution between the public and private sectors or for the use of international borrowing. Approaches that consider the opportunity cost of capital in the private sector assume that a transfer of resources between the public and private sectors would result in a change in private-sector investment rather than in private consumption. Furthermore, approaches based on the opportunity cost of capital consider only the demand price of capital and do not take account of the supply price.

The opportunity cost of capital approach is only valid if the domestic supply of investment funds is perfectly inelastic. If this is not the case, then any additional investment will have the effect partly of displacing other investments and partly of inducing more saving and therefore less consumption. These effects will be brought about through changes in the real rate of interest. It can therefore be argued that the economic cost of an additional investment should be the weighted average of the opportunity cost of the investment displaced and the opportunity cost of the additional saving generated.[5]

We have already considered the opportunity cost of displaced investment. What determines the supply price of saving or the price at which people are willing to sacrifice present consumption for future consumption? To answer this question we need to investigate the concept of time preference.

The Social Time Preference Approach

In considering the social time preference approach to estimating the discount rate we need to examine the underlying logic behind discounting. Why should income in the future have a lower value than present income?

One reason has already been considered. An alternative investment may be available giving a positive rate of return. But what if it is possible to transfer resources from consumption to investment and vice versa? In such cases the only reason for preferring present income to that of the future is if future consumption has a lower value than present consumption. Why should this be?

The first reason is that people might have an absolute preference for present income because of uncertainty about the future. This is sometimes described as *pure time preference*. It is usually argued that, while this may be important for people as individuals, it should not be a significant factor for the government because the government should take account of the interest of future generations as well as the present generation. For this reason it is usually argued that the rate of pure time preference (p) should be no more than 2% per annum.

The second reason why consumption may have a lower value in the future than in the present is that people may become richer in the future. It can be argued that the principle of diminishing marginal utility can be applied to consumption in general as well as to the individual items that make up that consumption. An extra unit of consumption to a poor person is more important and therefore of more value than an extra unit of consumption to someone who is rich. If per capita consumption is growing, then the value of additional consumption in each year in the future is declining at a rate related to the rate of growth of per capita consumption (g) and the elasticity of diminishing marginal utility of consumption (e).

From the above reasoning it is possible to construct a formula for i, the social rate of discount (also called the consumption rate of interest):

$$i = eg + p \qquad (12.1)$$

The problem with this formula is that two of the parameters in the formula, e and p, are essentially value judgments. Empirical determination of i is therefore very difficult. Nevertheless some indication of range is possible. Values for e of less than 0.5 and greater than 2.0 are not usually consistent with other indicators of government attitudes to distributional issues such as minimum wage levels or poverty lines. Values for p of greater than 2% imply an attitude toward future generations that might be regarded as socially irresponsible.

Empirical estimates for g are possible based on past performance. However, it should be recognized that, if the estimate is to be used for estimating the social discount rate, it is the expected future growth in per capita consumption that matters. Rates of per capita consumption growth of more than 4% are difficult to sustain in the long run, and so it might be assumed that long-run values for g would be in the range 0–4% for most developing countries, with most countries being at the lower end of the range.

From the above discussion it is possible to get an idea of the range of possible values for i. A possible range of values might be 0% to 10% with the most likely range being 2% to 6%. The latter range is significantly below the range usually used as a discount rate by developing countries and international funding agencies. The implication of this result is that the opportunity cost of capital could be significantly above the rate at which society as a whole would wish to discount the value of consumption. This would not be possible if there were a perfect capital market because an opportunity cost of capital higher than the social rate of discount would lead to higher investment. However, capital markets are not perfect, particularly in developing countries. People collectively may have a different view of time preference than they display as individuals.[6] There may also be institutional constraints on the level of savings that prevent the supply of savings from satisfying the demand for investment. These issues are examined in more detail in the next section.

Explaining the Difference:
The Uses of Additional Income

There are a number of reasons why capital markets do not function perfectly. The first and most obvious reason is that the criterion of perfect knowledge cannot be satisfied because to know the actual return on capital requires knowledge of the future. The impossibility of perfect knowledge of the future means that any future return to an investment is uncertain. Even if the chance of exceeding predictions is the same as the chance of doing worse, it is only large organizations that can afford not to have some degree of risk aversion. The time preference of people as individuals will therefore be affected by risk considerations, and this will lead to a higher rate of time preference than would be the case if the future were certain. It can be argued that such behavior, while rational for individuals, should be less important for people acting collectively both because of the need to consider the interests of future generations and because of the ability of large organizations to spread risk.

The difference between the individual and collective perception of time preference is also affected by what Sen (1967) has called the *isolation paradox*. People in isolation may exhibit a high rate of time preference because of their assumptions about the behavior of other people even though they would prefer a lower rate of time preference (higher savings) if they could guarantee that other people would behave in the same way. Observation of market behavior may therefore give an unreliable indication of the true perception of social time preference.

A further problem with using market behavior as a guide is that individual returns are affected by taxes and subsidies, including income tax on interest and profits. Savers will save less than they otherwise would because of taxes on interest, and investors will require a pretax rate of return that is higher than their target post-tax return because of company taxes. In general, taxes on interest and profits will lead to a level of investment that is lower than the optimal level.

It could be argued that the government can make up for the suboptimal investment level by using taxation revenue to increase public investment. However, this could lead to a situation where the return on public-sector investment might be lower than that of the private sector so that the distribution of investment expenditure between public and private sectors would be suboptimal. Furthermore, in many developing countries, the ability of the government to raise revenue from taxation to boost investment is severely constrained by the administrative capacity of the tax authorities as well as by political constraints and the poverty of much of the population.

For all of the above reasons it is quite possible that measures of the opportunity cost of capital (q) could exceed any estimates of the social rate of time preference (i) with the implication that the demand for investment funds will exceed the available supply. In economic efficiency analysis the opportunity cost of capital is used as the discount rate to ration capital among competing projects. However, this leads to the use of a discount rate that is higher than it otherwise would be with results that are not neutral for the choice of projects. In particular the higher the rate of discount, the less likely it is that projects with a long time horizon will be chosen. Yet in some cases these projects might be exactly the type of projects that generate returns that are more likely to be reinvested and could eventually contribute to resolving the investment constraint. Meanwhile, short-term projects imposing longer-term environmental costs might be selected because of their high IRR despite their potential costs to future generations. It is only if the use of income is identical between projects that capital rationing using an opportunity cost rate of discount will give an optimal result. It is therefore necessary to consider the implications of the use to which the income generated by different projects is put.

In principle any additional income generated by a project can be used to increase current consumption or to increase investment. A unit of investment, if invested to earn a return of q% per annum, can generate the equivalent of q units of consumption indefinitely. If this consumption is discounted at the social time preference rate i, it will give a present value of more than one as long as $q > i$. It can therefore be argued that, in conditions where investment is constrained, a unit of investment has more value than a unit of consumption. This idea provides the basis for the estimation of the *shadow price of investment* (P^{inv}), also known as the *value of public income* (v).

Public Investment Constraints and the Value of Public Income

In conditions where public investment is constrained we have seen that the use of an opportunity cost–based discount rate to ration investment funds may not provide the most appropriate solution. An alternative approach is to distinguish between income that is used for further investment and income that is used to increase consumption and then to apply different weights to reflect their relative value. The weights are determined by estimating the present value of the future consumption generated by a marginal unit of investment and discounted at the social rate of time preference i.

The present value (v) of the return on a unit of investment, q, received indefinitely and discounted at the social rate of discount i, is given by the formula:

$$v = \frac{q}{i} \qquad (12.2)$$

Furthermore a proportion of the return on investment (given by s, the marginal propensity to save) will be reinvested, giving further consumption gains. This leads to the formula:

$$v = \frac{(1-s)q}{(i-sq)} \qquad (12.3)[7]$$

The main problems with this formula are that it is extremely unstable with varying values of q and i and that it depends on the value judgments embodied in the formula for i. An example serves to illustrate the point. Assume that the value of i is believed to be between 4% and 6%, that the value of q is believed to be between 8% and 10%, and that the value of s is 20%. The following values for v are obtained:

	$q = 8\%$	$q = 10\%$
$i = 4\%$	2.67	4.00
$i = 6\%$	1.45	2.00

Relatively minor variations in assumptions about the key parameters in the formula for the shadow price of investment can therefore lead to considerable differences in the result. It should also be pointed out that the above formula is only correct on the assumption that the parameters are constant. Alternative versions of the formula have been put forward in which the difference between q and i tends to decline until the two are equated.[8] Such formulas give less extreme variations in the values, but it is difficult to see either how the decline in the difference between the two parameters can be determined or why such a decline should actually occur if the difference is a result of inherent deficiencies in the capital market.

Social Analysis, the Numeraire, and the Discount Rate

The process of attaching different weights to different uses of income was developed in the 1970s and described by Squire and van der Tak (1975) as *social analysis.* This process also involved attaching different weights to consumption by different income groups.[9] If such a process is adopted and different values are attached to consumption and investment, it is necessary to make a further choice of numeraire. The original UNIDO *Guidelines* (1972) suggested *consumption to people at the average income level* as the numeraire. Later UNIDO publications and the authors associated with the world price numeraire approach suggested that a unit of *uncommitted government income* should be used as the numeraire, in the former case measured in units of domestic resources and in the latter case measured in units of foreign exchange.

It can be shown that, where a distinction is made between the value of investment and the value of consumption and where the parameters determining the value of investment are assumed to be constant, the appropriate discount rate to be used is the social rate of discount *i*. An adjusted opportunity cost of capital (q') can be defined:

$$q' = \frac{(1-s)}{v} q + sq \qquad (12.4)$$

where the first part of the expression relates to the units of consumption generated per unit of investment each valued at $1/v$ in relation to a unit of investment, and the second part relates to the units of reinvestment generated. Equation 12.4 can be restated:

$$q' = \frac{(1-s)q(i-sq)}{(i-s)q} + sq = (i - sq) + sq = i$$

Consistency Checks and Alternative Estimation Approaches for V

The formula provided for estimating v has been seen to be potentially unstable and dependent on difficult value judgments. Is it therefore possible to obtain a more stable estimate of the value of v from alternative sources? Two alternative and very different approaches have been suggested.

The first approach is to check the results from the original formula with alternative indicators. Uncommitted government income is assumed to be of equal value to a unit of consumption at a base level of income, b, which is usually defined by a poverty datum line or an indicator of the level of income below which the government ceases to levy tax or provides some form of income subsidy. A consistency check can be made by comparing Equation 12.3 with

$$v = \left(\frac{c}{b} \right)^e \tag{12.5}$$

where c is the average level of consumption. The value of a unit of government investment[10] is equal to the ratio of the average level of consumption to the base level raised to the power of e, the rate at which the value of consumption declines as the level of consumption rises.[11]

Equations 12.4 and 12.5 will only be consistent for certain combinations of i, e, q, and s. Empirical estimates of q and s can be made, as can an estimate of the value of g to enter into the formula for i. This reduces the range of possible values for the parameters for which value judgments are needed. Various assumptions for the values of p and e can be introduced until consistent values are derived. Some data, partly taken from a real economy, serve to illustrate the approach (see Table 12.1):

- The value of q is estimated to be between 6% and 8%.
- The value of s is estimated to be about 15%.
- The value of g is estimated to be 1.4% currently and is expected to be about 1.5% in the medium term.

Table 12.1   Derivation of Shadow Price of Investment by Year (all figures in constant 1998 prices)

	1995	1998	Overall	Rate of Growth Population	Per Capita
Gross domestic product (GDP)	134,008	155,084	5.0%	3.2%	1.8%
Increase in GDP		21,076			
Total consumption	125,660	143,720	4.6%	3.2%	1.4%
Increase in consumption		18,060			
Per capita consumption	2,096	2,180			
Domestic savings	8,348	11,364			
Increase in saving		3,016			
Marginal propensity to save		14.3%			

Estimates for v	$q = 6\%$	$q = 7\%$	$q = 8\%$
$i = 3\%$	2.43	3.05	3.78
$i = 4\%$	1.65	2.02	2.43
$i = 5\%$	1.24	1.50	1.78

- The value of p is believed to be about 2%.
- The value of e is believed to be between 0.5 and 2.0.
- The base level of consumption (b) is estimated to be more than 1,200 and less than 1,600 compared with an average level (c) of 2,180.

On the basis of this information the value of i will range from 2.75% to 5%. Assume that this range can be narrowed down to 3%–5%. The following values of v could be calculated:

	$q = 6\%$	$q = 7\%$	$q = 8\%$
$i = 3\%$	2.43	3.05	3.78
$i = 4\%$	1.65	2.02	2.43
$i = 5\%$	1.24	1.50	1.78

The restrictions on the values of e and b mean that the range of possible values for v is from 1.24 to 3.05. The compatible combinations of q and i are shown in italics. The value for i of 3% is only compatible with the values for q of 6% and 7%. Further examination of the implications of particular values can narrow the range of values down further until an acceptable set of consistent parameters is derived. This process is shown in Table 12.2 where compatible values are shown in italics. A central value for v of 1.65 is compatible with values of $q = 6\%$, $i = 4\%$, $e = 1.0$, and $b = 1,200$–1,600. This is the value chosen for illustration purposes in Chapter 13. Alternative values for q of 7% and 8% give values for v of 2.02 and 2.43 respectively. These values are less likely to be compatible with the value for i because they imply either a higher rate of pure time preference or a higher rate of growth.

A totally different approach has been proposed by Devarajan et al. (1996). They argue that there is an economic cost of raising taxation rev-

Table 12.2   Consistency Check for Values for b

$b >$	1,200
$b <$	1,600
$c =$	2,180

Value for v	3.78	3.05	2.43	2.02	1.78	1.65	1.50	1.24
$e = 0.5$	1,122	1,248	1,399	1,535	1,635	1,700	1,780	1,957
$e = 1.0$	577	714	898	1,081	1,226	1,325	1,453	1,756
$e = 1.5$	297	409	576	761	919	1,033	1,186	1,576
$e = 2.0$	153	234	370	536	689	805	969	1,414

enue for government expenditure due to the distortionary effects of taxes and that measurement of this cost can provide an estimate of the opportunity cost of public funds. They suggest that the distortionary cost can be in the range 30%–50% for developed countries and even higher for developing countries. Measurement of such distortions requires rather strong assumptions about the nature and economic efficiency of the market mechanism, and the reliability of measurements of distortionary costs is open to question. Nevertheless the implications in terms of the existence of a scarcity value of public investment funds are similar to those derived from earlier approaches.

It can be seen that there may be a case for adding a premium to costs and benefits that are likely to affect the availability of investment funds, particularly the scarce funds available to the government. Various approaches are available for measuring this premium, but they are all subject to a significant margin of error. One way of approaching the problem is to test for consistency with other measures related to the value of income at different income levels. In all cases it is impossible to use the investment premium effectively without identifying the distribution of the costs and benefits of projects. Chapter 13 will consider the issues surrounding estimation of distributional impacts and how and whether to use distributional weights.

Further Reading

Most major texts on the economic analysis of projects cover the issue of the discount rate. Perkins (1994: chap. 13) provides a useful and comprehensive review of different approaches. Price (1993) provides a thorough and critical review of the whole issue of discounting. Jenkins and Harberger (1991) describe a weighted cost of capital approach to estimation of the discount rate. Feldstein (1964) is the classic exposition of the social time preference rate approach. Kula (1996) provides a historical approach to the development of ideas on discounting. Scott (1977) examines the evidence on the basis for the test rate of discount for the UK. Livingstone and Tribe (1995) give a critical assessment of conventional assumptions about the level of the rate of discount and examine some of the implications.

The idea for the shadow price of investment was developed by Marglin (1963a, 1963b, and 1967), and this idea was incorporated into the UNIDO *Guidelines* (1972: chaps. 13 and 14). Little and Mirrlees (1974: chaps. 13 and 14) discuss the same concept in a slightly different framework and with different assumptions. The same issues are also covered by Squire and van der Tak (1975: chaps. 7 and 10).

Notes

1. Due to the circularity problem it is advisable that when estimates of shadow prices for an economy are made, estimation of the discount rate should be included as part of the exercise to ensure the internal consistency of the estimates. In principle the issue of circularity also means that any set of shadow prices is only consistent with one discount rate and therefore that an economic IRR cannot be calculated. For practical purposes this complication is usually ignored although the issue could be significant in the analysis of projects making use of the products of capital-intensive nontraded sectors.

2. A study by the FAO Investment Centre of seventy-five projects prepared between 1970 and 1980 and subsequently evaluated found that 75% of the projects achieved results that were worse than the original appraisal estimates (FAO 1989).

3. Measurement of the value of capital is one of the central theoretical problems of economics and is beset by logical difficulties associated with the impossibility of knowing the future return on a unit of capital invested. This does not stop economists from trying to measure it! The usual simplifying assumption is that the experience of the past provides a reasonable guide for expectations of the future.

4. When real interest rates were very high in the 1980s the average rate was still only about 7–8% in real terms. Allowing a risk premium of about 2% for high-risk countries still only gives rates of 9–10%. Rates in the 1990s have been significantly lower. The concept of real interest rates is discussed in Chapter 16.

5. This approach is associated with Jenkins and Harberger (1991).

6. The issue of the difference between individual and collective time preference is also related to the mortality of individuals. While society can be assumed to have an infinite life, it consists of cohorts of individuals with finite lives. This difference provides the basis for a modified approach to discounting suggested by Kula. Kula's approach has been the subject of debate (particularly in *Project Appraisal* 1988–1989) but has not been used in practice. The modified discounting method gives similar discount factors in the early years of a project's life, but they do not tend to zero, and, after a period defined by average life expectancy, they become constant.

7. This formula is closely associated with the work of Marglin and is reflected in the 1972 UNIDO *Guidelines*. For a general derivation of this formula from first principles see Potts (1979).

8. See, for example, Little and Mirrlees (1974).

9. The estimation of such weights is discussed in Chapter 13.

10. It is usually assumed that government income is equally valuable whether it is used for investment or consumption. To assume otherwise would be to assume irrationality of the government in its allocation of expenditure—a rather dangerous view to put forward in practice. It is possible also to distinguish between public and private investment, but this complicates the analysis without usually adding any significant increase in accuracy.

11. The rationale for the parameter e is discussed in Chapter 13.

13

Alternative Approaches to Economic Analysis and the Distribution of Costs and Benefits

Who Gets What?
Identification of Distribution Effects

In recent years concern with the impact of structural adjustment policies on the distribution of income and the availability of public investment funds has led to a revival of interest in the distributional impact of projects. The focus of the original project analysis literature on the distributional impact of projects was largely on the calculation of income distribution weights and their use in adjusting shadow prices. Relatively little attention was paid to the process of actually estimating distributional impact in a comprehensive manner.[1] Implementation of distribution weighting approaches proved difficult because of the value judgments involved. More recent concerns with fiscal impact have led to a revival of interest in measuring distributional effects without necessarily introducing any weighting system.

In practice, estimating the distribution effects is the difficult part of the analysis and the subsequent application of weights is relatively easy if sufficient agreement can be obtained to determine the basis for calculating the weights. Estimation of distribution effects is particularly difficult using the world price numeraire approach to economic analysis because the units that costs and benefits are counted in do not correspond to the units that the recipients actually spend. The use of composite conversion factors also obscures the nature of distribution effects. For these reasons a domestic price numeraire approach is preferable if direct estimation of distributional impact is to be undertaken.[2]

The distributional impact of a project can be assessed by identifying the most important stakeholders and estimating both the direct income effects of the project and the indirect effects caused by externalities and the divergence of prices from economic values. In principle the economic NPV of any project can be divided among the various recipients of benefits. For example,

$$ENPV = NPV_{MP} + NPV_X + (NPV_F * AF_F) +$$
$$\Sigma_i(NPV_{Li} * AF_{Li}) - \Sigma_j NPV_{Tj} \tag{13.1}$$
$$\text{and } NPV_{MP} = \Sigma_k NPV_{Sk} + NPV_B + NPV_{CT} + NPV_{ND} \tag{13.2}$$

where $ENPV$ is the economic NPV; MP refers to market prices; X refers to externalities; F refers to foreign exchange; Li refers to different categories of labor; Tj refers to different categories of transfer payments; AF refers to adjustment factors; S refers to stakeholders affected directly, including the owners of the project; B refers to the bank or lenders to the project; CT refers to government income from company taxes; and ND refers to net debtors as the recipients of accounts receivable net of accounts payable.

Equation 13.1 identifies the economic analysis adjustments to the market price NPV, and Equation 13.2 identifies the immediate beneficiaries from the financial analysis. Obviously Equation 13.2 would become more complicated for an enabling project with a larger number or categorization of beneficiaries than for a directly productive commercial project. Nevertheless the principle remains the same. The market price NPV is the sum of the NPVs to all the individual stakeholders directly affected by the project.

It should be noted that, in more sophisticated calculations of the shadow wage rate, not all of the adjustment to unskilled labor represents a change in the income of workers. This is because the difference between the market price and the shadow price of the goods produced by workers in their alternative occupation might involve elements of foreign exchange or transfer payments. One way to take such considerations into account is to treat labor as a nontraded good and to present information on labor costs in terms of foreign exchange, domestic resources, and various categories of transfer payments, one of which would be additional income to labor. An illustration of an alternative way of dealing with income effects deriving from the use of unskilled labor through the use of primary and secondary breakdowns is given below.

Particularly important aspects of distribution analysis are the analysis of fiscal impact and the assessment of the impact on poverty reduction. These are discussed in turn.

Fiscal Impact

In many countries concern has been expressed over the constraints facing governments in funding public-sector activities, partly as a result of structural adjustment and programs of economic liberalization. In principle a thorough economic analysis should provide the information needed to identify the impact of a project on government income (i.e., the fiscal impact). Considering Equations 13.1 and 13.2 above the fiscal impact (NPV_G) can be defined as

$$NPV_G = NPV_{CT} + (NPV_F * AF_F) - \Sigma_j NPV_{Tj} \qquad (13.3)$$

Equation 13.3 assumes that the difference between the shadow exchange rate and the official exchange rate is entirely due to taxes and subsidies on traded goods and therefore that any change in foreign exchange availability has a direct effect on government income from this source. If part of this difference is due to quantitative controls on trade, some of this income could accrue to traders and/or rent seekers profiting from artificial scarcity.

Impact on Poverty Reduction

Another recent trend has been the revival of interest in poverty reduction. In principle the contribution of projects to poverty reduction objectives can be assessed by estimating the direct income effects on stakeholders at market prices as well as the indirect effects of projects in terms of their contribution to the incomes of workers, particularly through induced employment of unskilled labor. It would then be possible to state clearly the direct and indirect impact of the project on target groups.

Part of the problem of assessing the impact of projects on poverty lies in the definition of target groups. What are the characteristics that define a poor group? Is income the most important factor or are other characteristics such as gender, ethnic group, or age equally important in defining the groups affected by poverty? Resolution of these issues is beyond the scope of this book, but they need to be addressed by anyone wishing to make a serious analysis of the impact of projects on poverty reduction. Targeted approaches to poverty alleviation are unlikely to have any success if the groups defined do not have any social meaning.

If the income effects of a project are to be estimated, a methodology is required that allows the analyst to make such estimates. To some extent such a methodology is provided by the UNIDO approach. However, the published expositions of this methodology summarize all of the effects of a project in present values when the timing of these income changes may well be of interest. Published case studies also tend to assume that the entire difference between the shadow wage and the market wage is an income gain to workers, an unnecessary simplification. The methodology therefore needs to be adapted to take account of these issues. The next two sections will describe a modified version of the UNIDO approach and then outlines an alternative approach that tries to measure income directly.

A Modified UNIDO Approach

It was suggested that it was possible to estimate income effects using the UNIDO approach but that the approach would have to be modified in the following way:[3] (1) The income effects would have to be indicated on a year-by-year basis. This would require the disaggregation of costs and benefits into primary factors on a year-by-year basis. (2) The disaggregation of costs and benefits would have to take account of the distributional implications of transfer payments. Transfer payments would therefore have to be classified according to the nature of the recipients of the transfer while labor costs would have to be decomposed into other primary factors and various transfer payments, of which one would be income to labor.

The process can be illustrated using the example developed in previous chapters. The breakdown into primary factors is given in Table 11.2. By multiplying the percentage breakdown for each cost or benefit item by the market price value, it is possible to obtain an overall breakdown into primary factors on a year-by-year basis. This is shown as the primary breakdown in Table 13.1. The disaggregation of labor costs into primary factors and transfer payments was outlined in Table 10.4. Assuming that no similar information is available on skilled labor it can be assumed that skilled labor costs are a domestic resource cost. A secondary breakdown of the costs and benefits into foreign exchange, domestic resources, and various categories of transfer payments can then be obtained by applying the breakdown for unskilled labor given in Table 10.4 to the unskilled labor costs. The resulting secondary breakdown shown in Table 13.1 consists of foreign exchange, domestic resources, and three categories of transfer payment relating to income to government, unskilled workers, and landowners.

Two different values for the foreign exchange premium are applied in Table 11.1 so that the results can be tested for variations in the assumptions about the relative scarcity of foreign exchange and so that the domestic resource cost of foreign exchange can be estimated. Three different discount rates are also used.

The results are shown in a matrix so that a balanced view of the sensitivity of the project to changes in key parameters can be obtained. Since most of the values for the NPV are negative the project is unlikely to be accepted unless there are very strong distributional grounds for accepting it. This issue can be examined in Table 13.2.

The distribution of the direct costs and benefits between equity, the bank, other enterprises, the government, different categories of farmers, the ginnery, and the villages was shown in Table 8.4. These values can be amended to take account of the indirect costs and benefits traced through the shadow pricing exercise and indicated in Table 13.1. The negative values of the transfer payments shown in Table 13.1 represent income changes

Table 13.1 Economic Analysis Using Modified UNIDO Approach by Year

	1	2	3	4	5	6	7	8	9	10	11	12
Primary Breakdown												
Foreign exchange	-11,764	-9,459	6,013	8,606	9,778	9,723	8,123	9,723	9,723	9,723	13,769	3,900
Domestic resources	-2,636	213	1,330	1,706	1,676	1,651	1,551	1,651	1,651	1,651	1,561	
Skilled labor	-708	-1,627	-2,463	-2,499	-2,502	-2,502	-2,502	-2,502	-2,502	-2,502	-2,502	
Unskilled labor	-1,776	-3,257	-4,906	-6,493	-6,497	-6,497	-6,497	-6,497	-6,497	-6,497	-5,874	
Taxes	-3,140	502	5,129	6,909	6,961	6,941	6,141	6,941	6,941	6,941	6,581	
Land adjustment	-276	24	24	24	24	24	24	24	24	24	24	300
Net benefits (market prices)	-20,300	-13,604	5,128	8,253	9,440	9,340	6,840	9,340	9,340	9,340	13,559	4,200
Secondary breakdown												
Foreign exchange	-12,252	-10,354	4,664	6,820	7,991	7,936	6,336	7,936	7,936	7,936	12,153	3,900
Domestic resources	-4,179	-2,945	-3,438	-3,845	-3,880	-3,905	-4,005	-3,905	-3,905	-3,905	-3,701	1,645
Transfers to unskilled labor	-497	-912	-1,374	-1,818	-1,819	-1,819	-1,819	-1,819	-1,819	-1,819	-1,819	
Taxes	-3,076	583	5,252	7,072	7,124	7,104	6,304	7,104	7,104	7,104	6,727	
Land adjustment	-276	24	24	24	24	24	24	24	24	24	24	300
Net benefits (market prices)	-20,300	-13,604	5,128	8,253	9,440	9,340	6,840	9,340	9,340	9,340	13,559	4,200
Foreign exchange premium (SER = 1.10)	-1,225	-1,035	466	682	799	794	634	794	794	794	1,215	
Foreign exchange premium (SER = 1.20)	-2,450	-2,071	933	1,364	1,598	1,587	1,267	1,587	1,587	1,587	2,431	
Net benefits (SER/OER = 1.10)	-17,656	-14,334	1,693	3,658	4,911	4,825	2,965	4,825	4,825	4,825	9,667	3,900
Net benefits (SER/OER = 1.20)	-18,882	-15,370	2,159	4,340	5,710	5,619	3,599	5,619	5,619	5,619	10,883	3,900

				IRR
Discount Rate	4.0%	8.0%	12.0%	5.7%
NPV (SER/OER = 1.10)	3,397	-3,541	-8,067	7.1%
NPV (SER/OER = 1.20)	6,488	-1,563	-6,867	
DRC of FE	0.99	1.28	1.77	

273

Table 13.2 Distribution Analysis by Year—Modified UNIDO Approach

	0	1	2	3	4	5	6	7	8	9	10	11
Income to equity	−10,000	−3,060	3,085	1,555	3,011	2,399	−131	2,305	2,235	2,159	8,320	3,074
Income to bank	−10,000	−12,000		4,285	4,285	4,285	4,285	4,285	4,285	4,285	4,285	
Government income												
Company taxes					137	716	746	810	880	956	1,038	1,126
Other taxes and public enterprise profits	3,096	−583	−5,252	−7,072	−7,124	−7,104	−6,304	−7,104	−7,104	−7,104	−6,727	
FE adjustment	−2,450	−2,071	933	1,364	1,598	1,587	1,267	1,587	1,587	1,587	2,431	
Income to other enterprises		573	422	367	68						−1,429	−300
Income to landowners	276	−24	−24	−24	−24	−24	−24	−24	−24	−24	−24	
Income to hand cultivators		634	634	634	634	634	634	634	634	634	634	
Income to ox cultivators		1,088	1,096	1,096	1,096	1,096	1,096	1,096	1,096	1,096	1,096	
Income to ginnery		−518	−66	359	253	253	253	253	253	253	−342	
Income to villages	−300	−321	−42	−42	−42	−42	−42	−42	−42	−42	−42	
Income to unskilled labor	497	912	1,374	1,818	1,819	1,819	1,819	1,819	1,819	1,819	1,645	
Net benefits	−18,882	−15,370	2,159	4,340	5,710	5,619	3,599	5,619	5,619	5,619	10,883	3,900

	NPV at		
	4%	8%	12%
Equity	7,936	3,346	294
Bank	4,937	0	−3,344
Government income	−33,226	−26,423	−21,360
Income to other enterprises	345	529	618
Income to landowners	−109	−13	48
Income to hand cultivators	4,941	3,937	3,196
Income to ox cultivators	8,540	6,803	5,523
Income to ginnery	680	480	331
Income to villages	−874	−778	−702
Income to unskilled labor	13,316	10,556	8,530
Total NPV	6,488	−1,563	−6,867

to the government in the form of tax and public enterprise profits, to the unskilled workers in the form of increased wages, and to the landowners in the form of the value of land sales less the foregone rent. The overall distribution of costs and benefits to different stakeholders is shown in Table 13.2 both on a year-by-year basis and in present value form. The main beneficiaries are the unskilled workers and the farmers, and the main losers are the government. There is also some gain to equity and the ginnery. The largest share of the benefits to farmers accrues to the relatively well-off ox cultivators. A conclusion might be that the project could only be justified if the unskilled workers were very poor without the project and if government income were not very scarce, an unlikely combination of circumstances.

It should be noted that the hand cultivators have been assumed to be poor in this case and the ox cultivators to be relatively affluent. In practice such assumptions would have to be verified to ensure that the categorization of groups really did correspond to their relative incomes. Otherwise the poverty impact of the project would remain uncertain. More reliable results could be obtained through more detailed examination of the characteristics of the two groups.

How Much Is Consumption Worth?
Estimation of Distribution Weights

We have seen that there are various ways of estimating the distribution of the benefits from projects, including both direct and indirect effects. Judgments can be made on the desirability or otherwise of such a distribution by analyzing the proportion of net benefits accruing to different income groups as shown in Table 13.2. However, it could be suggested that such judgments could be made more systematically using a clearly defined weighting system. Such a system could be based on the economic principle of *diminishing marginal utility.* This principle states that the more that someone has of something, the less value (or utility) an extra unit of that thing will have. If this principle can be applied to the consumption of individual commodities, why not also apply it to consumption as a whole and to comparisons between people with different levels of consumption? On this basis an extra unit of consumption to a poor person would be considered more valuable than an extra unit to a rich person.

The idea that the principle of diminishing marginal utility can be applied in comparisons between people is probably intuitively acceptable to most people with any concern for raising the living standards of the poor. Whether that idea can and should be introduced into project appraisal is an open question. Some people certainly would argue that policy changes are more likely to have an effect on income distribution than projects. Nevertheless weighting systems can be devised whereby projects could be select-ed according to their impact on income distribution. The idea is simple. Just as savings or government income may be regarded as more valu-able than consumption and weighted correspondingly, so consumption could be weighted according to the level of income of the recipient. The issues are how to decide what the weights are and how to apply them to projects.

Estimating Consumption Weights

There is no objective way in which consumption weights can be estimated. All estimates involve subjective judgment. For this reason almost any set of weights could potentially be chosen. Nevertheless, most economists who have attempted to use consumption weights have chosen to use a relatively systematic method with some basis in economic theory.

Consumption weights are generally estimated in relation to the value of consumption at the average level of per capita consumption (c). Consumption of people at this level may be allocated a weight of one; con-sumption of people at incomes below the average would be allocated a weight greater than one; consumption of people at incomes above the aver-age would be allocated a weight of less than one.[4] The normal method for calculating a weight (d_i) for group i with an income level of c_i is

$$d_i = \left(\frac{c}{c_i}\right)^e \tag{13.4}$$

where e determines the rate at which the weight changes with changes in the income level. According to Equation 11.4, where $c_i < c$,

$$d_i > 1;$$

where $c_i > c$,
$$d_i < 1.$$

Also the higher the value of e, the greater the variation in d_i according to income levels. For example, if $c = 1,000$ and $c_i = 500$,

$$d_i = \left(\frac{1,000}{500}\right)^e$$

when $e = 1$, $d_i = 2$;
when $e = 2$, $d_i = 4$;

if $c_i = 2,000$;
when $e = 1$, $d_i = 0.5$;
when $e = 2$, $d_i = 0.25$.

Applying Consumption Weights

Two approaches to the application of consumption weights have been used. The first approach was to adjust the conversion factors of those items including significant elements of labor costs, particularly the shadow wage rate for unskilled labor. This approach suffers from the limitation that, unless attempts are made to measure other distribution effects directly, it is assumed that the only distributional effects that matter are those relating to unskilled labor.[5] The approach also does not give any information on the income effects themselves.

An alternative approach, closely associated with the use of the domestic price numeraire, is to estimate the distribution effects first before applying weights. The first step is then to estimate the distribution costs and benefits among different groups by the project. Savings effects can be separated out and dealt with separately. Consumption effects can be revalued by multiplying the value of the consumption effect for each group by the distribution weight estimated on the lines outlined above.

At this stage there is a choice of numeraire. There are two possible choices—either savings or consumption at the average level of income. Thus

1. Savings numeraire	→	Savings unchanged
		Consumption $\times d_i \div v$
2. Average consumption numeraire	→	Savings $\times v$
		Consumption $\times d_i$

In practice, where such analysis has been undertaken, uncommitted income (savings) in the hands of the government has usually been assumed to be the numeraire and so is valued at 1, while consumption is valued at the level given by the distribution weight divided by the value of a unit of savings in terms of a unit of consumption (v). The major problem is to determine the value of v. The issues surrounding the estimation of v were discussed in Chapter 12. In our example a value of 1.65 is used for illustration purposes.

The first approach to applying distribution weights is shown in Table 13.3. A new distribution weighted conversion factor for unskilled labor is estimated using the formula:

$$CF_L = ma + (1 - m)\left(1 - \frac{d}{v}\right)\beta \tag{13.5}$$

Table 13.3   Income Distribution Weighted Conversion Factors

	F 1.00	D 0.83	SL 0.83	UL 0.74	T 0.00	CF(w)
Groundnuts	125.0%	−12.5%			−12.5%	1.15
Other agricultural costs		100.0%				0.83
Agricultural labor (hired and family)	55.0%	50.0%			−5.0%	0.97
Ginning costs		100.0%				0.83
Transport costs	68.3%	13.0%	7.9%	7.1%	3.7%	0.91
Cotton seed		100.0%				0.83
Land opportunity cost (urban)		100.0%				0.83
Site development	56.0%	20.0%	8.0%	10.0%	6.0%	0.87
Buildings	18.0%	30.0%	10.0%	26.0%	16.0%	0.70
Machinery (including purchase of tubewells)	80.0%	4.0%			16.0%	0.83
Vehicles	64.0%	4.0%			32.0%	0.67
Exported cotton lint	115.0%	−3.5%			−11.5%	1.12
Chemicals (and pesticides)	87.0%	4.3%			8.7%	0.91
Labor				100.0%		0.74
Utilities	72.0%	15.0%	10.0%	20.0%	−17.0%	1.08
Maintenance (including tubewell operation)	55.0%	25.0%			20.0%	0.76
Management			100.0%			0.83
Sales	75.8%	5.3%			18.9%	0.80

where m is the opportunity cost of labor at market; a is the conversion factor applying to the opportunity cost of labor; d is the distribution weight applied to the consumption of unskilled workers; and β is the conversion factor applying to workers' consumption (assumed to be the standard conversion factor of 0.83).

Table 10.4 shows the value of m to be $(600 + 192 + 64 + 8) = 864$, or 72% of the monthly market wage of D\$1,200. The value of a can be determined from the breakdown of m into primary factors (from Table 10.4 this is 330 foreign exchange, 564 domestic resources, and −30 transfers). The value for a is then $(330 + (564 * 0.83))/864 = 0.89$.

The value of d is determined by the national annual average per capita consumption level (c) of 2,180, divided by the average per capita consumption level of the unskilled workers (estimated in this case to be 1,880) and raised to the power of e, which, for the value of v assumed here, is 1.0.

The distribution weighted conversion factor for unskilled labor derived from the above values is

$$(0.72 * 0.89) + (0.28 * \frac{2,180}{1,880} \div 1.65 * 0.83) = 0.74$$

The distribution weighted conversion factor for unskilled labor is then applied to the labor content of all the other cost items, including an unskilled labor component to derive the new distribution weighted conversion factors shown in Table 13.3. These are then multiplied by the market price values to obtain a distribution weighted NPV at the discount rate appropriate for distribution analysis. Since the value of v used of 1.65 implies a social discount rate of 4% the resulting net benefits are discounted using a 4% discount rate. The results are shown in Table 13.4. It can be seen that the NPV is positive and therefore that, with the assumptions used, the project can apparently be justified on distributional grounds. However, the analysis is neither very informative nor very transparent. A fairly complicated set of calculations yields a new answer, but it has only considered distributional issues insofar as they relate to the employment of unskilled labor. Other distributional effects have not been considered because it is too complicated to include the weights in any of the conversion factors. The process of moving from the unweighted values in Table 11.4 to the weighted values in Table 13.4 has also not actually defined the distribution of income.

A more informative result can be derived much more simply from the modified UNIDO analysis given in Table 13.2. The change in income to the different groups is already set out. All that is required is to adjust this value for the distribution weight $(d_i/v)^e$. Thus:

$$NB_D = NB_E + \Delta Y_i \left(1 - \left(\frac{d_i}{v} \right)^e \right) \tag{13.6}$$

where NB_D is the distribution weighted value of net benefits; NB_E is the unweighted economic value of net benefits; and Y_i refers to the income change to income group i. The process is illustrated in Table 13.5 with distribution weighting adjustments made to all income changes. The following distribution weights were used:

Shareholders and other enterprises:	0.40
Landowners:	0.25
Hand cultivators:	1.25
Ox cultivators:	0.60
Ginnery:	0.85
Unskilled labor:	0.70

The results show that the NPV at 4% discount rate is negative. The project cannot be justified on distribution grounds, and it can be seen that the restriction of income distribution weighting to adjusting the conversion factor for unskilled labor gives misleading results because it does not take account of other income changes.

Table 13.4 Distribution Weighted Analysis Using Conversion Factors by Year (D$ '000 world price numeraire)

	0	1	2	3	4	5	6	7	8	9	10	11
Groundnuts		-1,031	-2,063	-2,063	-2,063	-2,063	-2,063	-2,063	-2,063	-2,063	-2,063	
Pesticide		-38	-76	-76	-76	-76	-76	-76	-76	-76	-76	
Other agricultural costs		11	22	22	22	22	22	22	22	22	22	
Hired agricultural and family labor		-138	-276	-276	-276	-276	-276	-276	-276	-276	-276	
Ginning costs		-120	-240	-240	-240	-240	-240	-240	-240	-240	-240	
Transport costs		38	-203	-44	-84	-84	-84	-84	-84	-84	-306	
Cotton seed		336	672	672	672	672	672	672	672	672	672	
Exports of cotton lint		-4,792	-5,170	-7,692	-7,061	-7,061	-7,061	-7,061	-7,061	-7,061	-3,531	
Tubewells	-250	-250										
Tubewell operating costs		-16	-32	-32	-32	-32	-32	-32	-32	-32	-32	
Land opportunity cost	-20	-20	-20	-20	-20	-20	-20	-20	-20	-20	-20	
Site development	-520											520
Buildings	-4,651											2,326
Machinery	-10,417	-10,417										
Vehicles		-1,683					-1,683					
Chemicals		-1,374	-1,955	-2,589	-2,536	-2,536	-2,536	-2,536	-2,536	-2,536	-2,071	
Unskilled factory labor		-2,208	-3,312	-4,416	-4,416	-4,416	-4,416	-4,416	-4,416	-4,416	-3,975	
Utilities		-1,398	-2,097	-2,635	-2,635	-2,635	-2,635	-2,635	-2,635	-2,635	-2,420	
Maintenance		-379	-758	-910	-1,062	-1,138	-1,138	-1,138	-1,138	-1,138	-1,138	
Management		-1,250	-1,875	-1,875	-1,875	-1,875	-1,875	-1,875	-1,875	-1,875	-1,875	
Sales		11,696	18,843	25,340	25,990	25,990	25,990	25,990	25,990	25,990	25,990	
Net benefits	-15,858	-13,034	1,459	3,166	4,308	4,232	2,549	4,232	4,232	4,232	8,662	2,846

NPV at 4% = 1,855

Table 13.5 Distribution Weighted Net Benefits by Year—Direct Adjustment of Benefits (D$ '000 domestic price numeraire)

	1	2	3	4	5	6	7	8	9	10	11	12
Net benefits (unweighted)	-18,882	-15,370	2,159	4,340	5,710	5,619	3,599	5,619	5,619	5,619	10,883	3,900
Distribution adjustment												
Shareholders and other enterprises (-60%)	6,000	1,492	-2,104	-1,153	-1,847	-1,440	78	-1,383	-1,341	-1,295	-4,134	-1,845
Landowners (-75%)	-207	18	18	18	18	18	18	18	18	18	18	225
Hand cultivators (+25%)		158	158	158	158	158	158	158	158	158	158	
Ox cultivators (-40%)		-435	-438	-438	-438	-438	-438	-438	-438	-438	-438	
Ginnery (-15%)		78	10	-54	-38	-38	-38	-38	-38	-38	51	
Unskilled labor (-30%)	-148	-271	-408	-540	-541	-541	-541	-541	-541	-541	-489	
Adjusted net benefits	-13,236	-14,330	-605	2,331	3,023	3,339	2,837	3,396	3,438	3,483	6,049	2,280

NPV at 4% = -4,640

Whether there is any advantage in applying distribution weights in practice is questionable. It is impossible to avoid the fact that value judgments are involved, and it can be argued that it is more efficient to implement the most economically efficient set of projects and use policies to achieve redistribution.[6] Nevertheless a strong case can be made for investigating the distributional impact of projects, particularly if it is intended to implement an investment strategy oriented toward poverty alleviation. It is by no means certain that most developing countries have the flexibility in policy choice to implement a strategy that will ensure that growth is accompanied by equitable distribution. Distribution weights are unlikely to be adopted on a systematic basis, but they could be of use in determining whether a project that was otherwise economically marginal could conceivably be justified on distributional grounds.

Further Reading

Estimation of distributional effects is considered in Curry and Weiss (2000: chap. 11). A thorough exposition of the issues involved with some examples is given in Londero (1996a). Fujimura and Weiss (2000) also gives a good review of the issues. Londero (1996b) has some interesting insights. Potts (1999) shows how distributional effects can be estimated using an example from Latvia.

There are many expositions of the distribution weighting approach. Early texts include UNIDO (1972: chap. 15), Little and Mirrlees (1974: chap. 13), Squire and van der Tak (1975: chaps. 7 and 10), and a comprehensive illustration in Scott, MacArthur, and Newbery (1976). The subject was extensively discussed in a special issue of *World Development* (1978: vol. 6, no. 2) including articles by Amin, MacArthur, Mirrlees, and Stewart. Other articles relating to the usefulness and validity of this approach include Potts (1978), Weiss (1979), and Harberger (1978 and 1984). The issue is also discussed in Ray (1984: chaps. 2 and 3). Practical application of distribution weighting is illustrated in UNIDO (1980: chap. 5).

Appendix: The Effects Method

The *effects method* was developed in France using a national income accounting approach to project analysis. The method has rarely been used outside Francophone countries, but it provides the basis for the economic analysis methodology set out in the 1997 Commission of the European Communities (CEC) *Manual on Financial and Economic Analysis of Projects*. Both the original authors of the method and the more recent EC manual recommend the use of assumptions that many economists would regard as extreme or unrealistic, and for this reason Anglophone economists have tended to ignore this approach.[7] Nevertheless the effects method tries to address directly the issue of the distributional impact of projects and does have some valuable insights into the way project analysis is conducted. It is also possible to use different assumptions from those commonly recommended and through this to arrive at results that are equivalent to those from shadow pricing approaches.[8]

The starting point for an analysis using the effects method is an estimate of the direct value added generated by the project, consisting of wages, interest, taxes, depreciation, and profits. This is illustrated for the project example in Table 13.6 concentrating initially on the textile factory.

To the direct value added must be added the indirect value added derived from purchases of goods and services from the ginnery and from other suppliers. The ginnery in turn makes purchases from the farmers. Indirect value added is obtained by decomposing the costs of intermediate goods and services using the same information used to derive Table 11.2.[9] Indirect value added is included in Table 13.7. Table 13.7 also includes a residual not broken down that is equivalent to the part of costs defined as "domestic resources" in Table 11.2. This is described as a "change in domestic consumption," assuming that expenditure on these costs deprives consumers elsewhere in the economy of an equivalent value of consumption.[10]

The next step is to set out the value added without the project. This is shown in Table 13.8. Without the project, the farmers sell their cotton to the ginnery, which exports the cotton lint. An export tax is levied on the proceeds. The cloth produced by the project would be imported without the project and an import tax is levied on cloth imports. Table 13.8 shows the value of imports net of exports without the project as well as the value of export and import taxes. There are also some residual values of intermediate goods and services associated with the transport and handling of the traded goods that are not broken down. These are described as a change in domestic consumption. The foregone product of land used by the project is assumed to be equivalent to the rent foregone by the landowners as a result of selling their land and is included as value added without the project.

The next stage is to deduct the without project situation from the with project situation to derive the incremental effects of the project. The incremental value added provides an indication of the distribution of the income gains of the project. An economic rate of return can be obtained by deducting the investment costs associated with the project (net of any investment costs without the project). This is shown in Table 13.9.

Two aspects of this stage are unclear in the manual. First of all it is not clear how the indirect value added associated with the investment costs

Table 13.6 Direct Effects by Year—With the Project (D$ '000)

	1	2	3	4	5	6	7	8	9	10	11	
Intermediate goods and services												
Cotton lint			4,500	7,250	9,750	10,000	10,000	10,000	10,000	10,000	10,000	10,000
Chemicals			1,260	2,030	2,730	2,800	2,800	2,800	2,800	2,800	2,800	2,800
Utilities			1,200	1,900	2,400	2,450	2,450	2,450	2,450	2,450	2,450	2,450
Maintenance			500	1,000	1,200	1,400	1,500	1,500	1,500	1,500	1,500	1,500
Total IGS			7,460	12,180	16,080	16,650	16,750	16,750	16,750	16,750	16,750	16,750
Value added												
Unskilled labor wages			2,700	4,350	5,850	6,000	6,000	6,000	6,000	6,000	6,000	6,000
Skilled labor wages			1,500	2,250	2,250	2,250	2,250	2,250	2,250	2,250	2,250	2,250
Taxes					137	716	746	810	880	956	1,038	1,126
Loan interest			800	1,824	1,970	1,785	1,585	1,369	1,135	883	611	317
Depreciation			3,330	3,330	3,330	3,330	3,330	3,330	3,330	3,330	3,330	3,330
Profits to project owners			−1,210	−444	1,973	1,670	1,740	1,891	2,054	2,231	2,421	2,627
Total direct value added			7,120	11,310	15,510	15,750	15,650	15,650	15,650	15,650	15,650	15,650
Total effects			14,580	23,490	31,590	32,400	32,400	32,400	32,400	32,400	32,400	32,400

Table 13.7 Total Effects by Year—With the Project (D$ '000)

	1	2	3	4	5	6	7	8	9	10	11
Imports net of exports	-46,209	-37,913	-34,722	-31,175	-31,585	-31,530	-31,530	-31,530	-31,530	-31,530	-34,985
Change in domestic consumption	2,457	2,284	2,192	2,246	2,331	2,356	2,356	2,356	2,356	2,356	2,499
Change in stocks		-1,750	-875	-875							3,500
Value added											
Unskilled labor wages	892	3,829	5,638	7,226	7,389	7,389	7,389	7,389	7,389	7,389	7,406
Skilled labor wages	993	2,609	3,450	3,487	3,495	3,495	3,495	3,495	3,495	3,495	3,514
Farm labor wages	2,720	2,868	3,016	3,016	3,016	3,016	3,016	3,016	3,016	3,016	3,016
Net income to hand cultivators	19,952	20,586	20,586	20,586	20,586	20,586	20,586	20,586	20,586	20,586	20,586
Net income to ox cultivators	21,975	23,058	23,061	23,061	23,061	23,061	23,061	23,061	23,061	23,061	23,061
Profits to ginnery	5,940	5,423	5,875	6,300	6,193	6,193	6,193	6,193	6,193	6,193	5,598
Income to villages		-21	-42	-42	-42	-42	-42	-42	-42	-42	-42
Taxes and public enterprise surplus	6,219	5,627	5,541	5,429	6,111	6,161	6,226	6,296	6,372	6,453	6,913
Loan interest		800	1,824	1,970	1,785	1,585	1,369	1,135	883	611	317
Depreciation		3,330	3,330	3,330	3,330	3,330	3,330	3,330	3,330	3,330	3,330
Profits to project owners		-1,210	-444	1,973	1,670	1,740	1,891	2,054	2,231	2,421	2,627
Total value added	58,692	66,899	71,835	76,335	76,594	76,514	76,514	76,514	76,514	76,514	76,327
Total effects	14,940	29,520	38,430	46,530	47,340	47,340	47,340	47,340	47,340	47,340	47,340

Table 13.8 Total Effects by Year—Without the Project (D$ '000)

	1	2	3	4	5	6	7	8	9	10	11
Imports net of exports	-46,209	-35,158	-28,404	-22,264	-21,650	-21,650	-21,650	-21,650	-21,650	-21,650	-21,650
Change in domestic consumption	2,433	3,206	3,678	4,108	4,151	4,151	4,151	4,151	4,151	4,151	4,151
Value added											
Rent to lanowners	24	24	24	24	24	24	24	24	24	24	24
Unskilled labor wages	892	892	892	892	892	892	892	892	892	892	892
Skilled labor wages	993	993	993	993	993	993	993	993	993	993	993
Farm labor wages	2,720	2,720	2,720	2,720	2,720	2,720	2,720	2,720	2,720	2,720	2,720
Net income to hand cultivators	19,952	19,952	19,952	19,952	19,952	19,952	19,952	19,952	19,952	19,952	19,952
Net income to ox cultivators	21,975	21,975	21,975	21,975	21,975	21,975	21,975	21,975	21,975	21,975	21,975
Profits to ginnery	5,940	5,940	5,940	5,940	5,940	5,940	5,940	5,940	5,940	5,940	5,940
Taxes and public enterprise surplus	6,219	8,975	10,659	12,189	12,343	12,343	12,343	12,343	12,343	12,343	12,343
Total value added	58,716	61,472	63,156	64,686	64,840	64,840	64,840	64,840	64,840	64,840	64,840

Table 13.9 Incremental Total Effects by Year (D$ '000)

	1	2	3	4	5	6	7	8	9	10	11	12
Incremental foreign exchange		2,755	6,318	8,911	9,935	9,880	9,880	9,880	9,880	9,880	13,335	
Change in domestic consumption	−24	922	1,486	1,862	1,819	1,794	1,794	1,794	1,794	1,794	1,652	
Change in stocks		1,750	875	875							−3,500	
Incremental total effects	−24	5,428	8,680	11,648	11,754	11,674	11,674	11,674	11,674	11,674	11,487	
Value added												
Unskilled labor wages		2,937	4,746	6,333	6,497	6,497	6,497	6,497	6,497	6,497	6,514	
Skilled labor wages		1,617	2,458	2,494	2,502	2,502	2,502	2,502	2,502	2,502	2,522	
Rent to landowners	−24	−24	−24	−24	−24	−24	−24	−24	−24	−24	−24	
Farm labor wages		148	296	296	296	296	296	296	296	296	296	
Incremental income to hand cultivators		634	634	634	634	634	634	634	634	634	634	
Incremental income to ox cultivators		1,083	1,086	1,086	1,086	1,086	1,086	1,086	1,086	1,086	1,086	
Profits to ginnery		−518	−66	359	253	253	253	253	253	253	−342	
Income to villages		−21	−42	−42	−42	−42	−42	−42	−42	−42	−42	
Taxes and public enterprise surplus		−3,348	−5,117	−6,761	−6,231	6,181	−6,116	6,047	−5,971	−5,889	−5,430	
Loan interest		800	1,824	1,970	1,785	1,585	1,369	1,135	883	611	317	
Depreciation		3,330	3,330	3,330	3,330	3,330	3,330	3,330	3,330	3,330	3,330	
Profits to project owners		−1,210	−444	1,973	1,670	1,740	1,891	2,054	2,231	2,421	2,627	
Incremental total effects	−24	5,428	8,680	11,648	11,754	11,674	11,674	11,674	11,674	11,674	11,487	
Less investment costs	20,300	15,300					2,500					−4,200
Less incremental working capital		2,980	1,625	1,570	68						−6,243	
Net benefits	−20,324	−12,852	7,055	10,078	11,687	11,674	9,174	11,674	11,674	11,674	17,730	4,200

NPV at 4% = 48,025
NPV at 8% = 30,661
NPV at 12% = 18,589
IRR = 23.5%

should be treated. Second, working capital seems to disappear from the analysis. In Table 13.9 working capital has been included in the investment costs. Even so, the resultant NPV is positive at all three discount rates used, and the IRR is 23.5%.

Why does this approach give such a different result? The main reason is that all workers are assumed to be otherwise unemployed unless, as in the case of farm production without the project, some direct employment effects can be identified. This is equivalent to assuming a shadow wage of zero for any additional work by all categories of worker. The result would have been even more extreme if the overcapacity assumption had been adopted in determining the breakdowns of operating costs.

It can be seen that a conventional effects method analysis has a consistent tendency to overstate the net benefits of projects and therefore provides an unreliable guide for project selection. However, such extreme assumptions do not have to be used, and it is quite possible to modify the approach to generate results that are equivalent to those of the shadow pricing methods.

Another problem is that the emphasis on the value added concept, while providing a good correspondence with national income accounting concepts, does not correspond very well with the concept of benefits used in project analysis where capital expenditures are recorded as and when they are incurred. As a result the treatment of different types of capital expenditure in the effects method is not always clear from the literature.

Some modifications to the basic approach are made in Tables 13.10 and 13.11 to obtain an equivalent result to Table 13.2. The modifications are: (1) Table 13.10 includes the investment and working capital costs of the project and the value added associated with them as well as the income changes derived from the sale of land and transfers to and from the bank, the debtors, and the creditors. The depreciation and profit values are replaced by the return to equity capital. (2) Table 13.11 includes the value added produced by workers without the project identified through the estimation of the shadow wage. The foreign exchange content of the output produced by workers without the project is included, as is the production of domestic consumption goods. The value added from taxes on the output of labor is also included. Table 13.11 also includes a premium on net foreign exchange earnings implied by the shadow exchange rate. This could also have been included by adding an additional domestic consumption value in Tables 13.10 and 13.8 and an equivalent item in the tax line of value added.

The results of the analysis are identical because equivalent assumptions have been made. Income changes have been measured directly through a modified version of the value added concept; however, the process of obtaining the results is very complicated. It might be concluded that a simple version of the effects method gives unreliable results, while

Table 13.10 Modified Total Effects by Year—With the Project (D$ '000)

	1	2	3	4	5	6	7	8	9	10	11	12
Imports net of exports	-34,445	-25,778	-34,574	-31,027	-31,585	-31,530	-29,930	-31,530	-31,530	-31,530	-35,576	
Change in domestic consumption	5,069	2,922	2,205	2,259	2,331	2,356	2,456	2,356	2,356	2,356	2,446	-3,900
Incomes												
Unskilled labor wages	2,668	4,149	5,798	7,386	7,389	7,389	7,389	7,389	7,389	7,389	6,766	
Skilled labor wages	1,701	2,619	3,455	3,492	3,495	3,495	3,495	3,495	3,495	3,495	3,494	
Farm labor wages	2,720	2,868	3,016	3,016	3,016	3,016	3,016	3,016	3,016	3,016	3,016	
Income to landowners	300											-300
Net income to hand cultivators	19,952	20,586	20,586	20,586	20,586	20,586	20,586	20,586	20,586	20,586	20,586	
Net income to ox cultivators	21,975	23,058	23,061	23,061	23,061	23,061	23,061	23,061	23,061	23,061	23,061	
Profits to ginnery	5,940	5,423	5,875	6,300	6,193	6,193	6,193	6,193	6,193	6,193	5,598	
Income to villages	-300	-321	-42	-42	-42	-42	-42	-42	-42	-42	-42	
Taxes and public enterprise surplus	9,359	8,480	5,544	5,294	5,532	6,131	6,961	6,226	6,296	6,372	6,814	
Benefits to debtors net of creditors		573	422	367	68						-1,429	1,126
Income to bank	-10,000	-12,000		4,285	4,285	4,285	4,285	4,285	4,285	4,285	4,285	
Return to project owners	-10,000	-3,060	3,085	1,555	3,011	2,399	-131	2,305	2,235	2,159	8,320	3,074
Total value added	44,316	52,376	70,800	75,299	76,594	76,514	74,814	76,514	76,514	76,514	80,470	3,900
Total effects	14,940	29,520	38,430	46,530	47,340	47,340	47,340	47,340	47,340	47,340	47,340	

Table 13.11 Modified Incremental Total Effects by Year (D$ '000)

	1	2	3	4	5	6	7	8	9	10	11	12
Incremental foreign exchange	-11,764	-9,380	6,171	8,763	9,935	9,880	8,280	9,880	9,880	9,880	13,926	
Change in domestic consumption	-2,636	284	1,473	1,849	1,819	1,794	1,694	1,794	1,794	1,794	1,704	3,900
Incremental total effects	-14,400	-9,096	7,644	10,613	11,754	11,674	9,974	11,674	11,674	11,674	15,630	3,900
Incremental incomes												
Unskilled labor wages	1,776	3,257	4,906	6,493	6,497	6,497	6,497	6,497	6,497	6,497	5,874	
Skilled labor wages	708	1,627	2,463	2,499	2,502	2,502	2,502	2,502	2,502	2,502	2,502	
Farm labor wages		148	296	296	296	296	296	296	296	296	296	
Income to landowners	276	-24	-24	-24	-24	-24	-24	-24	-24	-24	-24	-300
Net income to hand cultivators		634	634	634	634	634	634	634	634	634	634	
Net income to ox cultivators		1,083	1,086	1,086	1,086	1,086	1,086	1,086	1,086	1,086	1,086	
Profits to ginnery		-518	-66	359	253	253	253	253	253	253	-342	
Income to villages	-300	-321	-42	-42	-42	-42	-42	-42	-42	-42	-42	
Taxes and public enterprise surplus	3,140	-494	-5,115	-6,895	-6,810	-6,211	-5,381	-6,116	-6,047	-5,971	-5,529	1,126
Benefits to debtors net of creditors		573	422	367	68						-1,429	
Income to bank	-10,000	-12,000		4,285	4,285	4,285	4,285	4,285	4,285	4,285	4,285	
Return to project owners	-10,000	-3,060	3,085	1,555	3,011	2,399	-131	2,305	2,235	2,159	8,320	3,074
Incremental total effects	-14,400	-9,096	7,644	10,613	11,754	11,674	9,974	11,674	11,674	11,674	15,630	3,900
Values adjusted for labor OC												
Incremental foreign exchange	-12,252	-10,354	4,664	6,820	7,991	7,936	6,336	7,936	7,936	7,936	12,153	
Change in domestic consumption	-4,179	-2,945	-3,438	-3,845	-3,880	-3,905	-4,005	-3,905	-3,905	-3,905	-3,701	3,900
Unskilled labor incremental benefit	497	912	1,374	1,818	1,819	1,819	1,819	1,819	1,819	1,819	1,645	
Skilled labor incremental benefit												
Farm labor incremental benefit												
Net benefit to ox cultivators		5	10	10	10	10	10	10	10	10	10	
Taxes and public enterprise surplus	3,096	-583	-5,252	-7,072	-6,987	-6,388	-5,558	-6,293	-6,223	-6,148	-5,690	1,126
Foreign exchange premium	-2,450	-2,071	933	1,364	1,598	1,587	1,267	1,587	1,587	1,587	2,431	
Total net benefits	-18,882	-15,370	2,159	4,340	5,710	5,619	3,599	5,619	5,619	5,619	10,883	3,900

NPV at 4% = 6,488; NPV at 8% = -1,563; NPV at 12% = -6,867; IRR = 7.1%.

less simplistic assumptions complicate the analysis. However, such a conclusion is judging the effects method on the basis of the information it gives on single-figure criteria of project worth. Part of the critique of the proponents of the method is that single-figure criteria such as the NPV or IRR do not tell the whole story. The effects method applies multiple criteria by making specific measurement of factors such as the contributions to the foreign exchange balance, to public funds, and to the distribution of income. Specific measures are proposed related to such criteria.[11] Whether these measures can be interpreted readily by decisionmakers is open to question.

Further Reading

Chervel and Le Gall (1978) is the clearest exposition of the effects method and provides the basis for the methodology outlined in Commission of the European Communities (1997). Franck (1996) provides a useful comparison of the effects method and shadow pricing approaches. A highly critical assessment of the effects method is given in Balassa (1976). This provoked a reply by Chervel (1977) and a further response by Balassa (1977). See also Jenkins (1999).

Notes

1. An honorable exception to the general neglect of measuring distributional impact can be found in the work of Londero (1996a, but originally published in 1987).
2. The issue is discussed in Potts (1999).
3. The basic features of this approach are described in Potts (1990).
4. Strictly speaking, consumption is not the same as income; however, information on income levels is sometimes more readily available than information on consumption levels and so income levels are used as a proxy for consumption levels. For relatively poor groups the difference is likely to be small.
5. A significant early attempt to measure other distribution effects directly is described in Scott, MacArthur, and Newbery (1976).
6. This viewpoint is associated particularly with Harberger (1978).
7. Prou and Chervel are the original authors. See Chervel and Le Gall (1978) for an exposition of this method in English.
8. The possibility of equivalence between the two approaches is demonstrated by Franck (1996). Unfortunately Franck does not provide a numerical example.
9. In practice, some of the assumptions used for deriving the percentage breakdowns would be different if the recommendations of the authors of the method were to be followed. In particular the composition of nontraded goods would be based on short-run marginal cost rather than long-run marginal cost if the recommendation to assume the existence of excess capacity in nontraded sectors were to be followed. See Commission of the European Communities (1997: 129) for a justification of this assumption. Many would disagree.

10. The case study in the CEC *Manual* includes a very small amount described as a residual not broken down. In practice, given the likely availability of data in most developing countries, such residuals are likely to be much larger.

11. A total of twenty-two "principal indicators" are listed on page 215 of the CEC *Manual*.

14

The Limitations of Economic Analysis

Economics Is Not Everything

Economic analysis attempts to identify and measure the economic effects of a project. Often the results are brought together in a single-figure estimate of project worth, usually an economic NPV or an economic IRR. Such figures give an indication of the economic value of a project, but they cannot take account of all issues. Although it is possible to take account of distributional considerations through a weighting system, many would argue that such issues cannot be summarized in a single figure. Furthermore, not all social issues relevant to project appraisal are of a distributional nature. Questions of social or political acceptability can be fundamental for the success of a project. It is sometimes possible to measure and value environmental effects, but it is not always possible. There are also many projects for which valuation of benefits is difficult and controversial. It is therefore likely to be important for many projects to take proper account of noneconomic issues and to include these issues in the process of making judgments about the desirability of the project.

If noneconomic issues are to be brought into judgments about projects, it is important to determine what sort of criteria can be used and how these can be combined with economic criteria. In this chapter some noneconomic approaches will be discussed, first of all considering what has come to be known as social analysis and then considering the multicriteria analysis approach.

Social Analysis and Social Impact Assessment

The term *social analysis* has been used in different ways by different disciplines. It was used by economists in the 1970s to mean economic analysis including distribution weights. This is not what a sociologist or an anthropologist would understand by the term.[1]

In the 1970s economists writing about cost-benefit analysis tried to encompass many different objectives in their measures of project worth. This proved to be problematic because of the inherent value judgments involved and because it is extremely difficult to put values on some of the unquantifiable effects that might be very important for the people involved. In the field of environmental economics the technique of contingent valuation has been used to try to circumvent the problem, but it is not obvious that it is either possible or desirable to put a value on every kind of impact.

An alternative approach is to deal with such issues separately. This is not to say that a social analysis should be entirely divorced from the economic analysis but that there may be some aspects of a project where qualitative assessment is both more relevant and more informative.[2] In practice a dialogue between economists and social analysts can be very helpful both in identifying key groups affected by a project and in assessing the implications. The process of assessing potential social effects can be described as *social impact assessment.*

Social impact assessment (SIA) can be viewed as a similar process to environmental impact assessment. The starting point is public involvement.[3] Without some form of interaction with the affected population it is impossible to say anything meaningful about social impact. Chapter 3 discussed some of the approaches that may be used by social analysts in the identification and design of projects. Stakeholder analysis is particularly useful in determining the relevant interest groups and the type and extent of their participation.

Assessment of alternatives is also important. Some of the objective oriented project planning techniques can be useful in determining relevant alternatives to the problem or opportunity identified.

The next stage is to collect relevant social baseline information on the affected population. These will include basic economic and social data as well as more qualitative assessments of social structures, cultures, and attitudes. If integration of social, environmental, and economic assessment approaches is considered important, the determination of data requirements should involve representatives from all three disciplines. A range of participatory approaches to learning about the local context can be used, but existing secondary sources are also important, and data collection should be restricted to what is relevant to the proposal under consideration and not already available.[4]

On the basis of the identified alternatives and baseline information the range of potential social impacts is assessed (this is called "scoping"), and effects are projected. Predictions are then made of the likely responses to the potential impacts as well as any indirect impacts.

Judgments on impact and responses are then used to make recommendations on appropriate alternatives as well as any amendments or mitigating actions to minimize negative effects.

During implementation the process is completed with monitoring and evaluation. A summary of the SIA process might be

consultation → definition of alternatives →
collection of baseline information →
scoping of potential impacts → judgment on impact and response →
amendments and mitigating actions →
monitoring and evaluation

The next step is to consider what issues are likely to be important in assessing the social impact of projects, particularly as they affect the appraisal process.

In project appraisal it is important to assess whether the advantages of a project (usually realized in the form of future benefits) outweigh the disadvantages (often incurred in the form of initial investment costs and the subsequent costs of maintaining activities). Through cost-benefit analysis or cost-effectiveness analysis economists try to quantify and value these advantages and disadvantages. A social analyst might look at some of these issues from the point of view of different stakeholders but might also look at issues that are more difficult to quantify. In assessing social impact, distributional and motivational concerns and the issues of vulnerability and cultural acceptability are particularly important, as is the institutional structure in which the project is supposed to function.

Distributional Issues

Distributional questions do not just involve estimation of the effects of a project on the incomes of different groups. Definition of the groups themselves is important. Have the relevant groups been defined in a way that is helpful in understanding the social dynamics of the affected communities? Income level is not necessarily the most helpful indicator to use in defining the groups affected by a project. People may also be differentiated by social status, gender, and ethnic background. Involvement in a project may have implications for the social status of people that may not be reflected in income gains.

Definition of units for analysis is also important. Typically the household is used as a unit of measurement with the assumption that the interests of all household members are the same. In reality the definition of a household may be complicated by factors such as kinship obligations. The interests of household members may also be affected by the division of labor by age and gender as well as the division of the rewards from labor.[5] A social analyst will be interested in the division of income, resources, and obligations within households as well as among different groups.

An important question for the social appraisal of a project is therefore whether the distributional outcome is acceptable to the affected groups. This has important implications for both motivation and for assessing the impact of the project on vulnerability. If the distributional outcome is not acceptable to some groups, what steps will be taken to ensure that their interests are taken into account?

Motivation and Conflict

Cost-benefit analysis assesses the costs and benefits to different stakeholders in monetary terms. Where the objective of a project is understood by all concerned to be straightforward income earning this may be sufficient. However, many projects have complex or multiple objectives, particularly in the social sectors. How do the affected people perceive the purpose of the project? What do they understand to be the benefits and costs to them? Is there a common understanding of the purpose of the project, or do different groups have different perceptions and attitudes? Where such differences arise there is potential for conflict.

Many social-sector projects change the social status of the affected population. This is not something that can be measured easily in monetary terms, but it may be very important for the perceptions of the beneficiaries and their attitude to participation.

An important task for the social analyst is therefore to assess the likely motivational response of key stakeholders. Are they likely to support the project sufficiently to contribute what is assumed? Will there be significant opposition to the project? How can or should such opposition be contained or taken into account? Are arrangements for participation and/or consultation sufficient?

Vulnerability

A secure income or livelihood is more valuable than one that is insecure. There is therefore a potential trade-off between vulnerability and income earning opportunities. Often projects that can lead to higher incomes can have a negative effect on the income security of the poorest and most vulnerable groups. An obvious example is the possible expansion of cash crops at the expense of food crops. The problem may be exacerbated by intrahousehold distribution questions. A male head of household may be the principal beneficiary of a project designed to increase earnings from cash crops, while women and children may bear the risk to food security from reduced attention to food crops.

The impact of projects on health can be an important issue.[6] Projects that affect water supplies often have indirect effects on health even where the major purpose might be increased irrigated crop production. Does the project affect access to water and the quality of water available? Are there risks of waterborne diseases?

Projects can also have behavioral consequences for affected populations. What changes in behavior can be expected as a result of the project? Will these changes increase or reduce the risks affecting the most vulnerable people? Improved road access to remote areas can induce significant changes in affected populations, including an increase in social problems such as crime, alcoholism, and drug addiction.

Land tenure and erosion of customary rights can also be important. Will a project threaten access to land or grazing rights for the poorest people? Commercialization of forests can also be an issue where people have assumed a customary right to forest products.

A social analyst might therefore be expected to make an assessment of the potential impact of a project on the most vulnerable people. If a project has potential negative consequences, how significant are they, and what actions can be taken to mitigate against their effect?

Cultural Acceptability

Projects are normally implemented within a complex cultural environment. Inadequate understanding of the cultural norms and expectations of the affected population can lead to conflicts and sometimes to complete project failure. Since planners are usually outsiders they are unlikely to have more than a partial understanding of local cultures. It is therefore important for any social analysis to address the issue of cultural acceptability and to make a conscious effort to use existing local knowledge.

Institutional Structures

Projects do not exist within a vacuum. Local institutions already exist and fulfill functions. It is therefore important to know what those functions are and how they might relate to the proposed project. What are the authority structures of different institutions? What are their roles? Are they perceived to be legitimate by the population they serve? Normally the strengthening of existing institutions is likely to be more sustainable than the establishment of new ones, but do they have the capacity to do what is asked? Does the project strengthen or undermine local institutions?

Institutions also often serve particular client groups. Which groups do they serve? Does this help or hinder the achievement of project objectives, particularly in relation to target groups? Institutional appraisal is likely to concentrate on the extent to which any project contributes to the development of sustainable institutions that serve the target groups.

Mixing Criteria—Multicriteria Analysis

Financial and economic analyses of projects produce quantitative criteria based on monetary values. Social and environmental considerations can be included in these criteria to some extent, but it is unlikely that every aspect can be taken into account, and the cost of undertaking such comprehensive studies may be excessive for all but the largest projects. Some considerations may be quantifiable but difficult to value while others may only be amenable to qualitative assessment. What should be the response to this dilemma?

One response is to conduct different analyses entirely separately and to rely on judgment or negotiation to define the trade-off. This is the most common response, but it suffers from several defects.

First of all it does not require that specialists from different disciplines engage in dialogue and use each other's work in arriving at their conclusions. Lack of communication between different members of a project team is caused by compartmentalization of work and is very common, particularly when project preparation teams have to meet tight deadlines.

Second, the criteria on which a decision is eventually reached are not transparent. What is the relative importance of the contribution of different disciplines to decisionmaking? How can we be sure that decisionmaking is not entirely arbitrary?

Third, the criteria for determining the overall extent to which a project has achieved its objectives are not clear. They can only be defined in relation to specific indicators. An alternative approach is to try to take account of different criteria in a systematic way. Multicriteria analysis (MCA) provides such an approach.

What Is MCA?

MCA is a method of analysis that considers separately a variety of different criteria for assessing a project and then attempts to define the trade-offs between the criteria in order to decide on the best course of action. Criteria are defined by the objectives of the project and in principle should have minimal interdependence. There are many different variants of MCA, and what is described here is only an outline of a general approach.

In order to undertake an MCA it is necessary to establish the important impacts of a project. One way to do this is to draw up an *impact matrix.* Such a matrix, originally drawn up to support a conventional economic cost-benefit analysis (ECBA) for the tea project described at the end of Chapter 3, is shown as Figure 14.1. This particular matrix indicates what has been taken into account in the ECBA and what has not and indicates the implications of the issues that have not been taken into account. These include some of the issues outlined above. For MCA an impact matrix would be drawn up indicating the *criteria* to be considered and the scale to be used for assessing the project according to each criterion. Preferably the analysis would also show various alternatives for comparison. One of the alternatives could be "without the project."

Goal Criteria and Veto Criteria

MCA distinguishes between *goal criteria* and *veto criteria.* Veto criteria are those criteria that have to be satisfied if the project is not to be rejected. All forms of feasibility criteria are veto criteria because if the project is not feasible, it will not work and therefore must be rejected. Once a veto criterion has been satisfied it takes no further part in the analysis unless it is also a partial goal criterion.

Some veto criteria can be framed in such a way that they are also goal criteria. For example, a funding agency may have a rule that all projects for which CBA can be undertaken must have an NPV above zero at a rate of discount of 8%. This is a veto criterion, but the NPV can also be included as a goal criterion when the minimum acceptability criterion has been met.

A goal criterion is defined when the extent to which a project satisfies a particular goal becomes a weight in the analysis. For example the NPV may be a goal criterion so long as it is above zero, and the size of the NPV may determine the value of its weight in the MCA.

Scales

Various scales for measuring the impact of a project can be used. In CBA and cost-effectiveness analysis (CEA) all criteria are *quantitative.* In CBA all quantitative measures are also *monetary,* while in CEA some quantitative measures may be partly *physical* (see the health example below). Quantitative scales can be linear or nonlinear and may or may not be truncated.

In MCA there may be a mix between quantitative ("hard") data and *qualitative* ("soft") data. Qualitative scales can be established in the form of an *ordinal* ranking (1, 2, 3, etc.) or in a *nominal* form. Nominal scales in some cases may be impossible to rank (e.g., if they are purely descriptive terms such as color). In other cases the scores may be *binary.* These can be

Figure 14.1 Impact Matrix for the Tea Project

Issue	Likely Effect on Result of Analysis	Taken into Account in CBA (Y/N)	Gainers	Losers	Implications
Production of tea from smallholder green leaf without the project	Negative	Yes		Private sector	Need to consult with private-sector factory
Difference in quality between existing and new factory	Positive	No	Reduces estimated value of private-sector losses		
Difference in processing cost between existing and new factory	Positive	No	Reduces estimated value of private-sector losses		
Smallholder crop production without the project	Negative	Yes		Farmers (foregone output)	
Smallholder labor/input use without the project	Positive	Yes	Farmers (reduced net cost)		Need to investigate labor availability
Environmental impact	Positive	No	Farmers (output without the project might decline)		Need to examine land-use patterns
Food security	Negative	No		Farmers—women and children (increased cost/reduced availability of food)	Investigate food security and improve support services to areas suitable for maize
Estate labor supply	Not certain	No	Estate workers	Private sector, government (Forex)	Need to examine mutually beneficial ways of ensuring adequate labor supply
Feeder roads	Positive	No	Local population		Need to investigate likely traffic and to define maintenance responsibilities

used in ranking (e.g., values of 0 and 1, or for veto criteria "yes" and "no").

Weights

The outcome of an MCA depends on the weight attached to particular criteria. Usually weights are defined in such a way that the total value of the weights for all the criteria adds up to one. The weight attached to each individual criterion must therefore lie between zero and one. The determination of appropriate weights is obviously a subjective one, but it can be made more systematic by a process of iteration in which the people and interest groups involved in a project are asked to rank criteria in order of importance.

Application of MCA to the Health Project Example

The health project example used in Chapter 4 to illustrate cost-effectiveness analysis can also be used to illustrate some of the potential advantages and drawbacks of MCA.

If we apply CEA to the health project we assume that we can determine reasonably accurately the effect of each project on the reduction of infant and maternal mortality. In fact these assumptions are open to a wide margin of error and sometimes the difference between alternatives may not be very significant. It is also assumed that the projects would have no other effects on the operation of the health service, which is clearly not true. The results of CEA are therefore not always very conclusive. How might MCA help us?

Criteria

First of all we must define the criteria to be adopted. The following criteria might be considered: (1) cost per death avoided, (2) effect on morbidity reduction, (3) effect on other health service activities, (4) social impact, (5) distributional effect. Other criteria could be considered (e.g., sustainability), but, for the purpose of the example, these five will suffice.

The next stage is to work out how to assess these criteria. Program A is the biggest, but it consists of a number of subprojects. A similar situation applies to the other programs. Should we consider each option as one program or a number of subprojects? In this case, for simplicity, each program has been treated as one entity, but they are judged on the basis of relative efficiency on the grounds that for any volume of available funds the programs are potentially divisible. The implication is that with a given volume of funds it might be possible to implement one program fully and one or both of the others in part. The need is therefore to determine priorities. On the basis of cost effectiveness in relation to one criterion (effect on mortality) Program C clearly has highest priority. Could other considerations have any effect on prioritization?

It is likely that both Program A, the rural health center program, and Program B, the district hospital prenatal and delivery care program, would have a strong positive effect on morbidity reduction and on other health service activities. Improvement of rural health centers would no doubt have a beneficial effect on the other activities of the health centers, and it is likely that improvement of prenatal and delivery care at the district hospitals would deliver other benefits to the affected population. Program C, the district hospital equipment and training program, would probably have a relatively small but positive effect beyond the immediate purpose because it is restricted to the activities of one particular department. However, it should have some positive effect on morbidity reduction because presumably the equipment and training will contribute to more than just preventing deaths.

In principle it might be possible to quantify the effect on morbidity, particularly where it relates to mothers and infants; however, there may also be wider health education effects that would be more difficult to quantify.

Program C would be unlikely to have any significant social impact, the effect being broadly neutral. Program B might have some positive social impact in terms of the health education of pregnant women. Program A would probably have a significant positive social impact by bringing more women to the health centers and improving the general standard of health education.

It is unlikely that there would be any strong distributional impact of the programs. The programs based at district hospitals are more likely to benefit the urban population who might be relatively affluent, while the rural health center program is more likely to serve the rural poor. Program A therefore might have some positive distributional effect. For this criterion there might be a case for considering the individual projects within each program to determine the hospitals and health centers that serve the poorest people.

The assessment of the project on the basis of different criteria can then be shown in an impact matrix before attempting to apply weights and scores. Such an impact matrix is shown in Figure 14.2, indicating a mixture of quantifiable and nonquantified criteria.

Weights and Scores

The relative weights to be used are essentially subjective, but it is probable that the major objectives would be the first two, and so a weight of 0.5 has been given to cost per death avoided and a weight of 0.25 to the effect on morbidity. The remaining weights, adding to 0.25, are divided between the effect on other health service activities (0.1), social impact (0.1), and distributional impact (.05).

The score for cost per death avoided was based on giving 0.5 to Program C (the lowest cost per avoided death) and adjusting the other two scores on a pro-rata basis.

Scores for impact on morbidity were rated as highest for Program A, fairly high for Program B, and small but positive for Program C. Similar relative scores were given for impact on other health service activities.

For social impact Program A scores highest, Program B also has a positive score, and Program C has no effect and therefore no score. For distributional impact only Program A scores anything. On the above basis the following scores were obtained (Table 14.1).

When multiple criteria are considered Program A appears to contribute most toward overall objectives although it is significantly less cost-effective than Program C in terms of lives saved. Of course the result is very heavily dependent on the choice of weights and scores for qualitative indicators, but it does give a wider picture of the impact of the different programs.

The scoring system used here is only one of many that could be used and is only used for illustration purposes. Other systems rely on simple

Figure 14.2   Impact Matrix for the Health Project

	Program A	Program B	Program C
Cost per death avoided	2,883	2,929	1,156
Effect on morbidity	+++	++	+
Effect on other health service activities	+++	++	+
Social impact	+++	++	0
Distributional impact	+	0	0

+ indicates positive; 0 indicates no significant effect

Table 14.1   Scores for Different Health Programs

	Program A	Program B	Program C
Cost per death avoided	0.18	0.18	0.40
Effect on morbidity	0.25	0.17	0.08
Effect on other health service activities	0.10	0.07	0.03
Social impact	0.10	0.07	—
Income distribution effect	0.02	—	—
Total score	0.65	0.49	0.51

ranking, but it does appear that where quantifiable data are available they should be used in calculating the scores. The analysis has not solved the problems of project analysis, and it has brought in some very subjective judgments, but it has considered explicitly some criteria that otherwise might have been left out.

Limitations of Multicriteria Analysis

The limitations of MCA are also its strengths. It introduces considerations that might be left out of a CBA or a CEA, but in doing so it introduces strong value judgments. It is probably quite useful for investigating alternative ways of achieving a particular main objective and for looking at projects with multiple objectives. It is not very good at comparing completely different projects with each other because the applicability of particular criteria will vary from one situation to another. It can be used in conjunction with CBA and CEA to cover the aspects of the project that are sometimes difficult for those techniques to deal with, and it can be used on its own for projects where CBA and CEA are not readily applicable.

A general conclusion of this brief review of noneconomic approaches to project appraisal might be that those involved in appraising projects must be aware both of the limitations of their discipline and of the potential contribution of other disciplines. Such awareness is important in ensuring that all relevant considerations are taken into account when assessing the advantages and disadvantages of projects.

Further Reading

Overseas Development Administration (1995) provides a very good introduction to the subject of social analysis. Howlett and Nagu is also a useful source. Other valuable sources include Cernea (1991 and 1994), Pretty (1995), and Vanclay and Bronstein (1995). See also the Interorganisational Committee on Guidelines and Principles for Social Impact Assessment (1995). For ideas on participatory appraisal see Chambers (1983 and 1994).

Good introductions to MCA can be found in van Pelt et al. (1990) and van Pelt (1993 and 1994). The subject is also covered in Snell (1997: app. F). See also Petry (1990).

Notes

1. The ODA *Guide* defines the term *social analysis* to refer to approaches derived from sociology, anthropology, and human geography (Overseas Development Administration 1995: 1).

2. In Chapter 8 the issue of the interrelationship between environmental and social impact assessment was also mentioned.

3. The sequence outlined here is based on that put forward by Burdge and Vanclay in Vanclay and Bronstein (1995: 41).

4. Commonly used terms for such approaches are *participatory rural appraisal* (PRA) and *rapid rural appraisal* (RRA).

5. A detailed discussion of gender issues is beyond the scope of this book. Moser (1993) provides a comprehensive review of gender issues in development.

6. A useful guide to health impact assessment is provided by Birley (1995).

PART 4

Allowing
Assumptions to Vary

15

Sensitivity and Risk Analysis

Risk and Uncertainty

In all the examples used so far the estimates of costs and benefits used in the different approaches to project analysis have been assumed to be correct. Of course we know that all projections into the future are actually uncertain and that any estimate is subject to a margin of error. How can such uncertainty be taken into account in project analysis?

A distinction is often made between *risk* and *uncertainty*. Risk is related to the probability of an occurrence whereas uncertainty is inherently unpredictable. If uncertainty can be reduced to risk, it is possible to estimate the probability of a particular range of outcomes and, if necessary, to insure against an adverse outcome. If information on probabilities is unavailable, it is only possible to examine the consequences of particular outcomes and to make a qualitative judgment on the implications. Risk can therefore be subjected to *risk analysis* whereas areas of uncertainty are subjected to *sensitivity analysis*. In this chapter sources of uncertainty and risk will be investigated first and then the various approaches to dealing with them will be considered.

Sources of Uncertainty and Risk

Since uncertainty relates to the assumptions made about a project, the key areas of uncertainty are often identified in the assumptions column of the logical framework. The major sources of uncertainty affecting a project can be categorized as technical, economic, sociopolitical, and environmental. These will be considered in turn.

Technical Uncertainty

All projects have a technical basis, which will be subject to some uncertainty. Typical areas of uncertainty include the quality and availability of materials, the quality and availability of labor and managerial skills, and the type and reliability of technology. Uncertainty increases if a project adopts a new approach and is reduced if tried and tested approaches are replicated. As in all forms of uncertainty, it is important to identify the potential margin of error in the assumptions made or the potential consequences of technical conditions not being met. Issues of technical uncertainty generally require tests relating to technical efficiency and output performance.

Economic Uncertainty

The major areas of economic uncertainty affecting projects relate to prices, demand levels, and market conditions. These in turn can be affected by macroeconomic policies particularly in relation to exchange rates and interest rates. Projects in the social and infrastructure sectors often depend on assumptions about levels of demand, while projects in the directly productive sectors are affected by competitive conditions for both inputs and outputs as well as international prices. Issues of economic uncertainty generally require tests on assumptions about prices and quantities.

Sociopolitical Uncertainty

Sociopolitical uncertainty relates to the acceptability of a project to the affected groups and the potential for disruption either by affected groups or through outside political interventions, conflicts, and bureaucratic delay. It can be difficult to devise tests relating to such uncertainty, but possible approaches include tests for the effect of delay or for the failure of sensitive components of a project.

Environmental Uncertainty

Environmental uncertainty relates to climatic and ecological issues and the potential for natural disaster. Particularly important areas include rainfall; water availability and quality; soil conditions; the impact of pests and diseases; and the incidence of earthquakes, floods, and volcanoes. Potential tests for environmental uncertainty include tests for production and yield variations and tests for disruption to project operations.

Nonsystematic Approaches to Uncertainty

Various approaches to the issue of uncertainty are commonly used but can be described as unsystematic. These include the use of contingencies, the addition of a "risk premium" to the discount rate, and varying the assumed life of a project either by reducing the project life or by using the payback criterion.

Contingencies

The proper use of physical contingencies was discussed in Chapter 4. The use of price contingencies is discussed in Chapter 16. In general it is not a good idea to add on contingencies to costs to account for uncertainty because whatever figure is added on is essentially arbitrary. Base costs should be estimated on the basis of their expected value, not on the basis of expected value plus a margin of error. The expected value can then be tested to determine the impact of potential variations in a systematic manner.

Increasing the Discount Rate

Use of a higher discount rate as a means of taking uncertainty into account is a very common practice, particularly for banks. This is understandable in the case of banks where the profit margin is derived from the difference between the borrowing rate and the lending rate. However, from the national point of view or from the viewpoint of an investor facing a given opportunity cost of capital, the use of a higher discount rate imparts a bias in decisionmaking toward short-term projects. Furthermore, it assumes that uncertainty is a function of time rather than of other factors. Increasing the discount rate is therefore not an appropriate way to deal with uncertainty.

Shortening the Time Period of Analysis

Another common method of dealing with uncertainty is to assume a shorter project life or to use shortcut methods that have a similar effect, such as the payback period. Such approaches also assume that uncertainty is a direct function of time and are even more arbitrary than raising the discount rate because all net benefits beyond the specified period are completely ignored.

Nonsystematic approaches to dealing with uncertainty are therefore not very reliable nor are they very helpful in identifying measures that could increase the level of certainty and improve the chances of project success. Sensitivity analysis provides a more systematic approach to the issue.

Sensitivity Analysis

Sensitivity analysis involves identifying important areas of uncertainty and testing key assumptions in a systematic way to determine the factors that are most likely to affect project success and to identify possible measures that could be taken to improve the chances of success.

There are various approaches to sensitivity analysis. These are described below.

Range of Estimates

In this approach the variable being tested might be tested using three different values, a "best" estimate, an "optimistic" value, and a "pessimistic" value. These values could be determined by the likely order of variation of the variable being tested. Such an approach is useful in defining the possible impact of changes in a particular parameter, but, without further analysis, such tests do not provide any additional information, and it is difficult to make comparisons of sensitivity to changes in different variables if the percentage variations are different.

Change by a Fixed Percentage

Another approach is to choose a percentage variation (usually ± 10%) and to test each important variable for that percentage change. This approach makes it possible to compare the sensitivity of the project to changes in different variables and therefore to determine which variables are most important in determining project profitability. It has the disadvantage that it says nothing about the likelihood of the assumed change or the size of potential variations.

Linear Tests and Switching Values

Some changes in variables have a linear relationship to the NPV while others do not. Where a linear relationship exists it is possible to make a test by a fixed percentage and then to estimate the percentage change in the variable required to change the NPV to zero (the switching value) by interpolation. In general, linear relationships can be assumed for prices, yields, and production levels. This can be seen fairly easily from the following relationship:

$$PV_i = \sum_{t=1}^{n} \frac{P_i Q_i}{(1 + r)^t} \tag{15.1}$$

where PV_i is the present value of cost or benefit item i, P_i is the price of i, Q_i is the quantity of i, r is the rate of discount, and t is the year.

A fixed percentage change in either P or Q will give the same percentage change in the present value of the item concerned. Therefore the absolute value of the change in the NPV from a change in either variable will have a linear relationship with the assumed change in that variable.

Thus when NPV_1 is the base value for the project NPV and NPV_2 is the new value resulting from an assumed price change from P_1 to P_2, the switching value for the item is given by:

$$\left(\frac{NPV_1}{(NPV_2 - NPV_1)} \right)\left(\frac{P_1 - P_2}{P_1} \right) * 100\% \qquad (15.2)$$

The approach can be illustrated using our example project. Sensitivity tests for variations in the sales price, the cost of machinery, the cost of cotton lint, and the cost of labor are shown in Table 15.1 covering the NPV of the project at market prices, the NPV to equity, and the NPV at shadow prices. The results for the sales price at market prices are also shown graphically in Figure 15.1. It can be seen that the project is very sensitive to changes in the sales price and also quite sensitive to changes in the price of cotton lint and in the level of production.[1] It is least sensitive to changes in the price of machinery.

In conducting these tests it is useful to indicate results for a range of different discount rates, particularly for marginal projects. At the test rate of discount a marginal project will be sensitive to changes in almost anything. For marginal projects it is important to know if a project is also sensitive to a change in a parameter at lower rates of discount. This will give an indication as to the possibility that a change in that parameter could lead to totally unacceptable results.

Switching-value tests are also useful for examining projects that appear to be unacceptable. This is a relevant issue for the economic analysis of our example. The project appears to be at best marginal from an economic point of view. What change in assumption is required for the project to be acceptable? Table 15.1 shows that relatively small changes in assumptions about sales prices, production, and the cotton lint export price could lead to an acceptable NPV.

Nonlinear Tests

Not all relationships are linear and switching values cannot be calculated for all sensitivity tests because they are not relevant. Examples of sensitivity tests where the relationship to the NPV is nonlinear include tests involving delays and growth rates. The benefits of many infrastructure and social-sector projects depend on rates of growth of demand or need. The change in NPV in moving from a 1% growth rate to a 2% growth rate is not the same

Table 15.1 Sensitivity Tests for Project Example by Discount Rate

	NPV			Change in NPV			Switching Value		
	4%	8%	12%	4%	8%	12%	4%	8%	12%
NPV at market prices									
Base value of NPV	17,352	6,539	-733						
Sales price-10%	-5,342	-11,195	-14,853	-22,693	-17,734	-14,120	-7.6%	-3.7%	0.5%
Production-10%	9,358	391	-5,552	-7,993.3	-6,147.3	-4,818.7	-21.7%	-10.6%	1.5%
Machinery price +10%	14,994	4,310	-2,845	-2,357.6	-2,229.1	-2,112.6	73.6%	29.3%	-3.5%
Cotton lint price +10%	10,261	932	-5,247	-7,090.9	-5,606.7	-4,514.2	24.5%	11.7%	-1.6%
Labor costs +10%	13,122	3,213	-3,397	-4,229.7	-3,325.8	-2,663.7	41.0%	19.7%	-2.8%
NPV to equity capital									
Base value of NPV	7,936	3,346	294						
Sales price-10%	-10,279	-11,195	-11,509	-18,215.2	-14,541.9	-11,802.9	-4.4%	-2.3%	-0.2%
Production-10%	2,248	-1,101	-3,250	-5,688.3	-4,447.2	-3,543.4	-14.0%	-7.5%	-0.8%
Machinery price +10%	5,932	1,726	-1,044	-2,004.7	-1,620.4	-1,337.9	39.6%	20.7%	2.2%
Cotton lint price +10%	2,837	-788	-3,113	-5,099.7	-4,134.6	-3,407.3	15.6%	8.1%	0.9%
Labor costs +10%	4,905	909	-1,699	-3,031.5	-2,437.2	-1,993.2	26.2%	13.7%	1.5%
NPV at shadow prices									
Base value of NPV	6,488	-1,563	-6,867						
Sales price-10%	-15,421	-18,732	-20,574	-21,908.5	-17,168.6	-13,706.5	-3.0%	0.9%	5.0%
Production-10%	-21	-6,565	-10,785	-6,508.4	-5,001.8	-3,917.9	-10.0%	3.1%	17.5%
World price of cotton lint +10%	543	-6,288	-10,689	-5,944.3	-4,724.8	-3,822.4	10.9%	-3.3%	-18.0%
Machinery price +10%	4,130	-3,792	-8,980	-2,357.6	-2,229.1	-2,112.6	27.5%	-7.0%	-32.5%
Labor costs +10%	3,104	-4,224	-8,998	-3,383.7	-2,660.7	-2,131.0	19.2%	-5.9%	-32.2%

Figure 15.1   Graphical Estimation of Switching Values

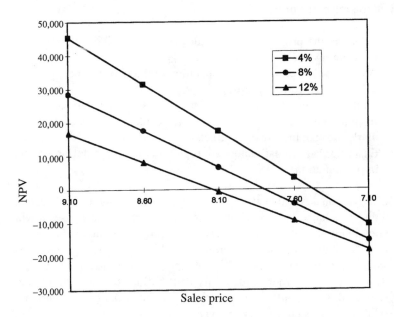

as the change caused by a move from a 2% growth rate to a 3% growth rate. Large projects are often subject to delay. The effect of a one-year delay on the NPV is not necessarily half that of a two-year delay. It is therefore difficult, but not necessarily impossible, to calculate switching values for such tests, although the tests may be very relevant.

For some tests a switching value has no meaning. To test the effect of removing a project component is very useful for projects involving multiple but separable components. Similarly, to test the effect of using a different technology may also be very useful. Sensitivity tests for such changes can be one-off tests, but they may provide very useful information.

Responses to Uncertainty

It is quite common to see the results of sensitivity tests stated without comment. In such cases the job is only half done. What are the implications of the results? How can they inform those planning and implementing the project so that the project is likely to be more successful?

The first point is that sensitivity analysis allows identification of the critical areas that will influence the success or failure of the project. This should provide those planning and managing projects with ideas about the areas that need to be studied in more depth or where actions may be required to protect the project. Such actions could include:

- Adapting the project design to allow greater flexibility in response to changing circumstances
- Adopting a different scale of operation in the first instance, perhaps using a pilot project approach
- Exploring alternative sources of materials, energy, or services
- Institutional adjustments to reduce the degree of uncertainty, particularly through the use of contracts
- Ensuring that critical factors are regularly monitored during project implementation

Sensitivity analysis also allows the identification of the critical factors that might be included in a risk analysis of the project. In many cases it will not be possible to undertake risk analysis for a project because information will not be available to establish a probability distribution for the variables under consideration. In such cases it is only possible to undertake sensitivity analysis. However, where probability distributions can be determined, sensitivity analysis provides the first step by defining the critical parameters that should be tested in a risk analysis.

The Limitations of Sensitivity Analysis

There are two major limitations of sensitivity analysis: (1) It is partial. Sensitivity analysis usually tests one variable at a time. Even where more than one variable is tested there are limits to the number of combinations of changes that can be tested to provide manageable results. (2) It says nothing about the likelihood that the changes tested for will happen. Of course qualitative judgments about likelihood can be made, but the information provided is limited.

In certain circumstances these limitations can be taken into account through the use of risk analysis.

Risk Analysis

Risk analysis is used to determine the probability of different outcomes for a project. On the basis of the information obtained from the risk analysis it is then possible to make a judgment on the project related to the degree of risk aversion of those involved in proposing the project. As with sensitivity analysis it is also possible to use the results to amend the design of the project. The process of undertaking a risk analysis can be defined in a number of steps. These are:

1. Determine the parameters to which the project is most sensitive through sensitivity analysis.
2. Assign a probability distribution to the selected range of values.
3. Undertake a Monte Carlo simulation of the project using random numbers to select the values of different variables. Normally such a simulation requires at least 200 runs to obtain a reasonably representative result.
4. Calculate the expected value of the NPV (mean value), the standard deviation, the probability of a negative NPV, and the expected size of the negative NPV (the mean value of the negative NPVs).

Having defined the areas to which a project is most sensitive, the next step in risk analysis is to determine a probability distribution for the variable in question. For some types of project this may not be a major problem, particularly if statistical data have been used in the estimation of the costs and benefits. Major infrastructure projects are usually subjected to careful demand analysis using time series data such as traffic counts for roads, port handling data for ports, and past sales data for utilities. Cross-sectional data can also be used for determining variations in demand levels. However, such data are not always available for all projects.

Strictly speaking, risk analysis cannot be undertaken in the absence of statistical data on probabilities. Given the absence of such data and the computational complexities of risk analysis, attempts to undertake risk analysis have tended to be restricted to large-scale infrastructure projects. However, advances in computer software have reduced the computational problems, and, if the standard of data input required is not set too high, it is now possible to undertake a form of risk analysis on a wide range of projects.[2]

In the absence of good statistical data to determine a probability distribution it is possible to obtain a reasonable estimate by defining the range in which the value of the parameter is expected to lie and the expected shape of the distribution. For example, most estimates of prices for project inputs and outputs are likely to be "best estimates." In the absence of information to the contrary it is reasonable to assume that the distribution of possible values will approximate to a normal distribution. Different assumptions might be made for some other variables. For example, experience suggests that the range of variation of investment costs around the best estimate is likely to be greater upward than it is downward. The scope for costs to exceed the best estimate is much greater than the scope for costs to be

lower. Similarly, for a manufacturing project, the range of potential variation above the best estimate of the production level is less than the range of
potential variation below the best estimate because of capacity constraints.
Biological limitations impose similar constraints on agricultural production. There are therefore good reasons why skewed distributions might be
used for some variables.

The tests undertaken in the sensitivity analysis for our project example
have been used in an illustration of risk analysis. The values for the sales
price and the prices of cotton lint and labor were assumed to be distributed
approximately normally. Five possible values for each variable were given
probabilities with the following distribution:[3]

	5%	25%	40%	25%	5%
Sales price	7.29	7.695	8.10	8.505	8.91
Cotton lint price	2.00	2.25	2.50	2.75	3.00
Unit labor cost	1.20	1.35	1.50	1.65	1.80

The above distribution assumes that the percentage variation in the
range of values is greater for cotton lint and labor than it is for the sales
price. This implies that the sales price is known with a greater degree of
certainty than the cotton lint and labor prices.

The other two variables included in the risk analysis were the value of
machinery costs and the level of production. These parameters were
assumed to have skewed distributions. The possible variation upward for
machinery costs was greater than the possible variation downward, and the
possible variation downward for the production level was greater than the
possible variation upward. The distribution assumed was based on an
approximation to a Poisson distribution. The assumptions used are outlined
below:

	13%	20%	25%	21%	12%	6%	3%
Machinery costs	−20%	−10%	Base	+10%	+20%	+30%	+40%
Production level	+20%	+10%	Base	−10%	−20%	−30%	−40%

The Monte Carlo simulation was undertaken by assigning the value of
random numbers to particular outcomes. A total of 500 runs were undertak-
en and the results recorded for the return to the project as a whole at constant market prices, the return to equity capital, and the return to the project
at shadow prices.[4] The results are outlined in Tables 15.2 and 15.3 and
illustrated graphically for the NPV at an 8% discount rate (Figures 15.2
through 15.4) and for the IRR (Figures 15.5 through 15.7).

The expected value for the NPV is in all cases lower than the value
obtained by using the best estimates for all the different parameters. This is
because two of the distributions are skewed. Even using a 4% discount rate
the probability of a negative NPV at market prices is 20%. The probability

Table 15.2 Frequency Distribution for Values of the NPV at Selected Discount Rates

	NPV at Market Prices			NPV to Equity			Economic NPV		
	4%	8%	12%	4%	8%	12%	4%	8%	12%
Less than −30,000				4			4	4	5
−30,000 to −20,000	11	25	34	23	25	16	26	43	56
−20,000 to −10,000	30	55	86	38	55	69	64	104	166
−10,000 to 0	57	113	187	97	135	195	110	164	175
0 to 10,000	105	138	130	156	179	170	121	119	82
10,000 to 20,000	111	104	51	115	91	48	101	53	15
20,000 to 30,000	85	51	11	53	13	2	49	11	1
30,000 to 40,000	56	12	1	12	2		19	2	
40,000 to 50,000	35	2		2			5		
More than 50,000	10						1		
Total observations	500	500	500	500	500	500	500	500	500
Expected value of NPV	14,694	4,370	−2,543	5,212	1,187	−1,449	4,129	−3,502	−8,497
Standard deviation	17,651	13,817	11,056	13,880	10,951	8,798	15,459	12,162	9,786
Probability NPV < 0	20%	39%	61%	32%	43%	56%	41%	63%	80%
Average value of loss	10,223	9,288	9,528	10,286	8,702	7,515	10,534	10,913	11,916

Table 15.3 Frequency Distribution for Values of the IRR

	IRR at Market Prices	IRR to Equity	Economic IRR
Less than −28%		9	
−28% to −24%		9	
−24% to −20%		6	
−20% to −16%		12	1
−16% to −12%	2	10	7
−12% to −8%	5	16	17
−8% to −4%	19	25	21
−4% to 0%	19	26	66
0% to 4%	53	49	92
4% to 8%	95	53	111
8% to 12%	114	65	87
12% to 16%	83	52	57
16% to 20%	66	51	31
20% to 24%	31	43	8
24% to 28%	11	25	2
28% to 32%	2	29	
32% to 36%		8	
36% to 40%		7	
More than 40%		5	
Total observations	500	500	500
Expected value of IRR	10.0%	9.2%	5.6%
Standard deviation	7.6%	14.9%	7.5%

Figure 15.2   Frequency Distribution of Values for the Project NPV at Market Prices at 8% Discount Rate

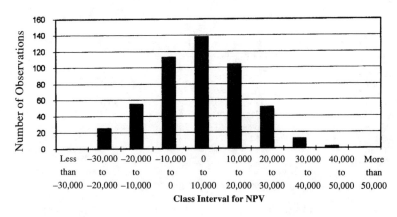

Figure 15.3   Frequency Distribution of Values for the NPV to Equity at 8% Discount Rate

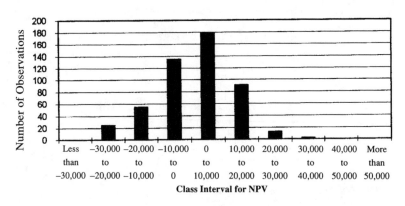

Figure 15.4   Frequency Distribution of Values for the Economic NPV at 8% Discount Rate

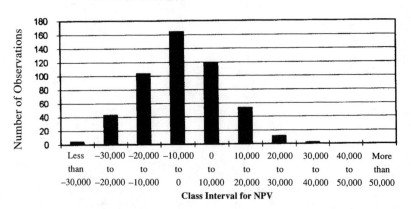

Figure 15.5   Frequency Distribution of Values for the Project IRR at Market Prices

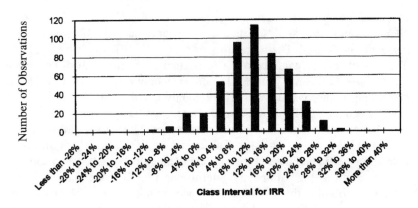

Figure 15.6   Frequency Distribution of Values for the IRR to Equity

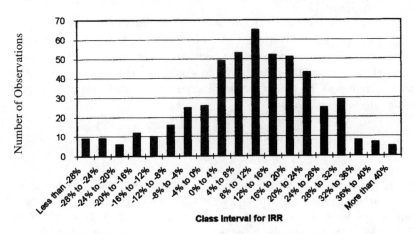

Figure 15.7   Frequency Distribution of Values for the Economic IRR

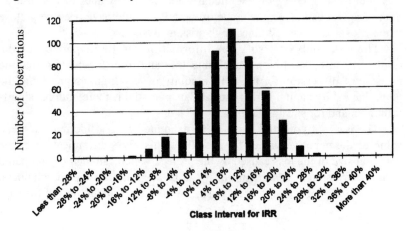

of a negative IRR is 9%. For the shareholders the probability of a negative NPV is even higher at 32% with a 4% discount rate and 43% when an 8% discount rate is used. The probability of a negative IRR to equity is 22.6%. The project is clearly quite risky. The original economic analysis suggested that the project was not worthwhile from an economic point of view. This is confirmed by the risk analysis. There is only a 37% chance of obtaining a positive economic NPV at 8% discount rate.

One of the implications of the risk analysis is that the simple use of best estimates (or modal values) to determine the project NPV does not give an unbiased estimate of the expected value of the NPV when some of the distributions for parameters determining the NPV are skewed. For a skewed distribution the mean and the mode are not the same. We have seen that there are good reasons why some distributions might be skewed and that the unmodified use of best estimates could give a systematic tendency toward overoptimism.[5]

Where information on the probability distribution for parameters determining the project NPV is available it is better to use the expected value rather than the best estimate of the parameter concerned. For the estimate of machinery costs the expected value would be the weighted average of the different possible values for machinery costs with the probabilities providing the weights. Thus

$$EV_{MC} = \sum_i P_i MC_i \qquad (15.3)$$

where EV_{MC} is the expected value of machinery costs and P_i is the probability attached to the machinery cost value MC_i. Using the parameters already provided the expected value of machinery costs turns out to be 2.9% higher than the modal value, and the expected quantity of production turns out to be 2.9% below the modal value. If these values had been used in the original estimates, the value of the NPV would have been very close to the expected values obtained in the risk analysis.

The risk analysis also gives information on the dispersion of the results. It can be seen both from Table 15.3 and from Figure 15.6 that the measure of dispersion for the IRR to equity is very high, emphasizing the point that equity capital is risk capital. The potential is there both for significant gain and for substantial loss.

The issue of potential loss can be examined by considering the mean value of the negative values for the NPV. This gives an indication of the potential size of the loss caused by the project, which can then be compared with the investment cost incurred. It can be seen that for the shareholders, at an 8% discount rate, the average size of the loss is about 58% of the capital they invested. Given that the probability of loss is 50% it is clear that the shareholders face a significant risk of losing a substantial part of their initial investment.

Once a risk analysis has been undertaken the next step is to examine the implications for decisionmaking. How important is the risk of loss compared to the potential for gain? The answer to this question depends on the attitude of the investors toward risk. In general the larger the investor and the more investments the investor has to spread the risk, the less risk averse the investor is likely to be. At the other extreme, a poor farmer is likely to be extremely risk averse because the investment under consideration may be the only one he or she is able to make. Clearly any decision rules have to take account of risk aversion.

It is often argued that risk should not be a consideration for a government because the public investment program (PIP) will include a large number of projects. The overall NPV for all the projects in the PIP will be maximized by choosing projects in such a way as to maximize the expected NPV. As long as the expected value of the NPV of each project selected is positive, the projects that exceed expectations should compensate for the projects that do worse than expected. Any other approach is likely to lead to a smaller overall NPV.

The argument for using the expected NPV as the criterion is valid for large economies where no one project has a dominant effect on the final outcome. The argument is less valid for very small countries or where a project is so large that it has a substantial effect on the overall investment budget.

Another significant issue is that of the localized effect of projects. A small project for a government may have very significant implications for the population affected by it. The government may be risk neutral, but the people affected are unlikely to have the same perspective.

Various criteria have been put forward for making judgments about risk, particularly in relation to the choice among alternatives. The *maximin* principle provides a conservative criterion whereby the option chosen is that which maximizes the returns from the worst possible outcome. This criterion pays no attention to the potential gains from different alternatives and is only concerned with minimizing losses. An alternative approach is the *minimax* approach whereby the alternative chosen is that which minimizes the maximum possible loss from making a wrong decision. Both the maximin and the minimax principles suffer from logical defects, and neither is particularly useful in determining whether or not to go ahead with a particular project.[6]

In principle the trade-off between the risk of loss and the potential gain represented by the expected value of the NPV can be determined through an indifference map of preferences. In practice it is difficult to set out such a map because preferences are not usually expressed in a way that can be easily measured.

There is no universally satisfactory way of dealing with the problem of risk from all perspectives. A risk analysis will give some information on the possible range of outcomes resulting from an investment project. This may be used to make a judgment on whether or not a project should go ahead or on which of a number of alternatives should be chosen.

It should be noted that such questions can be considered from a number of points of view and that different viewpoints may be associated with different attitudes to risk. It is only when all these viewpoints are considered that a balanced judgment can be made.

Further Reading

Reutlinger (1970) and Pouliquen (1970) are early sources setting out the techniques and the theory. Most cost-benefit analysis texts include some discussion of risk, uncertainty, and sensitivity analysis. Useful sources include Curry and Weiss (2000: chap. 9), Perkins (1994: chap. 15), Snell (1997: app. A), Brent (1996: chap, 11), Overseas Development Administration (1988: chap. 6), Dobbins and Pike (1986), Hull (1986), and Sugden and Williams (1978: chaps. 5 and 12). FAO (1989) provides an interesting analysis of the causes of differences between appraisal estimates and actual outcomes. Clarke and Low (1993) and Savvides (1994) illustrate the application of risk analysis.

Notes

1. Note that the relevant test for the cotton lint price for the economic analysis is the change in the export price used in Table 8.1. A change in the price paid by the factory just affects the distribution of the benefits between the factory and the ginnery.

2. It is relatively easy to perform a simple risk analysis using standard spreadsheet software as in the case illustrated here. A more sophisticated approach is also possible using software such as Crystal Ball, which is designed to add on to spreadsheet packages.

3. A distribution sometimes called the "beta distribution" can also be used. This has only three values (lowest, best estimate, and highest) with probabilities of 20%, 60%, and 20% respectively. The problem with this distribution is that it tends not to give a very smooth distribution of results because the number of possible combinations is reduced and the probability of the central value is very high.

4. It should be noted that the implications of the variations in different parameters are different for different aspects of the analysis. Where risk analysis is under-

taken on the economic analysis it has been assumed that changes in market prices are reflected in changes in shadow prices. This does not necessarily have to be the case. For example it is quite possible that the market wage could change without any change in the opportunity cost of labor. In such a case there would be a change in the ratio of the shadow price to the market price. It is therefore necessary to be careful when interpreting risk analysis applied to economic analysis.

5. An FAO Investment Centre study of seventy-two projects showed that for most of the projects analyzed, the expost evaluation results were worse than the exante appraisal expectations. Perhaps the use of simple best estimates provides one reason for this result (FAO: 1989).

6. A very useful discussion of the various approaches to decisionmaking, including the logical defects of the minimax and maximin criteria, is given by Dorfman in Layard (1972).

16

Changes in Prices and Exchange Rates

Constant and Current Prices

Constant prices are defined as prices of a particular base year, usually the year in which planning is taking place. Economic analysis is normally conducted in constant prices because it is important to measure costs and benefits in standard units that allow the comparison of one project with another even though the projects may have different time profiles covering periods with different price levels. In a constant price statement of costs and benefits, prices may be adjusted for changes in relative prices but they will not be adjusted for general inflation.

Current prices are those that actually occur. However, since project analysis is about prediction, the term *current prices* also refers to expected future prices. Although project analysis is usually conducted in constant prices it is necessary to take account of inflation in financial planning, otherwise projects are likely to run out of money. Some estimation of costs and benefits in current prices is therefore required to ensure that financial resources match financial requirements.

Changes in Relative Prices

Sometimes the price of a cost or benefit item may be expected to increase at more (or less) than the general level of inflation over the life of a project. This implies a change in the relative price of the item in question. For example, if a project is being planned at a time when the price of the main output is unusually high (or low), it may be expected that the price of the output will decrease (increase) relative to all other prices. It would then be wrong to use the base year price as a reasonable indicator of the constant price value of the output over the rest of the life of the project. What is

327

required is an estimate of the real price (RP_t) of the item in question for each year of the project life in relation to the base year price (RP_0). This can be defined by

$$RP_t = RP_0 \frac{(1 + r_1)(1 + r_2)......(1 + r_t)}{(1 + i_1)(1 + i_2)......(1 + i_t)} \qquad (16.1)$$

where r refers to the percentage change in price of the item in each year and i refers to the percentage change in domestic prices in general in each year.

The problem, of course, is how to predict such changes in relative prices. A number of international organizations, including the World Bank, make regular projections of commodity prices in constant price terms but including expected changes in relative prices. Such projections may be used in economic analysis but they should be used with care, particularly in the case of agricultural primary commodities. Price fluctuations are often caused by weather conditions in the major producing countries, and sometimes the predictions of international agencies can themselves influence the decisions of producers in such a way that the medium-term price moves in the opposite direction to the prediction.

The effect of a 2% annual change in real wages is illustrated in Table 16.1. Table 16.2 contains a line that allows for the possibility that real wages and salaries change at a different rate than the general inflation rate, but the real wage change is not carried forward from Table 16.1 into Table 16.2 in order to maintain comparability between the distribution of costs and benefits at constant prices and those adjusted for inflation. A change in real wage rates would affect the real costs of labor and management in each year as well as the cost of stocks of finished goods. Such adjustments have to be made carefully if a full financial analysis is to be undertaken because changes in unit costs from one year to another have implications for the valuation of operating costs and stocks of finished goods. Similar issues

Table 16.1   Unit Prices and Unit Costs by Year ($ including 2% annual real wage change)

	0	1	2	3	4	5	6	7
Growth in real wages	2.0%	2.0%	2.0%	2.0%	2.0%	2.0%	2.0%	2.0%
Escalation factor for real wages	1.000	1.020	1.040	1.061	1.082	1.104	1.126	1.149
Unit costs (constant prices)								
Labor	1.50	1.53	1.56	1.59	1.62	1.66	1.69	1.72

Table 16.2 Unit Prices and Unit Costs by Year ($)

	0	1	2	3	4	5	6	7	8	9	10	11	12
Growth in real wages													
Escalation factor for real wages	1.000	1.000	1.000	1.000	1.000	1.000	1.000	1.000	1.000	1.000	1.000	1.000	1.000
Unit prices/costs (constant prices)													
Sales	8.10	8.10	8.10	8.10	8.10	8.10	8.10	8.10	8.10	8.10	8.10	8.10	8.10
Cotton lint	2.50	2.50	2.50	2.50	2.50	2.50	2.50	2.50	2.50	2.50	2.50	2.50	2.50
Chemicals	0.70	0.70	0.70	0.70	0.70	0.70	0.70	0.70	0.70	0.70	0.70	0.70	0.70
Labor	1.50	1.50	1.50	1.50	1.50	1.50	1.50	1.50	1.50	1.50	1.50	1.50	1.50
Utilities	0.50	0.50	0.50	0.50	0.50	0.50	0.50	0.50	0.50	0.50	0.50	0.50	0.50
Inflation rate	10.0%	10.0%	8.0%	6.0%	6.0%	6.0%	6.0%	6.0%	6.0%	6.0%	6.0%	6.0%	6.0%
Inflation factor—general	1.000	1.100	1.188	1.259	1.335	1.415	1.500	1.590	1.685	1.786	1.893	2.007	2.128
Inflation factor—wages and salaries	1.000	1.100	1.188	1.259	1.335	1.415	1.500	1.590	1.685	1.786	1.893	2.007	2.128
Base costs of overheads													
Utilities	450												
Maintenance	1,500												
Management	2,250												
Unit prices/costs													
Sales	8.10	8.91	9.62	10.20	10.81	11.46	12.15	12.88	13.65	14.47	15.34	16.26	
Cotton lint	2.50	2.75	2.97	3.15	3.34	3.54	3.75	3.97	4.21	4.47	4.73	5.02	
Chemicals	0.70	0.77	0.83	0.88	0.93	0.99	1.05	1.11	1.18	1.25	1.33	1.40	
Labor	1.50	1.65	1.78	1.89	2.00	2.12	2.25	2.38	2.53	2.68	2.84	3.01	
Utilities	0.50	0.55	0.59	0.63	0.67	0.71	0.75	0.79	0.84	0.89	0.95	1.00	

arise in the valuation of material costs and stocks of materials if changes in the relative price of materials are assumed. These issues are examined in more detail later in the chapter.

Exchange Rate Changes

Project costs and benefits are not just affected by internal inflation. The prices of traded goods can also be affected by changes in exchange rates and changes in prices in the economies of trading partners. As long as any difference in the inflation rates between the domestic economy and the trading partners is balanced by compensating changes in the exchange rate, it can be said that the *real exchange rate* remains the same. In such a situation the domestic prices of traded goods will change at the same rate as the prices of nontraded goods, and there will be no change in relative prices. If the real exchange rate remains constant, the competitive position of the country remains the same, and the expected actual exchange rate in relation to a particular trading partner can be determined using a very similar equation to Equation 16.1:

$$ER_t = ER_0 \frac{(1 + i_1)(1 + i_2)......(1 + i_t)}{(1 + j_1)(1 + j_2)......(1 + j_t)} \qquad (16.2)$$

where ER_t refers to the exchange rate in Year t and j_t refers to the rate of inflation in the economy of the trading partner in the same year.

In the absence of information to the contrary, it is easiest to assume no change in the real exchange rate when planning projects. This would mean no change in relative prices due to exchange rate changes. However, whether or not this is a reasonable assumption will depend on the macroeconomic policy of the country concerned. In particular, such an assumption is unlikely to hold where a country does not have a policy of exchange rate flexibility. Where a country maintains a fixed exchange rate, it may be assumed that the prices of traded goods will change at the average rate applying to the currency in which the transactions are being conducted. However, a fixed exchange rate cannot be maintained indefinitely with a persistent difference between internal and external inflation and so, in the medium to long term, it will be necessary to assume either that internal and external inflation rates converge or that the fixed exchange rate policy is discontinued.

Even if the real exchange rate is assumed to be stable some adjustments will have to be made to the financial analysis of any project involving foreign exchange loans whenever changes in the actual exchange rate are expected. This is because the local currency value of payments on the loan will change when the exchange rate changes. A particular difficulty arises in accounting for the foreign exchange loss that occurs when loan repayments have to be made at a less favorable rate than that ruling when the loan was taken out. This issue is described in more detail below.

In principle, therefore, the financial analysis of a project should take account not just of internal inflation but also of any changes brought about by expected changes in exchange rates.

Inflation and Financial Planning

Financial planning is concerned with money and in particular with the answers to two key questions: Are the financial resources available sufficient to meet the expected expenditure on the project and its financing? Are the financial returns to the entities involved in the project sufficient to maintain their interest in implementing the project?

Inflation has an impact on both of these questions. It should not be ignored although it often is, partly because of the difficulty in predicting inflation rates over the life of the project.

There are two main approaches to dealing with the issue of inflation in financial analysis. These are: (1) use of price contingencies to work out financial requirements and (2) inflating part or all of the cash flow. These approaches are discussed below.

Price Contingencies

Price contingencies are allowances that are added on to cost estimates to take account of expected price changes. They should not appear in any analysis that uses constant prices, but they may be used in financial planning to assess financial requirements. Usually they are estimated by multiplying the constant price value of financial requirements by an inflation factor, taking into account the cumulative effect of inflation from the base year to the year in question. Thus the inflation factor (IF_t) in Year t is given by

$$IF_t = (1+i_1)(1+i_2)..............(1+i_t) \qquad (16.3)$$

The inflation factor is the same as a compounding factor if a constant rate of inflation is assumed, but it is not necessary to assume the same inflation rate in each year. Price contingencies are often expressed as a percentage. An example showing the estimation of price contingencies is given below:

	1	2	3	4
Constant prices financial requirement	100	200	150	50
Expected inflation rate	25%	20%	15%	10%
Inflation factor	1.250	1.500	1.725	1.898
Price contingency (%)	25.0%	50.0%	72.5%	89.8%
Current prices financial requirement	125	300	259	95

The advantage of using a price contingency is its simplicity. It is necessary just to inflate the costs and benefits for the investment period and to adjust the financial plan to cover expected escalation during the investment period. Usually such an approach would not involve recalculation of any indicators of project profitability, which would be worked out at constant prices. The price contingencies are therefore only used for the estimation of disbursement requirements.

The disadvantages of just using price contingencies are

- They may be unreliable. Inflation has effects on the distribution of costs and benefits and sometimes causes changes in the cash flow that are not immediately obvious or that lie outside the immediate investment period.
- There may be problems of consistency if constant and current price measures of costs and benefits are mixed together.
- Use of a price contingency does not resolve the potential confusion surrounding real and nominal rates of interest. Nominal interest rates partly reflect inflation. How then can internal rates of return calculated on the basis of constant price cost and benefit estimates be compared with nominal rates of interest?

Real and Nominal Rates of Interest

Financial rates of return are often compared with interest rates. The nominal rate of interest is the rate of interest actually charged (r). Suppose this is 15% and the rate of inflation (i) is 9%. The real rate of interest is

$$\left(\frac{1+r}{1+i}\right) - 1 = \left(\frac{1.15}{1.09}\right) - 1 = 0.055 \equiv 5.5\% \qquad (16.4)$$

Any internal rate of return calculated that is calculated at constant prices should only be compared with a real rate of interest. Comparisons with nominal rates of interest are not valid because actual payments of interest are in current price units, not constant price units. This distinction between nominal and real rates of interest can lead to serious problems in countries with relatively high rates of inflation because the distinction is not always recognized by those dealing with loan requests. As a result, borrowers may be asked to show unrealistically high rates of return from their projects, and it becomes impossible to finance projects with long gestation periods without presenting unrealistic estimates of costs and benefits.

An alternative to presenting costs and benefits in constant prices is to inflate the cash flow. This procedure allows proper estimates of financial requirements to be made and also allows the comparison of the internal rate of return to the borrowers with the nominal rate of interest because current price units are being used.

Inflating the Benefits and Costs

The most comprehensive way of taking account of inflation is to inflate the cash flow. Unfortunately, apart from the general problem of predicting the rate of inflation, there are also problems of inflation accounting. For these reasons the most common approach in practice is just to look at the first few years of the project when finance may be a problem and to assume that the project will always generate a surplus in subsequent years so that financing is not a problem.

In this case the easiest thing to do is simply to multiply all the relevant items from the annual statement (investment costs, sales, operating cost, and incremental working capital) by the inflation factor for the year in question. This procedure is not strictly correct for working capital and operating costs, but, for the purposes of estimating financial requirements, it does not matter very much because the errors cancel each other out.

Loan payments are not changed directly by the rate of inflation because loan terms are specified in current price units, although there is of course an indirect link between internal and external rates of inflation, exchange rates, and the rate of interest.

Depreciation will be calculated on the basis of the inflated investment costs even though the allowances themselves will not inflate. The profit and loss account and cash flow for the first five years can then be recalculated to ensure that the financial plan is sound.

The disadvantages of the approach of just inflating the first few years of the project life are that it does not take account of the redistributional effect of inflation and that it assumes that all financial problems are confined to the early years. It is also not possible to estimate an internal rate of return because there are no estimates for the later years of the project life in equivalent units. It is also not possible to construct a projected balance sheet for the life of the project.

The alternative is to inflate the whole cash flow for the life of the project, recognizing that any assumption about inflation rates becomes more and more uncertain the further into the future the projection is made.

Tables 16.2 through 16.12 show how this can be done for our textile project, assuming an annual rate of inflation that starts at 10% and falls to 6% over a period of four years, after which the inflation rate is assumed to remain constant. The tables also illustrate how to deal with exchange rate changes. For simplicity it is assumed that all price and exchange rate changes occur at the beginning of each year. This assumption could be relaxed, but it would increase the complexity of the calculations without making any substantial improvement in accuracy.

In Table 16.2 a set of inflation factors is calculated for use in all subsequent tables. These are applied to all of the items of investment costs, including the salvage value (see below). The unit prices for variable costs and sales are also multiplied by the inflation factor.

In Table 16.3 the inflated value of sales revenue is shown. This value is obtained simply by multiplying the constant price value of sales by the inflation factor for the year in question.

In Table 16.4 the value of operating costs is inflated. However, simply to multiply the constant price values by the inflation factor would overstate the inflation of operating costs for two reasons. First of all, part of the sales in any year after the first year will consist of the sale of stocks of finished goods manufactured in the previous year at the previous year's prices. Second, some of the new production will involve the use of stocks of materials (cotton lint and chemicals) purchased at the previous year's prices.

In Table 16.4 the value of material costs for Year t (MC_t) is therefore given by

$$MC_t = (PN_t - S_t - MS_{t-1})MP_t + (S_{t-1} + MS_{t-1})MP_{t-1} \qquad (16.5)$$

where PN refers to the production level, S refers to the level of stocks of final goods, MS refers to the level of production covered by material stocks, and MP refers to the price of materials. Similar formulas could be used for other direct cost items, but the material stock element would be unnecessary for costs such as labor and utilities where stocks are not held. It should be noted that this procedure is also required even for constant price estimates of operating costs in cases where a change in relative prices is assumed.

An alternative approach to estimating the inflated value of operating costs, which is easier from a computational point of view but can be more difficult to understand, is to use a *stock valuation adjustment*. The stock valuation adjustment is shown in Table 16.5, but it is calculated through the

Table 16.3 Production and Sales by Year

	0	1	2	3	4	5	6	7	8	9	10	11
Capacity ('000 units)		4,000										
Production ('000 units)			2,000	3,000	4,000	4,000	4,000	4,000	4,000	4,000	4,000	3,600
Stock ('000 units)			200	300	400	400	400	400	400	400	400	400
Increase in stock ('000 units)			200	100	100							−400
Sales ('000 units)			1,800	2,900	3,900	4,000	4,000	4,000	4,000	4,000	4,000	4,000
Sales value ($ '000)			17,321	29,580	42,167	45,844	48,594	51,510	54,601	57,877	61,349	65,030

Table 16.4 Operating Costs by Year ($ '000)

	0	1	2	3	4	5	6	7	8	9	10	11
Variable costs												
Cotton lint			5,346	9,005	12,816	13,869	14,701	15,583	16,518	17,509	18,560	19,673
Chemicals			1,497	2,538	3,615	3,921	4,156	4,405	4,670	4,950	5,247	5,562
Labor			3,208	5,456	7,775	8,442	8,948	9,485	10,054	10,657	11,297	11,974
Utilities			1,069	1,819	2,592	2,814	2,983	3,162	3,351	3,552	3,766	3,991
Overheads												
Utilities			356	567	601	637	675	715	758	804	852	903
Maintenance			594	1,259	1,602	1,981	2,250	2,385	2,528	2,679	2,840	3,011
Management			1,782	2,833	3,003	3,184	3,375	3,577	3,792	4,019	4,260	4,516
Total operating costs			13,852	23,478	32,004	34,846	37,087	39,312	41,671	44,171	46,821	49,631

Table 16.5 Operating Costs Showing Stock Valuation Adjustment by Year ($ '000)

	0	1	2	3	4	5	6	7	8	9	10	11
Constant prices												
Variable costs												
Cotton lint			4,500	7,250	9,750	10,000	10,000	10,000	10,000	10,000	10,000	10,000
Chemicals			1,260	2,030	2,730	2,800	2,800	2,800	2,800	2,800	2,800	2,800
Labor			2,700	4,350	5,850	6,000	6,000	6,000	6,000	6,000	6,000	6,000
Utilities			900	1,450	1,950	2,000	2,000	2,000	2,000	2,000	2,000	2,000
Overheads												
Utilities			300	450	450	450	450	450	450	450	450	450
Maintenance			500	1,000	1,200	1,400	1,500	1,500	1,500	1,500	1,500	1,500
Management			1,500	2,250	2,250	2,250	2,250	2,250	2,250	2,250	2,250	2,250
Total operating costs			11,660	18,780	24,180	24,900	25,000	25,000	25,000	25,000	25,000	25,000
Current prices												
Inflated operating costs			13,852	23,649	32,276	35,232	37,496	39,745	42,130	44,658	47,337	50,178
Stock valuation adjustment				172	273	386	409	433	459	487	516	547
Adjusted inflated operating costs			13,852	23,478	32,004	34,846	37,087	39,312	41,671	44,171	46,821	49,631

working capital schedule. In Table 16.5 it has been assumed that the stock valuation adjustment applies only to variable costs.

In Table 16.6 the value of each item of working capital at constant prices is inflated in each year, and incremental working capital is calculated by deducting the total value in one year from the previous year's values. There is an increase in the value of working capital every year, even when there is no physical increase in stocks, because prices are increasing. This treatment corresponds to FIFO (first-in-first-out) stock valuation, which is what must be used in most countries. Due to this procedure, stock appreciation appears in the working capital schedule, and operating costs are correspondingly lower than they would be otherwise. As a result profits appear to be higher as are taxes on profits.

If the operating costs have been inflated by the full value as in Table 16.5, the stock valuation adjustment for operating costs can be calculated as follows (see Table 16.7):

- Take the total value of stocks at constant prices and inflate them.
- Estimate the value of incremental stocks on this (FIFO) basis.
- Take the value of incremental stocks at constant prices and inflate them. This is equivalent to LIFO (last-in-first-out) stock valuation.
- The stock valuation adjustment is the difference between the LIFO and FIFO valuations and will reduce the value of operating costs, giving an equivalent value to Table 16.4.

The stock valuation adjustment is usually relatively small except at very high rates of inflation, and in most cases it will not have a big effect on project profitability. However, without this adjustment, it is impossible to have an inflation-adjusted financial analysis that is both consistent with the annual statement of costs and benefits at constant prices and will give a balance sheet that will balance. Where the rate of inflation is fairly high the effect of changes in the value of stocks can also have a significant effect on apparent profitability. The trading profit appears higher than it otherwise would be, and effectively the FIFO approach to stock valuation leads to taxation of stock appreciation.

The main advantage of the stock valuation adjustment approach is that it can be used for projects where it may be difficult to define unit costs in the way that is possible for relatively simple manufacturing processes. Although the approach is conceptually more complicated, it is computationally easier than an approach using adjusted unit prices, and for this reason it is operationally more useful.

Table 16.6 Working Capital by Year ($ '000)

	0	1	2	3	4	5	6	7	8	9	10	11
Stocks												
Cotton lint			1,485	2,361	3,337	3,537	3,750	3,975	4,213	4,466	4,734	4,734
Chemicals			139	220	311	330	350	371	393	417	442	442
Output			1,236	1,964	2,776	2,943	3,120	3,307	3,505	3,716	3,938	3,938
Accounts receivable			1,443	2,465	3,514	3,820	4,050	4,292	4,550	4,823	5,112	5,112
Accounts payable			762	1,212	1,696	1,798	1,906	2,020	2,142	2,270	2,406	2,406
Total working capital			3,540	5,799	8,243	8,833	9,363	9,924	10,520	11,151	11,820	11,820
Incremental stocks												
Cotton lint			1,485	876	976	200	212	225	238	253	268	−4,734
Chemicals			139	82	91	19	20	21	22	24	25	−442
Output			1,236	729	812	167	177	187	198	210	223	−3,938
Incremental accounts receivable			1,443	1,022	1,049	306	229	243	258	273	289	−5,112
Incremental accounts payable			762	450	484	102	108	114	121	128	136	−2,406
Incremental working capital			3,540	2,259	2,444	590	530	562	595	631	669	−11,820

Table 16.7 Working Capital Showing Stock Valuation Adjustment by Year ($ '000)

	0	1	2	3	4	5	6	7	8	9	10	11
Constant prices												
Stocks												
Cotton lint			1,250	1,875	2,500	2,500	2,500	2,500	2,500	2,500	2,500	
Chemicals			117	175	233	233	233	233	233	233	233	
Output			1,040	1,560	2,080	2,080	2,080	2,080	2,080	2,080	2,080	
Total stocks			2,407	3,610	4,813	4,813	4,813	4,813	4,813	4,813	4,813	
Incremental stocks			2,407	1,203	1,203							−4,813
Accounts receivable			1,215	1,958	2,633	2,700	2,700	2,700	2,700	2,700	2,700	
Accounts payable			642	963	1,271	1,271	1,271	1,271	1,271	1,271	1,271	
Total working capital			2,980	4,605	6,175	6,243	6,243	6,243	6,243	6,243	6,243	
Incremental working capital			2,980	1,625	1,570	68						−6,243
Current prices												
Total stocks			2,859	4,546	6,425	6,811	7,219	7,652	8,111	8,598	9,114	
Incremental stocks (1) (FIFO)			2,859	1,687	1,879	386	409	433	459	487	516	−9,114
Incremental stocks (2) (LIFO)			2,859	1,515	1,606							−9,661
Stock valuation adjustment				172	273	386	409	433	459	487	516	547
Accounts receivable			1,443	2,465	3,514	3,820	4,050	4,292	4,550	4,823	5,112	
Accounts payable			762	1,212	1,696	1,798	1,906	2,020	2,142	2,270	2,406	
Total working capital			3,540	5,799	8,243	8,833	9,363	9,924	10,520	11,151	11,820	
Incremental working capital			3,540	2,259	2,444	590	530	562	595	631	669	−11,820

Depreciation and Inflation

Table 16.8 gives the inflated value of investment costs. The depreciation schedule, Table 16.9, is worked out in exactly the same way as it would be without inflation, only this time it is based on the inflated value of investment costs. There is a small problem in that there is likely to be a difference between the book value of assets in the terminal year and the inflated salvage value. This difference can be described as a *balancing charge,* and this would be subject to tax in the final year of the project or at any time that the assets of the enterprise were revalued. The tax on the balancing charge is shown in the final year of the cash flow (Table 16.12). Where the inflated salvage value is greater than the original purchase price of the asset the difference is a *capital gain,* and this might be subject to capital gains tax. The most obvious case where this arises is in the value of land, but it can also happen with the valuation of buildings. In our example it has been assumed for simplicity that appreciation in the land value is taxed at the same rate as company taxation and hence no attempt has been made to distinguish between the balancing charge and capital gains.

Foreign Exchange Loss

An extra complication that may be caused by differential rates of inflation is that of changes in the exchange rate on loans denominated in foreign currency. When the internal rate of inflation is significantly above the international rate of inflation, it is likely that a country will have to devalue its currency periodically unless the rate of inflation is brought quickly into line with the international rate. This means that the value in local currency of payments of interest and principal repayment will increase, and the value of the outstanding loan principal will also increase. The difference between the local currency value of the loan at the new exchange rate and what it would have been at the old rate is known as an *exchange loss.* The exchange loss will have to be included in the profit and loss account, otherwise the balance sheet will not balance.

Table 16.10 shows the calculation of the loan interest and repayment schedule in $US and also the calculation of the expected exchange rate assuming that all differences between local and international inflation are reflected in the exchange rate (i.e., the real exchange rate remains the same). In Table 16.9 the exchange rate is calculated as indicated in Equation 16.3 above. The loan schedule is then recalculated in local currency, and the exchange loss (EL_t) in each year is calculated by multiplying the balance outstanding in the previous year (B_{n-1}) by the difference in the exchange rate between the current year and the previous year $(ER_n - ER_{n-1})$. Thus

$$EL_t = B_{n-1}(ER_n - ER_{n-1}) \qquad (16.6)$$

Table 16.8 Investment Costs by Year ($ '000)

	0	1	2	3	4	5	6	7	8	9	10	11	12
Land		300											−300
Site development		600											−600
Buildings		6,600	12,500										−3,300
Machinery		12,500						2,500					
Vehicles			2,500										−4,200
Total investment cost		20,000	15,000					2,500					
Current prices													
Land		330											−638
Site development		660											−1,277
Buildings		7,260	14,850										−7,021
Machinery		13,750						3,975					
Vehicles			2,970										
Total investment cost		22,000	17,820					3,975					−8,936

Table 16.9 Depreciation Schedule by Year ($ '000)

	0	1	2	3	4	5	6	7	8	9	10	11	12
Buildings			363	363	363	363	363	363	363	363	363	363	363
Machinery			2,860	2,860	2,860	2,860	2,860	2,860	2,860	2,860	2,860	2,860	2,860
Vehicles			594	594	594	594	594	795	795	795	795	795	795
Total depreciation			3,817	3,817	3,817	3,817	3,817	4,018	4,018	4,018	4,018	4,018	4,018
Book value of assets		22,000	36,003	32,186	28,369	24,552	20,735	20,692	16,674	12,656	8,638	4,620	
Balancing charge/capital gain													4,316

Table 16.10 Loan Interest and Repayment Schedule by Year

	0	1	2	3	4	5	6	7	8	9	10	11
External $'000												
Interest rate		8.0%										
Loan principal		1,000	1,200									
Total payment					428	428	428	428	428	428	428	428
Unpaid interest			80	182								
Interest paid					197	178	158	137	114	88	61	32
Loan repayment					232	250	270	292	315	340	367	397
Balance outstanding		1,000	2,280	2,462	2,231	1,981	1,711	1,419	1,104	764	397	0
External inflation rate		3.0%	3.0%	3.0%	3.0%	3.0%	3.0%	3.0%	3.0%	3.0%	3.0%	3.0%
Inflation factor		1.030	1.061	1.093	1.126	1.159	1.194	1.230	1.267	1.305	1.344	1.384
Exchange rate	10.00	10.68	11.20	11.52	11.86	12.21	12.56	12.93	13.30	13.69	14.09	14.50
Domestic $'000												
Loan principal		10,680	13,438									
Unpaid interest			896	2,102								
Exchange loss			518	744	827	771	704	626	534	428	305	163
Interest paid					2,336	2,178	1,991	1,769	1,510	1,209	861	460
Loan repayment					2,746	3,052	3,392	3,770	4,190	4,657	5,176	5,753
Balance outstanding		10,680	25,532	28,377	26,458	24,177	21,490	18,346	14,690	10,461	5,590	0

Inflating the Main Financial Schedules

The profit and loss account, Table 16.11, is exactly the same in its format as it would be without price changes except that it is based on the inflated values, and exchange losses are included as a cost.

The layout of the cash flow, Table 16.12, is also the same except that a line has been included where the current price return to equity is deflated back to constant prices. It can be seen that the current-price internal rate of return to equity is now 20.9% but that at constant prices the rate of return is only 13.7%. The owners of the project should be able to repay their loan without any problem and make a reasonable profit. However, the financial plan, as initially set out, will not work because the project runs out of money in Year 2. Inflation affects both the liquidity of projects and the distribution of the benefits. If the owners of the project are to realize their profit, they will have to change their financial plan and find some more money. In this case the owners of the project gain slightly in real terms from inflation. Equity holders can gain from moderate rates of inflation when real rates of interest are low but are likely to lose from very high rates of inflation. There are a number of distributional effects caused by inflation. These include

- Increased taxation caused by the reduced real values of loan interest and depreciation allowances and the effect of FIFO stock valuation in transferring costs from tax-deductible operating costs into non-tax-deductible working capital.
- A decrease in the real value of tax payments caused by the effect of inflation on the delay in tax payment.
- A change in the real value of loan interest and repayment. This is likely to be less significant when an enterprise takes out loans denominated in foreign currencies with low inflation rates as long as the real exchange rate remains the same. If the real exchange rate depreciates, the real value of interest and loan repayments in the local currency will increase. Another distributional effect of the high interest rates often associated with high rates of inflation is that the real value of payments on loans becomes more "front loaded." This makes financing projects more difficult.
- An increase in the real cost of delayed payments (accounts receivable) and an increase in the real value of credit received (accounts payable).

The balance sheet (Table 16.13) can be drawn up in exactly the same way as before and should present no problem so long as all the other adjustments have been made correctly. This is easier said than done!

Table 16.11 Trading and Profit and Loss Account by Year ($ '000)

	0	1	2	3	4	5	6	7	8	9	10	11
Sales revenue			17,321	29,580	42,167	45,844	48,594	51,510	54,601	57,877	61,349	65,030
Less variable costs			11,120	18,818	26,798	29,045	30,788	32,635	34,593	36,669	38,869	41,201
Gross or trading profit			6,201	10,762	15,370	16,799	17,807	18,875	20,007	21,208	22,480	23,829
Less overheads			2,732	4,659	5,206	5,801	6,299	6,677	7,078	7,503	7,953	8,430
Less depreciation			3,817	3,817	3,817	3,817	3,817	4,018	4,018	4,018	4,018	4,018
Less loan interest			896	2,102	2,336	2,178	1,991	1,769	1,510	1,209	861	460
Exchange loss			518	744	827	771	704	626	534	428	305	163
Net pretax profit			−1,762	−560	3,184	4,232	4,996	5,785	6,867	8,050	9,344	10,758
Cumulative taxable profit			−1,762	−2,322	862	5,093	10,089	15,874	22,741	30,791	40,135	50,893
Tax @ 30%					259	1,269	1,499	1,735	2,060	2,415	2,803	3,228
Net profit after tax			−1,762	−560	2,926	2,962	3,497	4,049	4,807	5,635	6,541	7,531
Cumulative net profit after tax			−1,762	−2,322	603	3,565	7,062	11,112	15,918	21,554	28,094	35,625

Table 16.12 Cash Flow for Financial Planning by Year ($ '000)

	0	1	2	3	4	5	6	7	8	9	10	11	12
Cash inflow													
Equity capital	15,000												
Loan	10,680	13,438											
Sales		17,321	29,580	42,167	45,844	48,594	51,510	54,601	57,877	61,349	65,030		
Total annual cash inflow	25,680	30,759	29,580	42,167	45,844	48,594	51,510	54,601	57,877	61,349	65,030		
Cash outflow													
Investment	22,000	17,820					3,975						−8,936
Incremental working capital		3,540	2,259	2,444	590	530	562	595	631	669	−11,820		
Operating costs		13,852	23,478	32,004	34,846	37,087	39,312	41,671	44,171	46,821	49,631		
Loan interest				2,336	2,178	1,991	1,769	1,510	1,209	861	460		
Loan repayment				2,746	3,052	3,392	3,770	4,190	4,657	5,176	5,753		
Tax					259	1,269	1,499	1,735	2,060	2,415	2,803		
Total annual cash outflow	22,000	35,212	25,736	39,529	40,925	44,269	50,886	49,702	52,729	55,943	46,827	−4,413	
Annual net cash flow	3,680	−4,454	3,844	2,638	4,919	4,326	624	4,898	5,148	5,406	18,203	4,413	
Cumulative balance C/F	3,680	−774	3,070	5,708	10,627	14,953	15,577	20,475	25,623	31,029	49,233	53,646	
Return to equity	−11,320	−4,454	3,844	2,638	4,919	4,326	624	4,898	5,148	5,406	18,203	4,413	
Return to equity (constant)	−10,291	−3,749	3,053	1,977	3,476	2,884	392	2,907	2,882	2,855	9,069	2,074	

	Current	Constant
NPV to equity at 4% =	24,035	9,741
NPV to equity at 8% =	14,414	4,594
NPV to equity at 12% =	7,961	1,135
IRR =	20.9%	13.7%

Table 16.13 Projected Balance Sheet by Year ($ '000)

	0	1	2	3	4	5	6	7	8	9	10	11	12
Employment of funds (assets)													
Fixed assets (net of depreciation)		22,000	36,003	32,186	28,369	24,552	20,735	20,692	16,674	12,656	8,638	4,620	
Current assets													
Cash balance		3,680	−774	3,070	5,708	10,627	14,953	15,577	20,475	25,623	31,029	49,233	53,646
Current assets			4,303	7,011	9,939	10,631	11,269	11,945	12,661	13,421	14,226		
Total current assets		3,680	3,529	10,081	15,647	21,258	26,222	27,522	33,137	39,044	45,256	49,233	53,646
Current liabilities													
Accounts payable			762	1,212	1,696	1,798	1,906	2,020	2,142	2,270	2,406		
Tax payable					259	1,269	1,499	1,735	2,060	2,415	2,803	3,228	
Total current liabilities			762	1,212	1,955	3,068	3,405	3,756	4,202	4,685	5,209	3,228	
Net working capital		3,680	2,766	8,869	13,692	18,191	22,817	23,766	28,935	34,359	40,046	46,005	53,646
Total assets		25,680	38,769	41,055	42,061	42,743	43,552	44,457	45,609	47,015	48,684	50,625	53,646
Funds employed (liabilities)													
Equity capital		15,000	15,000	15,000	15,000	15,000	15,000	15,000	15,000	15,000	15,000	15,000	15,000
Accumulated profits			−1,762	−2,322	603	3,565	7,062	11,112	15,918	21,554	28,094	35,625	38,646
Loans		10,680	25,532	28,377	26,458	24,177	21,490	18,346	14,690	10,461	5,590	0	0
Total liabilities		25,680	38,769	41,055	42,061	42,743	43,552	44,457	45,609	47,015	48,684	50,625	53,646

Table 16.14 Distribution of Costs and Benefits Adjusted for Inflation by Year ($ '000, constant prices)

	0	1	2	3	4	5	6	7	8	9	10	11	12
Equity	-10,291	-3,749		3,053	1,977	3,476	2,884	392	2,907	2,882	2,855	9,069	2,074
Bank	-9,709	-11,311			3,807	3,696	3,589	3,484	3,383	3,284	3,188	3,096	
Government (taxes)						183	846	943	1,030	1,153	1,275	1,397	2,126
Debtors		1,215		811	786	217	153	153	153	153	153	-2,547	
Creditors		-642		-357	-363	-72	-72	-72	-72	-72	-72	1,199	
Net benefits	-20,000	-14,487		3,507	6,207	7,500	7,400	4,900	7,400	7,400	7,400	12,213	4,200

	NPV at		
	4%	8%	12%
Equity	9,741	4,594	1,135
Bank	927	-2,804	-5,308
Government (taxes)	6,195	4,375	3,148
Debtors	1,599	1,733	1,749
Creditors	-764	-831	-840
Total NPV	17,697	7,067	-115

The distribution of costs and benefits at market prices, after adjusting for inflation but deflated back to constant prices, is shown in Table 16.14. This can be compared with Table 7.1. The overall level of benefits is the same, indicating that the changes made are consistent with the overall estimate of costs and benefits at constant market prices. The distribution has changed. The main gainers are the shareholders, the government, and the debtors. The main losers are the bank (or more likely those that lend their money to the bank) and the creditors. There are significant distributional changes even though the inflation rates assumed are not particularly high by the standards of developing countries.

Adjusting for inflation is difficult, and because of this it is unusual to see it done on a consistent basis. As a result it is often difficult to reconcile financial statements drawn up by financial analysts and economic statements drawn up by economists. Nevertheless we ignore inflation at our peril—the world is full of projects that have run out of money.

Further Reading

The subject of inflation and changes in exchange rate is a neglected one, and there are very few comprehensive attempts to deal with the subject in relation to the financial appraisal of projects. This chapter is based on Potts (1996). Some of the basis for this article can be seen in Yaffey (1992: 172–177). Other relevant references include Phillips (1986) and Sell (1992). Some recognition of the issue can also be found in Overseas Development Administration (1988: 19, 80–81, and 124–127).

PART 5
Conclusion

17

Project Planning and Appraisal for Development

Project Planning and Appraisal: A Summary of the Issues

Project planning and appraisal is of necessity a multidisciplinary activity. Even a simple project requires the cooperative efforts of people with different skills and expertise. While much of the academic literature has concentrated on the economic analysis of projects, it has often been perceived by noneconomists to be too complex and inaccessible. This is true for some aspects of project analysis, but it is unfortunate if a flexible and useful toolkit is completely discarded because some of the tools in the kit are difficult to use. What is needed is to use the appropriate tools at the right time and in the right places. This book has tried to show what the tools are and how they can be used. It has also tried insofar as possible to make those tools accessible to a wide range of potential users. It is hoped that the book will contribute to constructive dialogue and cooperation among disciplines rather than any attempt to assert the primacy of one discipline over another.

Project planning and appraisal is a practical activity. It therefore involves the application of ideas and techniques. However, underlying any set of ideas is a theoretical framework. This can be a matter of convention as in accounting practice, but it can also be a more fundamental expression of a value system. The latter case applies particularly to the economic valuation of projects, but it also relates to sociological perspectives on class and conflict. Projects are sometimes used to challenge the existing order, but more often they are used to reinforce it. This book has tried to present techniques and approaches in relation to the information they provide. Such information can be used by different interest groups for different purposes. It is hoped that users of this book will recognize the fundamental importance of taking into account the interests of the poorest sections of the community and listening to their views. It is only when these interests are taken into account that project planning and appraisal can make its full contribution to the development process.

The process of taking account of the interests of the poorest must start at the project identification stage (Chapter 2) and will be enhanced to the extent that sectoral strategies are informed by poverty reduction concerns and a genuine willingness to listen to those affected by poverty. The willingness to listen and engage in dialogue must continue into the stage of project design where a number of approaches can be used to enhance participation, analyze problems, and ensure logical design (Chapter 3).

Basic project appraisal techniques provide the building blocks for all subsequent financial and economic analysis. If the initial estimation of costs and benefits at constant market prices (Chapter 4) is not sound, no amount of sophisticated techniques will cover up the deficiencies of the analysis. Sometimes benefit valuation is problematic, and in these cases cost-effectiveness techniques can often be used.

Projects do not work if they run out of money. Financial planning is therefore essential for all projects to ensure both timely completion and long-term sustainability (Chapter 5). Adaptations to financial appraisal techniques may be required when considering small producers who face particular constraints, especially in relation to seasonal factors and the integration of productive activities with the needs of household maintenance (Chapter 6). Projects oriented to the needs of small producers may have significant potential for raising the incomes of poor people, although it is often the case that the poorest people do not get the greatest share of the benefits.

The process of economic analysis is most likely to be done for medium- to large-scale projects or for small-scale projects where they are likely to be replicated. The opportunity cost of the time and effort involved in conducting an economic analysis may make it too expensive to be applied to one-off small-scale projects. Nevertheless the economic analysis of projects can provide valuable insights into the relative priority of different types of projects and their contribution to different national goals (Chapter 7).

A major justification for public-sector intervention is the concept of externalities (Chapter 8). These include environmental externalities and externalities associated with the development of the infrastructure and social sectors (Chapter 9). Some of these sectors provide services for which benefits may be based on consumer willingness to pay, while for others a cost-effectiveness approach to benefit assessment may be more realistic. Effective use of limited funds in the infrastructure and social sectors is particularly important to ensure that the poorest sections of the community have access to basic needs.

Sometimes the prices actually paid for goods and services are poor indicators of their economic value. Economic values can be investigated using the opportunity cost concept, which provides the basis for the estimation shadow prices (Chapter 10). Different procedures can be used (Chapter 11), but it can be shown that with common assumptions they all give equivalent results. All mainstream procedures use the process of discounting to take account of time preference, but there are differences in approach to the estimation of the rate of discount, and they can have different implications for the choice of projects (Chapter 12). An important issue in choosing the rate of discount and in considering environmental issues is to ensure that the interests of future generations are given adequate consideration.

The issue of the distribution of the benefits arising from projects is clearly important when poverty reduction is regarded as a central aim of development. While there has been a rich theoretical literature on the rationale for and use of income distribution weights, insufficient attention has been paid in practice to the estimation of the costs and benefits to different stakeholder groups. Chapter 13 outlines an approach to economic analysis that allows the necessary information to be derived. These issues relate to the social analysis of projects (Chapter 14), which is important for the identification of target groups as well as for an understanding of the impact of projects on such groups. The criteria used by social analysts may not correspond to those used by economists, but through a dialogue between the disciplines a common understanding can be reached. One way of building different criteria into decisionmaking is to use multicriteria analysis, although this type of analysis cannot yield the single decision rule that some economists seem to believe is required.

All projects are subject to uncertainty, and it is important that full account is taken of the possibility that the assumptions underlying cost-and-benefit estimates might not turn out to be correct (Chapter 15). The implications of such outcomes for project design also need to be examined. High rates of inflation might not be as widespread as they used to be, but it does not take too big a change in costs to undermine a financial plan, especially when exchange rates may also change (Chapter 16). To take full account of such changes can be quite complex, but failure to take inflation into account properly is one of the main causes of project failure.

Economic Value Systems and the Use of Economic Analysis

Cost-benefit analysis has developed as a branch of welfare economics, and as such the literature is dominated by the concepts of neoclassical economics. Ultimately economic values are determined through some form of prices in terms of willingness to pay. Willingness to pay of course presupposes ability to pay and therefore could be said to depend on the existing distribution of income. To some extent this issue can be avoided through reference to world prices as opportunity costs on the grounds that the world economic order and the prices it delivers are a given factor for individual countries. Nevertheless valuation of the benefits of the nontraded sectors is likely to be derived from internal price relationships and therefore reflects internal economic conditions.

The imperfections of developing country markets are often described as "distortions," but in some cases these distortions may be the results of attempts to redress the much greater real distortion manifested in the unequal distribution of wealth and power both within and among countries. Since the neoclassical framework takes the existing distribution of income and wealth as a given condition, a very one-sided perspective of distortions can be obtained if too many value judgments are made about "distorted" markets. The emphasis taken in this book has therefore been to try to identify the income gains and losses associated with particular prices and to use the concept of opportunity cost to define the difference between the position with and without a project. In this way the assumed source of any differences in income or welfare can be traced. In practice this emphasis makes little or no difference to the overall NPV or IRR of a project, but the information provided by the approach described in Chapter 13 provides a more multidimensional view of economic analysis, and the language used implies less faith in single value results. Ultimately appraisal of a project involves much more than a judgment about an NPV or IRR. These are just pieces of relevant information to be used and taken into account.

In 1991 Little and Mirrlees concluded that "the extent to which social cost benefit analysis is used and has real influence is not great, even in the World Bank." This conclusion can be interpreted in different ways.

It could be argued that this is a reflection of the poor standard of project analysis in an institution that might be expected to have the highest standards. This may be partly true, although there is some evidence to suggest that the economic analysis of more than half of World Bank projects is good and that good economic analysis is correlated with good outcomes (Devarajan et al. 1996: 40).

It could be argued that the organizations in developing countries supposed to engage in economic analysis do not have the capacity to do the job properly. This is certainly true in many cases, but it begs the question as to whether the problem is lack of capacity, the complexity of the analysis, or the usefulness of the results. The latter factor could certainly be affected by the presentation of the results. Single-figure values for measures of project worth do not convey much information and might not be regarded as being very useful. Lack of capacity and complexity of analysis are related, but it is also possible that problems are experienced in matching the complexity of the analysis with the scale of the project. Choosing appropriate tools from the project analysis toolkit is an important skill.

It could also be argued that the relative usefulness of economic appraisal techniques in relation to work on policy analysis and sectoral programs has been overstated and therefore that work on these areas is more important than project appraisal. One reason for this argument is that economic liberalization has reduced the size of the difference between shadow prices and market prices. This reason of course applies to only one aspect of project appraisal, and the argument can be overstated.[1] Economic analysis of projects is also not just about the use of shadow prices. Measurement of externalities, particularly those associated with environmental effects, has taken on increasing significance in project analysis in recent years. Nevertheless it is worth asking the question whether project planning and analysis matters.

Does Project Planning and Analysis Matter?

It is clearly in the interest of anyone writing about project planning and analysis to assert that project planning matters. Nevertheless it is worth considering the counterfactual argument that project planning does not matter. If project planning does not matter, there is no purpose in trying to make a systematic assessment of investment requirements or to make a serious attempt to ask whether the investment is worth doing. Are investment funds so abundant in developing and transitional economies (or anywhere else for that matter) that a rigorous analysis of spending proposals is unnecessary? Is getting policies and prices "right" a guarantee that public- and private-sector investment will be productive? Are the consequences of such investments so obvious that such analysis is unnecessary?

Just as attempts to assert the supremacy of one discipline over another are counterproductive, so too suggestions that planning resources should be expended primarily on the analysis of policies and programs are misguided. In the late 1960s and early 1970s, debates took place about the relative importance of macroeconomic planning and microeconomic analysis of projects in a very different context. The attention of donor agencies switched to microeconomic analysis, resulting in neglect of the macroeconomic policy and program framework within which projects were supposed to work. It was not until the 1980s that serious attention returned to the policy framework, and then it was introduced in a way that led to the imposition of donor-determined structural adjustment policies on often reluctant recipient governments. There was an asymmetry of power in the relationship that continues to have serious implications for any concept of genuine partnership.

The subsequent switch of emphasis by donor agencies away from funding projects and toward policy-conditional program lending carries the risk of neglecting the micro issues, with potentially serious consequences for the effectiveness of investment unless adequate in-country project planning capacity is developed. The policy and program context within which projects are developed is vitally important, but so too are the planning and analysis of the investment projects that make up much of the programs. It is the combination of coherent locally led macro-level policies and programs and sound micro-level planning and analysis that is likely to deliver the most effective results. It is hoped that this book will make some contribution to the capacity building needed for the micro-level part of such a combination.

Notes

1. A useful summary of the arguments about the effect of liberalization can be found in Curry and Weiss (2000: 326–328).

Bibliography

The sources outlined below are the sources used in writing this book. Some of the institutional sources are also available on the World Wide Web. The websites of the World Bank (www.worldbank.org) and the Asian Development Bank (www.adb. org) are particularly useful.

Abelson, P. (1996) *Project Appraisal and Valuation of the Environment*. London: Macmillan.

Adhikari, R., P. Gertler, and A. Lagman (1999) "Economic Analysis of Health Sector Projects—A Review of Issues, Methods, and Approaches." Asian Development Bank Economic Staff Paper Series, no. 58.

Adler, H. (1987) *Economic Appraisal of Transport Projects*. Baltimore: Johns Hopkins University Press.

Akroyd, D. (1995) "Steps Towards the Adoption of the Logical Framework Approach in the African Development Bank: Some Illustrations for Agricultural Sector Projects." *Project Appraisal* 10, no. 1.

Ali, Ifzal (1991) "Economic Analysis of Investment in Power Systems." Asian Development Bank Staff Paper, no. 49.

Allan, B., and K. Hinchliffe (1982) *Planning Policy Analysis and Public Spending*. Aldershot, England: Gower.

Amin, G. (1978) "Project Appraisal and Income Distribution." *World Development* 6, no. 2.

Anand, S., and K. Hanson (1998) "DALYs: Efficiency Versus Equity." *World Development* 26, no. 2.

Ashworth, A., and S. Khanum (1997) "Cost-Effective Treatment for Severely Malnourished Children: What Is the Best Approach?" *Health Policy and Planning* 12, no. 2.

Asian Development Bank (1996) *Economic Evaluation of Environmental Impacts: A Workbook*. Manila: ADB.

——— (1997) *Guidelines for the Economic Analysis of Projects*. Manila: ADB.

——— (1998a) *Guidelines for the Economic Analysis of Telecommunications Projects*. Manila: ADB.

——— (1998b) *Guidelines for the Economic Analysis of Water Supply Projects*. Manila: ADB.

——— (1999) *Handbook for the Economic Analysis of Water Supply Projects*. Manila: ADB.

────── (2000) *Handbook for the Economic Analysis of Health Sector Projects.* Manila: ADB.

Baird, A., and D. Potts (1978) "The Project Spiral." Discussion Paper No. 24. University of Bradford, Project Planning Centre.

Balassa, B. (1976) "The 'Effects Method' of Project Evaluation." *Oxford Bulletin of Economics and Statistics* 38, no. 4.

────── (1977) "The 'Effects Method' of Project Evaluation Once Again." *Oxford Bulletin of Economics and Statistics* 39, no. 4.

Baum, W. (1970) "The Project Cycle." *Finance and Development* 7, no. 2.

────── (1978) "The World Bank Project Cycle." *Finance and Development* 15, no. 4.

Baum, W., and S. Tolbert (1985) *Investing in Development: Lessons of World Bank Experience.* Oxford: Oxford University Press.

Behrens, W., and P. Hawranek (1991) *Manual for the Preparation of Industrial Feasibility Studies.* Vienna: UNIDO.

Belli, P., J. Anderson, H. Barnum, J. Dixon, and Tan Jee-Peng (1998) *Handbook on Economic Analysis of Investment Operations.* Washington: World Bank.

Benjamin, McDonald P. (1981) *Investment Projects in Agriculture.* Harlow, England: Longman.

Bennell, P. (1995) "Using and Abusing Rates of Return: A Critique of the World Bank's 1995 Education Sector Review." Institute of Development Studies Working Paper, no. 22.

Birley, M. (1995) *The Health Impact Assessment of Development Projects.* London: HMSO.

Brent, R. (1996) *Project Appraisal for Developing Countries.* Cheltenham: Edward Elgar.

Bridger, G., and J. Winpenny (1983) *Planning Development Projects.* London: HMSO.

Brown, M. (1979) *Farm Budgets: From Farm Income Analysis to Agricultural Project Analysis.* Baltimore: Johns Hopkins.

Caiden, N., and A. Wildavsky (1974) *Planning and Budgeting in Poor Countries.* New York: Wiley.

Carrin, G. (1984) *Economic Evaluation of Health Care in Developing Countries.* London: Croom Helm.

Cernea, M. (1994) "Using Knowledge from Social Science in Development Projects." *Project Appraisal* 9, no. 2.

──────, ed. (1991) *Putting People First: Sociological Variables in Rural Development.* Oxford: Oxford University Press.

Chambers, R. (1983) *Rural Development: Putting the Last First.* London: Longman.

────── (1994) "The Origins and Practice of Participatory Rural Appraisal." *World Development* 22, no. 7.

Chervel, M. (1977) "The Rationale of the Effects Method: A Reply to Bela Balassa." *Oxford Bulletin of Economics and Statistics* 39, no. 4.

Chervel, M., and M. Le Gall (1978) *Manual of Economic Evaluation of Projects: The Effects Method.* Paris: Ministère de la Cooperation.

Clarke, R., and A. Low (1993) "Risk Analysis in Project Planning: A Simple Spreadsheet Application Using Monte Carlo Techniques." *Project Appraisal* 8, no. 3.

Coleman, G. (1987) "Project Planning: Logical Framework Approach to the Monitoring and Evaluation of Agricultural and Rural Development Projects." *Project Appraisal* 2, no. 4.

Colman, D., and F. Nixson (1994) *Economics of Change in Less Developed Countries.* London: Harvester Wheatsheaf.

Commission of the European Communities (1993) *Project Cycle Management: Integrated Approach and Logical Framework.* Brussels: Commission of the European Communities: Evaluation Unit, Methods, and Instruments for Project Cycle Management, no. 1.

—— (1997) *Manual, Financial and Economic Analysis of Development Projects.* Brussels: Commission of the European Communities, Methods and Instruments for Project Cycle Management.

—— (1998) *Guidelines for Water Resources Development Co-operation— Towards Sustainable Water Resources Management.* Brussels: Commission of the European Communities.

Cook, P., and P. Mosley (1989) "On the Valuation of External Effects." *Project Appraisal* 4, no. 3.

Cracknell, B. (1989) "Evaluating the Effectiveness of the Logical Framework System in Practice." *Project Appraisal* 4, no. 3.

Cummings, R., A. Dinar, and D. Olson (1996) "New Evaluation Procedures for a New Generation of Water Related Projects." World Bank Technical Paper, no. 349.

Curry, S., and J. Weiss (2000) *Project Analysis in Developing Countries.* London: Macmillan.

Cusworth, J., and T. Franks, eds. (1993) *Managing Projects in Developing Countries.* Harlow: Longman.

Dallago, B., and J. Kovacs, eds. (1990) *Economic Planning in Transition: Socio-Economic Development and Planning in Post-Socialist and Capitalist Societies.* Aldershot, England: Dartmouth.

Dasgupta, P. (1972) "A Comparative Analysis of the UNIDO Guidelines and the OECD Manual." *Bulletin of the Oxford University Institute of Economics and Statistics* 34, no. 1.

Delp, P., A. Thesen, J. Motiwalla, and N. Seshari (1977) *Systems Tools for Project Planning.* Bloomington, IN: PASITAM.

Devarajan, S., L. Squire, and S. Suthiwart-Narueput (1996) "Project Appraisal at the World Bank." In C. Kirkpatrick and J. Weiss, eds., *Cost Benefit Analysis and Project Appraisal in Developing Countries.* Cheltenham: Edward Elgar.

Development Project Management Center (1979) *Elements of Project Management.* Washington, DC: U.S. Department of Agriculture, DPMC.

Dickey, J., and L. Miller (1984) *Road Project Appraisal for Developing Countries.* Chichester, England: Wiley.

Dinwiddy, C., and F. Teal (1996) *Principles of Cost Benefit Analysis for Developing Countries.* Cambridge: Cambridge University Press.

Dixon, J., R. Carpenter, L. Fallon, and P. Sherman (1994) *Economic Analysis of Environmental Impacts.* London: Earthscan.

Dobbins, R., and R. Pike (1986) *Investment Decisions and Financial Strategy.* Oxford: Philip Allan.

Dorfman, R. (1972) "Decision Rules Under Uncertainty." In R. Layard, ed., *Cost Benefit Analysis.* Harmondsworth, England: Penguin.

Ellis, F. (1988) *Peasant Economics.* Cambridge: Cambridge University Press.

FAO (1986) *Guide for Training in the Formulation of Agricultural and Rural Investment Projects.* Rome: FAO.

—— (1989) "The Design of Agricultural Investment Projects: Lessons from Experience." FAO Investment Centre Technical Paper, no. 6. Rome: FAO.

—— (1991) "Guidelines for the Design of Agricultural Investment Projects." FAO Investment Centre Technical Paper, no. 7. Rome: FAO.

Feldstein, M. (1964) "The Social Time Preference Rate in Cost Benefit Analysis." *Economic Journal* 74.

Foster, M., and J. Knowles (1982) *Railway Sector Appraisal Manual*. London: ODA.

Franck, B. (1996) "The Effects Method and Economic Cost-Benefit Analysis: Substitutes or Complements?" In C. Kirkpatrick and J. Weiss, eds., *Cost Benefit Analysis and Project Appraisal in Developing Countries*. Cheltenham: Edward Elgar.

Fujimura, M., and J. Weiss (2000) "Integration of Poverty Impact in Project Economic Analysis: Issues in Theory and Practice." EDRC Methodology Series, no. 2. Manila: ADB.

Gittinger, J. P. (1982) *Economic Analysis of Agricultural Projects*. Baltimore: Johns Hopkins.

Goodman, L., and R. Love, eds. (1979) *Management of Development Projects: An International Case Study Approach*. Oxford: Pergamon.

GTZ (1987) *ZOPP Flipcharts*. Eschborn, Germany: GTZ.

—— (1988) *ZOPP (An Introduction to the Method)*. Eschborn, Germany: GTZ.

—— (1990) *Moderation Course: Objective Oriented Project Planning (ZOPP)*. Eschborn, Germany: GTZ.

Hammer, J. (1993) "The Economics of Malaria Control." *World Bank Research Observer* 8, no. 1.

Hanley, N., and C. Spash (1993) *Cost Benefit Analysis and the Environment*. Cheltenham: Edward Elgar.

Harberger, A. (1978) "On the Use of Distributional Weights in Social Cost Benefit Analysis." *Journal of Political Economy* 86, no. 2.

—— (1984) "Basic Needs Versus Distributional Weights in Cost-Benefit Analysis." *Economic Development and Cultural Change* 32, no. 3.

Harris, J., and M. Todaro (1970) "Migration, Unemployment and Development: A Two-Sector Analysis." *American Economic Review* (March).

Hicks, J. (1972) "The Valuation of the Social Income." *Economica* (May).

Howlett, D., and J. Nagu (1997) *Agricultural Project Planning in Tanzania*. Bradford, England: DPPC, and Mzumbe, Tanzania: IDM.

Hull, J. (1986) *The Evaluation of Risks in Business Investment*. Oxford: Pergamon.

Interorganisational Committee on Guidelines and Principles for Social Impact Assessment (1995) "Guidelines and Principles for Social Impact Assessment" *Environmental Impact Assessment Review* 15.

Irvin, J. (1976) *Modern Cost-Benefit Methods*. London: Macmillan.

Jenkins, G. (1999) "Evaluation of Stakeholder Impacts in Cost-Benefit Analysis," *Impact Assessment and Project Appraisal*, 17, no. 2.

Jenkins, G., and A. Harberger (1994) *Manual—Cost Benefit Analysis of Investment Decisions*. Cambridge, MA: Harvard Institute for International Development. Mimeographed.

Jha, P., O. Bangoura, and K. Ranson (1998) "The Cost-Effectiveness of Forty Health Interventions in Guinea." *Health Policy and Planning* 13, no. 3.

Johnes, G. (1993) *The Economics of Education*. Oxford: Macmillan.

Jones, G. (1991) *Starting Up*. London: Pitman NatWest Business Handbooks.

Joshi, H. (1972) "World Prices as Shadow Prices: A Critique." *Bulletin of the Oxford University Institute of Economics and Statistics* 34, no. 1.

Kaldor, N. (1939) "Welfare Propositions of Economists and Interpersonal Comparisons of Utility." *Economic Journal* (September).

Karatas, C. (1989) "Third Bosphorus Bridge Versus Bosphorus Road Tube Tunnel and Combined Alternative." *Project Appraisal* 4, no. 2.

Kim, A., and B. Benton (1995) "Cost Benefit Analysis of the Onchocerciasis Control Program." World Bank Technical Paper, no. 282.

Kirkpatrick, C., and J. Weiss, eds. (1996) *Cost Benefit Analysis and Project Appraisal in Developing Countries.* Cheltenham: Edward Elgar.

Klumper, S-A. (1996) "Analysis of Water Supply Projects in Practice." In C. Kirkpatrick and J. Weiss, eds., *Cost Benefit Analysis and Project Appraisal in Developing Countries.* Cheltenham: Edward Elgar.

Kula, E. (1996) "Social Project Appraisal and Historical Development of Ideas on Discounting—A Legacy for the 1990s and Beyond." In C. Kirkpatrick and J. Weiss, eds., *Cost Benefit Analysis and Project Appraisal in Developing Countries.* Cheltenham: Edward Elgar.

———— (1997) *Time, Discounting and Future Generations: The Harmful Effects of an Untrue Economic Theory.* Westport, CT: Quorum.

Lal, D. (1974) "Methods of Project Analysis: A Review." World Bank Staff Occasional Papers, no. 16.

Layard, R., ed. (1972) *Cost Benefit Analysis.* Harmondsworth, England: Penguin.

Layard, R., and S. Glaister, eds. (1994) *Cost Benefit Analysis.* Cambridge: Cambridge University Press.

Lewis, W. (1966) *Development Planning.* London: Allen and Unwin.

Little, I., and J. Mirrlees (1969) *Manual of Industrial Project Analysis in Developing Countries,* vol. 2. Paris: OECD.

———— (1974) *Project Appraisal and Planning in Developing Countries.* London: Heinemann.

———— (1991) "Project Appraisal and Planning Twenty Years On." In R. Layard and S. Glaister, eds., *Cost Benefit Analysis.* Cambridge: Cambridge University Press.

Little, I., and M. Scott (1976) *Using Shadow Prices.* London: Heinemann.

Livingstone, I., and M. Tribe (1995) "Projects with Long Time Horizons: Their Economic Appraisal and the Discount Rate." *Project Appraisal* 10, no. 2.

Loevinsohn, B., R. Sutter, and M. Costales (1997) "Using Cost-Effectiveness Analysis to Evaluate Targeting Strategies: The Case of Vitamin A Supplementation." *Health Policy and Planning* 12, no. 1.

Londero, E. (1994) "'Estimating the Accounting Price of Foreign Exchange': An Input-Output Approach." *Economic Systems Research* 6, no. 4.

———— (1996a) *Benefits and Beneficiaries.* Washington: Inter American Development Bank.

———— (1996b) "Reflections on Estimating Distributional Effects." In C. Kirkpatrick and J. Weiss, eds., *Cost Benefit Analysis and Project Appraisal in Developing Countries.* Cheltenham: Edward Elgar.

MacArthur, J. (1978) "Appraising the Distributional Aspects of Rural Development Projects: A Kenya Case Study." *World Development* 6, no. 2.

———— (1993) "The Logical Framework—A Tool for the Management of Project Planning and Evaluation." New Series Discussion Paper, no. 42. Bradford, England: Development and Project Planning Centre, University of Bradford.

———— (1994) "The Project Sequence: A Composite View of the Project Cycle." In J. MacArthur and J. Weiss, eds., *Agriculture, Projects and Development.* Aldershot, England: Avebury.

——— (1997) "Stakeholder Roles and Stakeholder Analysis in Project Planning: A Review of Approaches in Three Agencies." New Series Discussion Paper, no. 42. Bradford, England: Development and Project Planning Centre, University of Bradford.

Maddock, N., and F. Wilson, eds. (1994) *Project Design for Agricultural Development.* Aldershot, England: Avebury.

Marglin, S. (1963a) "The Social Rate of Discount and the Optimal Rate of Reinvestment." *Quarterly Journal of Economics* 77.

——— (1963b) "The Opportunity Costs of Public Investment." *Quarterly Journal of Economics* 77.

——— (1967) *Public Investment Criteria.* London: Unwin.

Mathur, Om Prakash (1985) *Project Analysis for Local Development.* Boulder, CO: Westview.

McCulloch, M. (1986) "Project Frameworks—A Logical Development for More Effective Aid." *British Overseas Aid in 1985.* London: HMSO.

Mirrlees, J. A. (1978) "Social Benefit Cost Analysis and the Distribution of Income." *World Development* 6, no. 2.

Moser, C. (1993) *Gender Planning and Development: Theory, Practice and Training.* London: Routledge.

NORAD (1996) *The Logical Framework Approach (LFA): Handbook for Objectives-Oriented Project Planning.* Oslo: NORAD.

Overseas Development Administration (1984) *Manual for the Appraisal of Rural Water Supplies.* London: HMSO.

——— (1988) *Appraisal of Projects in Developing Countries.* London: HMSO.

——— (1989) *Manual of Environmental Appraisal.* London: HMSO.

——— (1995a) *A Guide to Social Analysis for Projects in Developing Countries.* London: HMSO.

——— (1995b) *Guidance Note on How to Do Stakeholder Analysis of Aid Projects and Programmes.* London: Overseas Development Administration, Social Administration Department.

Pearce, D. (1993) *Economic Values and the Natural World.* London: Earthscan.

Pearce, D., E. Barbier, and A. Markandya (1990) *Sustainable Development.* London: Earthscan.

Pearce, D., A. Markandya, and E. Barbier (1989) *Blueprint for a Green Economy.* London: Earthscan.

Perkins, F. (1994) *Practical Cost Benefit Analysis.* Macmillan.

Petry, F. (1990) "Who Is Afraid of Choices? A Proposal for Multi-Criteria Analysis as a Tool for Decision-Making Support in Development Planning." *Journal of International Development* 2, no. 2.

Phillips, D. (1986) "Inflation, Income Distribution, and Cost Benefit Analysis." *Project Appraisal* 1, no. 4.

Picciotto, R., and R. Weaving (1994) "A New Project Cycle for the World Bank?" *Finance and Development* 31, no. 4.

Potts, D. (1978) "Politics Social Cost Benefit Analysis and Planners." *IDS Bulletin* 10, no. 1.

——— (1979) "The Discount Rate and the Shadow Price of Investment in Integrated Systems of Social Cost-Benefit Analysis." Occasional Paper, no. 5. Bradford, England: University of Bradford, Project Planning Centre for Developing Countries.

——— (1990) "Shadow Pricing Agricultural Projects: An Approach Using Unknown Parameters." *Project Appraisal* 5, no. 3.

——— (1992) "'Let Us Assume ...': A Case Study of With and Without Assumptions in Project Appraisal." *Uongozi: Journal of Management Development* 4, no. 1.

——— (1994a) "Assumptions of Causality and the Phasing and Aggregation of Farm Models in Project Analysis," In J. MacArthur and J. Weiss, eds., *Agriculture, Projects and Development.* Aldershot, England: Avebury.

——— (1994b) "Real Interest Rates and the Pattern of Agricultural Investment." In N. Maddock and F. Wilson, eds., *Project Design for Agricultural Development.* Aldershot, England: Avebury.

——— (1996a) "Estimating Shadow Prices in a Transitional Economy: The Case of Lithuania." In C. Kirkpatrick and J. Weiss, eds., *Cost Benefit Analysis and Project Appraisal in Developing Countries.* Cheltenham, England: Edward Elgar.

——— (1996b) "When Prices Change: Consistency in the Financial Analysis of Projects." *Project Appraisal* 11, no. 1.

——— (1999) "Forget the Weights, Who Gets the Benefits? How to Bring a Poverty Focus to the Economic Analysis of Projects." *Journal of International Development* 11.

Pouliquen, L. (1970) "Risk Analysis in Project Appraisal." IBRD Occasional Paper, no. 11.

Powers, T., ed. (1981) *Estimating Accounting Prices for Project Appraisal.* Washington, DC: Inter-American Development Bank.

Pretty, J. (1995) "Participatory Learning for Sustainable Agriculture." *World Development* 23, no. 8.

Price, C. (1993) *Time, Discounting and Value.* Oxford: Blackwell.

——— (1996a) "Discounting and Project Appraisal: From the Bizarre to the Ridiculous." In C. Kirkpatrick and J. Weiss, eds., *Cost Benefit Analysis and Project Appraisal in Developing Countries.* Cheltenham, England: Edward Elgar.

——— (1996b) "Long Time Horizons, Low Discount Rates and Moderate Investment Criteria." *Project Appraisal* 11, no. 3.

Prou, C., and M. Chervel (1970) *Etablissement des Programmes en Économie Sous-Dévelopée, Tome 3, L'Étude des Grappes de Projets.* Paris: Dunod.

Psachoropoulos, G., and M. Woodall (1985) *Education for Development: An Analysis of Investment Choices.* Oxford: Oxford University Press.

——— (1994) "Returns to Investment in Education: A Global Update." *World Development* 22, no. 9.

——— (1995) "The Profitability of Investments in Education: Concepts and Methods." World Bank Human Capital Development and Operations Policy Working Paper, no. 63.

Ray, A. (1984) *Cost Benefit Analysis: Issues and Methodologies.* Baltimore: Johns Hopkins University Press.

Reutlinger, S. (1970) "Techniques for Project Appraisal Under Uncertainty." IBRD Occasional Paper, no. 10.

Rondinelli, D., ed. (1977) *Planning Development Projects.* Stroudsburg, PA: Dowden, Hutchinson and Ross.

——— (1983) *Development Projects as Policy Experiments.* London: Methuen.

(Roskill) Commission on the Third London Airport (1971) *Report.* London: HMSO.

Saerbeck, R. (1988) "Estimating Accounting Price Ratios with a Semi-Input-Output Table: Botswana." *Project Appraisal* 3, no. 4.

Savvides, S. (1994) "Risk Analysis in Investment Appraisal." *Project Appraisal* 9, no. 1.

Scott, M. (1977) "The Test Rate of Discount and Changes in the Base Level of Income in the United Kingdom." *Economic Journal* 87 (June).

Scott, M., J. MacArthur, and D. Newbery (1976) *Project Appraisal in Practice.* London: Heinemann.

Sell, A. (1991) *Project Evaluation: An Integrated Financial and Economic Analysis.* Aldershot, England: Avebury.

——— (1992) "Planning and Evaluation of Projects in Countries with High Inflation Rates." *Project Appraisal* 7, no. 1.

Selvavinayagam, K. (1991) "Financial Analysis in Agricultural Project Preparation." FAO Investment Centre Technical Paper, no. 8.

Sen, A. (1967) "Isolation, Assurance and the Social Rate of Discount." *Quarterly Journal of Economics* 81.

Snell, M. (1997) *Cost-Benefit Analysis.* London: Thomas Telford.

Squire, L., and H. van der Tak (1975) *Economic Analysis of Projects.* Baltimore: Johns Hopkins University Press.

Stewart, F. (1978) "Social Cost Benefit Analysis in Practice: Some Reflections in the Light of Case Studies Using the LM Techniques." *World Development* 6, no. 2.

Stewart, F., and P. Streeten (1972) "Little-Mirrlees Method and Project Appraisal." *Bulletin of the Oxford University Institute of Economics and Statistics,* 34, no. 1.

Sugden, R., and A. Williams (1978) *The Principles of Practical Cost Benefit Analysis.* Oxford: Oxford University Press.

Tan Tok Shiong and J. MacArthur (1995) "Extended Semi-Input-Output Method for Estimating Shadow Prices." *Project Appraisal* 10, no. 1.

Tinbergen, J. (1967) *Development Planning.* London: Weidenfeld and Nicholson.

Transport and Road Research Laboratory (1988) "A Guide to Road Project Appraisal." *Overseas Road Note,* no. 5.

Turvey, R., and D. Anderson (1977) *Electricity Economics.* Baltimore: Johns Hopkins.

UNDP (1990) *Human Development Report.* New York: United Nations.

UNEP (1988) *Environmental Impact Assessment: Basic Procedures for Developing Countries.* New York: United Nations.

UNIDO (1972) *Guidelines for Project Evaluation.* New York: United Nations.

——— (1978) *Guide to Practical Project Appraisal.* New York: United Nations.

——— (1980) *Practical Appraisal of Industrial Projects.* New York: United Nations.

Upton, M. (1987) *African Farm Management.* Cambridge: Cambridge University Press.

USAID (1974) *Project Evaluation Guidelines.* Washington, DC: USAID.

——— (1985) *Selected Materials on the Logical Framework.* Washington, DC: USAID.

van Pelt, M. (1993) *Ecological Sustainability and Project Appraisal—Case Studies in Developing Countries.* Aldershot, England: Avebury.

——— (1994) "Sustainability-Oriented Appraisal for Agricultural Projects." In N. Maddock and F. Wilson, eds., *Project Design for Agricultural Development.* Aldershot, England: Avebury.

van Pelt, M., A. Kuyvenhoven, and P. Nijkamp (1990) "Project Appraisal and Sustainability: Methodological Challenges." *Project Appraisal* 5, no. 3.

Vanclay, F., and D. Bronstein, eds. (1995) *Environmental and Social Impact Assessment.* Chichester, England: Wiley.

Weiss, J. (1979) "Project Selection and the Equity Objective—The Use of Social Analysis." *Pakistan Development Review* (summer).

——— (1988) "An Introduction to Shadow Pricing in a Semi-Input-Output Approach." *Project Appraisal* 3, no. 4.

———, ed. (1994) *The Economics of Project Appraisal and the Environment.* Cheltenham, England: Edward Elgar.

West, A. (1988) *A Business Plan.* London: Pitman NatWest Business Handbooks.

Whittington, D., and V. Swarna (1994) "The Economic Benefits of Potable Water Supply Projects to Households in Developing Countries." *Asian Development Bank Staff Paper,* no. 53.

Wiggins, S., and D. Shields (1995) "Clarifying the Logical Framework as a Tool for Planning and Managing Development Projects." *Project Appraisal* 10, no. 1.

Winpenny, J. (1983) *Planning Development Projects.* London: HMSO.

——— (1991) *Values for the Environment.* London: HMSO.

World Bank (1991) *Environmental Assessment Sourcebook.* World Bank Technical Paper, no. 139.

——— (1998) *Environmental Assessment Sourcebook Update.* Washington, DC: World Bank Environment Department.

World Commission on Environment and Development (1987) *Our Common Future.* Oxford: Oxford University Press.

Yaffey, M. (1989) "Variants of the Cash Flow Statement." *Project Appraisal* 4, no. 2.

——— (1992) *Financial Analysis for Development: Concepts and Techniques.* London: Routledge.

Yaffey, M., and M. Tribe (1992) *Project Rehabilitation in Adverse Environments.* Aldershot, England: Avebury.

Index

Accounting rate of interest, 235
Accounts payable, 59, 62*tab;* as current
liability, 96; incremental, 62*tab;*
transfer payments and, 149; value of,
61
Accounts receivable, 59, 61, 62*tab;* as
current asset, 96; incremental,
62*tab;* transfer payments and, 149
Activity budget, 117, 118*tab,* 119–120;
gross margins in, 119; indicators of
profitability in, 119, 120; seasonality
and, 119; standard units in, 117
Adjustment factors, 238–239
Annual Statement of Project Costs and
Benefits at Constant Market Prices,
64–66
Average incremental cost, 110–111

Balance of payments: economic analysis and, 144, 145. See also Foreign
exchange
Benefit cost ratio, 69–71, 74*tab,*
Benefits: categories of, 55–63; in commercial transport, 182; distribution
analysis and, 281*tab;* distribution of,
7, 150*tab,* 173, 176*tab,* 353; economic, 157; of energy projects,
187–188; estimates of, 57*tab,* 58,
179–197; external, 63, 157; health
projects, 194–195; overestimation
of, 258; road construction and
improvement, 183–185, 187; for
small producers, 115–117; in transport projects, 181–187; valuation of,
84, 352; water supply/sanitation
projects, 188–194

Blueprint projects, 6, 36–38; participation and, 37; time and, 37
Brundtland Commission, 165

Canadian International Development
Agency, 31
Capital: cost of, 66, 70, 93, 213; critical
natural, 166; environmental,
165–166; equity, 101, 105, 314*tab;*
gains, 340; human, 159, 168, 179,
180, 187, 195, 196; man-made, 166;
opportunity cost of, 206, 255–259;
rationing, 77, 258, 262; return on,
105, 257, 261, 268*n3;* small-scale
production and, 123, 126; stock,
165, 257; value of, 268*n3;* working,
59–63, 65*tab,* 70, 86*n4,* 116, 123,
126, 177*n2,* 288, 338*tab,* 339*tab*
Capital recovery factor, 81, 86*n9,* 97,
214
Cash: availability, 101; flow, 89, 90, 98,
100*tab,* 116, 123, 126, 127*tab,* 333;
shortages, 98; small-scale production
and, 123, 126
Commission of the European
Communities, 14, 282
Commodity: prices, 23; primary, 328;
shadow prices, 226; trade, 23, 203
Consumer surplus, 158, 179–180; in
energy projects, 188; in water projects, 190–191
Contingent valuation, 170–171, 189,
294
Conversion factors, 253*n3;* composite,
235; in distribution analysis, 280*tab;*
Cost-benefit analysis, 47, 294, 295, 353;

About the Book

In this comprehensive, practical guide to project planning and appraisal in developing countries, David Potts focuses on economic and financial analysis but also gives serious weight to such key factors as sustainability and social impact.

Part 1 of the book considers a range of approaches to project identification and design and introduces basic techniques for determining costs and benefits. Part 2 provides an outline for the financial analysis of commercial projects, incorporating the issue of possible noncommercial objectives; here, Potts includes a discussion of methods for assessing projects that involve small-scale producers. Part 3 explores the economic and social analysis of projects.

The final section of the book addresses the practicalities of dealing with risk and uncertainty in project planning, including ways to account for the realities of inflation and exchange-rate fluctuations.

David Potts is senior lecturer at the Bradford Centre for International Development, University of Bradford. He has had extensive field experience in Africa, Asia, the Caribbean, and Eastern Europe.